Criminal Disclosure R

Second Edition

Criminal Disclosure Referencer

Second Edition

Tom Wainwright
Barrister, Garden Court Chambers

Emma Fenn
Barrister, Garden Court Chambers

Shahida Begum
Barrister, Garden Court Chambers

Bloomsbury Professional

Bloomsbury Professional

An imprint of Bloomsbury Publishing Plc

Bloomsbury Professional Ltd
41–43 Boltro Road
Haywards Heath
RH16 1BJ
UK

Bloomsbury Publishing Plc
50 Bedford Square
London
WC1B 3DP
UK

www.bloomsbury.com

**BLOOMSBURY and the Diana logo are trademarks of
Bloomsbury Publishing Plc**

© Bloomsbury Professional Ltd 2017

British Library Cataloguing-in-Publication Data

A catalogue record for this book is available from the British Library.

ISBN: PB: 978 1 78451 879 0
ePDF: 978 1 78451 881 3
ePub: 978 1 78451 880 6

Typeset by Compuscript Ltd, Shannon
Printed and bound by CPI Group (UK) Ltd, Croydon, CR0 4YY

To find out more about our authors and books visit
www.bloomsburyprofessional.com. Here you will find extracts, author information,
details of forthcoming events and the option to sign up for our newsletters

Foreword to the first edition

Issues involving disclosure arise in many criminal trials. They can be very difficult indeed. Given the extensive work that has been done in this area over recent years, a publication that brings together all the relevant material is to be welcomed. It will undoubtedly assist everyone involved in the process of criminal justice to navigate through the complex issues that arise; something which is essential to ensure a correct and just outcome in every case.

The correct approach to disclosure is crucial for a fair trial. However, the process must be managed intelligently if it is not to overwhelm the system. It is essential that everyone clearly understands the principles and applies them appropriately. As Lord Justice Gross stated in his 2011 Disclosure Review:

> 'Improvements in disclosure must be prosecution led or driven, in such a manner as to require the defence to engage – and to permit the defence to do so with confidence. The entire process must be robustly case managed by the judiciary. The tools are available; they need to be used.'

The available tools are of course the Criminal Procedure Rules (the application of which it is worth underlining is mandatory), the Code of Practice issued under Part II of the CPIA, the Attorney General's Guidelines (2005 and 2011) and the Judicial Protocol. They need both to be *understood* and *used* by practitioners. This book draws them together and underlines the important direction that they set down.

In short, full compliance with the duties of disclosure must be seen as fundamental for investigators, prosecution and defence lawyers and advocates. Each person engaged in the process has an individual responsibility. It will not always be easy. There is no 'quick fix'. Judges will provide the necessary leadership as is appropriate. The days of the 'ambush defence' are over. There should be no place for late or uninformative defence case statements.

I therefore welcome this comprehensive review of the relevant law and practice of disclosure. It has been prepared by two practitioners who, between them, have a wealth of experience and expertise. They have set out in a comprehensive and clear manner, both the broad principles and the details of the disclosure regime.

This will be an invaluable guide for all criminal practitioners in this difficult and challenging area.

Rt Hon Lord Justice Goldring QC
Senior Presiding Judge

Preface and acknowledgements

In July 2017, as this second edition of *Criminal Disclosure Referencer* was being finalised, a report was published by HM Inspectorate of Constabulary and the HM Crown Prosecution Service Inspectorate which found widespread failing by the police and Crown Prosecution Service in their duties of disclosure. One in five schedules compiled by the police were found to be inadequate and officers were 'routinely failing to comply with guidance and requirements'. The Crown Prosecution Service was found to suffer from poor decision making and poor supervision. Inadequate training and a lack of understanding were found to be key problems. The report emphasised that the 'importance of disclosure in the criminal justice system cannot be underestimated'.

Criminal practitioners do not need to be told why disclosure is important. It remains the 'golden thread' running through the criminal justice system and the battleground upon which trials can be won or lost. It is knowing this that defence advocates scrutinise and pursue requests for material held by the prosecution, if necessary trawling through reams or gigabytes of information, in order to ensure that every point which may assist their case is identified and deployed to maximum effect. This is despite the fact that this crucial and time-consuming aspect of case preparation remains unpaid under the legal aid system. And yet, despite the hard work and determination to leave no stone unturned, convictions are still quashed on a regular basis because material comes to light which, had it been used at trial, may have resulted in a not guilty verdict.

The question may not therefore be *why* disclosure is important but *how* to comply with disclosure obligations, *how* to pursue disclosure requests and *how* to do so effectively. What initially appears to be a simple procedure is surrounded by a maze of guidance, rules, protocols and codes. It was with the aim of helping all those involved in the disclosure process to follow the golden thread through this labyrinth that the authors of the first edition of this book, Caroline Bradley and Alastair Munt, produced a clear, practical and comprehensive guide in November 2012. We are indebted to their research, thought and precision.

Since that time, whether or not the maze has grown, it has certainly changed significantly. The Attorney General's Guidelines and the Judicial Protocol on Disclosure have been updated. Lord Justice Gross's review on Magistrates' Court Disclosure has been published. The Criminal Procedure and Investigations Act Codes of Practice, the Criminal Procedure Rules and the CPS Guidelines have been amended. Case law has continued to proliferate, including important cases such as *R v Boardman*, *R v R* and *R(Nunn) v Chief Constable of Suffolk*. An updated guide is therefore essential to ensure that police, prosecutors and defenders carry out their roles fairly and effectively.

Preface and acknowledgements

The authors would all like to thank our clerks and our colleagues at Garden Court Chambers for their support, their wisdom and their assistance. Individually:

- Tom would wish to thank Pippa and Milo for their inspiration and their patience;
- Shahida would like to thank her family and her mentor, Ali Bajwa QC, for all his guidance and support; and
- Emma wishes to thank her family, her partner Ali, and the Paris girls.

The authors believe that, at the time of going to press, the law is accurately stated.

Tom Wainwright
Shahida Begum
Emma Fenn
November 2017

Contents

Contents

Table of statutes

All references are to paragraph number.

Table of statutory instruments

All references are to paragraph number.

Table of cases

All references are to paragraph number.

H

J

L

M

P

R

Table of non-statutory sources of law

All references are to paragraph number.

Attorney General's Guidelines

Chapter 1

The criminal investigation

INTRODUCTION

1.01   The Criminal Procedure and Investigations Act 1996 (CPIA 1996) was enacted to 'make provision about criminal procedure and criminal investigations'.[1] Part I provides for disclosure and Part II is concerned with criminal investigations. The CPIA 1996 applies to all investigations that were commenced on or after 1 April 1997 but has been substantially amended by the Criminal Justice Act 2003 (CJA 2003) and the Criminal Justice and Immigration Act 2008 (CJIA 2008).

1.02   Under the provisions of the CPIA 1996 the accused is entitled, subject to some exceptions,[2] to all material and information that does not form part of the prosecution case against him and which satisfies the prosecution disclosure test. Material satisfies the prosecution disclosure test if it might reasonably be considered capable of undermining the case for the prosecution against the accused or assisting the case for the accused.[3] A number of roles and duties are imposed by the CPIA 1996 upon relevant participants which are designed to ensure that all information or material which may be relevant, whether obtained or generated, is properly recorded and retained. The procedure whereby unused material passes to the defence begins with the criminal investigation.

1.03   This chapter deals with:

• the criminal investigation	**1.04–1.08**
• specific roles	**1.09–1.10**
• specific duties	
– to pursue all reasonable lines of enquiry	**1.11–1.21**
	continued overleaf

---

1   Preamble to CPIA 1996.
2   See Chapters 8 and 13 in relation to public interest immunity and the Regulation of Investigatory Powers Act 2000 s. 17.
3   CPIA 1996, s 3(1).

– relevance of material	**1.22–1.28**
– to record information that may be relevant	**1.29–1.35**
– to retain material that may be relevant	**1.36–1.43**

THE CRIMINAL INVESTIGATION

1.04   A criminal investigation, as defined by CPIA 1996, s 22(1) is:

'… an investigation conducted by police officers[4] with a view to it being ascertained –

(a)   whether a person should be charged with an offence, or

(b)   whether a person charged with an offence is guilty of it.'[5]

1.05   A code of practice (the CPIA Code) has been issued under CPIA 1996, s 23 that sets out 'the manner in which police officers are to record, retain and reveal to the prosecutor material obtained in a criminal investigation' which may be relevant to the investigation, and related matters.[6] The current version of the CPIA Code was revised with effect on 19 March 2015, updating the previous version in effect from 4 April 2005.

1.06   CPIA Code, para 2.1 provides that a criminal investigation will include:

•   investigations into crimes that have been committed;

•   investigations whose purpose is to ascertain whether a crime has been committed, with a view to the possible institution of criminal proceedings; and

•   investigations which begin in the belief that a crime may be committed, for example when the police keep premises or individuals under observation for a period of time, with a view to the possible institution of criminal proceedings.

1.07   The CPIA Code is mandatory in relation to police officers. The CPIA 1996 also states that 'persons other than police officers' who are charged with the duty of conducting an investigation shall have regard to any relevant provision

---

4   *DPP v Metten* (unreported, 22 January 1999), per Buxton LJ – the instantaneous reaction of police officers to an incident that takes place in their presence is not part of an investigation of the type envisaged by CPIA 1996.

5   CPIA 1996, Part I, s 1(4) has an identical definition.

6   See the preamble to the CPIA Code.

of a Code which would apply if the investigation were conducted by police officers.[7] 'Persons other than police officers' will include those working in agencies such as the Health and Safety Executive, the Serious Fraud Office, the Financial Conduct Authority and the Royal Society for Protection of Animals.

1.08   In the early stages of an investigation there is often little or no prosecution supervision and no judicial oversight. Defence input is routinely limited to the accused's answers in interview. The police are entrusted with the responsibilities of gathering and preserving material that may point towards the innocence of the accused. It is imperative that this work is carried out with complete integrity.

SPECIFIC ROLES

1.09   The CPIA Code defines four distinct roles in the investigation:[8]

1   *An investigator*: An investigator is any police officer involved in the conduct of a criminal investigation. All investigators have a responsibility for carrying out the duties imposed on them under the CPIA Code including recording information and retaining records of information and other material.

2   *The officer in charge of an investigation (often referred to as the OIC)*: The officer in charge is responsible for directing the criminal investigation and ensuring that proper procedures are in place for recording information and retaining records of information together with other material in the investigation.

3   *The disclosure officer*: The disclosure officer is responsible for examining the material and revealing it to the prosecutor. He must certify that certain functions have been carried out and disclose material to the accused at the request of the prosecutor.

4   *The prosecutor*: The authority responsible for the conduct, on behalf of the Crown, of criminal proceedings resulting from a specific criminal investigation.

1.10   Although specific duties attach to each role, the first three roles are often performed by one and the same officer. It is dependent on the complexity of the case and administrative arrangements within each police force.[9]

---

7   CPIA 1996, s 26 and CPIA Code, para 1.1.
8   CPIA Code, para 2.1.
9   CPIA Code para 3.1.

SPECIFIC DUTIES

To pursue all reasonable lines of enquiry

1.11   One of the statutory objectives of the CPIA Code is to ensure that where a criminal investigation is conducted all reasonable lines of enquiry are pursued. The CPIA Code, para 3.5, provides:

> 'In conducting an investigation, the investigator should pursue all reasonable lines of enquiry, whether these point towards or away from the suspect. What is reasonable in each case will depend on the particular circumstances. For example, where material is held on computer, it is a matter for the investigator to decide which material on the computer it is reasonable to inquire into, and in what manner.'

1.12   The duty to pursue all reasonable lines of enquiry arises as soon as an investigation starts and cannot be avoided. In *R v Adam Joof* Hooper LJ stated:

> 'The responsibilities imposed by the Criminal Procedure and Investigations Act and by the Attorney General's Guidelines cannot be sidestepped by not making an enquiry. A police officer who believes that a person may have information which might undermine the case for the prosecution or assist the case for the suspect or defendant cannot decline to make enquiries of that person in order to avoid the need to disclose what the person might say.'[10]

1.13   The lines of enquiry must be reasonable as opposed to speculative. What would be a reasonable enquiry will depend on the circumstances of each case and, in particular, the information available at any particular time. In cases involving digital material it is not the duty of the prosecution to comb through all the material in its possession – e.g. every word or byte of computer material – for anything which might conceivably or speculatively assist the defence. In some cases a sift could be made by the disclosure officer manually assessing a computer or other digital material from its directory to determine which files may be relevant; in other cases, it would be proper to use search tools to identify relevant passages.[11]

1.14   The need to pursue reasonable lines of enquiry may arise at the scene. It may be necessary, inter alia, to make enquiries of potential eyewitnesses, seize CCTV footage or seek alternative suspects. Equally, what an accused says later in interview may give rise to further reasonable lines of enquiry.

---

10 [2012] EWCA Crim 1475 at para 17.
11 Attorney General's Guidelines on Disclosure (2013), para. 48 and Annex: Supplementary Guidelines on Digitally Stored Material (2011) A38–A44.

1.15 Before the accused is charged with an offence a prosecutor is required to consider the accuracy, reliability and credibility of the evidence, including witnesses, and any defence or information on which the defendant might rely.[12] This may give rise to further enquiries which may support or undermine the account of a witness.

1.16 Following service of the defence statement, prosecutors are under a specific duty to copy the defence statement to the disclosure officer and investigator as soon as practicable and advise the investigator if, in their view, reasonable and relevant lines of further enquiry should be pursued.[13] This should also apply upon the service or giving of an updated defence statement.[14]

1.17 An investigator should not show the defence statement to a non-expert witness. The extent to which the detail of a defence statement is made known to a witness will depend upon the extent to which it is necessary to clarify the issues disputed by the defence or assist the prosecutor in identifying further disclosable material or reasonable lines of enquiry. The investigator should seek guidance from the prosecutor if there is any doubt as to how the defence statement should be used in conducting further enquiries.[15]

1.18 Prosecution advocates should ensure that all material that ought to be disclosed under the CPIA 1996 is disclosed to the defence. They cannot, however, be expected to disclose material if they are not aware of its existence. As far as is possible, prosecution advocates must place themselves in a fully informed position to enable them to make decisions on disclosure.[16] Upon receipt of instructions, they should consider whether they can be satisfied that they are in possession of all relevant documentation and that they have been instructed fully regarding disclosure matters.[17]

1.19 Decisions already made regarding disclosure should be reviewed. If as a result, the advocate considers that further information or action is required, written advice should be promptly provided setting out the aspects that need clarification or action.[18] There is, by implication, a duty on the advocate to advise upon any further reasonable lines of enquiry whether they point towards or away from the accused.

---

12 Code for Crown Prosecutors (January 2013), para 4.5–4.6.
13 Attorney General's Guidelines on Disclosure (2013), paras 31.
14 CPIA 1996, s 6B which deals with updated defence statements is not yet in force.
15 CPS Disclosure Manual, para 15.19.
16 Attorney General's Guidelines on Disclosure (2013), para 35.
17 Attorney General's Guidelines on Disclosure (2013), para 36.
18 Attorney General's Guidelines on Disclosure (2013), para 36.

1.20   The duty of fairness to the accused, of which the duty to pursue all reasonable lines of enquiry forms a part, is contained in the Criminal Procedure Rules 2015 (CrimPR 2015). The police, the prosecutor and prosecution advocates are all participants[19] in the conduct of a criminal case and subject to a duty to prepare and conduct the case in accordance with the overriding objective.[20] The overriding objective '.... is that criminal cases be dealt with justly'.[21] Dealing with a criminal case justly includes:

- acquitting the innocent and convicting the guilty;

- dealing with the prosecution and the defence fairly;

- recognising the rights of an accused, particularly those under Article 6 of the European Convention on Human Rights.[22]

1.21   A serious and significant failure to pursue a reasonable line of enquiry which points away from the guilt of the accused or to take reasonable steps to secure material which satisfies the prosecution disclosure test may breach the duty to assist the court in achieving the overriding objective.

Relevance of material

1.22   There is a duty on an investigator to record information which may be relevant[23] and a duty to retain material which may be relevant.[24] The CPIA Code, para 2.1 provides:

> 'material is material of any kind, including information and objects, which is obtained or inspected in the course of a criminal investigation and which may be relevant to the investigation. This includes not only material coming into the possession of the investigator (such as documents seized in the course of searching premises) but also material generated by him (such as interview records)'.[25]

1.23   The terms 'information' and 'material' are intended to be all embracing to cover anything such as words, documents, objects and electronic records, whether obtained or seized during the investigation or generated by it.

---

19 CrimPR 2015, r 1.2(2): 'Anyone involved in any way with a criminal case is a participant in its conduct for the purposes of this rule.'
20 CrimPR 2015, r 1.2.
21 CrimPR 2015, r 1.1(1).
22 CrimPR 2015, r 1.1(2).
23 CPIA Code, para 4.1.
24 CPIA Code, para 5.1. See Attorney General's Guidelines on Disclosure (2013), paras 15 and 25.
25 CPIA Code, para 2.1. Under CPIA 1996, s 22(2), references to material means material of all kinds, and in particular references to information and objects of all descriptions.

1.24   The duties to record and retain material do not require that the material is relevant or that it passes the prosecution disclosure test. It is sufficient that it 'may be relevant' and this is a widely defined concept. The CPIA Code, para 2.1 provides:

> 'material may be *relevant to an investigation* if it appears to an investigator, or to the officer in charge of an investigation, or to the disclosure officer, that it has some bearing on any offence under investigation or any person being investigated, or on the surrounding circumstances of the case, unless it is incapable of having any impact on the case'.

1.25   Investigating officers, in determining whether material 'may be relevant' should consider:

- whether the information adds to the total knowledge of how the offence was committed, who may have committed it, and why;

- whether the information could support an alternative explanation, given the current understanding of events surrounding the offence; and

- what the potential consequences will be if the material is not preserved.[26]

1.26   It may not be possible to make a considered decision on the relevance of an item until later in the case when the facts are clearer.[27] Once an item is retained, the officer in charge, the disclosure officer or the investigator may seek the prosecutor's advice about whether a particular item 'may be relevant'.[28]

1.27   Investigators should always err on the side of caution, recording and retaining information where there is any doubt whether the material may be relevant.[29] This inclusive approach should reduce the risk of disclosable material failing to be recorded and retained and, if it is non-sensitive, will ensure the defence are aware of its existence by its appearance on the non-sensitive material schedule.[30]

1.28   As a general rule, pure opinion or speculation, eg police officers' theories about who committed the crime, is not unused material. If the opinion

---

26 CPS Disclosure Manual, para 5.15.
27 CPS Disclosure Manual, para 5.15.
28 CPIA Code, para 6.1.
29 Attorney General's Guidelines on Disclosure (2013), para 25; CPS Disclosure Manual, para 5.8.
30 Review of Disclosure in Criminal Proceedings, The Rt Hon Lord Justice Gross (September 2011), Executive summary, para 8(v) considered but decided against narrowing the relevance test.

or speculation is based on some other information or fact, not otherwise notified or apparent to the prosecutor, that information or fact might well be relevant to the investigation.[31] Likewise reports, advices and other communications between the CPS and police will usually be of an administrative nature or contain professional opinion based on evidential material or material already subject to revelation. They will usually have no bearing on the case and thus will not be relevant. However, a summary of charging advice may become disclosable if there is challenge to a prosecution decision.[32] Legal privilege does not apply to the Crown. If the material is disclosable but sensitive, public interest immunity would need to be asserted.

To record information that may be relevant

1.29   The duty to record information that may be relevant to the investigation in a durable or retrievable format is mandatory. The CPIA Code, para 4.1 provides:

> 'If material which may be relevant to the investigation consists of information which is not recorded in any form, the officer in charge of an investigation must ensure that it is recorded in a durable or retrievable form (whether in writing, on video or audio tape, or on computer disk).'[33]

1.30   Information will often consist of words spoken with a police officer, be they words at the scene of a crime, during a telephone conversation, before or after a witness makes a witness statement, or between a witness and a family liaison officer. Information may be within messages such as running commentaries and the details of a pursuit. Conversations with experts and other investigators, where the information discussed is likely to be relevant to the case and is not recorded elsewhere, should be recorded.[34]

1.31   Where it is not practicable to retain the initial record of information because it forms part of a larger record which is to be destroyed, its contents should be transferred as a true record to a durable and more easily-stored form before

---

31 CPS Disclosure Manual, para 5.12.

32 CPS Disclosure Manual, para 5.13. Note: If the content of any such document is relevant and not recorded elsewhere then the material should be described on the appropriate schedule. The prosecutor must not assume that there is no basis for disclosure. In relation to reasons for prosecution see R (on the application of Barons Pub Company Limited) v Staines Magistrates' Court v Runnymede Borough Council, Director of Public Prosecutions [2013] EWHC 898 (Admin) para. 51(iv).

33 See also CPIA 1996, s 22(3).

34 CPS Disclosure Manual, para 5.19.

that happens.[35] Such a larger record could include control room audio, custody suite tapes, traffic car videos of speeding offences or other similar recordings.[36] The officer in charge of the investigation should identify information that should be retained and ensure that it is transferred accurately to a durable and retrievable form before the tapes are destroyed.[37]

1.32 The impact of negative information can be significant and, where it may be relevant, must be recorded. Negative information may include:[38]

- information that a number of people present at the scene of an alleged offence state they saw nothing unusual;

- CCTV footage inconsistent with the prosecution case;

- the presence of fingerprints at a crime scene which cannot be identified as belonging to the accused; and

- crime scene samples that do not match those of the accused.

1.33 Where information which may be relevant is obtained, it must be recorded at the time it is obtained or as soon as practicable thereafter. This would include information obtained in house-to-house enquiries. The requirement to record information promptly does not require an investigator to take a statement from a potential witness where it would not otherwise be taken.[39]

1.34 Operations for intelligence purposes may, subject to public interest immunity considerations, become disclosable. Any officers involved in intelligence operations should regularly and actively consider whether information they possess has a bearing on any live investigations or prosecutions. If this is the case, the officer should act quickly to see that it is brought to the attention of the disclosure officer or prosecutor.[40]

1.35 Any information, once recorded in compliance with the CPIA Code, para 4, becomes material to which the duty to retain under the CPIA Code, para 5 applies.

---

35 CPIA Code, para 4.2.
36 CPS Disclosure Manual, para 5.18.
37 CPS Disclosure Manual, para 5.18.
38 CPIA Code, para 4.3; CPS Disclosure Manual, para 5.16.
39 CPIA Code, para 4.4.
40 See *R v Barkshire* [2011] EWCA Crim 1885 and R v Bard [2014] EWCA Crim 463 for the consequences of failing to disclose information received by an undercover officer or the fact of involvement of an undercover officer.

To retain material that may be relevant

1.36 The duty to retain material that may be relevant is mandatory. The CPIA Code, para 5 provides:

> 'The investigator must retain material obtained in a criminal investigation which may be relevant to the investigation. Material may be photographed, video-recorded, captured digitally or otherwise retained in the form of a copy rather than the original at any time, if the original is perishable; the original was supplied to the investigator rather than generated by him and is to be returned to its owner; or the retention of a copy rather than the original is reasonable in all the circumstances.'

1.37 The duty to retain material is subject to the Police and Criminal Evidence Act 1984, s 22 which details how anything seized under section 19 (general power of seizure) and section 20 (powers of seizure for computerized information) may be retained 'so long as is necessary in all the circumstances':

- for use as evidence at a trial;
- for forensic examination and for investigation in connection with an offence; and
- to establish its lawful owner.[41]

1.38 Previously examined material which was not retained, as it was not thought to be relevant, may become relevant as the case develops and issues are clarified. In such circumstances the officer in charge should take steps, wherever practicable, to obtain the material or ensure that it is retained for further inspection or for production in court if required.[42]

1.39 If the officer in charge believes that other persons may be in possession of material that may be relevant to the investigation which has not been obtained, he should ask the disclosure officer (if he is a different person) to invite those persons to retain the material in case it becomes relevant. The disclosure officer should inform the prosecutor that they may have such material.[43]

1.40 The developments in a case, triggering the responsibilities of the officer in charge to obtain and retain, may often derive from information provided by the accused in his interview or in his defence statement.

---

41 Police and Criminal Evidence Act 1984, s 22(1) and (2).
42 CPIA Code, para 5.3.
43 CPIA Code, para 3.6.

1.41   Some categories of material are specifically identified by the CPIA Code as material that should be retained where it 'may be relevant'.[44] These categories are:

- crime reports (including crime report forms, relevant parts of incident report books or police officer's notebooks);

- custody records;

- records which are derived from tapes of telephone messages (for example, 999 calls) containing descriptions of an alleged offence or offender;

- final versions of witness statements (and draft versions where their content differs from the final version), including any exhibits mentioned (unless these have been returned to their owner on the understanding that they will be produced in court if required);

- interview records (written records or audio or video tapes, of interviews with actual or potential witnesses or suspects);

- communications between the police and experts such as forensic scientists, reports of work carried out by experts, and schedules of scientific material prepared by the expert for the investigator, for the purpose of criminal proceedings;

- records of the first description of a suspect by each potential witness who purports to identify or describe the suspect, whether or not the description differs from that of subsequent descriptions by that or other witnesses;

- any material casting doubt on the reliability of a witness.[45]

1.42   The duty to retain material where it 'may be relevant' to the investigation specifically includes material which may satisfy the prosecution disclosure test.[46] This would include:

- information provided by an accused which indicates an explanation for the offence with which he has been charged;

- any material casting doubt on the reliability of a confession;

- any material casting doubt upon the reliability of a prosecution witness.[47]

---

44 CPIA Code, para 5.4.
45 CPIA Code, para 5.4.
46 i.e. any prosecution material which might reasonably be considered capable of undermining the case for the prosecution against the accused or of assisting the case for the accused.
47 CPIA Code, para 5.5.

1.43   Material which may be relevant to the investigation must be retained until a decision is taken whether to institute proceedings against a person for an offence.[48] If proceedings are instituted, the material must be retained at least until the accused is acquitted, convicted or the prosecutor decides not to proceed with the case.[49] If the accused is convicted, the material must be retained at least until six months from the date of conviction or upon his release from prison or discharge from hospital if the period is longer than six months.[50] In the event of an appeal against conviction (or referral to the Criminal Cases Review Commission) the material must be retained until the appeal or referral has concluded.[51]

---

48 CPIA Code, para 5.7.
49 CPIA Code, para 5.8.
50 CPIA Code, paras 5.9.
51 CPIA Code, paras 5.10.

Chapter 2

The role of the disclosure officer

INTRODUCTION

2.01　　The skill, competence and diligence of the disclosure officer are central to the operation of the disclosure process. They are responsible, amongst other things, for examining material and generating proper, accurate and transparent schedules of unused material that are integral to determining what is ultimately disclosed to the defence.

2.02　　This chapter deals with:

• the disclosure officer	**2.03–2.11**
• examination of material	**2.12–2.19**
• scheduling	
– timing	**2.20–2.25**
– contents and format	**2.26–2.30**
– non-sensitive material (MG6C)	**2.31–2.32**
– sensitive material (MG6D)	**2.33–2.39**
– block scheduling	**2.40–2.41**
• revelation to the prosecutor	
– schedules	**2.42**
– disclosure officer's report (MG6E)	**2.43–2.50**
– other police forms	**2.51–2.52**
• continuing disclosure	**2.53–2.55**
– amending and updating	**2.56–2.58**
• certifications by disclosure officer	**2.59–2.61**
• disclosure to the defence	**2.62–2.66**

THE DISCLOSURE OFFICER

2.03 The disclosure officer must:

- examine all relevant material that has been retained by the investigator and that does not form part of the prosecution case;

- create schedules that fully describe the material and detail its precise location;

- reveal this material to the prosecutor;

- continually review the schedules and retained material, particularly after service of the defence statement;

- certify that certain disclosure steps have been complied with; and

- disclose material to the defence as requested by the prosecutor.[1]

2.04 The disclosure officer should, in addition:

- alert third parties to the need to preserve material that may be relevant to the investigation and give consideration to obtaining it;[2]

- take reasonable steps to identify, secure and consider material held by any third party (including Government departments and other Crown bodies) where such material appears relevant to an issue in the case;[3] and

- consider whether relevant material may exist in relation to other linked investigations or prosecutions.[4]

2.05 The disclosure officer must discharge their responsibilities promptly and properly in order to ensure that justice is not delayed, denied or frustrated.[5]

2.06 The Chief Officer of Police for each police force is responsible for ensuring that disclosure officers and their deputies have sufficient skills and authority, commensurate with the complexity of the investigation, to discharge their functions effectively.[6] It is crucial that the police (and indeed all investigative

---

1 CPS Disclosure Manual, para 3.9.
2 CPS Disclosure Manual, para 4.7.
3 Attorney General's Guidelines on Disclosure (2013), paras 53–58. This responsibility is shared with investigators and the prosecutor.
4 CPS Disclosure Manual, paras 4.4–4.5. This responsibility is shared with investigators and the prosecutor.
5 Disclosure: A Protocol for the Control and Management of Unused Material in the Crown Court ('Disclosure Protocol'), para 16.
6 CPIA Code, para 3.3.

bodies) implement appropriate training regimes and appoint competent disclosure officers, who have sufficient knowledge of the issues in the case.[7] For instance, where a case involves the inspection of digital material, the disclosure officer will need to have the necessary skills to liaise with any computer forensic experts.[8] Likewise, in an enquiry using the 'Holmes2' system,[9] the disclosure officer must have completed training in the specific 'Holmes2' disclosure facility.[10]

2.07   The Chief Officer of Police is responsible for putting in place arrangements to ensure that in every investigation the appointment of the officer in charge and the disclosure officer is recorded. Any replacement must also be recorded.[11]

2.08   Practitioners commonly find that the officer in the case is also the disclosure officer. Whether the role of disclosure officer is performed by the officer in the case or by another officer depends on the complexity of the case and the administrative arrangements within each police force. Where more than one person undertakes these roles, close consultation between them is essential to the effective performance of the duties imposed by the CPIA Code.[12]

2.09   A person must not be appointed as disclosure officer or continue to act in that role if it is likely to result in a conflict of interest.[13] The advice of a more senior officer must always be sought about any potential conflict, as should the advice of a prosecutor where necessary.[14]

2.10   The officer in charge may delegate tasks to another investigator.[15] The CPS Disclosure Manual fixes the officer in charge with the responsibility of appointing the disclosure officer and, in particular, where there is more than one disclosure officer, for ensuring that there is a lead disclosure officer who is the focus for enquiries and responsible for ensuring that an investigator's disclosure obligations are complied with.[16] Whether the officer in charge appoints a

---

7 CPIA Code, para. 3.3.
8 CPS Disclosure Manual, para 30.4.
9 Home Office Large Major Enquiry System 2 – a computer database for large-scale investigations.
10 CPS Disclosure Manual, para 31.8.
11 CPIA Code, paras 3.3, 3.7.
12 CPIA Code, para 3.1.
13 CPIA Code, para 3.3; and see R v Joof [2012] EWCA Crim 1475 at para 29–32.
14 CPIA Code, para 3.3.
15 CPIA Code, para 3.4.
16 CPS Disclosure Manual, para 3.5; Attorney General's Guidelines on Disclosure (2013), para 18.

disclosure officer at the outset or later will depend on the seriousness, complexity and scale of the case.[17] A disclosure officer should be appointed at the beginning of an enquiry involving the Holmes2 system.[18]

2.11   The appointment must be in sufficient time to enable the disclosure officer, with the assistance of the officer in charge and investigators, to become fully familiar with the facts and background to the case and to prepare the unused schedules.

EXAMINATION OF MATERIAL

2.12   Disclosure officers, or deputy disclosure officers, must inspect, view or listen to all relevant material that has been retained by the investigator and the disclosure officer must provide a personal declaration to the effect that this task has been undertaken.[19] If the disclosure officer is uncertain whether all relevant material has been revealed to him, enquiries should be made of the officer in charge to resolve the matter.[20] It is the responsibility of the lead disclosure officer to ensure that an investigator's disclosure obligations are complied with.[21]

2.13   Generally, the disclosure officer will be required to examine in detail all relevant material retained by an investigator, however, the extent and manner of the examination will depend on the nature of the material and its form. With technological advances and the explosion of electronic materials the physical examination of every document in paper or electronic format, particularly but not exclusively in fraud cases, will be virtually impossible.[22] This would place unrealistic or disproportionate demands on the investigator and prosecutor.

2.14   To satisfy the prosecution disclosure test it may be reasonable to examine digital material using software search tools or to establish the contents of large volumes of material by dip sampling.[23]

---

17 CPS Disclosure Manual, para 3.11. The CPIA Code makes no provision as to when the disclosure officer must be appointed.
18 CPS Disclosure Manual, para 31.9.
19 Attorney General's Guidelines on Disclosure (2013), para 21; CPIA Code, para 2.1.
20 CPS Disclosure Manual, para 10.13.
21 Attorney General's Guidelines on Disclosure (2013), para 18.
22 Attorney General's Guidelines on Disclosure (2013), para 21; Review of Disclosure in Criminal Proceedings, The Rt Hon Lord Justice Gross (September 2011), Executive summary, para 8 (xxvi).
23 Attorney General's Guidelines on Disclosure (2013) Annex: Supplementary Guidelines on Digitally Stored Material (2011), paras A38–A44.

2.15   Where cases involve large quantities of data the officer in charge will develop a strategy setting out how the material should be examined to identify certain categories of data.[24] If search tools are used to examine digital material it will usually be appropriate to provide the accused with a copy of the search terms used, or to be used, and invite defence input of search terms to ensure that reasonable and proportionate searches are carried out.[25] The service of a defence statement is not a pre-condition to this defence input.

2.16   With vast quantities of electronic material, it is important that parties cooperate responsibly to see that the case is dealt with efficiently and expeditiously. As part of its case management function, the court should give a firm and clear steer as to what is required and short shrift to any party not engaging appropriately.[26]

2.17   If such material is not examined in detail, it must still be described on the disclosure schedules accurately and as clearly as possible. The extent and manner of the examination of the material must also be described together with justification for such action.[27]

2.18   The prosecutor is required to take action where he believes the disclosure officer has not examined all relevant material retained by the investigator and request that it be done.[28]

2.19   A disclosure officer's examination of material retained by an investigator must be at least sufficient for him to:

•   decide whether the material may be relevant;

•   describe the material that may be relevant adequately on the appropriate schedule;

•   decide whether the material satisfies the prosecution test for disclosure; and

•   decide whether the material is non-sensitive or sensitive (in whole or in part) and, if it is sensitive, to explain why.

---

24 Attorney General's Guidelines on Disclosure (2013) Annex: Supplementary Guidelines on Digitally Stored Material (2011), para 43 ; CPS Disclosure Manual, Chs 29–31.
25 Attorney General's Guidelines on Disclosure (2013) Annex: Supplementary Guidelines on Digitally Stored Material (2011), para A43.
26 Review of Disclosure in Criminal Proceedings, The Rt Hon Lord Justice Gross (September 2011), Executive summary, para 8(xxvii); CrimPR 2015, r 3.2.
27 Attorney General's Guidelines on Disclosure (2013) Annex: Supplementary Guidelines on Digitally Stored Material (2011), para A43–A49.
28 Attorney General's Guidelines on Disclosure (2013), para 30.

SCHEDULING

Timing

2.20   The disclosure officer is responsible for preparing the schedules and they must give them, signed and dated, to the prosecutor. They must ensure that a schedule is prepared where:

- the accused is charged with an offence which is triable only on indictment;

- the accused is charged with an offence which is triable either way, and it is considered that the case is likely to be tried on indictment.[29]

2.21   If the accused is charged with a summary offence or an either-way offence that is likely to remain in the magistrates' court, and it is considered that they are likely to plead not guilty, a streamlined disclosure certificate must be completed. If it is considered that they are likely to plead guilty (e.g. because they have admitted the offence), a schedule or streamlined disclosure certificate is not required.[30]

2.22   In every case, irrespective of the anticipated plea, if there is material known to the disclosure officer that might assist the defence with the early preparation of their case or at a bail hearing (for example, a key prosecution witness has relevant previous convictions or a witness has withdrawn his or her statement) a note must be made on the MG5. The material must be disclosed to the prosecutor who will disclose it to the defence if they think it meets the common law test.[31] Where there is no such material a certificate to that effect must be completed.[32]

2.23   The duty to prepare a schedule does not arise under the CPIA Code until the accused has been charged. The streamlined disclosure certificate must be disclosed to the accused either at the hearing where a not guilty plea is entered or as soon as possible following a formal indication of a not guilty plea.[33]

---

29 CPIA Code, para 6.9.
30 CPIA Code para 6.3–6.5.
31 CPIA Code 6.6.
32 CPIA Code 6.3.
33 CPIA Code para. 10.1.

2.24   The submission of the schedules by the disclosure officer should be at the same time,[34] wherever practicable,[35] as they give the prosecutor the full file containing the material for the prosecution case.[36]

2.25   Discussions between the police and prosecution before the schedules are prepared may help greatly in large or complicated cases and the disclosure officer or officer in charge should not hesitate to contact the prosecution for early advice.[37]

Contents and format

2.26   Material must be listed on a schedule if:

*   it may be relevant and has been retained in accordance with the CPIA Code; and

*   the disclosure officer believes that it will not form part of the prosecution case.[38]

2.27   Material may be relevant if it appears to an investigator, the officer in charge or the disclosure officer that it has some bearing on any offence under investigation or any person being investigated, or on the surrounding circumstances of the case, unless it is incapable of having any impact on the case.[39]

2.28   The officer in charge, disclosure officer or an investigator may seek advice from the prosecutor about whether any particular item of material may be relevant to the investigation and this should take place as soon as practicable.[40]

2.29   It is essential that the disclosure officer ensures that, subject to the exception of block scheduling (see **2.40**), individual items are listed separately on the schedule and are numbered consecutively. It is crucial that descriptions by disclosure officers in non-sensitive schedules are detailed, clear and accurate. The descriptions may require a summary of the contents of the retained material

---

34 Or as soon as reasonably practicable after the decision on mode of trial or the plea, in cases to which CPIA Code, para 6.9 applies.
35 The Disclosure Protocol, para 14 states that 'wherever possible' the schedules should be sent to the prosecutor at the same time as the file. The CPS Disclosure Manual, paras 3.11, 6.1 anticipate that the schedules will be included with the full file.
36 CPS Disclosure Manual, para 6.1.
37 CPS Disclosure Manual, para 10.11.
38 CPIA Code, para 6.2.
39 As defined in CPIA Code, para 2.1.
40 CPIA Code, para 6.1; CPS Disclosure Manual, para 6.2.

to assist the prosecutor to make an informed decision on disclosure.[41] Where continuation sheets are used or additional schedules sent in later submissions, the numbering of items must be consecutive to the numbering on the earlier schedules.[42]

2.30   Sensitive schedules must contain sufficient information to enable the prosecutor to make an informed decision as to whether or not the material itself should be viewed, to the extent possible without compromising the confidentiality of the information.[43]

Non-sensitive material (MG6C)

2.31   Material which the disclosure officer does not believe to be sensitive must be listed on a schedule of non-sensitive material (MG6C).[44] The schedule must contain a statement that the disclosure officer does not believe the material to be sensitive.[45] Material which contains some sensitive information (such as personal contact details) but is otherwise non-sensitive should be edited and the edited material scheduled on the MG6C. The unedited version can be scheduled on the MG6D.[46]

2.32   In practice, the non-sensitive schedules are valuable to the defence in that they allow the defence to request hitherto undisclosed material which might satisfy the prosecution disclosure test as well as to point out inadequately described items.

Sensitive material (MG6D)

2.33   Sensitive material is material the disclosure of which the disclosure officer believes would give rise to a real risk of serious prejudice to an important public interest.[47] For detailed consideration of this issue see **Chapter 8**.

2.34   Any material believed to be sensitive must be listed either on a schedule of sensitive material – the MG6D[48] – or, in exceptional circumstances,

---

41 Attorney General's Guidelines on Disclosure (2013), para 13. See CPIA Code, para 6.11–6.13; Attorney General's Guidelines on Disclosure (2013) Annex: Supplementary Guidelines on Digitally Stored Material (2011), para A49; CPS Disclosure Manual, paras 7.2–7.3.
42 CPS Disclosure Manual, para 7.2.
43 Attorney General's Guidelines on Disclosure (2013), para 24.
44 For a copy of an MG6C form see Appendix 7.
45 CPIA Code, para 6.10.
46 CPS Disclosure Manual, para 8.21.
47 For a copy of an MG6D form see Appendix 8.
48 CPIA Code, para 6.15.

revealed to the prosecutor separately. Where there is no sensitive material, the disclosure officer must record this fact on a schedule of sensitive material.[49] The schedule must include a statement that the disclosure officer believes the material to be sensitive and the reason for that belief.[50]

2.35   The CPIA Code, para 6.15 provides a list of examples of material which might be sensitive:[51]

'–   material relating to national security;

–   material received from the intelligence and security agencies;

–   material relating to intelligence from foreign sources which reveals sensitive intelligence gathering methods;

–   material given in confidence;[52]

–   material relating to the identity or activities of informants, or undercover police officers, or witnesses, or other persons supplying information to the police who may be in danger if their identities are revealed;

–   material revealing the location of any premises or other places used for police surveillance, or the identity of any person allowing a police officer to use them for surveillance;

–   material revealing, either directly or indirectly, techniques and methods relied upon by a police officer in the course of a criminal investigation, for example covert surveillance techniques, or other methods of detecting crime;

–   material whose disclosure might facilitate the commission of other offences or hinder the prevention and detection of crime;

–   material upon the strength of which search warrants were obtained;

–   material containing details of persons taking part in identification parades;

–   material supplied to an investigator during a criminal investigation which has been generated by an official of a body concerned with the regulation or supervision of bodies corporate or of persons engaged in

---

49   CPIA Code, para 6.14.
50   CPIA Code, para 6.14.
51   This list is not determinative and each item must be considered independently before it is included in the sensitive schedule.
52   Any doubts as to whether the information was given in confidence should be clarified with the provider of the information: see CPS Disclosure Manual, para 8.8.

financial activities, or which has been generated by a person retained by such a body;

–   material supplied to an investigator during a criminal investigation which relates to a child or young person and which has been generated by a local authority social services department, an Area Child Protection Committee or other party contacted by an investigator during the investigation;

–   material relating to the private life of a witness.'

2.36   To assist the prosecutor in deciding how to deal with sensitive material that satisfies the prosecution disclosure test, the CPS Disclosure Manual, para 8.13 advises that the investigator and disclosure officer should provide detailed information of:

'•   the reasons why the material is said to be sensitive;

•   the degree of sensitivity said to attach to the material, in other words, why it is considered that disclosure will create a real risk of serious prejudice to an important public interest;

•   the consequences of revealing to the defence:

  •   the material itself;

  •   the category of the material;

  •   the fact that an application may be made;

•   the apparent significance of the material to the issues in the trial;

•   the involvement of any third parties in bringing the material to the attention of the police;

•   where the material is likely to be the subject of an order for disclosure, what the police view is regarding continuance of the prosecution; and

•   whether it is possible to disclose the material without compromising its sensitivity.'

2.37   There is no requirement to include material on the sensitive schedule where the investigator considers the material so sensitive that it would be inappropriate to record it. This exception will only apply where compromising the material would be likely to lead directly to the loss of life, or directly threaten national security.[53]

---

53   CPIA Code, para 6.16.

2.38   The investigator who knows the details of the 'highly' sensitive material should inform the prosecutor as soon as is reasonably practicable after the file containing the material for the prosecution case is sent to the prosecutor. Such material should be listed and described on a separate 'highly sensitive' MG6D. It must be ensured that the prosecutor is able to inspect the material to assess its disclosability.[54]

2.39   Where there is no sensitive material the disclosure officer should still submit the MG6D endorsed and signed to that effect.[55]

Block scheduling

2.40   It may not be practicable to list each item of material separately when there are many items of a similar or repetitive nature. These items may be listed in a block and described by a quantity and generic title.[56] Block scheduling is subject to the caveat that the disclosure officer must ensure that any items among the material that is listed in a block which might satisfy the prosecution disclosure test are listed and described individually.[57]

2.41   The inappropriate use of generic listing by the disclosure officer is likely to lead to requests from the prosecutor and the defence to see the items in question which may lead to wasted resources and unnecessary delay.[58]

REVELATION TO THE PROSECUTOR

Schedules

2.42   The disclosure officer must give the schedules concerning unused material to the prosecutor. Wherever possible this should be done at the same time as the prosecution file in preparation for the first hearing and any case management that the judge may wish to conduct at that stage.[59]

---

54 CPIA Code, para 6.17.
55 CPS Disclosure Manual, para 8.3.
56 CPIA Code, para 6.12. Review of Disclosure in Criminal Proceedings, The Rt Hon Lord Justice Gross (September 2011), paras 8(vi), 57–58 and 120 called for the greater use of block listing.
57 CPIA Code, para 6.13; see Attorney General's Guidelines on Disclosure (2013) Annex: Supplementary Guidelines on Digitally Stored Material (2011), A50; CPS Disclosure Manual, paras 7.5, 31.40–42.
58 CPS Disclosure Manual, para 7.4.
59 CPIA Code, para 7.1B.

Disclosure officer's report (MG6E)

2.43   The disclosure officer is required to submit the disclosure officer's report (MG6E)[60] detailing any material an investigator has retained, including sensitive material not listed on the MG6D,[61] which may satisfy the prosecution disclosure test.[62] They should also explain on the MG6E, with reference to the relevant item number, why they have come to that view.[63] Copies of the material that the disclosure officer believes satisfies the prosecution disclosure test should accompany the MG6E.

2.44   Material that can satisfy the prosecution disclosure test will include anything that tends to show a fact inconsistent with the elements of the case that must be proved by the prosecution.[64] This can be through its use in cross-examination or by its capacity to support a legal argument or suggest an explanation for the accused's actions.[65]

2.45   Unless this material has already been supplied in the prosecution file, certain categories of material are so self-evidently capable of satisfying the prosecution disclosure test that the CPIA Code, para 7.3 expressly stipulates that it must be given to the prosecutor, namely:

'–   information provided by an accused person which indicates an explanation for the offence with which he has been charged;

–   any material casting doubt on the reliability of a confession;[66]

–   any material casting doubt on the reliability of a prosecution witness;

–   any other material which the investigator believes may satisfy the test for prosecution disclosure in the Act.'

---

60   For a copy of an MG6E form see Appendix 9.
61   CPIA Code, para 7.2. Note this is in contrast to CPIA Code, para 6.16 which states that the responsibility for informing the prosecutor of material too sensitive to be entered on the sensitive schedule lies with the investigator. See also CPIA Code, para 6.14.
62   i.e. any prosecution material which might reasonably be considered capable of undermining the case for prosecution against the accused or of assisting the case for the accused.
63   CPIA Code, para 7.2; CPS Disclosure Manual, para 10.7.
64   Attorney General's Guidelines on Disclosure (2013), para 4–5; CPS Disclosure Manual, para 10.3.
65   Attorney General's Guidelines on Disclosure (2013), para 6.
66   This may include the accused's mental or physical health, his intellectual capacity or any alleged ill-treatment in custody; see CPS Disclosure Manual, para 10.1.

2.46 Other examples of material that would satisfy the prosecution disclosure test are:

- material which may point to another person, whether charged or not (including a co-accused) having involvement in the commission of the offence;[67]

- material that might support a defence that is either raised by the defence or apparent from the prosecution papers;[68]

- material which may have a bearing on the admissibility of any prosecution evidence;[69]

- any previous convictions and cautions for prosecution witnesses;[70]

- any motives for making false allegations by prosecution witnesses;[71] and

- whether the witness has sought, been offered or received a reward.[72]

2.47 To assist prosecutors to review the case, copies of the crime report and the log of messages (edited if necessary) should routinely be copied to the prosecutor in every case in which a full file is provided.[73] If sensitive material cannot be edited the material should be listed on the MG6D.[74] Local arrangements between the police and CPS may provide for other types of material to be routinely disclosed.

2.48 The disclosure officer should use a wide interpretation when identifying material that might satisfy the prosecution disclosure test.[75] They should consult with the prosecutor where necessary to help identify material that may require disclosure.[76] While items of material when viewed in isolation may not satisfy the prosecution disclosure test they may do so when viewed together.[77]

2.49 If the prosecutor asks to inspect material which has not already been copied to him, the disclosure officer must allow him to inspect it. If the prosecutor asks for a copy of material (which has not already been copied to him) he must

---

67 CPS Disclosure Manual, para 10.1.
68 CPS Disclosure Manual, para 10.3.
69 CPS Disclosure Manual, para 10.1.
70 CPS Disclosure Manual, para 10.1.
71 CPS Disclosure Manual, para 10.1.
72 CPS Disclosure Manual, para 10.1.
73 CPS Disclosure Manual, paras 10.8–10.9.
74 CPS Disclosure Manual, paras 10.9–10.10.
75 CPS Disclosure Manual, para 10.5.
76 CPS Disclosure Manual, para 10.5.
77 Attorney General's Guidelines on Disclosure (2013), para 7.

be given a copy unless the disclosure officer believes, having consulted with the officer in charge, that the material is too sensitive to be copied and can only be inspected.[78]

2.50   Where material consists of information, which is recorded other than in writing, it is for the disclosure officer and prosecutor to agree whether the information should be given in its original form or in relevant extracts in the same form or in a transcript.[79]

Other police forms

2.51   The disclosure officer should submit an MG6 in the prosecution file. The MG6 contains any observations or explanations regarding the contents of the schedules and indicates whether the investigation commenced on or before 4 April 2005.[80] Where a relevant officer has misconduct or disciplinary findings against him these should be recorded on the MG6B.[81] The disclosure officer should inform the prosecutor of any additional enquiries that have been carried out in response to the defence statement and any results. This should be done on the MG20.[82]

2.52   The schedules and accompanying material should be brought to the attention of the prosecutor 'as soon as possible'.[83]

CONTINUING DISCLOSURE

2.53   The CPIA 1996, s 7A imposes a continuing duty on the prosecutor, for the duration of criminal proceedings against the accused, to disclose material which satisfies the prosecution disclosure test (subject to public interest immunity and the Regulation of Investigatory Powers Act 2000, s 17). To enable the prosecutor to discharge this continuing duty of disclosure, any new material coming to light after the initial investigations should be treated in the same way as the earlier material.[84]

---

78 CPIA Code, para 7.4.
79 CPIA Code, para 7.5.
80 Prior to 4 April 2005, different disclosure provisions apply. See CPS Disclosure Manual, paras 6.6–6.7.
81 CPS Disclosure Manual, para 11.6 and Ch 18 generally.
82 CPS Disclosure Manual, para 15.21.
83 CPS Disclosure Manual, para 11.7.
84 CPIA Code, para 8.2.

2.54 New material, which may be relevant to the investigation but which does not form part of the prosecution case, must be described on a further MG6C, MG6D or a continuation sheet and signed and dated before being submitted to the prosecutor. A further MG6E should be submitted even if none of the new material satisfies the prosecution disclosure test.[85]

2.55 After a defence statement has been served, the CPIA Code places a specific duty on the disclosure officer to look again at the material (sensitive and non-sensitive) that has been retained and draw the attention of the prosecutor to any material which satisfies the prosecution disclosure test.[86]

Amending and updating

2.56 The disclosure officer is responsible for keeping the schedules accurate and up-to-date. As the investigation progresses schedules may need to be amended and any such amendments should be done promptly and returned to the prosecutor as soon as possible.[87] If the disclosure officer is required by the prosecutor to remedy defects in the schedules, he must immediately take all necessary remedial action to furnish the prosecutor with properly completed schedules.[88]

2.57 When the schedules are first submitted to the prosecutor, the disclosure officer may not know exactly what material will form the case against the accused and the prosecutor may not have given advice about the likely relevance of particular items. Once these matters have been determined, the CPIA Code, para 8.1 provides that:

'the disclosure officer must give to the prosecutor, where necessary, an amended certificate or schedule listing any additional material:

–   which may be relevant to the investigation,

–   which does not form part of the case against the accused,

–   which is not already listed on the schedule, and

–   which he believes is not sensitive,

unless he is informed in writing by the prosecutor that the prosecutor intends to disclose the material to the defence.'

---

85 CPS Disclosure Manual, para 10.25–10.26.
86 CPIA Code, para 8.3; CPS Disclosure Manual, para 15.20.
87 CPS Disclosure Manual, para 10.18.
88 CPS Disclosure Manual, para 10.22.

2.58   If the prosecutor creates unused material by extracting statements or documents from the evidence bundle in the prosecution file and disclosing it straight to the defence, he can do so without waiting for the disclosure officer to amend the schedules but should advise the disclosure officer accordingly.[89]

CERTIFICATIONS BY DISCLOSURE OFFICER

2.59   The purpose of certification is to provide an assurance to the prosecutor that all relevant material that has been retained and made available to the disclosure officer has been identified, considered and revealed to the prosecutor.[90]

2.60   Certifications are required to show:

(i)   that the disclosure officer has revealed to the prosecutor all relevant retained material. He should certify on the MG6E –

> 'To the best of my knowledge and belief, all relevant material which has been retained and made available to me has been inspected, viewed or listened to and revealed to the prosecutor in accordance with the Criminal Procedure and Investigations Act 1996 as amended, the Code of Practice and the Attorney General's Guidelines.'[91]

(ii)   that the disclosure officer believes that there is no material that satisfies the disclosure test. He should certify on the MG6E –

> 'I have reviewed all the relevant material which has been retained and made available to me and there is nothing to the best of my knowledge and belief that might reasonably be considered capable of undermining the prosecution case against the accused or assisting the case for the accused.'[92]

(iii)   that the disclosure officer believes that there is no material that satisfies the disclosure test following receipt of the defence statement. He should certify on a further MG6E –

> 'I have considered the defence statement and further reviewed all the retained relevant material made available to me and there is nothing to the best of my knowledge and belief which might reasonably

---

89 CPS Disclosure Manual, para 10.21.
90 CPIA Code, para 9.1; CPS Disclosure Manual, para 10.16.
91 CPS Disclosure Manual, para 10.16.
92 CPS Disclosure Manual, para 10.17.

be considered capable of undermining the case for the prosecution against the accused or of assisting the case for the accused.'[93]

2.61   The disclosure officer must sign and date each certification. Further certifications are necessary when any later schedule or material is revealed to the prosecutor and must also be signed and dated.[94] The case against each accused must be considered and certified separately.[95]

DISCLOSURE TO THE DEFENCE

2.62   The prosecutor is responsible for ensuring the disclosure of material under the CPIA 1996.[96] The disclosure officer, however, must disclose it to the accused[97] where the material has not already been copied to the prosecutor and the prosecutor requests its disclosure on the grounds that:

(i)   the material satisfies the prosecution disclosure test; or

(ii)   the court has ordered disclosure after considering an application from the accused.

2.63   If material has been copied to the prosecutor and it is to be disclosed, whether the prosecutor or disclosure officer discloses it is a matter of agreement between the two of them.[98]

2.64   The disclosure officer must disclose material to the accused either by giving him a copy or by allowing him to inspect it. Where the accused asks for a copy of any material which he has been allowed to inspect, the disclosure officer must give it to him, unless in the opinion of the disclosure officer that is not practicable (e.g. the material consists of an object which cannot be copied or the volume of material is too great) or it is not desirable (e.g. a statement of a child witness in relation to a sexual offence).[99]

2.65   Where the accused has been allowed to inspect material consisting of information which is recorded other than in writing, whether it should be given to the accused in its original form or in the form of a transcript is a matter

---

93   CPS Disclosure Manual, paras 10.14, 15.22.
94   CPIA Code, para 9.1.
95   CPS Disclosure Manual, para 10.15.
96   CPIA 1996, s 3.
97   CPIA Code, para 10.1A.
98   CPIA Code, para 10.2.
99   CPIA Code, para 10.3.

for the discretion of the disclosure officer. If the material is transcribed, the disclosure officer must ensure that the transcript is certified to the accused as a true record of the material which has been transcribed.[100]

2.66   Where a court concludes that a sensitive document must be disclosed to the defence, it will be necessary to disclose this material if the case is to proceed. The document need not be disclosed in its original form. The court may agree that sensitive details still requiring protection should be blocked out or the contents of the documents summarised or that the prosecutor makes an admission about the substance of the material.[101]

---

100 CPIA Code, para 10.4.
101 CPIA Code, para 10.5.

Chapter 3

Receipt and review by the prosecutor

INTRODUCTION

3.01   When the prosecutor receives the prosecution file from the police they have a number of functions to perform to ensure that the disclosure process runs smoothly.

3.02   This chapter deals with:

• role of the prosecutor	**3.03–3.05**
• obligations of the prosecutor	**3.06–3.12**
• continuing duty to disclose	**3.13–3.18**
• endorsements to the schedules	**3.19–3.23**
• disclosure record sheet	**3.24–3.28**

ROLE OF THE PROSECUTOR

3.03   The prosecutor is responsible for making proper disclosure in consultation with the disclosure officer and for ensuring that advocates in court are properly instructed as to disclosure issues.[1]

3.04   The prosecutor must also be alert to the need to provide advice to, and where necessary probe the actions of, the disclosure officers to ensure that their disclosure obligations are met.[2]

---

1   Attorney General's Guidelines on Disclosure (2013), para 28. The description of the prosecutors duty as set out in the 2005 guidelines, to '*do all that they can to facilitate proper disclosure, as part of their general and personal professional responsibility to act fairly and impartially, in the interests of justice and in accordance with the law*' has not been reproduced in the 2013 guidelines.
2   Attorney General's Guidelines on Disclosure (2013), para 28.

3.05   The (lead) disclosure officer is the first point of contact for all enquiries regarding the contents of the schedules and access to material which has not been copied. The prosecutor should liaise closely with him and consult him regularly during the disclosure process.[3] Where the prosecutor has reason to believe that the disclosure officer has not inspected, viewed or listened to material, he should raise the matter immediately with the disclosure officer and request him to do so.[4]

OBLIGATIONS OF THE PROSECUTOR

3.06   Upon receiving the full prosecution file from the disclosure officer, the file should contain:

- a certification on the police report (MG5/SDF), where an accused is charged with a summary or either way offence that is likely to remain in the magistrates' court and is likely to plead guilty, confirming whether there is any material arising pursuant to the common law duty;[5]

- a streamlined disclosure certificate where an accused is charged with a summary or either way offence that is likely to remain in the magistrates' court and is likely to plead not guilty or was expected to plead guilty but pleads not guilty at the first hearing[6]

- an MG6 which contains any comments, observations or explanations of the schedules;[7]

- an MG6B which details any criminal conviction, caution or relevant misconduct of police officers;

- copies of all material that satisfies the prosecution disclosure test and a brief explanation for that belief on form MG6E (disclosure officer's report);

- an MG6C (schedule of non-sensitive material);[8]

- an MG6D (schedule of sensitive material or declaration that there is no sensitive material);[9]

---

3   Attorney General's Guidelines on Disclosure (2013), para 18; CPS Disclosure Manual, para 11.5.
4   Attorney General's Guidelines on Disclosure (2013), para 30; CPS Disclosure Manual, para 12.2.
5   CPIA Code, para 6.3 and 6.6: material that may assist the defence at bail hearings or in the early preparation of their case.
6   CPIA Code, para. 6.4–6.5.
7   The MG forms are found in the CPS/ACPO Manual of Guidance. See **Appendix 7–9**.
8   For a copy of an MG6C form see **Appendix 7**.
9   For a copy of an MG6D form see **Appendix 8**.

- copies of disclosable sensitive material (where appropriate);

- copies of the crime report and log of messages (edited where appropriate); and

- certifications of compliance by the disclosure officer on the MG6E (disclosure officer's report).[10]

3.07   Upon receipt of the prosecution file, the prosecutor's specific obligations under Attorney General's Guidelines on Disclosure (2013), para 29 are to:

- review the schedules thoroughly;

- be alert to the possibility that relevant material may exist which has not been revealed to him or material included which should not have been;

- take action at once to obtain properly completed schedules if no schedules have been provided or there are apparent omissions from the schedules;[11]

- take action at once if documents or other items are inadequately described or are unclear;

- return schedules for amendment if irrelevant items are included; and

- raise the matter with a senior investigator if the prosecutor remains dissatisfied with the quality or content of the schedules.

3.08   In addition to the above obligations, the prosecutor should check for items which ought to be listed on the MG6C[12] but have been wrongly included on the MG6D[13] and vice versa.[14] As the MG6D is not served on the defence, it is important that items erroneously appearing on the MG6D are identified as otherwise the defence may not be aware of their existence.

3.09   The prosecutor must always inspect, view or listen to any material, whether sensitive or non-sensitive, which they believe might reasonably be considered capable of undermining the prosecution case against the accused or assisting the case for the accused.[15] They should not simply rely on its description in the schedule. They should also satisfy themselves that the prosecution

---

10 CPS Disclosure Manual, paras 6.6–6.7, 11.6; see CPS Disclosure Manual, Ch 18.
11 CPS Disclosure Manual, para 11.8 – omissions should not delay disclosure as a continuation schedule can be provided.
12 Schedule of non-sensitive material.
13 Schedule of sensitive material.
14 CPS Disclosure Manual, paras 10.22, 11.12.
15 i.e. the prosecution disclosure test.

can properly be continued having regard to the disclosability of the material reviewed.[16] The judgment as to what other material to inspect, view or listen to will depend on the circumstances of each case.[17]

3.10   The prosecutor should always inspect any material, whether sensitive or non-sensitive, where:

•   the description (or the reasons given as to its sensitivity) remains inadequate despite requests for clarification;

•   he is unsure of whether the material satisfies the prosecution disclosure test.[18]

3.11   The review and preparation of unused material for disclosure to the defence should start as soon as possible after it becomes apparent that disclosure will be required .[19]

3.12   Care must be taken to ensure that sensitive material is handled with the commensurate level of security.[20]

CONTINUING DUTY TO DISCLOSE

3.13   The CPIA 1996, s 7A imposes a continuing duty on the prosecutor to keep the issue of disclosure under constant review until the accused is convicted or acquitted, or the case is discontinued. If at any given time there is prosecution material which satisfies the prosecution disclosure test and it has not been disclosed to the accused, the prosecutor must disclose it as soon as is reasonably practicable.[21]

3.14   Any new material coming to light after the initial prosecution file has been compiled should be treated in the same way as material received earlier. It must be described on a further MG6C, MG6D or a continuation sheet and submitted to the prosecutor together with a further MG6E.[22] Numbering of items submitted at a later stage should be consecutive to those on the previously submitted schedules.

---

16 Attorney General's Guidelines on Disclosure (2013), para 69; CPS Disclosure Manual, para 12.1.
17 Attorney General's Guidelines on Disclosure (2013), para 37.
18 CPS Disclosure Manual, paras 11.13, 12.1.
19 CPS Disclosure Manual, para 11.16.
20 CPS Disclosure Manual, paras 11.10–11.11, 11.17–11.28.
21 CPIA 1996, s 7A(2), (3).
22 CPIA Code, para 8.2; CPS Disclosure Manual, paras 10.25–10.26.

3.15   The CPIA 1996, s 7A places particular significance upon the need to review disclosure after service of a defence statement.[23] Once the prosecutor is in receipt of a defence statement, a copy of it should be sent immediately to the lead disclosure officer. At the same time the prosecutor should draw the attention of the disclosure officer to any key issues raised by the defence statement and, where appropriate, give advice to the disclosure officer in writing as to the type of material to look for.[24]

3.16   Advice to the disclosure officer may include:

• guidance on what material might have to be disclosed;

• advice on whether any further lines of enquiry need to be followed, e.g. where an alibi has been given;

• suggestions on what to look for when reviewing the unused material;

• suggestions on whether an alibi witness be interviewed; and

• the appropriate use of a defence statement in conducting further enquiries, particularly when it is necessary to speak again to prosecution witnesses[25] (the defence statement should not be shown to a non-expert witness).[26]

3.17   Upon receipt of the defence statement, the CPIA Code places a specific duty on the disclosure officer to re-visit the unused material (sensitive and non-sensitive) that has been retained and draw the attention of the prosecutor to any material which satisfies the prosecution disclosure test.[27] The disclosure officer should inform the prosecutor of any additional enquiries that have been carried out in response to the defence statement and any results. This should be done on form MG20. If no further enquiries are made the disclosure officer should explain why.[28]

3.18   Where the accused has reasonable cause to believe that there is prosecution material which is required by the CPIA 1996, s 7A to be disclosed

---

23 CPIA 1996, s 7A (2), (5).
24 Attorney General's Guidelines (2013), para 31;CPS Disclosure Manual, para 15.14.
25 CPS Disclosure Manual, para 15.15.
26 CPS Disclosure Manual, para 15.19. Whilst the CPS Guidance on Speaking to Witnesses at Court (March 2016) provides that witnesses should be informed of the general nature of the defence case, which may be determined from the defence statement, it is also made clear that the prosecutor must not enter into any discussion of the factual basis of the defence case.
27 i.e. any prosecution material which might reasonably be considered capable of undermining the prosecution case against the accused or of assisting the case for the accused. CPIA Code, para 8.3; CPS Disclosure Manual, para 15.20.
28 CPS Disclosure Manual, para 15.21.

to him and has not been, he may apply to the court for an order requiring the prosecutor to disclose it under the CPIA 1996, s 8.[29]

ENDORSEMENTS TO THE SCHEDULES

3.19   When considering their duty to disclose, the prosecutor should record all decisions on the MG6C, giving brief reasons for each decision in the 'comment' column where:

- the disclosability or otherwise of an item may not be apparent from its description;

- the prosecutor has decided to disclose material not identified as disclosable by the disclosure officer; or

- reasons might otherwise be helpful.[30]

3.20   Where an item is to be 'disclosed' the prosecutor should mark it with a 'D' and indicate whether a copy is attached. If the prosecutor considers that disclosure by 'inspection' is more appropriate the item should be marked with an 'I'.[31] The MG6C should be signed and dated by the prosecutor upon completion.[32]

3.21   Items that are 'clearly not disclosable' should be marked 'CND'.[33] Where the schedule description of an item is inadequate and there is insufficient time for the schedule to be amended, the item should be viewed and, if the material does not satisfy the prosecution disclosure test, be marked 'ND'.[34] The prosecutor must note that the disclosure test has been applied and that the item neither undermines the prosecution case nor assists the case for the defence.[35]

3.22   Where the defence are entitled to an item under the Police and Criminal Evidence Act 1984, eg a tape of the police interview or the custody record, yet the item does not satisfy the prosecution disclosure test, the prosecutor is instructed to mark it as 'CND' or 'ND' to ensure that there is no confusion between automatic entitlement and disclosure under the CPIA 1996.[36] In practice, the prosecutor

---

29 See Chapter 7 for Section 8 applications.
30 CPS Disclosure Manual, para 12.27.
31 CPS Disclosure Manual, para 12.29.
32 CPS Disclosure Manual, para 12.28.
33 CPS Disclosure Manual, para 12.30.
34 CPS Disclosure Manual, para 12.31.
35 CPS Disclosure Manual, para 12.31.
36 CPS Disclosure Manual, para 12.32.

will usually make a note that the item is available under the Police and Criminal Evidence Act 1984.

3.23   The decision of a prosecutor that an item is 'clearly not disclosable' (CND) should be based upon the disclosure officer's description of the item in the schedule. This applies both to sensitive and non-sensitive schedules. In practice, and in breach of the CPS Disclosure Manual, it is not uncommon to see items, whose descriptions are plainly inadequate for any proper assessment to be made upon disclosure, to be marked 'CND'.

DISCLOSURE RECORD SHEET

3.24   A single disclosure record sheet should be completed in respect of all unused material, whether sensitive or non-sensitive.[37] The disclosure record sheet should record all decisions, enquiries or requests and the date upon which they are made relating to:

- the disclosure of material to the defence;

- the withholding of material from the defence;

- the inspection of material; and

- the transcribing or recording of information into a suitable form.[38]

3.25   The disclosure record sheet should also record all actions and events that occur in the discharge of prosecution disclosure responsibilities.[39]

3.26   For sensitive material, the CPS Disclosure Manual, para 11.26 provides that:

'... the disclosure record sheet is used to record all events and actions, which will include the following:

- receipt of the MG6D;

- that a disclosure review has taken place (the outcome of such reviews will be recorded on the schedule itself);

- the receipt and review of any addenda to the MG6D;

---

37 CPS Disclosure Manual, para 11.15.
38 CPS Disclosure Manual, para 11.14.
39 CPS Disclosure Manual, para 11.14.

- contact with the disclosure officer or investigating officer in relation to sensitive unused material;

- receipt of defence statements and further reviews;

- any consultation with the prosecution advocate;

- any discussions with any other parties regarding sensitive unused material such as the court, the defence advocate or third parties;

- receipt of the prosecution advocate's advice in relation to sensitive unused material;

- details of any informal disclosure, should it occur;

- the fact of any PII applications.'

3.27   Unlike the non-sensitive material schedule, the disclosure record sheet entries should not contain sensitive information and will only record the fact that an event occurred as opposed to detailing the reasons. The reasons and decisions should be detailed on the MG6D and cross-referenced to the disclosure record sheet.[40]

3.28   The disclosure record sheet is an important document in any disclosure challenge as it provides a chronological paper trail of the disclosure process from start to finish.

---

40 CPS Disclosure Manual, para 11.25.

Chapter 4

Non-statutory disclosure

INTRODUCTION

4.01   A suspect has certain entitlements to disclosure upon arrest and at the police station before charge or caution. If a person is charged with an offence, the common law duty of disclosure applies prior to statutory disclosure taking place under the Criminal Procedure and Investigation Act 1996 (CPIA 1996), s 3 (see **Chapter 5**) and this sits alongside a defendant's right to be provided with initial details of the prosecution case under the Criminal Procedure Rules.

4.02   This chapter deals with:

• pre-charge disclosure	**4.03–4.14**
• pre-caution disclosure	**4.15–4.17**
• initial disclosure of prosecution case	**4.18–4.22**
• common law disclosure	**4.23–4.31**

PRE-CHARGE DISCLOSURE

4.03   Although there is no legal obligation under the CPIA 1996 or the CPIA Code to disclose material to the suspect prior to charge,[1] certain disclosure must be provided following the arrest of a suspect under the Police and Criminal Evidence Act 1984 (PACE) Codes of Practice, namely:

•   A person who is arrested, or further arrested, must be informed at the time, or as soon as practicable thereafter, that they are under arrest and the grounds for their arrest.[2]

---

1   *R v Ara* [2001] EWHC Admin 493, per Rose LJ, para 25. Although disclosure of a police interview record was required in this case to enable legal representatives to advise on the acceptability of a caution. The Magistrates' decision to stay proceedings as an abuse of process was upheld.
2   PACE 1984 Code C, para 10.3 – where the issue is identification this may include the first description of the suspect.

• An arrested person must be given sufficient information to enable them to understand that they have been deprived of their liberty and the reason they have been arrested, e.g. when a person is arrested on suspicion of committing an offence they must be informed of the nature of the suspected offence, when it was committed and where. The suspect must also be informed of the reason or reasons why the arrest is considered necessary. Vague or technical language should be avoided.[3]

• The legal representative or the appropriate adult must be permitted to consult a detainee's custody record[4] as soon as practicable after their arrival at the station and at any other time whilst the person is detained. Arrangements for this access must be agreed with the custody officer and may not reasonably interfere with the custody officer's duties.[5]

4.04   The legal adviser's right to view the custody record should never be overlooked as matters may be contained therein over and above any disclosure provided by an interviewing officer.

4.05   Sufficient disclosure should be provided to a suspect before his police interview to enable a solicitor to properly advise him.[6] A lack of police disclosure at a suspect's interview is particularly significant as it may prevent an adverse inference being drawn under of the Criminal Justice and Public Order Act 1994, s 34 where the accused has failed to mention in his interview a fact which he later relies on in court. In *R v Nottle* Simon J stated:

'The purpose of the pre-interview disclosure derives from the realisation by the police that, without proper disclosure, solicitors cannot properly advise their clients. They [*the police*] voluntarily provide disclosure in order to counter an argument at trial that no adverse inferences should be drawn under section 34 of the Criminal Justice and Public Order Act 1994 from the suspect's failure to answer questions … The quality and quantity of disclosure will depend on the case. The officer must assess the risk of giving inadequate disclosure, namely that no adverse inferences will be drawn.'[7]

---

3   PACE 1984 Code C, note 10B.

4   At the police station the custody officer shall record on the custody record the offences and the reasons that the detainee has been arrested, note any comment the detainee makes in relation to the arresting officer's account and, if the custody officer authorizes a person's detention, the detainee must be informed of the grounds as soon as practicable and before he is questioned about any offence.

5   PACE 1984 Code C, para 2.4.

6   *R v Argent* [1997] 2 Cr App R 27, per Lord Bingham CJ.

7   [2004] EWCA Crim 599 at para 14. See also *R v Hoare and Pierce* [2004] EWCA Crim 784, per Auld LJ, para 53 for the rationale behind Criminal Justice and Public Order Act 1994, s 34.

4.06   The Court of Appeal in *R v Argent* rejected the argument that insufficient disclosure by the police prior to interview should render evidence of the accused's silence inadmissible.[8]

4.07   The term 'sufficient disclosure' does not require the police to disclose the case against the suspect before interview[9] or to give his legal representative a full briefing.[10] The police must not actively mislead the suspect,[11] but they do not need to present him with all the evidence they have to prevent him from lying to them.[12]

4.08   There is no rule of law that requires the police to reveal to a suspect the questions that they may wish to put to him in interview nor are they required to reveal in advance the topics that they wish to cover, even in the most general terms.[13] In some cases providing those details in advance of an interview will prejudice the police enquiries, but this is a judgment that must be left to the police.[14] Interviews must be conducted fairly but advance notice is not regarded as a pre-requisite to fairness.[15]

4.09   The CPS legal guidance on pre-interview disclosure advises that if an investigator feels that it is necessary to withhold information from the legal representative during a pre-interview briefing, he should be able to explain clearly the reasons supporting this approach in any further proceedings. Prosecutors should be made aware of all pre-interview disclosure in order to assess whether adverse inferences may properly be drawn at trial and to anticipate or prepare for any defence arguments on the point.[16]

4.10   There may be good reason to prevent an adverse inference being drawn where a solicitor cannot 'usefully advise' their client because the interviewing officer has disclosed little or nothing of the nature of the case against their client[17] or where the suspect is unable to sensibly respond to the questions as a

---

8   [1997] 2 Cr App R 27, per Lord Bingham CJ.

9   *R v Ara* [2001] EWHC Admin 493, per Rose LJ, para 25.

10 *R v Imran and Hussain* [1997] Crim LR 754; [1997] EWCA Crim 1401, per Rougier J.

11 *R v Imran and Hussain* [1997] Crim LR 754; [1997] EWCA Crim 1401.

12 *R v Imran and Hussain* [1997] Crim LR 754; [1997] EWCA Crim 1401; see *R v Farrell* [2004] EWCA Crim 597.

13 *Ward v Police Service of Northern Ireland* [2007] UKHL 50, per Appellate Committee, para 22.

14 *Ward v Police Service of Northern Ireland* [2007] UKHL 50.

15 *Ward v Police Service of Northern Ireland* [2007] UKHL 50.

16 See CPS Legal Guidance, Adverse Inferences.

17 *R v Roble* [1997] Crim LR 449, per Rose LJ. The words 'usefully advise' are not defined.

result of the complexity of the case,[18] the lapse of time,[19] the suspect's condition (ill-health, mental disability, confusion, intoxication, shock, etc.)[20] or their inability genuinely to recollect events without reference to documents which are not to hand or communication with other persons who may be able to assist his recollection.[21]

4.11   In complex or heavy fraud cases, the Protocol for the control and management of heavy fraud and complex criminal cases[22] recognizes the need to provide disclosure before the interview and to properly structure the interview to bring about some reduction in the length of trials. The protocol is primarily aimed at jury trials likely to last eight or more weeks but should also be followed in all cases estimated to last longer than four weeks. Paragraph 1(ii), Protocol states:

'Interviews

a)   At present many interviews are too long and too unstructured. This has a knock-on effect on the length of trials. Interviews should provide an opportunity for suspects to respond to the allegations against them. They should not be an occasion to discuss every document in the case. It should become clear from judicial rulings that interviews of this kind are a waste of resources.

b)   The suspect must be given sufficient information before or at the interview to enable them to meet the questions fairly and answer them honestly; the information is not provided to give the suspect the opportunity to manufacture a false story which fits undisputable facts.

c)   It is often helpful if the principal documents are provided either in advance of the interview or shown as the interview progresses; asking detailed questions about events a considerable period in the past without reference to the documents is often not very helpful.'

4.12   The less complex the case, the more prepared the court will be to permit the drawing of adverse inferences where minimal disclosure has been made pre-interview.[23]

---

18   *R v Roble* [1997] Crim LR 449, per Rose LJ.

19   *R v Roble* [1997] Crim LR 449, per Rose LJ.

20   *R v Howell* [2003] EWCA Crim 1, per Laws LJ, para 24.

21   *R v Howell* [2003] EWCA Crim 1, per Laws LJ, para 24.

22   Issued by the Lord Chief Justice (22 March 2005): 'The Protocol supplements the Criminal Procedure Rules and summarises good practice which experience has shown may assist in bringing about some reduction in the length of trials of fraud and other crimes that result in complex trials.' (Introduction to the Protocol).

23   See *R v Argent* [1997] 2 Cr App R 27 and *R v Farrell* (2004) EWCA Crim 597.

4.13   Laws LJ in *R v Howell*[24] observed that legal advisers should always bear in mind that there must be soundly-based objective reasons for silence, such as the accused's infirmness, his age or the complexity of the case which are sufficiently cogent and telling to weigh in the balance against the clear public interest in an account being given to the police. This observation must be considered in light of note 6D, PACE 1984 Code C, which stipulates that the solicitor's only role in the police station is to protect and advance the legal rights of his client. This may require the solicitor to give advice which has the effect of the client avoiding giving evidence which strengthens the prosecution case.

4.14   The PACE 1984 Code C, para 11.4A provides that at the beginning of an interview the interviewer, after cautioning the suspect, shall put to him any significant statement or silence[25] which occurred in the presence or hearing of a police officer or other police staff before the start of the interview and which has not been put to the suspect in a previous interview. The interviewer shall ask the suspect whether he confirms or denies that earlier statement or silence and if he wants to add anything. This does not prevent the interviewer from putting significant statements and silences to a suspect again at a later stage or in further interviews.[26]

PRE-CAUTION DISCLOSURE

4.15   A caution is a non-statutory disposal that, though not classified as a conviction, may cause significant adverse consequences to the accused in that it may be used in subsequent court proceedings and appear on a criminal record check.[27] Cautions may also place the accused on the sex offender's register or handicap their employment prospects on the job market.

4.16   For the police to be in a position to give a caution, there must be sufficient evidence for a realistic prospect of conviction if the suspect were prosecuted, there must be a clear and reliable admission of the offence, the accused must understand the significance of the caution and give an informed consent to being cautioned.[28]

---

24 [2003] EWCA Crim 1, at para 24.
25 A significant statement is one which appears capable of being used in evidence against the suspect, in particular a direct admission of guilt. A significant silence is a failure or refusal to answer a question or answer satisfactorily when under caution, which might give rise to an inference under the Criminal Justice and Public Order Act 1994, Part III.
26 PACE 1984 Code C, para 11.4, note 11A.
27 Ministry of Justice Guidance 'Simple Cautions for Adult Offenders' para. 13.
28 Ministry of Justice Guidance 'Simple Cautions for Adult Offenders' paras. 9 and 13.

4.17   Although there is no general obligation on the police to disclose material prior to charge,[29] the question of whether or not an accused should accept a caution is inextricably linked to his entitlement to informed legal advice. In *R v Ara*[30] the Divisional Court held that the justices were correct to have stayed proceedings for abuse of process where the police refused to supply a copy of the accused's interview to his legal adviser. In order for informed legal advice to be given, a legal adviser needs to know accurately the terms of the interview which form the basis of the caution. Without such disclosure, informed advice from a legal adviser is not possible and an informed consent from the accused cannot follow.

INITIAL DISCLOSURE OF PROSECUTION CASE

4.18   So that a Defendant can be properly advised in relation to plea, allocation of venue and sentence, they are entitled, prior to the first hearing taking place, to Initial Details of the Prosecution Case (IDPC).

4.19   CrimPR r8.2 provides that:

'(1)   The prosecutor must serve initial details of the prosecution case on the court officer—

    (a)   as soon as practicable; and

    (b)   in any event, no later than the beginning of the day of the first hearing.

(2)   Where a defendant requests those details, the prosecutor must serve them on the defendant—

    (a)   as soon as practicable; and

    (b)   in any event, no later than the beginning of the day of the first hearing.

(3)   Where a defendant does not request those details, the prosecutor must make them available to the defendant at, or before, the beginning of the day of the first hearing.'

---

29 *R v Ara* [2001] EWHC Admin 493, per Rose LJ, para 25.
30 [2001] EWHC Admin 493, per Rose LJ, para 25.

4.20   Rule 8.3 sets out the required contents of IDPC and states that:

'Initial details of the prosecution case must include—

(a)   where, immediately before the first hearing in the magistrates' court, the defendant was in police custody for the offence charged—

    (i)   a summary of the circumstances of the offence, and

    (ii)   the defendant's criminal record, if any;

(b)   where paragraph (a) does not apply—

    (i)   a summary of the circumstances of the offence,

    (ii)   any account given by the defendant in interview, whether contained in that summary or in another document,

    (iii)   any written witness statement or exhibit that the prosecutor then has available and considers material to plea, or to the allocation of the case for trial, or to sentence,

    (iv)   the defendant's criminal record, if any, and

    (v)   any available statement of the effect of the offence on a victim, a victim's family or others.'

4.21   The CPS Guidance: IDPC Guidance for Advocates (25 July 2016) advises that:

'If necessary the case should be stood down so that the defence can take proper instructions… The court should be supportive as it is also in their interest to avoid unnecessary adjournments or tactical not guilty pleas.'

4.22   The Magistrates Court Disclosure Review,[31] para 92 recommends that:

'If the first hearing is to be effective, with the aim of achieving proper case management, details of the case should be available to the defence in advance of [the day of hearing], save in unavoidable circumstances, such as overnight custody cases.'

---

31 Conducted by Lord Justice Gross, May 2014.

COMMON LAW DISCLOSURE

4.23   The common law duty of disclosure arises before initial statutory disclosure is triggered.[32] Initial statutory disclosure by the prosecutor under the CPIA 1996 is triggered where[33] –

- a person pleads not guilty in the magistrates' court or the youth court;

- a person is charged with an offence for which he is sent for trial;[34]

- a count charging a person with a summary offence is included in an indictment;[35] and

- a bill of indictment charging a person with an indictable offence is preferred.[36]

4.24   The wording of the CPIA 1996, s 3(1) that the prosecutor 'must (a) disclose to the accused any prosecution material which has not previously been disclosed to the accused' clearly envisages the possibility that some disclosure (common law disclosure) may have already occurred.

4.25   The extent of the common law duty of disclosure is not clear but the principled origin of the duty is fairness and it is tailored to the needs of the stage of the proceedings in question.[37]

4.26   The Criminal Procedure and Investigations Act 1996 Code of Practice 2015 provides that:

'6.6 In every case, irrespective of the anticipated plea, if there is material known to the disclosure officer that might assist the defence with the early preparation of their case or at a bail hearing (for example, a key prosecution witness has relevant previous convictions or a witness has withdrawn his or her statement), a note must be made on the MG5 (or other format agreed under the National File Standards). The material must be disclosed to the

---

32 And continues after conviction. See **Chapter 12.**

33 *R(Nunn) v Chief Constable of Suffolk Constabulary* [2014] 2 Cr. App. R. 22, para 22–23.

34 CPIA 1996, s 1. The provisions dealing with committal to the Crown Court were repealed by schedule 37(4) para 1, in force as of 18 June 2012. The effect of this repeal is that all relevant cases are sent to the Crown Court under the Crime and Disorder Act 1998, as amended.

35 Crime and Disorder Act 1998, s 51.

36 Criminal Justice Act 1988, s 40.

37 Administration of Justice (Miscellaneous Provisions) Act 1933, s 2(2); Prosecution of Offences Act 1985, s 22B(3)(a); This also includes where a suspension in proceedings is lifted after initial approval of a deferred prosecution agreement under paragraph 2(3) of Schedule 17 to the Crime and Courts Act 2013.

prosecutor who will disclose it to the defence if he thinks it meets this Common Law test.'

4.27   In Magistrates' Court cases, a streamlined disclosure certificate will now be provided to prosecutors in anticipated not guilty plea cases. This disclosure process sits between the common law disclosure test and the initial duty of disclosure.[38] This should be provided to the defence at the hearing where a not guilty plea is entered or as soon as possible following a formal indication a not guilty plea will be entered.[39]

4.28   Kennedy LJ in *R v DPP ex parte Lee*[40] reviewed the common law duty of disclosure and the following propositions emerged. These propositions must now be considered in light of the abolition of committals as well as the requirements in the Criminal Procedure Rules for disclosure of Initial Details of the Prosecution Case (see **4.18–4.22** above).[41]

'(1)   The 1996 Act considerably reduced the ability of the defence to take an active part in committal proceedings, so the need for disclosure prior to committal was also reduced.

(2)   Part I of the 1996 Act introduced a completely new regime in relation to disclosure. It replaces most if not all of the provisions of the common law from the moment of committal with a two stage process set out in sections 3 and 7 of the Act. The second stage only occurs in response to a defence statement.

(3)   The disclosure required by the Act is and is intended to be less extensive than would have been required prior to the Act at common law.

(4)   Although some disclosure may be required prior to committal (and thus prior to the period to which the Act applies) it would undermine the statutory provisions if the pre-committal discovery were to exceed the discovery obtainable after committal pursuant to the statute.

(5)   The 1996 Act does not specifically address the period between arrest and committal, and whereas in most cases prosecution disclosure can wait until after committal without jeopardising the defendant's right

---

38 Criminal Procedure and Investigations Act 1996 (section 23(1)) Code of Practice 2015, paras 6.3–6.7.
39 Criminal Procedure and Investigations Act 1996 (section 23(1)) Code of Practice 2015, para 10.1.
40 [1999] 1 WLR 1950, section 9 'Conclusion'.
41 Part 8 CrimPR 2015.

to a fair trial the prosecutor must always be alive to the need to make advance disclosure of material of which he is aware (either from his own consideration of the papers or because his attention has been drawn to it by the defence) and which he, as a responsible prosecutor, recognises should be disclosed at an earlier stage. Examples canvassed before us were –

(a)   Previous convictions of a complainant or deceased if that information could reasonably be expected to assist the defence when applying for bail;

(b)   Material which might enable a defendant to make a pre-committal application to stay the proceedings as an abuse of process;

(c)   Material which might enable a defendant to submit that he should only be committed for trial on a lesser charge, or perhaps that he should not be committed for trial at all;

(d)   Material which will enable the defendant and his legal advisors to make preparations for trial which may be significantly less effective if disclosure is delayed (e.g. names of eye witnesses who the prosecution do not intend to use).

(6)   Clearly any disclosure by the prosecution prior to committal cannot normally exceed the primary disclosure which after committal would be required by section 3 of the 1996 Act (i.e. disclosure of material which in the prosecutor's opinion might undermine the case for the prosecution). However, to the extent that a defendant or his solicitor chooses to reveal what he would normally only disclose in his defence statement the prosecutor may in advance if justice requires give the secondary disclosure which such a revelation would trigger, so whereas no difficulty would arise in relation to disclosing material of the type referred to in sub-paragraph 5(a)(b) and (c) above, and I accept that such material should be disclosed, the disclosure of material of the type referred to in sub-paragraph 5(d) would depend very much on what the defendant chose to reveal about his case.

(7)   No doubt additions can be made to the list of material which in a particular case ought to be disclosed at an early stage, but what is not required of the prosecutor in any case is to give what might be described as full blown common law discovery at the pre-committal stage. Although the 1996 Act has not abolished pre-committal discovery the provisions of the Act taken as whole are such as to require that the common law obligations in relation to the pre-committal period be radically recast in the way that I have indicated.

(8)   Within the framework which I have attempted to outline I would accept [the] submission that even before committal a responsible prosecutor should be asking himself what if any immediate disclosure justice and fairness requires him to make in the particular circumstances of the case. Very often the answer will be none, and rarely if at all should the prosecutor's answer to that continuing piece of self examination be the subject matter of dispute in this court. If the matter does have to be ventilated it should, save in a very exceptional case, be before the trial judge.'[42]

4.29   To suggest that matters of early disclosure be ventilated before the trial judge 'save in a very exceptional case' (in proposition 8 above) will, in practice, be difficult to implement as trial judges are rarely identified until well after the plea and trial preparation hearing.

4.30   The CrimPR 2015 impose an obligation to deal with a case efficiently and expeditiously[43] and parties must actively assist the court in the early identification of the real issues and are subject to a duty to engage.[44] Notwithstanding the absence of any established procedure to trigger common law disclosure, an early identification of issues by the defence should allow relevant material or information to be obtained and disclosed sooner rather than later.[45]

4.31   The defence should be mindful that to reveal the accused's defence to the prosecution at an early stage in a letter requesting early disclosure may carry a risk of sanctions being applied should a different defence be put forward either in a defence statement or at trial. As the disclosure letter should be based on the accused's instructions, the prosecution, though unable to rely on the CPIA 1996, s 11 (defence sanctions), may seek to adduce it as an inconsistent or a hearsay statement. Although the chances of a prosecution application succeeding are remote, good practice dictates that such disclosure letters must be carefully worded and submitted only after their potential significance has been explained to the accused and a signed endorsement obtained.[46]

---

42 See CPS Disclosure Manual, Ch 2.
43 CrimPR 2015, r 1.1(2)(e).
44 CrimPR 2015, rr 1.2(1), 3.2, 3.3, 3.10(2).
45 See Attorney General's Guidelines on Disclosure (2013), paras 42 and 43.
46 See *R v Newell* [2012] EWCA Crim 650, per Sir John Thomas P, para 36: 'provided the case is conducted in accordance with the letter and spirit of the Criminal Procedure Rules … information or a statement written on a PCMH form should in the exercise of the Court's discretion under s 78 [Police and Criminal Evidence Act 1984] not be admitted in evidence as a statement that can be used against the defendant.'

Chapter 5

Statutory disclosure

INTRODUCTION

5.01   The prosecutor must disclose material to the defence where it satisfies the prosecution disclosure test under the Criminal Procedure and Investigations Act (CPIA) 1996, ie any prosecution material which might reasonably be considered capable of undermining the case for prosecution against the accused or of assisting the case for the accused.

5.02   This chapter deals with:

• initial disclosure	**5.03–5.17**
• continuing disclosure	**5.18–5.22**
• time for service	**5.23–5.25**

INITIAL DISCLOSURE

5.03   Once initial statutory disclosure is triggered under the CPIA 1996, s 3(1) the prosecution must –

(a)   disclose to the accused any prosecution material which has not previously been disclosed to the accused and which might reasonably be considered capable of undermining the case for the prosecution against the accused or assisting the case for the accused, or

(b)   give to the accused a written statement that there is no material of a description mentioned in paragraph (a).

5.04   The Crown are only required to send the non-sensitive schedule (MG6C) to the defence when it is in the prosecutor's possession when initial disclosure occurs. It is not a necessary component nor mark of initial disclosure.[1]

---

1   *DPP v Wood, DPP v McGillicuddy* [2006] EWHC 32 (Admin), per Ouseley J, paras 23.

Therefore, while the CPS Disclosure Manual advises that the MG6C should be served upon the defence, a failure to do so will not be regarded as a failure on the part of the prosecution to provide initial statutory disclosure.[2]

5.05   In determining what material must be disclosed to the defence, the CPS Disclosure Manual, para 12.4 states that it will always be necessary to consider:

- the nature and strength of the case against the accused;

- the essential elements of the offence alleged;

- the evidence upon which the prosecution relies;

- any explanation offered by the accused, whether in formal interview or otherwise; and

- what material or information has already been disclosed.

5.06   Under the Attorney General's Guidelines on Disclosure (2013), para 6:

In deciding whether material satisfies the disclosure test, consideration should be given amongst other things to:

(a)   the use that might be made of it in cross-examination;

(b)   its capacity to support submissions that could lead to:

  (i)   the exclusion of evidence; or

  (ii)   a stay of proceedings where the material is required for a proper application to be made; or

  (iii)   a court or tribunal finding that any public authority had acted incompatibly with the accused's rights under the ECHR;[3] or

(c)   its capacity to suggest an explanation or partial explanation of the accused's actions; or

(d)   the capacity of the material to have a bearing on scientific or medical evidence in the case

5.07   It is not intended that disclosure be an open-ended trawl of unused material. The defence must play their role to ensure the prosecution are directed to material which may pass the disclosure test.[4] However, prosecutors must

---

2   *DPP v Wood, DPP v McGillicuddy* [2006] EWHC 32 (Admin), per Ouseley J, paras 23, 66.
3   European Convention of Human Rights. *R v Barkshire* [2011] EWCA Crim 1885.
4   Attorney General's Guidelines on Disclosure (2013), para 9.

play an active role in scrutinising the disclosure exercise conducted by the disclosure officer. Inadequate schedules of unused material must be challenged and prosecutors must ensure the disclosure exercise goes beyond a signing-off exercise.[5]

5.08 Examples of material that might reasonably be considered capable of undermining the case for the prosecution against the accused or assisting the case for the accused are:[6]

- any material casting doubt upon the accuracy of any prosecution evidence;

- any material which may point to another person, whether charged or not, (including a co-accused) having involvement in the commission of the offence;

- any material which may cast doubt upon the reliability of a confession;

- any material that might go to the credibility of a prosecution witness;

- any material that might support a defence that is either raised by the defence or apparent from the prosecution papers;

- any material which may have a bearing on the admissibility of any prosecution evidence;

- any material that might assist the accused to cross-examine prosecution witnesses as to credit and/or substance;

- any material that might enable the accused to call evidence or advance a line of enquiry or argument; and

- any material that might explain or mitigate the accused's actions.[7]

5.09 The CPS Disclosure Manual[8] instructs disclosure officers and prosecutors to give careful consideration to:

- recorded scientific or scenes of crime findings retained by the investigator;

- where identification is or may be in issue, all previous descriptions of suspects, however recorded, together with all records of identification procedures in respect of the offence(s) and photographs of the accused taken at the time of arrest;

---

5 HM Crown Prosecution Inspectorate *Making it Fair: The Disclosure of Unused Material in Volume Crown Court Cases* published 18 July 2017. The report was heavily critical of the conduct of disclosure of unused material in Crown Court cases.
6 ie the prosecution disclosure test in CPIA 1996, s3.
7 CPS Disclosure Manual, para 12.11.
8 CPS Disclosure Manual, para 12.14.

- information that any prosecution witness has received, been promised or requested any payment or reward in connection with the case;

- plans of crime scenes or videos made by investigators of crime scenes;

- names, within the knowledge of the investigators, of individuals who may have relevant information and whom the investigators do not intend to interview; and

- records, which the investigator has made, of information provided by any individual which may be relevant. This will include records of conversations with individuals such as expert witnesses.

5.10   Where material satisfies the prosecution disclosure test, it should be disclosed even if it suggests a defence inconsistent with or alternative to one already advanced by the accused.[9] While items of material viewed in isolation may not satisfy the disclosure test, several items together can have the effect of making such material disclosable.[10]

5.11   Material relating to the accused's mental or physical health or intellectual capacity, or to any ill treatment that the accused may have suffered when in the investigator's custody, is likely to fall within the prosecution disclosure test.[11]

5.12   In *R v Olu, Wilson and Brooks*[12] the Court of Appeal held that the defence should be provided with all notes, records and statements in relation to the evidence of eyewitnesses irrespective of whether or not the prosecution deemed them disclosable under the provisions of the CPIA 1996. Thomas LJ stated:

'45.   ... what a witness says when first seen, even informally, in a case which depends on eyewitness evidence, is often the most reliable. Thus it was important that all of these notes and statements were obtained (where available) and scheduled at the outset. .... Once scheduled, it would have been a pointless exercise and a waste of police resources to go through each note of contact with the eyewitnesses (as opposed to the other witnesses) to decide whether it did or did not undermine the prosecution case or whether it assisted or did not assist the defence. All the statements in relation to the eyewitnesses should have

9 CPS Disclosure Manual, para 12.9.
10 Attorney General's Guidelines on Disclosure (2013), para 7; CPS Disclosure Manual para.
11 Attorney General's Guidelines on Disclosure (2013), para 8. CPS Disclosure Manual, para 12.16.
12 [2011] 1 Cr. App. R. 33; [2010] EWCA Crim 2975.

been obtained, scheduled and disclosed as unused material so that the defence could determine whether such notes, records or statements assisted or did not assist …

46.   We also recognise that a failure to disclose the material documentation prior to a trial has two adverse consequences for the defence. Without proper disclosure a defence advocate cannot plan how the trial is to be conducted and what to put to the witnesses called by the Crown. Secondly, disclosure during the trial distracts a defence advocate from the proper and expeditious conduct of a trial. Experience shows it inevitable that there may be some late disclosure, but late disclosure on the scale that occurred in this case is unacceptable.'

5.13   In light of this the defence can expect that all notes, records and statements of eyewitnesses that do not form part of the case against the accused will be served as part of initial disclosure.

5.14   Material relating to prosecution witnesses which will ordinarily satisfy the test for disclosure includes:

•   records of discussions with a prosecution witness, or a co-defendant who gives evidence for the Crown, about a reward to be paid for giving evidence; and[13]

•   such previous convictions of and outstanding charges against witnesses whom it intended to call, and such warnings or other measures adopted as alternatives to prosecution of such witnesses, has materially weakened the prosecution case or materially strengthened that of the defence.[14]

5.15   Further guidance on material which should be disclosed as part of the prosecution's duty of disclosure was given in *R v Makin* in which it was held that:

'there is an obligation to disclose material if it assists the defence by allowing the defendant to put forward a tenable case in the best possible light or if the material could assist the defence to make further enquiries and those enquiries might assist in showing the defendant's innocence or avoid a miscarriage of justice.'[15]

---

13 *R v Allan* [2004] EWCA Crim 2236, at para 141; *R v Smith* [2004] EWCA Crim 2212, at para 17.

14 *HM Advocate v Murtagh (HM Advocate General for Scotland intervening)* [2011] 1 A.C. 731 and *Allison (Steven Edward) v HM Advocate* [2010] H.R.L.R. 16.

15 [2004] EWCA Crim 1607, para 30.

5.16   When deciding what material is to be disclosed, prosecutors should resolve any doubts in favour of disclosure 'unless the material is sensitive and to be placed before the court in a PII application'.[16] If material substantially undermines the prosecution case, assists the accused or raises a fundamental question about the prosecution, the prosecutor will need to re-assess the case in accordance with the Code for Crown Prosecutors and decide, after consultation with the police, whether the case should continue.[17]

5.17   In cases where there are large quantities of documents, in particular electronic material, it is essential that the Crown takes a grip on disclosure from the outset and considers an appropriately resourced approach to initial disclosure. A strategy for disclosure should be adopted as well as appropriate use of technology and isolating material subject to legal professional privilege ("LPP") at an early stage in proceedings[18]. Such an approach must be tailored to the individual requirements of each case. Early communication with the defence as to the approach to be taken by the Crown (ideally in a disclosure management document) will be crucial in ensuring this process is effective. The defence will be under a duty to engage with the prosecution's approach. Judges will be encouraged to robustly manage cases of this nature although preparatory hearings are generally to be discouraged save for in exceptional cases.

CONTINUING DISCLOSURE

5.18   Once the prosecutor has complied or purported to comply with initial disclosure, the CPIA 1996, s 7A[19] requires him to keep disclosure under review at all times applying the same prosecution disclosure test as that applied to initial disclosure.[20] The statutory duty of continuing disclosure exists until the accused is acquitted or convicted or the case is discontinued.[21]

5.19   If material which has not previously been disclosed to the accused is identified as satisfying the prosecution disclosure test, the prosecutor must, unless disclosure is prohibited under the Regulation of Investigatory Powers Act 2000

---

16 CPS Disclosure Manual, para 12.18.
17 CPS Disclosure Manual, para 12.19.
18 *R v R* (Practice Note) [2015] EWCA Crim 1941; [2016] 1 W.L.R. 1872 paragraphs 34–36, strongly endorsing the approach in *R. v Pearson (Brendan)* [2006] EWCA Crim 3366.
19 Inserted by Criminal Justice Act 2003, s 37.
20 i.e. any prosecution material which might reasonably be considered capable of undermining the case for prosecution against the accused or of assisting the case for the accused.
21 CPIA 1996, s 7A(1)(b).

(RIPA 2000), s 17[22] or is subject to public interest immunity considerations,[23] disclose it to the accused as soon as is reasonably practicable.[24]

5.20 Prosecutors should be alert to the possibility that further unused material may be generated or come to light after initial statutory disclosure as a result of investigations being conducted following advice from the prosecutor or, for example, upon the receipt of negative fingerprint and forensic results.[25]

5.21 The duty to keep disclosure under review is a continuing one, but it is particularly important after the service of a defence statement[26] as it may identify issues not apparent at the outset of the disclosure procedure. The prosecutor should consider the defence statement carefully and promptly provide a copy to the disclosure officer, to assist the prosecution in its continuing disclosure obligations.[27] However, as stated in *R v H and C:*[28]

> 'If material does not weaken the prosecution case or strengthen that of the defendant, there is no requirement to disclose it. For this purpose the parties' respective cases should not be restrictively analysed. But they must be carefully analysed, to ascertain the specific facts the prosecution seek to establish and the specific grounds on which the charges are resisted. The trial process is not well served if the defence are permitted to make general and unspecified allegations and then seek far-reaching disclosure in the hope that material may turn up to make them good. Neutral material or material damaging to the defendant need not be disclosed and should not be brought to the attention of the court.'

5.22 Where the accused has reasonable cause to believe that there is prosecution material that should be disclosed to him pursuant to the CPIA 1996, s 7A which has not been disclosed, he may apply to the court for an order requiring the prosecutor to disclose it under the CPIA 1996, s 8. (see **Chapter 7**).

TIME FOR SERVICE

5.23 Although there is provision[29] for the Secretary of State to make regulations to prescribe time limits for the service of initial disclosure, as none

---

22 CPIA 1996, s 7A(9).
23 CPIA 1996, s 7A(8).
24 CPIA 1996, s 7A(3).
25 CPS Disclosure Manual, para 14.3.
26 CPIA 1996, s 7A(2).
27 Attorney General's Guidelines on Disclosure (2013), para 31.
28 *R v H and C* [2004] UKHL 3; [2004] 2 AC 134; [2004] 2 Cr App R 10, at paragraph 35.
29 CPIA 1996, s 12.

are in force, the default position is that the prosecutor must act 'as soon as is reasonably practicable'.[30] This should be considered alongside the Crime and Disorder Act 1998 (Disclosure of Prosecution Evidence) Regulations 2005, regulation 2 which provides that the prosecution should disclose the documents containing the evidence upon which the charge is based within 70 days of the date of sending (for bail cases) or 50 days of the date of sending (custody cases).

5.24   The CPS Disclosure Manual envisages that initial disclosure will be served by the prosecutor 'as soon as possible' after a not guilty plea in the magistrates' court or immediately after the sending or service of the prosecution case in cases sent to the Crown Court.[31] This initial disclosure will consist of[32] –

•   the endorsed schedule of non-sensitive material (MG6C); and

•   copies of any documents which satisfy the prosecution disclosure test.

5.25   Where cases are sent to the Crown Court, the court will ordinarily require the service of initial disclosure as the date set for compliance with Stage 1. This is in furtherance of the 'Better Case Management' initiative and in order to act with the spirit of the overriding objective.[33] Stage 2 includes the service of the defence statement which is itself predicated on the receipt of initial disclosure and is ordinarily set for 28 days after Stage 1. A defence statement must be served within 28 days of receipt of initial disclosure unless an extension of time is granted by the court.[34] Initial disclosure will be deemed served and the time for service of the defence statement starts running from the date on which the s 3 letter is served.[35] This will be determined by CrimPR 4.11 which provides that:

•   where disclosure is served in person, it is served on the day it is handed over;

•   where disclosure is served electronically, it is served on the day it is sent so long as it is sent before 2:30pm on a business day, otherwise it is served the following business day; and

•   where disclosure is served by first class post or by document exchange, it is served on the second business day after it is posted.

---

30 CPIA 1996, ss 3(8), 13.
31 CPS Disclosure Manual, para 12.36.
32 CPS Disclosure Manual, para 12.35.
33 CrimPR 2015, part 1.
34 The time for service of a defence statement is prescribed by section 12 of the 1996 Act(c) and by the Criminal Procedure and Investigations Act 1996 (Defence Disclosure Time Limits) Regulations 2011(d).
35 *DPP v Wood, DPP v McGillicuddy* [2006] EWHC 32, para 66.

Chapter 6

Defence statements and witness notices

DEFENCE STATEMENTS: INTRODUCTION

6.01   The courts have stated that trial by ambush is no longer an acceptable defence trial tactic.[1] The defence need to adopt a proactive 'cards on the table approach'. The defence statement,[2] which is mandatory in the Crown Court, is a formal document that sets out the accused's defence and the issues with the prosecution case. It can also be used to identify areas of disclosure or reasonable lines of enquiry for the prosecution to consider.

6.02   This chapter deals with:

continued overleaf

---

1   *R v Penner* [2010] EWCA Crim 1155, per Thomas LJ, para 19; *R (on application of DPP) v Chorley Justices* [2002] EWHC 2162 (Admin).

2   Often erroneously referred to as the defence case statement; *R v Rochford* [2010] EWCA Crim 1928, per Hughes LJ, para 1.

COMPULSORY DISCLOSURE OF DEFENCE STATEMENT

6.03   Under the CPIA 1996, ss 1(2) and 5(1), an accused in a trial on indictment in the Crown Court must give a defence statement to the court and prosecutor where:

•   the provisions of CPIA 1996, Part 1 apply; *and*

•   the prosecutor complies or purports to comply with his initial duty of disclosure under the CPIA 1996, s 3(1).

6.04   The CPIA 1996, s 1[3] provides that Part 1 applies where:

•   a person pleads not guilty in the magistrates' court or the youth court and the court proceeds to summary trial;

•   a person is charged with an offence for which they are sent for trial in the Crown Court;[4]

•   a count charging a person with a summary offence is included in an indictment;[5]

---

3   This section's previous version was amended by Criminal Justice Act 2003, s 41 and Sch 3 and came into force on 18 June 2012 (see SI 2012/1320). Its effect was to abolish committal proceedings which used to trigger CPIA 1996, Part 1. All relevant cases are now sent to the Crown Court under the Crime and Disorder Act 1998. The latest version of the section came into force on 24 February 2014.
4   Crime and Disorder Act 1998, s 51.
5   Criminal Justice Act 1988, s 40.

- a bill of indictment charging a person with an indictable offence is preferred;[6] or,

- a judge lifts the suspension of prosecution imposed after a bill of indictment is preferred following initial approval for a deferred prosecution agreement.[7]

6.05   Where a person is charged with an offence for which he is sent to trial, the accused is not required to serve a defence statement unless:

- copies of the documents containing the evidence have been served on him;[8] and

- notice pursuant to the Crime and Disorder Act 1998, s 51D has been served on him.[9]

6.06   To comply with, or purport to comply with,[10] the initial duty of disclosure under the CPIA 1996, s 3(1) the prosecutor must:

(a)   disclose to the accused any prosecution material which has not previously been disclosed to the accused and which might reasonably be considered capable of undermining the case for the prosecution against the accused or of assisting the case for the accused;[11] or

(b)   give to the accused a written statement that there is no material of a description mentioned in paragraph (a).

If either of the above conditions is not satisfied the defence are not required to serve a defence statement.

6.07   The defence cannot ignore any failure by the prosecution to provide initial disclosure. Under the CrimPR 2015, each party must actively assist the court in fulfilling its case management duties[12] in furtherance of the

---

6   Administration of Justice (Miscellaneous Provisions) Act 1933, s 2(2)(b) or Prosecution of Offences Act 1985, s 22B(3)(a).
7   Added by Crime and Courts Act 2013 c. 22 Sch.17(3) para.37(2), including the power relevant to lifting the suspension of deferred prosecution agreements contained in paragraph 2(2) of Sch. 17.
8   CPIA 1996, s 5(3A)(a) and Crime and Disorder Act 1998, Sch 3, para 1.
9   CPIA 1996, s 5(3A)(b). The notice details the offences for which the accused is sent for trial and the place where he is to be tried.
10   CPIA 1996, s 5(1)(b).
11   i.e. the statutory test for disclosure.
12   See CrimPR 2015, rr 1.2(1)(c), 3.2–3.3.

overriding objective.[13] The defence must immediately notify the court and all parties where there is a 'significant' failure in the disclosure process and, if necessary, apply for a direction for disclosure. A failure is 'significant' where it might hinder the court in furthering the overriding objective.[14]

6.08 There is a statutory duty on the prosecutor to serve the non-sensitive schedule (MG6C) in order to comply with his duties of initial disclosure if it is in his possession at the time when he complies with section 3 (initial) disclosure.[15] A failure by the prosecutor to serve the MG6C will not prevent time beginning to run for the service of the defence statement as the 'schedule is not itself a necessary component of nor the mark of primary [initial] disclosure'.[16] The CPS Disclosure Manual envisages that the MG6C will be served at the time of initial disclosure.[17]

6.09 When the prosecutor complies or purports to comply with his duty of initial disclosure by either disclosing material to the defence or serving a written statement that there is no such material, he must at the same time inform the court officer.[18]

CONTENTS OF A DEFENCE STATEMENT

6.10 The CPIA 1996, s 6A(1)(a)-(d) provides:

'... a defence statement is a written statement –

(a) setting out the nature of the accused's defence, including any particular defences on which he intends to rely,

(b) indicating the matters of fact on which he takes issue with the prosecution,

(c) setting out, in the case of each such matter, why he takes issue with the prosecution,

(ca) setting out particulars of the matters of fact on which he intends to rely for the purposes of his defence, and

---

13 Which includes dealing with cases 'efficiently and expeditiously'; CrimPR 2015, r 1.1(2)(e).
14 CrimPR 2015, r 1.2(1)(c).
15 CPIA 1996, ss 4(1), (2) and 24.
16 *DPP v Wood and McGillicuddy* [2006] EWHC 32 (Admin), per Mr Justice Ouseley, para 23.
17 CPS Disclosure Manual, paras 12.35–12.36.
18 CrimPR 2015, r 15.2(2).

(d)   indicating any point of law (including any point as to admissibility or an abuse of process) which he wishes to take, and any authority on which he intends to rely for that purpose.'[19]

6.11   Where a defence statement is served, details of any alibi must also be provided. The CPIA 1996, s 6A(2) provides:

'A defence statement that discloses an alibi must give particulars of it, including –

(a)   the name, address and date of birth of any witness the accused believes is able to give evidence in support of the alibi, or as many of those details as are known to the accused when the defence statement is given;

(b)   any information in the accused's possession which might be of material assistance in identifying or finding any such witness in whose case any of the details mentioned in paragraph (a) are not known to the accused when the statement is given.'

6.12   Evidence in support of an alibi is evidence tending to show that by reason of the presence of the accused at a particular place or in a particular area at a particular time he was not, or was unlikely to have been, at the place where the offence is to have been committed at the time of its alleged commission.[20] The obligation to provide the details is not based on a willingness or ability of that witness to give evidence, but of the defendant's belief that the witness is able to assist.[21]

6.13   For a copy of a defence statement form for use with CrimPR 2015, Pt 15.4 see **Appendix 10.**

DEFENCE OBLIGATIONS

Generally

6.14   What the accused is required to disclose by the CPIA 1996, s 6A is what is going to happen at the trial.[22] Where the accused advances a positive

---

19 As amended by Criminal Justice Act 2003, s 33 and Criminal Justice and Immigration Act 2008, s 60.

20 CPIA 1996, s 6A(3).

21 *Re Joseph Hill & Co Solicitors* [2014] 1 WLR 786.

22 *R v Rochford* [2010] EWCA Crim 1928, per Hughes LJ, para 21.

case there must be compliance with the statutory obligations, clearly set out in section 6A, or the accused is at risk of the sanctions available under the CPIA 1996, s 11.[23] Judges expect a defence statement to contain a clear and detailed exposition of the issues of fact and law. Defence statements that merely rehearse the suggestion that the defendant is innocent do not comply with the requirements of the CPIA.[24]

6.15   The accused is not required to disclose confidential discussions with his advocate nor is he obliged to incriminate himself if he does not want to. The fundamental rights of legal professional privilege and the accused's privilege against self-incrimination have not been taken away by section 6A, CPIA 1996.[25]

6.16   The accused is under a statutory obligation to serve a defence statement and his lawyers must not advise him against doing so. In *R v Rochford*, Hughes LJ stated:[26]

'Can the lawyer properly advise an accused not to file a defence statement? The answer to that is "No". The obligation to file a defence statement is a statutory obligation on the accused. It is not open to a lawyer to advise his client to disobey the client's statutory obligation. It is as simple as that.'

6.17   The accused equally cannot be advised to omit something from the defence statement which the CPIA 1996, s 6A requires. In *R v Rochford*, Hughes LJ stated:[27]

'... the lawyer's duty is first of all never to advise either the absence of a defence statement or the omission from it of something which section 6A requires to be there because of the way the trial is going to be conducted. The lawyer's duty is not to give the accused advice on what to do. The lawyer's duty is to explain the statutory obligation that he has and to explain the consequences which follow from disobedience of it.'

6.18   Where the accused admits guilt to their lawyer within the cloak of legal privilege but refuses to plead guilty they cannot be prevented from this course of

---

23 *R v Patrick Malcolm* [2011] EWCA Crim 2069; *R v Rochford* [2010] EWCA Crim1928, per Hughes LJ, paras 16, 24.
24 Judicial Protocol on the Disclosure of Unused Material in Criminal Cases, October 2013, para 17.
25 *R v Rochford* [2010] EWCA Crim 1928, per Hughes LJ, para 21; see the reasoning in the context of the Criminal Procedure Rules in *R (Kelly) v Warley Magistrates Court* [2007] EWHC 1836 (Admin).
26 [2010] EWCA Crim 1928, at para 22.
27 [2010] EWCA Crim 1928, at para 25. See also *R v Essa* [2009] EWCA Crim 43, para 18.

action. They are entitled to sit through the trial to see whether the prosecution can prove the case or not. They are not under an obligation to declare an admission of guilt in their defence statement.[28] Likewise, an accused who refuses to give instructions, either at all or on specific points, is not obliged to declare their refusal to answer questions in their defence statement.[29]

6.19   In *R v Rochford*, Hughes LJ laid down general guidance where the accused advances no positive case:[30]

> 'The defence statement must say that the defendant does not admit the offence or the relevant part of it as the case may be, and calls for the Crown to prove it. But it must also say that he advances no positive case because if he is going to advance a positive case that must appear in the defence statement and notice of it must be given. Unless the requirement is that the statement is made but no positive case is advanced it would be open to defendants simply to ignore sections 5(5) and 6A.'

6.20   The CrimPR 2015 require 'a cards on the table' approach and rigorous case management in each case where there is a plea of not guilty. At the Plea and Trial Preparation Hearing (PTPH) the accused will be required to identify the trial issue on the PTPH form. This is further to the principles of 'Better Case Management' and the general case management duties that the parties are subject to.[31] The defence statement will then be expected to be served in line with 'Stage 2' of the judge's case management directions.

6.21   Where an accused's solicitor purports to provide a defence statement on behalf of the accused the defence statement shall, unless the contrary is proven, be deemed to be given with the authority of the accused.[32] Although it is good practice for the defence statement to be signed by the accused,[33] a court has no power to order that a defence statement be signed.[34] A judge can require an accused where a statement is unsigned to satisfy him that the document really is his statement.[35]

---

28 *R v Rochford* [2010] EWCA Crim 1928, per Hughes LJ, para 24.
29 *R v Rochford* [2010] EWCA Crim 1928, per Hughes LJ, para 24.
30 *R v Rochford* [2010] EWCA Crim 1928, per Hughes LJ, para 24. See also *R v Wayne Patrick Malcolm* [2011] EWCA Crim 2069.
31 Criminal Practice Directions 2015, 3A.
32 CPIA 1996, s 6E(1);
33 *R v Wheeler* [2001] 1 Cr App R 10, per Potter LJ, paras 52–53.
34 *R (on the application of Sullivan) v Maidstone Crown Court* [2002] EWHC 967, Kennedy LJ, para 17.
35 *R v Alan Newell* [2012] EWCA Crim 650, per Sir John Thomas P, para 32.

Privilege against self-incrimination

6.22   The privilege against self-incrimination cannot be used to justify non-compliance with the disclosure requirements under the CPIA 1996. In *R v Rochford*, Hughes LJ, in considering the disclosure that an accused is required to give in a defence statement, said:[36]

> 'Do legal professional privilege and the defendant's privilege against self-incrimination survive section 6A? The answer to that is "Yes". What the defendant is required to disclose by section 6A is what is going to happen at the trial. He is not required to disclose his confidential discussions with his advocate, although of course they may bear on what is going to happen at the trial. Nor is he obliged to incriminate himself if he does not want to. Those are fundamental rights and they have certainly not been taken away by section 6A ...'

6.23   A deficiency in the prosecution case that could give the accused an advantage must be identified in the defence statement even though it gives the prosecution the opportunity to rectify it. As Stanley Burton LJ stated in *Malcolm v DPP*:[37]

> 'Criminal trials are no longer to be treated as a game, in which each move is final and any omission by the prosecution leads to its failure. It is the duty of the defence to make its defence and the issues it raises clear to the prosecution and to the court at an early stage. That duty is implicit in rule 3.3 of the Criminal Procedure Rules ...'

6.24   His Lordship further stated:[38]

> 'A criminal trial is not a game under which a guilty defendant should be provided with a sporting chance. It is a search for truth in accordance with the twin principles that the prosecution must prove its case and that a defendant is not obliged to inculpate himself, the object being to convict the guilty and acquit the innocent.'

6.25   Where the accused has a defence but he refuses to allow his legal representative to disclose it, there is a positive duty under the CrimPR 2015, 1.2(1)(c) to notify the court. It is then for the court to decide how to proceed. The legal representative must not make himself complicit in a manipulation of the

---

36   [2010] EWCA Crim 1928, para 21.
37   [2007] EWHC 363 (Admin) at para 31.
38   At para 34.

court process.[39] The legal representative must also consider asking the court to list the case for non-compliance. The Law Society Practice Note states:[40]

'It is essential to appreciate that the purpose of Rule 1.2 (1) (c) is to enable the court to control the preparation process and avoid ineffective and wasted hearings.

When something goes wrong because of a failure of a defendant to co-operate with you the court should be made aware of this and if you fail to keep the court informed, you risk breaching your duty to the court under the provisions of the Rules.'

6.26   Where issues are not raised when they should be and unnecessary costs are incurred as a result, the court may consider a wasted costs order (see **Chapter 11**).[41]

Putting the prosecution to proof

6.27   Where an accused has no positive case to assert he is entitled to require the prosecution to prove its case but he must make his position clear to the court (see **6.19**). It is no longer sufficient to simply record on the defence statement that the prosecution are put to 'strict proof'.[42] The accused must state that he does not intend to assert a positive case. If he subsequently asserts a positive case at trial, it is likely that sanction will follow. A judge cannot require counsel to reveal his instructions if no positive case is going to be made. In *R v Rochford*, Hughes LJ stated:[43]

'The judge was entitled to ask, and indeed to ask insistently and trenchantly. He was not, however, entitled to require counsel to reveal his instructions if no positive case was going to be made in any of the ways which we have identified or any other. From a position of ignorance the judge was not in a position to know, any more than we are at this stage, whether there had been a breach of section 6A or not. Only time will tell as the trial, which has not yet begun, proceeds.'

---

39 See *R v SVS Solicitors* [2012] EWCA Crim 319.
40 Law Society Practice Note: Criminal Procedure Rules 2015: Solicitors' duties (29 February 2016), paras 4.3 and 4.4.
41 Costs in Criminal Cases (General) Regulations 1986 and Prosecution of Offences Act 1985, ss 19 and 19A.
42 In *Balogun v DPP* [2010] EWHC 799 (Admin), Leveson LJ, para 16 stated: 'For my part … I do not accept that the spirit or letter of the Criminal Procedure Rules is complied with by asserting that the Crown is put to "strict proof" …'.
43 [2010] EWCA Crim 1928 at para 17. See also *R v Essa* [2009] EWCA Crim 43, para 18.

6.28   Where the prosecution is simply being put to proof by the accused and no positive case is asserted, the accused may lose his right to determine which witnesses will be called. The 'Stop Delaying Justice' initiative states that in those circumstances the choice of witness:

'... would remain an issue for the CPS. They would be charged with deciding what evidence they wish to call and how. They may ... decide not to call a witness where the defence will not accept them section 9, if they feel they can conduct the trial without them.'[44]

6.29   If the evidence of a particular witness is not in dispute, it may more readily be admitted into evidence under the hearsay provisions of the Criminal Justice Act 2003 (CJA 2003), s 114. In *R v Ishmael Adams*,[45] where a witness could not be located on the day of trial and his statement could not be read under the provisions of the CJA 2003, s 116,[46] it was admitted under s 114. Hughes LJ, in giving judgment, stated at para 19:

'... the true issue in the case was not possession but intent to supply [drugs] ... it was plainly in the interests of justice for the uncontentious matter of possession to be proved by the Crown by the admission of the edited witness statement ... To hold otherwise would not be to do justice; it would rather be to afford a defendant an escape on purely technical grounds ... There is no question of relieving the Crown of the duty of proving the essential elements of the case. The question is not whether it is for the Crown to prove it, but how the Crown shall be permitted to prove it. If parts of the Crown's evidence are in dispute, it is quite likely that it will not be in the interests of justice to permit those parts to be proved by the reading of a hearsay statement when the witness cannot be cross-examined and properly challenged. But if parts of the Crown's case are not in dispute then it is plainly in the interests of justice that those parts shall be permitted to be proved by them by means of the hearsay statement as in this case.'

A similar approach was adopted by the Court of Appeal in *R v Moss*.[47] In that case, however, reference was also made to the case of *R v Tindle*,[48] where it was held that it would be only in rare circumstances, if any, that it would be right to allow evidence of central importance to be adduced when there has been a failure to take reasonable steps to secure the attendance of the witness.

---

44 'Stop Delaying Justice', p 11. This initiative was implemented in magistrates' courts with the support of the Senior Presiding Judge (Goldring LJ). It has not been implemented more widely at Crown Court level nor has it been given any statutory footing.
45 [2007] EWCA Crim 3025.
46 As such steps as were reasonably practicable had not been taken to locate him.
47 [2016] EWCA Crim 635.
48 *R v Tindle* [2011] EWCA Crim 2341, 175 JP 462 CA at paragraph 16.

6.30   It is unclear whether the provisions of the CJA 2003, s 114 may be deployed to prevent witnesses being listed as required simply to see if they turn up.[49] The Court of Appeal has made clear that hearsay evidence is not simply to be 'nodded through' which was a principle repeated in *R v Moss* above.[50]

6.31   If it becomes clear that there is a positive case to assert, not previously identified to the court, an adjournment may be necessary. If costs are incurred as a result, the court may impose a wasted costs order (see **Chapter 11**).[51]

TIME LIMITS

6.32   The accused must give a defence statement within 28 days (for trials in the Crown Court) from when the prosecutor complies or purports to comply with his initial duty to disclose.[52] The Criminal Procedure and Investigations Act 1996 (Defence Disclosure Time Limits) Regulations 2011/209 only provide for the power to extend the time limit for service of a defence statement. It is submitted therefore that there is no power to shorten the time period. The 28-day period applies to investigations commencing on or after 28 February 2011. In cases of any complexity, this time limit will often be too short, as it does not afford the defence sufficient time to assimilate the material and take an adequate proof of evidence from the accused.

6.33   The accused can apply for an extension of days in which to serve the defence statement. The court will only make an order if it is satisfied that it would be unreasonable to require the defence to comply within the specified time period.[53] The application must be made by the accused before the expiry of the time limit, specify the grounds and state the number of days of extension required.[54] There is no limit to the number of applications that can be made.[55]

---

49 'Stop Delaying Justice', p 13.
50 *R v Riyat and others* [2012] EWCA Crim 1509; [2013] 1 W.L.R. 2592 per Hughes LJ, para 25.
51 Costs in Criminal Cases (General) Regulations 1986 and Prosecution of Offences Act 1985, ss 19 and 19A.
52 CPIA 1996, s 3(3) and Criminal Procedure and Investigations Act 1996 (Defence Disclosure Time Limits) Regulations 2011.
53 Criminal Procedure and Investigations Act 1996 (Defence Disclosure Time Limits) Regulations 2011, r 3(2).
54 Criminal Procedure and Investigations Act 1996 (Defence Disclosure Time Limits) Regulations 2011, r 3(2) and (3).
55 Criminal Procedure and Investigations Act 1996 (Defence Disclosure Time Limits) Regulations 2011, r 3(4).

UPDATED DEFENCE STATEMENTS

6.34   The CPIA 1996, s 6B is not yet in force and, until implemented, the court has no power to order the service of an updated defence statement.[56] When in force, the CPIA 1996, s 6B(1) will impose a duty upon the defence to update the prosecution as to the defence case either by the service of an 'updated defence statement' or by the provision of a written statement to the effect that there are no changes to be made to the defence statement as initially served.

6.35   An updated defence statement must comply with the requirements imposed by the CPIA 1996, s 6A by reference to the state of affairs at the time when the statement is given.[57] The CPIA 1996, s 6B(5) and (6) allows the court to order the service of the updated defence statement on other co-accused either of its own motion or on the application of any party.

6.36   Additional prosecution evidence and unused material, which has significance to an accused's case, is regularly served after the initial defence statement. The CPIA 1996, s 6B will give the defence an opportunity to update their defence or provide further information that will allow the prosecutor to make informed decisions on disclosure or advise on further lines of enquiry. An updated defence statement can always be provided voluntarily.

SANCTIONS FOR FAULTS IN DEFENCE STATEMENT

6.37   The CPIA 1996, s 11 provides the sanctions for failing to comply with the statutory duty to (i) file a defence statement, and (ii) include those things which are required by the CPIA 1996, s 6A. It is not open to the court to add an additional extra-statutory sanction of punishment for contempt of court.[58] The fact that a defence statement is served late does not prevent sanctions applying pursuant to the CPIA 1996, s 11.[59]

6.38   The CPIA 1996, s 11(2) identifies nine triggers which will put the accused at risk of the sanction.[60] These include:

- the accused fails to give an initial defence statement;

- the accused is late in giving an initial defence statement;

---

56 As inserted by Criminal Justice Act 2003, s 33.
57 CPIA 1996, s 6B(3).
58 *R v Rochford* [2010] EWCA Crim 1928, per Hughes LJ, para 18.
59 *DPP v Wood; DPP v McGillicuddy* [2006] EWHC 32 (Admin).
60 Only seven triggers currently apply as s 6B is not yet in force.

- the accused sets out inconsistent defences in his defence statement; or

- at his trial the accused –

  - puts forward a defence which was not mentioned in his defence statement or was different from any defence set out in that statement;

  - relies on a matter which, in breach of the requirements imposed by or under section 6A,[61] was not mentioned in the defence statement;

  - adduces evidence in support of an alibi without having given particulars of the alibi in his defence statement; or

  - calls a witness to give evidence in support of an alibi without having complied with s 6A(2)(a) or (b)[62] as regards the witness in his defence statement.

6.39   The consequence of any of the above faults is that, unless the fault involves failing to mention a point of law, the court or any party (ie prosecution or co-accused) may make such comment as appears appropriate and the court or jury may draw such inferences as appear proper in deciding whether the accused is guilty of the offence concerned.[63] Whenever this amended CPIA regime applies, the prosecution may comment on any failure in defence disclosure (except where the failure relates to a point of law) without leave of the court, but counsel should use a measure of judgment as to whether it is wise to embark on cross-examination about such a failure. If the accused is cross-examined about discrepancies between his evidence and his defence statement, or if adverse comment is made, the judge must give appropriate guidance to the jury.[64]

6.40   Where the accused puts forward a defence which is different from any defence set out in his defence statement, before deciding or in deciding to do anything the court shall have regard to (a) the extent of the differences in the defence, and (b) whether there is any justification for it.[65]

6.41   If the fault involves reliance on a point of law (including any point on admissibility of evidence or abuse of process), which was not mentioned in the defence statement, leave of the court is required before another party can make comment.[66]

---

61 For the text of s 6A see **Appendix 1**.
62 For the text of s 6A(2)(a)(b) see **Appendix 1**.
63 CPIA 1996, s 11(5).
64 Judicial Protocol on the Disclosure of Unused Material in Criminal Cases, December 2013, para 21.
65 CPIA 1996, s 11(8).
66 CPIA 1996, s 11(6).

6.42   Where no defence statement has been served or the defence statement is lacking specificity or otherwise does not meet the requirements of the CPIA 1996, s 6A, prosecutors should challenge the lack of, or inadequate, defence statements in writing, copying the document to the court and the defence and seeking directions from the court to require the provision of an adequate statement from the defence.[67] The CPIA 1996, s 6E states that the judge, at a pre-trial hearing, should investigate the position in relation to defence statements and warn an accused if it appears to him that the accused has not fully complied with the statutory requirements relating to a defence statement so that there is a possibility of comment being made or inferences drawn and this result is likely if there is no justification for the deficiency. The fact that a warning has been given should be noted.[68]

6.43   Leave is not required for a party to cross-examine an accused on the differences between his defence and defence statement.[69] A judge may direct that a jury receive a copy of a defence statement, edited if appropriate, if it would help the jury to understand or resolve the issues in the case.[70] A judge's decision to exercise these powers (either on application or of his own motion) will not be appealable unless it can be shown that the judge was unreasonable to admit the defence statement.[71] The defence statement itself is not evidence, all it can ever do is to refer to matters which may become the subject of evidence.[72] It is sensible to take any defence statement(s) from the jury when they retire to deliberate.[73]

ADMINISTRATIVE SANCTIONS

6.44   The CrimPR 2015 3.5(6) provides that if a party fails to comply with a rule or a direction:

'the court may –

(a)   fix, postpone, bring forward, extend, cancel or adjourn a hearing;

(b)   exercise its power to make a costs order; and

(c)   impose such other sanctions as may be appropriate.'

---

67 Attorney General's Guidelines on Disclosure (2013), para 33.
68 As inserted by Criminal Justice Act 2003, s 36; see Judicial Protocol on the Disclosure of Unused Material in Criminal Cases, December 2013, para 20.
69 *R v Tibbs* [2000] 2 Cr App R 309, per Beldam LJ, para 34.
70 CPIA 1996, s 6E(4) to (6).
71 *Sanghera* [2012] 2 Cr App R 196, para 17.
72 *R v Sanghera* [2012] EWCA Crim 16, per Aikens LJ, para 51.
73 *R v Sanghera* [2012] EWCA Crim 16, per Aikens LJ, para 80.

6.45   The danger of breaching the Criminal Procedure Rules and the inherent conflict between the client/solicitor privilege and a solicitor's duty to the court is illustrated in *R v SVS Solicitors*.[74] In this case the solicitors objected to the admission of hearsay evidence but failed to comply with the Criminal Procedure Rules[75] in that they did not give their reasons for the objection or disclose their defence case.[76] A prosecution witness (Mr Amoako) was flown from Australia for the trial but ultimately not called to give evidence. The Court of Appeal upheld a wasted costs order against the solicitors. Field J in giving judgment stated, at para 24:

> '... No application setting out the grounds of objection to the admission of Mr Amoako's statement was served within the stipulated time or at all. This in our judgment, as the judge found, was a clear breach of CrimPR 34.3(2)(d). The judge was entitled to conclude that a cross-application setting out that part of Nseki's case [defendant] that he had to put to Mr Amoako should have been served or, if the client refused to sanction this step, the appellant firm should have ceased to act for him. The appellant's failure to take either of these steps was not a mere error of judgment. The defendant Nseki was manifestly seeking to manipulate the court's process. By insisting on the appearance of Mr Amoako without disclosing the defence case that was to be put to the witness, the appellant firm made itself complicit in the manipulation being practised by their client. The judge was entitled to hold that the failure to comply with the rule was deliberate and that it was a serious breach. He was also entitled to find that the appellant's conduct was improper, unreasonable and negligent, for the reasons he gave.'

6.46   The impact of *R v SVS*[77] is significant. The Law Society have issued an updated practice note advising solicitors to inform the court if their clients prevent them complying with their obligations under the Criminal Procedure Rules:

> '... a failure to do so, could be interpreted by the court as a manipulation of its process, and as improper, unreasonable or negligent conduct, could give rise to a Wasted Costs Order being made against the solicitor.'[78]

6.47   It must be borne in mind that the primary object of a wasted costs order is not to punish but to compensate. As the costs order can be regarded as having a penal element when it is ordered against a non-party, a mere mistake by a legal

---

74 [2012] EWCA Crim 319.
75 CrimPR 2010 applied at the relevant time.
76 As required by CrimPR 2010, r 34.3 (now incorporated into CrimPR 2015).
77 [2012] EWCA Crim 319.
78 Law Society Practice Note: Criminal Procedure Rules 2015: Solicitors' duties (29 February 2016), para 4.4

representative (or his employee) is not sufficient to justify an order. There must be a more serious error.[79]

6.48   For a wasted costs order to be made, the normal civil standard of proof applies but if the allegation is one of serious misconduct or crime, clear evidence will be required to meet the standard.[80] The procedure to be used is set out in the CrimPR 2015 45.9.

6.49   In relation to sanctions other than costs, where a party seeks to call an alibi witness not previously identified in the defence statement, a refusal to allow that witness to be called is likely to be regarded as a step too far and one that would require primary legislative sanction.[81] Different considerations apply to expert evidence and the CrimPR 2015 Part 19 applies.[82]

'SHOPPING LISTS'

6.50   Instructions permitting, the defence statement should be detailed, comprehensive and tailored to the issues in the case. The use of formulaic generalized 'shopping lists' is to be deprecated. Under the guidance available there is scope for focused and reasoned defence requests for disclosure linked to a comprehensive defence statement to which the prosecution must respond.[83]

6.51   The trial process is not well served if the defence make general and unspecified allegations and then seek far-reaching disclosure in the hope that material may turn up. The more detail a defence statement contains the more likely it is that the prosecutor will make an informed decision about disclosure and whether to advise the investigator to undertake further lines of enquiry.[84]

---

79 Practice Direction (Costs in Criminal Proceedings) [2015] EWCA Crim 15681 para 4.2.5 issued by Thomas LCJ (29 September 2015) applying the guidance in *re P (A Barrister)* [2001] EWCA Crim 1728; [2002] 1 Cr App R 207.

80 Practice Direction (Costs in Criminal Proceedings) [2015] EWCA Crim 15681 para 4.2.5(vi), issued by Thomas LCJ (29 September 2015) applying the guidance in *re P (A Barrister)* [2001] EWCA Crim 1728; [2002] 1 Cr App R 207.

81 *R (on the application of Tinnion) v Reading Crown Court* [2009] EWHC 2930 (Admin), per Mitting J, para 37; *R v Ullah* [2011] EWCA Crim 3275, per Moses LJ, para 13. Both cases were before the introduction of CrimPR 2015, r 3.5(6).

82 *R v Ensor* [2009] EWCA Crim 2519.

83 Attorney General's Guidelines on Disclosure (2013), para 39; Judicial Protocol on the Disclosure of Unused Material in Criminal Cases, December 2013, para 17; CPS Disclosure Manual, para 15.6-15.13.

84 Attorney General's Guidelines on Disclosure (2013), para 39. The essential need for a full and careful defence statement is spelt out in Judicial Protocol on the Disclosure of Unused Material in Criminal Cases, December 2013, para 19; see *R v H & C* [2004] Cr App R 10, per Lord Bingham CJ, para 35.

The prosecution can identify further material under their continuing duty to disclose under the CPIA 1996, s 7A and the need for an application under the CPIA 1996, s 8 (a section 8 application) may be eliminated, or at least, the areas of dispute narrowed.

6.52 A detailed defence statement assists not only the court in the management of the trial by focusing on the issues in dispute but also adds weight to defence submissions of prosecution failings in the disclosure process. In practice, the defence frequently serve requests for disclosure upon the prosecution within the body of the defence statement. Such requests are compliant with a party's duties under the CrimPR 2015 Parts 1 and 3.

6.53 Prosecution advocates frequently refer to defence requests for disclosure as 'shopping lists' or 'fishing expeditions' and often do so erroneously. A specific request for disclosure is not a 'fishing expedition' simply because the defence do not know whether or not the material requested will assist their case. By way of example, the defence will rarely know whether or not a prosecution witness has previous convictions but this does not mean that they are not entitled to request that this be reviewed to see if there is material which may assist the defence case or undermine the prosecution case. If the defence knew for certain that material would assist their case, there would often be no need to request it.

EXAMPLES OF DISCLOSURE REQUESTS

6.54 Listed below are examples of defence disclosure requests. Requests for disclosure must not be used indiscriminately and must be relevant and tailored to the issues in the case.

- Please provide the defence with copies of unused items (*insert numbers*) from the MG6C (*give date and reference number*).

- Has the complainant made previous false allegations against any other person? If so, please disclose copies of the relevant documentation.

- Please disclose the date, time, circumstances and any contemporaneous notes or record of every occasion when the complainant has given an account of the allegation.

- Has the complainant made any application to the CICA[85] or to any other agency for compensation? If so, please disclose details of the application

---

85 Criminal Injuries Compensation Authority (also sometimes referred to as the CICB).

including any account given of the alleged facts. Does the complainant intend to make any such application? Has the complainant received any advice from the police as to when and in what circumstances they might make such claims?

- Has the complainant received any counselling for the effects of the alleged offence? If so, provide details of when and by whom. Please supply all relevant documentation.

- Please provide copies of all notes and records of any contact the police have had with any civilian prosecution witnesses.

- Please confirm that all relevant entries in police notebooks have been read for disclosure purposes and are accurately and sufficiently described on the MG6C.

- Please give details of any investigations regarding contamination or collusion between the complainants.

- Has a major incident police book or equivalent record of actions or decisions been maintained and, if so, has it been reviewed for disclosure purposes?

- As far as the officer in the case, investigators or disclosure officers are aware, has there been any failure to record relevant material, such as a first complaint of witnesses, or has any relevant material been lost?

- Please confirm that the reviewing lawyer and/or prosecuting advocate has read the MG6D and the material described therein and satisfied himself that such material is properly categorized as sensitive as opposed to non-sensitive.

- Was any decision made as to what complainants should be told of the complaints of others? If so, please disclose full details.

- Please disclose details of all CCTV enquiries made in the case and if no enquiries were made, why not?

- Please identify the disclosure officer and the date of his appointment.

- Please confirm that the disclosure officer has been trained under an 'appropriate training regime' in accordance with paragraph 14, Disclosure Protocol and, if so, when?

- Please disclose copies of all police press releases and police copies of media broadcasts.

CROSS SERVICE OF DEFENCE STATEMENTS

6.55   The CPIA 1996 requires the accused to serve his defence statement on the court and the prosecutor,[86] not upon a co-accused. It is for the prosecutor to decide, and keep under review, whether the defence statement of one co-accused satisfies the test for disclosure to another, subject to issues of public interest immunity.[87]

6.56   Good practice would be for the prosecution to give the accused notice of any intention to disclose his defence statement to a co-accused, so that any issues of privilege, sensitivity, relevance and editing can be raised.

6.57   If the CJA 2003, s33 comes fully into effect, the CPIA 1996, ss 5(5A), 5(B) and (5D) will deal with the issues relevant to cross-service of defence statements as the court will have the power to order a defendant to serve a defence statement on a co-defendant, whether acting of its own motion or on application by a party to the proceedings.

6.58   If the judge is of the opinion that seeing a copy of a defence statement would help the jury to understand the case or to resolve any issue in the case,[88] he may direct that the jury be given a copy of any defence statement, edited if necessary, to exclude inadmissible evidence.[89]

DRAFTING THE DEFENCE STATEMENT

6.59   The Bar Council has issued a document (falling short of guidance)[90] which states that counsel should not draft a defence statement without adequate instructions, which should take the form of a signed proof of evidence or a note of instructions taken in conference. Such a note should also be signed by the defendant. Further, the Bar Standards Committee (BSC) via the Bar Standards Board has warned counsel that that there is no halfway house when accepting instructions to draft a defence statement and that the professional obligations are considerable. Where counsel accepts the brief for trial, his legal aid fee will be deemed to include all necessary preparation including the settling of a defence statement.[91]

---

86 CPIA 1996, s 5(5).
87 *R v Cairns* [2002] EWCA Crim 2838, per Keene LJ, para 78; CPIA 1996, s 11(5). See also CPS Disclosure Manual, para 15.29.
88 CPIA 1996, s 6E(5)(b).
89 CPIA 1996, s 6E(4).
90 Bar Council Ethics Committee note: Defence Statements (reviewed June 2016).
91 Bar Standards Board Code of Conduct, r c9, c23 and c29.

6.60 In their guidance[92] the BSC advises that when settling a defence statement counsel should recognise the crucial importance of obtaining all prosecution statements and documentary exhibits, a signed proof of evidence from the lay client (of sufficient detail to address properly the necessary issues) and statements from other material witnesses.

6.61 Counsel should ensure that the lay client realises the importance of the defence statement and the potential adverse consequences of an inaccurate or inadequate statement. There should be a proper informed approval of the draft by the lay client given the risks of professional embarrassment (should the lay client seek to disown the statement during cross examination).

6.62 Counsel ought to insist upon a written acknowledgement from the lay client that:

• he understands the importance of the accuracy of the defence statement; and

• he has had an opportunity of considering the contents of the defence statement carefully and approves it.

6.63 A conference may be necessary to ensure compliance with these fundamentals or, depending on the case, a written advice accompanying the defence statement may suffice.

WITNESS NOTICES: INTRODUCTION

6.64 The accused is required to give to the prosecutor a witness notice that indicates which witnesses he intends to call at trial and to provide their details. The requirement to give a witness notice is compulsory regardless of whether the case is in the magistrates' court or the Crown Court and is a further indication of the change effected through the provisions of the CPIA 1996 and CrimPR 2015 designed to abolish the alleged culture of trial by ambush.[93] Before its introduction the only obligation on the accused to give notice of a witness that he intended to call at trial related to alibi witnesses.

---

92 'The Preparation of Defence Statements', Bar Standards Committee (9 March 2011).
93 *R v Rochford* [2010] EWCA Crim 1928, per Hughes LJ, para 10.

CONTENTS OF A WITNESS NOTICE

6.65   A witness notice requires the accused to provide to the prosecutor and the court the identity and particulars of any witness whom he intends to call. The notice applies to witnesses of fact and character. The CPIA 1996, s 6C[94] states:

> (1)   The accused must give to the court and the prosecutor a notice indicating whether he intends to call any persons (other than himself) as witnesses at his trial and, if so –
>
> > (a)   giving the name, address and date of birth of each such proposed witness, or as many of those details as are known to the accused when the notice is given;
> >
> > (b)   providing any information in the accused's possession which might be of material assistance in identifying or finding any such proposed witness in whose case any of the details mentioned in paragraph (a) are not known to the accused when the notice is given.

6.66   The requirement is only to provide the particulars of the witness. There is no requirement to disclose the substance of the evidence a witness is expected to give or identify the issue(s) to which his evidence relates. Additional provisions apply to expert witnesses (see **6.101** below).

6.67   Details of alibi witnesses do not have to be given to the extent that they have already been given in the defence statement in accordance with the CPIA 1996, s 6A(2).

6.68   The requirement for an accused to give a witness notice is compulsory. It applies in all cases in which either the accused pleaded not guilty in the magistrates' court or was sent to the Crown Court on or after 1 May 2010. It does not apply to Newton hearings following a guilty plea. This requirement is separate to the requirement to provide witness requirements as directed at 'Stage 2' of the directions ordered at the Plea and Trial Preparation Hearing.[95]

---

94   As inserted by Criminal Justice Act 2003, s 34.
95   See 'Plea and Trial Preparation Hearings: Introductions and Guidance', December 2015.

DUTY TO AMEND

6.69   The provision of a witness notice is a continuing duty and an amended notice must be given if there are any changes to the witnesses it is intended to call. The CPIA 1996, s 6C(4) states:

If, following the giving of a notice under this section, the accused –

(a)   decides to call a person (other than himself) who is not included in the notice as a proposed witness, or decides not to call a person who is so included, or

(b)   discovers any information which, under subsection (1), he would have had to include in the notice if he had been aware of it when giving the notice,

he must give an appropriately amended notice to the court and the prosecutor.

INTENTION TO CALL A WITNESS

6.70   There is no authority as to what 'intends' means in the context of the CPIA 1996, s 6(C). Assistance may be obtained from *R v Ensor*,[96] in which Aikens LJ, in considering the late service of a defence expert's report under CPR 2005, Part 24,[97] stated at para 30:

'In our view the effect of CrimPR Parts 1.2 and 3.3[98] together is that it is incumbent upon both the prosecution and defence ... to alert the court and the other side at the earliest practicable moment if they are intending or may be intending to adduce expert evidence. That should be done if possible at a PCMH. If it cannot be done then it must be done as soon as the possibility [of calling expert evidence] becomes live.'[99]

6.71   In light of *Ensor*, the most likely interpretation of 'intends' would be that an accused intends to call a witness when he has decided that he might

96   [2010] 1 Cr App R 18.
97   CrimPR 2005, r 24.1 stated: '... *if any party to the proceedings who proposes to adduce expert evidence in the proceedings ... he shall as soon as practicable ... (i) furnish the other party or parties with a statement in writing of any finding or opinion which he proposes to adduce by way of such evidence ...*'
98   The wording of CrimPR 2005, rr 1.2 (duty of participants in a criminal case) and 3.3 (the duty of parties) is identical in CrimPR 2015.
99   The PCMH now having been abolished, it is assumed that the requirement to notify should be made in line with stage 2 of the proceedings.

call the witness. If a witness notice was required only after a final and settled intention had been reached, it would defeat the purpose of the CPIA 1996, s 6C to abolish ambush defences and may result in costly adjournments in order for the prosecution to interview the defence witness or investigate any potential bad character issues.[100]

6.72   Good practice dictates that a statement should be obtained from any potential defence witness before deciding whether it is intended to call him. To do otherwise is to risk giving the prosecutor details of a prospective witness who may support the prosecution case. However, practitioners should note that in *Re Joseph Hill & Co Solicitors*,[101] the Court of Appeal held that the obligation to provide the details of an alibi witness is not based on a willingness or ability of that witness to give evidence, but on the defendant's belief that the alibi witness is able to assist.

TIME LIMITS

6.73   The accused must give a witness notice within 28 days[102] for trials in the Crown Court from when the prosecutor complies or purports to comply with his initial duty to disclose.[103] The 28-day period applies to investigations commencing on or after 28 February 2011.[104] In cases of any complexity, this time limit will often be too short, as it does not afford the defence sufficient time to assimilate the material, take an adequate proof of evidence from the accused or obtain the contact details of potential eye-witnesses. Even when the solicitors or enquiry agents establish contact with potential defence witnesses, all too often the witnesses fail to maintain that contact or attend appointments. In any event, it is difficult to reconcile this time limit with the wording in section 6C which requires the defendant to notify the Crown of an *intention* to call a defence witness as the obligation can arguably only bite once the *intention* has been formed.

6.74   The accused can apply for an extension of days in which to serve the witness notice. The court will only make an order if it is satisfied that it would be unreasonable to require the defence to comply within the specified time period.[105]

---

100   See **6.84** 'Interviews of witnesses notified by the accused' below.
101   [2014] 1 WLR 786.
102   CPIA 1996, s 6C(3) – previously the time limit was 14 days.
103   CPIA 1996, s 3(3) and Criminal Procedure and Investigations Act 1996 (Defence Disclosure Time Limits) Regulations 2011.
104   Previously the time limit was 14 days.
105   Criminal Procedure and Investigations Act 1996 (Defence Disclosure Time Limits) Regulations 2011, r 3(2).

The application must be made by the accused before the expiry of the time limit, specify the grounds and state the number of days of extension required.[106] There is no limit to the number of applications that can be made.[107]

6.75   As the filing of a witness notice is a compulsory statutory obligation it is not open to an accused's lawyers to advise him to disobey it.[108]

SANCTIONS FOR FAULTS IN WITNESS NOTICE

6.76   The CPIA 1996, s 11(4) identifies two triggers which put the accused at risk of sanctions. These are where the accused:

(a)   is late in giving the witness notice; or

(b)   at his trial calls a witness (other than himself) not included, or not adequately identified, in a witness notice.

6.77   The consequence of either of the above faults is that the court or any party may make such comment as appears appropriate but the prosecution or co-accused may only do so with leave of the court.[109] The court may also direct the jury to draw such inferences as appear proper in deciding whether the accused is guilty of the offence concerned.[110]

6.78   Where the accused calls a witness whom he has failed to include, or to identify adequately in a witness notice, the court must have regard as to whether there is any justification for the failure before it allows any comment to be made or adverse inference to be drawn.[111]

6.79   An accused need not call a witness indicated in the witness notice and no sanction attaches under the CPIA 1996, s 11 or the CPIA Code for this failure. Having regard to the burden of proof, it is suggested that it would be inappropriate for either the judge or prosecution to comment upon this failure save, if necessary, for the standard jury direction not to speculate about what a witness might have said.[112]

---

106 Criminal Procedure and Investigations Act 1996 (Defence Disclosure Time Limits) Regulations 2011, r 3(2) and (3).
107 Criminal Procedure and Investigations Act 1996 (Defence Disclosure Time Limits) Regulations 2011, r 3(4).
108 *R v Rochford* [2010] EWCA Crim 1928, per Hughes LJ.
109 CPIA 1996, s 11(7).
110 CPIA 1996, s 11(5).
111 CPIA 1996, s 11(9).
112 *R v Paul Wheeler* (1968) 52 Cr App R 28, per Winn LJ; *R v Shani Wright* 1999 WL 1457234, per Kennedy LJ, para 14, Criminal Law Review 2010, p 690.

6.80   The judge, at a pre-trial hearing, shall warn an accused if it appears to him that the accused has not fully complied with the statutory requirements relating to a witness notice so that there is a possibility of comment being made or inferences drawn.[113]

ADMINISTRATIVE SANCTIONS

6.81   The CPR 2015 3.5(6) provides that if a party fails to comply with a rule or a direction:

… the court may –

(a)   fix, postpone, bring forward, extend, cancel or adjourn a hearing;

(b)   exercise its power to make a costs order; and

(c)   impose such other sanctions as may be appropriate.

6.82   Where a party seeks to call a witness not previously identified in the witness notice, a refusal to allow that witness to be called is likely to be regarded as a step too far and one which would require primary legislative sanction.[114] A party who does not call a witness indicated in a witness notice may be at risk of costs if there has been a clear wastage of police resources as a result of not amending the notice.

6.83   The Law Society issued a guidance note in relation to defence witness notifications and how legal representatives should treat their obligations to their client and to witnesses.[115]

INTERVIEWS OF WITNESSES NOTIFIED BY THE ACCUSED

6.84   The Code of Practice[116] for Arranging and Conducting Interviews of Witnesses Notified by the Accused (the Interview Code) came into force on

---

113   CPIA 1996, s 6E(2);

114   *R (on the application of Tinnion) v Reading Crown Court* [2009] EWHC 2930 (Admin), per Mitting J, para 37; *R v Ullah* [2011] EWCA Crim 3275, per Moses LJ, para 13. Both cases were before the introduction of CPR 2012, r 3.5(6).

115   Law Society Guidance Note: Defence witness notices, 21 December 2015.

116   For the text of the Code see **Appendix 2.**

1 May 2010.[117] Any police officer or other person charged with the duty of investigating offences who arranges or conducts an interview of a person notified by the accused either as an alibi witness[118] or as a witness identified in the witness notice[119] must have regard to the Interview Code.[120] The main provisions of the Interview Code, often drafted in mandatory terms, are summarised below.

6.85   The Interview Code, para 3.1 requires that before any interview may take place a witness must be:

•   asked whether he consents to being interviewed;

•   informed why the interview is being requested;

•   informed that he is not obliged to attend the proposed interview;

•   informed that he is entitled to be accompanied by a solicitor;[121] and

•   informed that a record will be made and he will be sent a copy.

6.86   The Interview Code, para 3.2 requires that if the witness consents to being interviewed he must be asked:

•   whether he wishes to have a solicitor present at the interview;

•   whether he consents to a solicitor attending on behalf of the accused as an observer; and

•   whether he consents to a copy of the record being sent to the accused and informed that it may nevertheless be required to be disclosed to the accused or any co-accused.

6.87   The Interview Code, para 4 requires that before any interview takes place the accused or, if he is legally represented, his legal representative must be notified:

•   that the interview has been requested;

•   whether the witness consented to the interview; and

117 The Criminal Procedure and Investigations Act 1996 (Code of Practice for Interviews of Witnesses Notified by Accused) Order 2010, pursuant to Criminal Procedure and Investigations Act 1996, s 21A, Code of Practice for Arranging and Conducting Interviews of Witnesses Notified by the Accused.
118 CPIA 1996, s 6A(2).
119 CPIA 1996, s 6C.
120 CPIA 1996, s 21A(3).
121 There is nothing in the LGFS scheme which provides funding for a solicitor's attendance at such an interview, nor is there any provision for independent legal aid funding for a witness to be separately represented.

whether he consented to a solicitor attending on behalf of the accused as an observer.[122]

6.88   The Interview Code, paras 5 and 6 deal with notification to the witness of the date, time and venue of the interview. There is no requirement to notify the accused's solicitor unless the witness has consented to his presence as an observer. Where the witness has consented to his presence, the accused's solicitor must be given reasonable notice of the date, time and venue of the proposed interview.

6.89   The Interview Code, para 7 requires that:

•   the identity of the investigator is recorded;

•   the investigator has sufficient skills and authority to discharge his functions effectively; and

•   the investigator must not conduct the interview if it is likely to lead to conflict of interest, eg if the investigator is the complainant for the allegation.

6.90   The Interview Code, para 8 provides:

•   the accused's solicitor may only attend if the witness has consented;

•   the interview may proceed in the absence of the accused's solicitor provided he was given reasonable notice of the interview;

•   if the witness withdraws his consent to the presence of the accused's solicitor the interview may continue in his absence; and

•   the accused's solicitor may only attend as an observer.

6.91   The Interview Code, para 9 requires that where a witness has indicated that he wishes to appoint a solicitor to be present, that solicitor must be permitted to attend.

6.92   The Interview Code, para 10 requires that a witness under the age of 18, or a witness who is mentally disordered or otherwise mentally vulnerable, must be interviewed in the presence of an appropriate person.

---

122 If the accused is not legally represented in the proceedings, and if the witness consents to a solicitor attending the interview on behalf of the accused, the accused must be offered the opportunity, a reasonable time before the interview is held, to appoint a solicitor to attend it. Code of Practice for Arranging and Conducting Interviews of Witnesses Notified by the Accused, Paragraph 4.2.

6.93   The Interview Code, para 11 requires an accurate record to be made of the interview whether it takes place at a police station or elsewhere. The record must be made, where practicable, by audio or visual recording with sound, or otherwise in writing. A copy of the record must be given to the witness within a reasonable time and, if the witness consents, to the accused.

6.94   Where the accused's solicitor is present as an observer in the interview of a potential defence witness, he has no right to intervene with the questioning as there is no solicitor/client relationship with the witness.[123] Provided there is no conflict of interest and the accused consents, the accused's solicitor can represent the witness if asked to do so and he can then intervene to protect the interests of the witness. The solicitor must withdraw if a conflict of interest arises between the witness and the accused.

6.95   The Interview Code does not contain any provision for warning witnesses of the potential consequences of withholding consent. Should any witness refuse their consent to be interviewed, it would be open to the prosecution or a co-accused to seek to cross-examine him on his reasons for the refusal to be interviewed. Further, any exchanges between the investigator and witness, particularly under paragraph 3 above (see **6.85** and **6.86** above), may be material relevant to the investigation and must be recorded by the investigator.[124]

6.96   The accused may be unaware of what a potential defence witness has said in interview because the witness's account does not satisfy the prosecution disclosure test[125] and the witness has refused to allow the accused's legal representative to attend the interview or has refused to allow a copy to be sent to the accused. To persist in calling the witness in such circumstances creates an obvious danger to the accused that the witness will be cross-examined by the prosecution or a co-accused on an undisclosed account adverse to his case.

INTERVIEWING WITNESSES FOR THE OTHER SIDE

6.97   There is no property in a witness[126] and it is permitted for either the prosecution or defence to take a statement from a witness for the other side

---

123 Law Society Guidance Note: Defence witness notices, 21 December 2015 sets out the obligations and ethical considerations that apply.
124 CPIA Code, paras 2.1 and 4.1.
125 i.e. any prosecution material which might reasonably be considered capable of undermining the case for the prosecution against the accused or of assisting the case for the accused. Where the interview satisfies the prosecution disclosure test in respect of a co-accused it will be disclosed to that co-accused.
126 *Connolly v Dale* [1996] QB 120, per Balcombe LJ.

who has given evidence or, it is known, will be giving evidence. Where it is intended to take this course of action, it is wise to give notice to the other side stating –

- that an interview is required;

- the reasons for the interview; and

- that a representative from the other side be present.[127]

6.98   The presence of a representative from the other side will help to avoid any suggestion of any attempt to change the account of a witness.

6.99   A witness can refuse his consent to be interviewed. CPS guidance[128] suggests that where a witness agrees only to be interviewed at a police station, this facility should be made available. Where the defence seek to interview a police officer who is a prosecution witness, a senior police officer may be present, who should preferably be unconnected with the proceedings in question.[129] If the defence wish to interview a police officer as a potential defence witness, CPS guidance suggests it is a matter for the Chief Constable or the CPS to determine the conditions for the interview, provided they are reasonable.

6.100   It may be a contempt of court for the prosecution to seek to prevent or discourage the defence from interviewing a prosecution witness or a potential prosecution witness.[130]

EXPERT WITNESSES

6.101   The advanced disclosure of expert evidence is governed by the CrimPR 2015 19.3 which requires a party who 'wants' to introduce expert evidence to serve the expert's report on the court officer and each other party as soon as practicable. A party may not adduce evidence if he has not complied with rule 19.3 unless every party agrees or the court gives permission.[131] This is in contrast to other defence witnesses where the substance of their evidence need not be disclosed to the prosecution (see **6.66** above).

---

127 CPS Legal Guidance, Interviewing Witnesses for the Other Side.
128 CPS Legal Guidance, Interviewing Witnesses for the Other Side.
129 CPS Legal Guidance, Interviewing Witnesses for the Other Side.
130 *Connolly v Dale* [1996] QB 120, per Balcombe LJ.
131 *R v Ensor* [2010] 1 Cr App R 18.

6.102   The CPIA 1996, s 6D,[132] which is not yet in force, will impose an obligation on the defence to notify the court of an expert's name and address if he 'instructs a person with a view to his providing any expert opinion for possible use as evidence at the trial'. This is different to the CPIA 1996, s 6C (defence witness notices) in that it does not require any intention on the part of the defence to call the expert.

---

132   As inserted by Criminal Justice Act 2003, s 35.

Chapter 7

Application for prosecution disclosure (section 8 application)

INTRODUCTION

7.01   Once the defence statement has been served, the defence has the opportunity to apply formally to the court for further disclosure where it believes that the prosecution has not fully complied with its obligations under the CPIA 1996.

7.02   This chapter deals with:

• application	• **7.03–7.07**
• procedure	• **7.08–7.18**

APPLICATION

7.03   Although the prosecution's continuing duty of disclosure under the CPIA 1996, s 7A exists from when the prosecution has purported to comply with initial disclosure until the conclusion of the trial process, where the accused believes there is material that should still be disclosed he should make an application to the court under the CPIA 1996, s 8 (a section 8 application).[1] The CPIA 1996, s 8(2) provides:[2]

> 'If the accused has at any time reasonable cause to believe that there is prosecution material which is required by section 7A[3] to be disclosed to him and has not been, he may apply to the court for an order requiring the prosecutor to disclose it to him.'

---

1   For a copy of the required form for an application for prosecution disclosure pursuant to rule 15.5 CrimPR 2015, Pt 15 see **Appendix 12**.
2   As amended by Criminal Justice Act 2003, s 38.
3   The prosecutor's continuing duty to disclose.

7.04   The section 8 application for disclosure can only be made *after* the accused has served a defence statement and the prosecutor has complied with, purported to comply with, or failed to comply with his duty to make disclosure as a result of the defence statement.[4] The Magistrates' Court Disclosure Review[5] noted that it was possible for the back page of the effective trial preparation form (usually completed at the first hearing in the Magistrates' Court when there will be a summary trial) to be used as a defence statement if completed in sufficient detail and that the use of the form in this way would enable a defendant to apply for further disclosure under section 8.

7.05   Prosecution material includes material which:[6]

• is in the prosecutor's possession and came into their possession in connection with the case for the prosecution against the accused;

• in pursuance of a code operative under the CPIA 1996, Part II, they have inspected in connection with the prosecution case against the accused; or

• in pursuance of a code operative under the CPIA 1996 Part II, if the prosecution asked for the material, they must be given a copy of, or be allowed to inspect that material, in connection with the case against the accused.

7.06   Before making a section 8 application the accused should have considered an informal approach to the prosecution for disclosure of the material sought. The CPS Disclosure Manual advises that the prosecutor should consider each approach on its merits and, wherever possible, the disclosure issues should be resolved without the need for a court hearing.[7] Any informal disclosure should be recorded on the disclosure record sheet. This approach is encouraged in the Disclosure Protocol.[8]

7.07   Section 8 applications should be limited to material which is referable to an issue in the case as identified by the defence statement. Blanket orders are inconsistent with the CPIA and the decision of the House of Lords in *R v H*.[9]

---

4   CPIA 1996, s 8(1); see CPIA 1996, s 7A(5).
5   Magistrates' Court Disclosure Review published May 2014 at paragraph 122.
6   CPIA 1996, s 8(3) and (4).
7   CPS Disclosure Manual, para 16.8.
8   Judicial Protocol on Disclosure of Unused Material in Criminal Cases, para 23.
9   *R v H and C* [2004] UKHL 3; [2004] 2 AC 134; [2004] 2 Cr App R 10; see also *DPP v Wood* (2006) 170 JP 177 where disclosure should have been refused where the defence statement did not raise any issue to which the material was relevant.

Defence requests which are not referable to an issue in the case identified in the defence statement should be rejected.[10] *R v H* made it clear that:

> 'the trial process is not well served if the defence are permitted to make general and unspecified allegations and then seek far-reaching disclosure in the hope that material may turn up to make them good'.[11]

Furthermore, 'there must be a proper evidential basis for concluding that the material sought is reasonably capable of undermining the prosecution or of assisting the defence, or that it represents a reasonable line of enquiry to pursue.'[12]

PROCEDURE

7.08   In order to make a section 8 application, the CrimPR 2015 15.5 provides:

> '(2)   The defendant must serve an application on—
>
>   (a)   the court officer; and
>
>   (b)   the prosecutor.
>
> (3)   The application must—
>
>   (a)   describe the material that the defendant wants the prosecutor to disclose;
>
>   (b)   explain why the defendant thinks there is reasonable cause to believe that—
>
>   (i)   the prosecutor has that material, and
>
>   (ii)   it is material that the Criminal Procedure and Investigations Act 1996 requires the prosecutor to disclose; and
>
>   (c)   ask for a hearing, if the defendant wants one, and explain why it is needed.
>
> (4)   The court may determine an application under this rule—
>
>   (a)   at a hearing, in public or in private; or
>
>   (b)   without a hearing.

---

10   Judicial Protocol on Disclosure of Unused Material in Criminal Cases, para 26.
11   *R v H and C* [2004] UKHL 3; [2004] 2 AC 134; [2004] 2 Cr App R 10 at paragraph 35.
12   *R (DPP) v Manchester and Salford MC* [2017] EWHC 1708 (Admin) at para 55.

(5)   The court must not require the prosecutor to disclose material unless the prosecutor—

  (a)   is present; or

  (b)   has had at least 14 days in which to make representations.'

7.09   It is good practice to enclose a copy of the defence statement and copies of any correspondence with the Crown about disclosure with the section 8 application. A section 8 application should generally be served within 14 days of receipt of a response to the defence statement in purported compliance with the CPIA 1996, s 7 and in advance of any oral hearing. Indeed, it is good practice for a judge to set a date by when any section 8 application is to be made as part of the timetabling exercise.[13] The PTPH system provides further support for this approach in that stage 4, the time when it is envisaged a section 8 application be served, is usually scheduled for 14 days after the Crown's response to a defence statement.[14]

7.10   The wording of the CrimPR 2015 15.5(5) allows the accused to make a section 8 application and for the court to seek an immediate determination provided the prosecutor is present or has had 14 days to respond to the application. In such circumstances, the CPS Disclosure Manual advises that the prosecution advocates should be robust in obtaining the necessary time to consider the matter properly and not allow the court to expedite timescales without good reason.[15]

7.11   Upon receipt of a section 8 application the prosecution has 14 days within which to contest the application or disclose the material.[16] The prosecutor should consider afresh the items requested by the defence in consultation with the disclosure officer and, if necessary, ask for copies of the items or inspect the material as appropriate.[17] If he concludes that all or part of the requested material should be disclosed, that decision should be formally communicated to the defence without delay.[18] The court should also be notified of the further disclosure and the appropriate letter sent to the defence, court and police.[19]

7.12   Material must not be disclosed as a result of a section 8 application to the extent that the court, on an application by the prosecutor, concludes that it is

---

13   Judicial Protocol on Disclosure of Unused Material in Criminal Cases, para 24.
14   Plea and Trial Preparation Hearings: Introduction and Revised Guidance, December 2015.
15   CPS Disclosure Manual, para 16.8B.
16   CPS Disclosure Manual, para 16.5.
17   CPS Disclosure Manual, para 16.2.
18   CPS Disclosure Manual, para 16.3.
19   CPS Disclosure Manual, Annex C4.

not in the public interest to disclose it and orders accordingly.[20] If the material has already been the subject of a public interest immunity ruling, the prosecutor should remind the defence to use the procedures that are available to review the public interest ruling to avoid the risk of jeopardizing the confidentiality of the material.[21]

7.13   Material must not be disclosed under a section 8 application to the extent that it is material the disclosure of which is prohibited by the Regulation of Investigatory Powers Act 2000, s 17.[22]

7.14   If at the hearing of a section 8 application agreement is reached between the advocates in respect of the material to be disclosed, the agreement should be incorporated into a formal consent order to prevent any misunderstanding by the parties as to what has been agreed.[23]

7.15   The defence can only seek disclosure of material of which they are aware. Often this knowledge will be predicated upon the material detailed in the non-sensitive schedule of unused material (MG6C). A failure by the prosecution to prepare the MG6C properly in accordance with its disclosure obligations may adversely affect the disclosure obtained by the defence.

7.16   An application for defence disclosure can be made at the same time as the court deals with a preparatory hearing but does not fall within the preparatory hearing for the purpose of any pre-trial issue appeal.[24]

7.17   In the course of an oral section 8 application, there may be cases where it is appropriate for the judge to press prosecution counsel, with or without the presence of the accused, in relation to issues of further disclosure. The final decision as to disclosure rests ultimately with the court.[25]

7.18   The consequences of non-disclosure are dealt with at **Chapter 11**.

---

20 CPIA 1996, s 8(5).
21 CPIA 1996, ss 14–15; CrimPR 2015, r 15.6; CPS Disclosure Manual, para 16.7.
22 CPIA 1996, s 8(6).
23 *R v O* [2007] EWCA Crim 3483.
24 *R v H* [2007] 2AC 270.
25 *R v Meshach; Braithwaite* [2002] EWCA Crim 1537.

Chapter 8

Public interest immunity (sensitive material)

INTRODUCTION

8.01   Sensitive material is material that, if disclosed, would give rise to a real risk of serious prejudice to an important public interest.[1] The golden rule of full disclosure, that the prosecution must disclose to the accused any material which may weaken the prosecution case or strengthens the defence case, is subject to two exceptions:

- 'Material must not be disclosed under this section to the extent that the court, on an application by the prosecutor, concludes it is not in the public interest to disclose it and orders accordingly';[2] and

- 'Material must not be disclosed under this section to the extent that it is material the disclosure of which is prohibited by section 17 of the Regulation of Investigatory Powers Act 2000'.[3]

8.02   There is obviously a potential conflict between this doctrine of 'public interest immunity' (PII) and the defendant's right to a fair trial. For consideration of the position in relation to the Regulation of Investigatory Powers Act 2000, see **Chapter 13**. This chapter deals with the following areas:

• relevance	**8.03–8.04**
• what is sensitive material?	**8.05–8.08**
• treatment of sensitive material	**8.09–8.15**
• role of the prosecutor	**8.16–8.23**
	continued overleaf

---

1   CPIA Code, para 2.1.
2   CPIA 1996, ss 3(6), 7A(8), 8(5).
3   CPIA 1996, ss 3(7), 7A(9), 8(6).

RELEVANCE

8.03   The first step is to determine whether the material may be relevant to the investigation. The CPIA Code, para 2.1 provides:

'Material may be relevant to an investigation if it appears to the investigator, or to the officer in charge of an investigation, or the disclosure officer, that it has some bearing on any offence under investigation or any person being investigated, or on the surrounding circumstances of the case, unless it is incapable of having any impact on the case.'

8.04   Material which is not relevant must not be scheduled or disclosed, regardless of its sensitivity. The officer in charge, disclosure officer or investigator may seek advice from the prosecutor about whether material may be relevant.[4]

WHAT IS SENSITIVE MATERIAL?

8.05   Material is only sensitive (ie subject to public interest immunity) where the disclosure officer believes its disclosure would give rise to a 'real risk of serious prejudice to an important public interest'.[5]

8.06   A non-exhaustive list of examples of material that *may*, but not necessarily *will*, be sensitive are set out in the CPIA Code, para 6.15 namely:

•   material relating to national security;

•   material received from the intelligence and security agencies;

•   material relating to intelligence from foreign sources which reveals sensitive intelligence gathering methods;

---

4   CPIA Code, para 6.1.
5   CPIA Code, para 2.1.

- material given in confidence;

- material relating to the identity or activities of informants, or undercover police officers, or witnesses, or other persons supplying information to the police who may be in danger if their identities are revealed;

- material revealing the location of any premises or other place used for police surveillance, or the identity of any person allowing a police officer to use them for surveillance;

- material revealing, either directly or indirectly, techniques and methods relied upon by a police officer in the course of a criminal investigation, for example covert surveillance techniques, or other methods of detecting crime;

- material whose disclosure might facilitate the commission of other offences or hinder the prevention and detection of crime;

- material upon the strength of which search warrants were obtained;

- material containing details of persons taking part in identification parades;

- material supplied to an investigator during a criminal investigation which has been generated by an official of a body concerned with the regulation or supervision of bodies corporate or of persons engaged in financial activities, or which has been generated by a person retained by such a body;

- material supplied to an investigator during a criminal trial which relates to a child or young person and which has been generated by a local authority social services department, an Area Child Protection Committee or other party contacted by an investigator during the investigation; and

- material relating to the private life of a witness.

8.07   To assist the officer in considering these examples, the CPS Disclosure Manual, para 8.4 provides that reference should be made to the following associated public interests:

- the ability of the security and intelligence agencies to protect the safety of the UK;

- the willingness of foreign sources to continue to cooperate with UK security and intelligence agencies, and law enforcement agencies;

- the willingness of citizens, agencies, commercial institutions, communications service providers etc to give information to the authorities in circumstances where there may be some legitimate expectation of confidentiality (eg Crimestoppers material);

• the public confidence that proper measures will be taken to protect witnesses from intimidation, harassment and being suborned;

• the safety of those who comply with their statutory obligation to report suspicious financial activity (whilst they are under a statutory obligation and therefore do not give suspicious activity reports in confidence, their safety is a consideration to be taken into account in disclosure decisions);

• national (not individual or company) economic interests;

• the ability of the law enforcement agencies to fight crime by the use of covert human intelligence sources, undercover operations, covert surveillance etc;

• the protection of secret methods of detecting and fighting crime; and

• the freedom of investigators and prosecutors to exchange views frankly about casework.

8.08 It is important to note that these are only examples and 'whether the disclosure of an individual document would be likely to give rise to a real risk of serious prejudice to an important public interest must be assessed in each case. Whilst some of the examples are always likely to carry that real risk, not all will and the prosecutor must assess the risk to the public interest of the disclosure of that document in the individual case, whilst also having regard to the risk of incremental or cumulative damage to the public interest'.[6]

TREATMENT OF SENSITIVE MATERIAL

8.09 If there is any sensitive material the disclosure officer must, subject to one exception below, list it on a schedule of sensitive material, also known as Form MG6D.[7] He must state in the MG6D that he believes the material to be sensitive and the reason for that belief.[8] In Crown Court cases, if there is no sensitive material, the disclosure officer must record this fact on the sensitive schedule or otherwise so indicate.[9]

---

6 CPS Disclosure Manual, para 8.18.
7 CPIA Code, para 6.7 in relation to magistrates court cases. CPIA Code, para 6.14 in relation to Crown Court cases.
8 CPIA Code, para 6.15.
9 CPIA Code, para 6.14.

8.10   The MG6D must be provided to the prosecutor.[10] It will not be served on the defence.[11]

8.11   The exception to listing sensitive material on the MG6D applies 'where compromising the material would be likely to lead directly to the loss of life, or directly threaten national security'.[12] In such exceptional circumstances, when the sensitivity of the material makes its recording on the MG6D inappropriate, its existence must be revealed to the prosecutor separately. The investigator who knows the detail of the sensitive material should not only inform the prosecutor as soon as is reasonably practicable after the file is sent to the prosecutor, he must also ensure that the prosecutor is able to inspect the material so that he can properly assess whether it is disclosable.[13] The CPS Disclosure Manual also provides that some police forces may wish to apply the same procedure to material which relates to a covert human intelligence source who, or whose family, may be injured, threatened or harassed if the material is compromised.[14]

8.12   To assist the prosecutor in deciding how to deal with disclosable sensitive material, the CPS Disclosure Manual, para 8.13 states that the investigator and disclosure officer(s) should set out:

- the reasons why the material is believed to be sensitive;

- the degree of sensitivity said to attach to the material, in other words, why it is considered that disclosure will create a real risk of serious prejudice to an important public interest;

- the consequences of revealing to the defence:

    - the material itself;

    - the category of the material;

    - the fact that an application may be made;

- the apparent significance of the material to the issues at trial;

- the involvement of any third parties in the bringing of the material to the attention of the police;

- where the material is likely to be the subject of an order for disclosure, what the police view is regarding continuance of the prosecution;

---

10 CPIA Code, para 7.1B.
11 CPS Disclosure Manual, para 8.2.
12 CPIA Code, para 6.16.
13 CPIA Code, para 6.14, 6.16, 6.17, 7.2. Such material should be included on a highly sensitive schedule and dealt with in accordance with the guidance in CPS Disclosure Manual, Ch 9.
14 CPS Disclosure Manual, para 9.4.

- whether it is possible to disclose the material without compromising its sensitivity.

8.13 To assist in determining the degree of sensitivity, consideration should be given as to whether the public interest may be prejudiced not only directly but also indirectly through incremental or cumulative harm.[15]

8.14 The CPS Disclosure Manual, para 8.15 lists examples of direct harm:

- exposure of secret information to enemies of the state;

- death of or injury to an intelligence source through reprisals;

- revelation of a surveillance post and consequent damage to the property or harm to the occupier;

- exposure of a secret investigative technique.

8.15 The CPS Disclosure Manual, para 8.16 provides examples of incremental or cumulative harm:

- exposure of an intelligence source that ... discourages others from giving information in the future because they lose faith in the system;

- revelation of a surveillance post leading to reluctance amongst others to allow their premises to be used;

- exposure of investigative technique that makes the criminal community more aware and therefore better able to avoid detection;

- exposure of material given in confidence or for intelligence purposes that may make the source of the material, or others, reluctant to cooperate in the future (eg Crimestoppers material);

- an active denial that a source was used in the instant case, leading to the inability to deny it in future cases where one was used, thereby impliedly exposing the use of a source. The Crown should neither confirm nor deny the use of a source.

ROLE OF THE PROSECUTOR

8.16 The prosecutor must consider, firstly, whether the material satisfies the prosecution disclosure test.[16] If the material does not satisfy the prosecution

---

15 CPS Disclosure Manual, para 8.14.
16 i.e. Any prosecution material which might reasonably be considered capable of undermining the case for the prosecution against the accused or of assisting the case for the accused.

disclosure test, there is no requirement to disclose it. Neutral material or material damaging to the accused need not be disclosed and, unless the issue of disclosability is 'truly borderline', should not be brought to the court's attention.[17]

8.17 Secondly, the prosecutor must consider whether the material is sensitive and that there is indeed a real risk of serious prejudice to an important public interest. The prosecutor must be satisfied that the risk is real, as opposed to fanciful.[18] They must be satisfied that the prejudice is serious, as opposed to trivial.[19] Such assessments are made on a document-by-document basis.

8.18 Thirdly, before any PII application is made, the prosecutor will need to consult with the police, normally at a senior level, and consider whether the material in question can be disclosed in an edited or summarised form or if formal admissions could be made. For the consultation with the police to be effective the prosecutor will need to be provided with the necessary information to make a proper decision.[20]

8.19 Where edited material is disclosed, the original must not be marked and the defence should be informed of the fact that editing has taken place. An application to the court will be required to withhold the remainder of the material if it is otherwise disclosable under the CPIA 1996.[21] It may be possible to separate non-sensitive and sensitive parts of a document and schedule them accordingly.[22]

8.20 Under the CPS Disclosure Manual, para 8.22, where the prosecutor decides:

- that sensitive material requires disclosure to the accused because it satisfies the disclosure test; and

- in consultation with the police, that it is not possible to disclose it in a way that does not compromise the public interest in question; and

- that disclosure should be withheld on public interest grounds;

the ruling of the court must be sought or the case abandoned.[23]

---

17 *R v H & C* [2004] UKHL 3, per Lord Bingham CJ, para 35; Attorney General's Guidelines on Disclosure (2013), para 65; CPS Disclosure Manual, para 8.23.
18 CPS Disclosure Manual, paras 8.17–8.18.
19 CPS Disclosure Manual, para 8.19.
20 CPS Disclosure Manual, paras 8.24–8.26.
21 CPS Disclosure Manual, para 8.20.
22 CPS Disclosure Manual, para 8.21.
23 CPS Disclosure Manual, para 8.22.

8.21 The above decision-making process for making a PII application may be summarised in the following flowchart:[24]

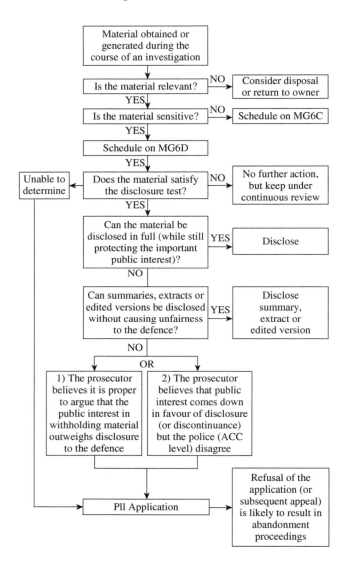

8.22 It is not clear whether there is provision for material which the prosecutor considers is sensitive but which should be disclosed to the defence, to be voluntarily disclosed without a court order. On the one hand, the CPS

---

24 Taken from CPS Disclosure Manual, Chapter 8.

Disclosure Manual, para 13.1 provides that where sensitive material is identified as meeting the disclosure test and the prosecutor is satisfied that disclosure would create a real risk of serious prejudice to an important public interest, the options are to:

- disclose the material in a way which does not compromise the public interest in issue;

- obtain a court order to withhold the material;

- abandon the case; or

- **disclose the material because the overall public interest in pursuing the prosecution is greater than abandoning it.**[25]

8.23   On the other hand, the High Court in *R (W.V.) v CPS*[26] *[2011]* stated in relation to informants that:

'... it is of the highest importance to public confidence in the administration of justice, that where the interests of justice require that an express or implied undertaking of confidence as to the identity of an informant or other provider of information has to be broken, unless there is informed consent from the informant/provider, the decision to break it is a decision of a judge.'

CPIA 1996, s 16 specifically allows for a person claiming to have an interest in the sensitive material to be heard by the court.[27]

PROCEDURE FOR APPLICATIONS TO THE COURT

8.24   Under the CrimPR 2015 15.3(2) the prosecutor's application to the court must be in writing and served on –

- the court officer;

- any person who the prosecutor thinks would be directly affected by disclosure of the material; and

- the defendant.[28]

---

25 CPS Disclosure Manual, para 13.32 provides that before such a decision is taken there must be consultation between the CPS and police at a senior level and, where appropriate, the owners of sensitive third party material.
26 [2011] EWHC 2480 (Admin).
27 See also CrimPR 2015, r 22.3(2)(b).
28 But only to the extent that serving it on the defendant would not disclose what the prosecutor thinks ought not to be disclosed.

8.25   The CrimPR 2015 15.3(3) requires that the application must describe the material and explain why the prosecutor thinks that:

- it is material that the prosecutor would have to disclose;

- it would not be in the public interest to disclose that material; and

- no measure such as the prosecutor's admission of any fact, or disclosure by summary, extract or edited copy would adequately protect both the public interest and the defendant's right to a fair trial.

8.26   Further details as to the required contents of the application are set out in CPS Disclosure Manual, paras 13.4–13.10. For examples of the need to ensure that the information provided to the court at all stages is accurate, see *R v Jackson*[29] and *R v Early*.[30] In the latter it was said that if in the course of a public interest immunity hearing or an abuse of process argument, whether on the *voir dire* or otherwise, prosecution witnesses lied in evidence to the judge, it was to be expected that, if the judge knew of that, or the Court of Appeal subsequently learnt of it, an extremely serious view would be taken. It was likely that the prosecution would be tainted beyond redemption, however strong the evidence against the defendant might be otherwise. This turned out not to be the case however in *R v Lawless (Reference by the Criminal Cases Review Commission),*[31] in which the court found that even if the judge had not been misled, no disclosure would have been ordered and the Prosecution case was strong in any event.

8.27   The extent to which the accused can, if at all, be made aware of the nature and content of the material was dealt with in *R v Davis, Johnson and Rowe*.[32] Three types of application were identified:

- Type 1: This application is served on the appropriate officer of the Crown Court and on the accused. It specifies the nature of the material to which the application relates.

- Type 2: The prosecutor believes that revealing to the accused the nature of the application to which the material relates would in effect disclose the information which the prosecutor contends should not, in the public interest, be disclosed. This application is served on the appropriate officer of the Crown Court and on the accused. The nature of the material is not specified.

---

29 [2000] Crim LR 377.
30 [2003] 1 Cr. App. R. 19.
31 [2016] EWCA Crim 2185.
32 [1993] 97 Cr App R 110.

- Type 3: The prosecutor believes that revealing to the accused the existence of an application would in effect disclose the information that the prosecutor contends should not be disclosed. The application is served on the appropriate officer of the Crown Court but not the accused.

8.28   Unless already done, the court may direct the prosecutor to serve an application on the accused and/or any person who the court considers would be directly affected by the disclosure of the material.[33]

8.29   Prior to the hearing the prosecutor and the prosecution advocate must examine all material which is the subject matter of the hearing and make any necessary enquiries of the investigator. The investigator must be frank with the prosecutor about the full extent of the sensitive material.[34]

8.30   Prior to, or at, the hearing the court must be provided with full and accurate information about the material.[35]

8.31   A written submission to the court should be prepared either by the reviewing prosecutor or the prosecuting advocate. The submissions should be signed by the CPS unit head or special casework lawyer and should be counter-signed by a police officer of at least substantive detective inspector (or equivalent) rank from each of the agencies or police units who have submitted information. The counter-signature should state that to the best of his knowledge and belief the assertions of fact on which the submission is based are correct. Whatever part the prosecution advocate may have played in the drafting of the submissions, responsibility for their form and content rests with the prosecutor.[36]

8.32   The written submissions should contain:[37]

- a summary of the facts of the case. Where a case summary or prosecution opening note has been served and this is believed still to be accurate and adequate, the background submission should refer to this document which should be annexed to the submission;

- a list of trial issues which the prosecutor has been able to identify;

- a summary of the defence case which has been advanced in a defence statement, section 8 application or correspondence;

---

33 CrimPR 2015, r 3(5).
34 Attorney General's Guidelines on Disclosure (2013), para 66;
35 Attorney General's Guidelines on Disclosure (2013), para 66;.
36 CPS Disclosure Manual, para 13.11 and 13.
37 CPS Disclosure Manual, para 13.14.

- in relation to Type Two and Three applications, reasons why it is considered inappropriate for there to be a Type One (or Type Two) application.

8.33   In relation to each item of material which is before the court for a ruling, the written submissions should also contain:[38]

- the number of the item as it appeared on form MG6D. Where more than one MG6D has been submitted, eg where the case has generated 'highly sensitive' material and involves more than one disclosure officer, each MG6D should be given its own reference;

- a detailed description of the material;

- in the case of lengthy items, a summary of their content;

- an assessment giving reasons why it is considered that the material satisfies the disclosure test, or why the reviewing prosecutor is unable to determine whether or not the disclosure test is satisfied;

- why it is considered that disclosure of the material will cause a real risk of serious prejudice to an important public interest and the degree of sensitivity that attaches to the material;

- why it would not be appropriate to provide to the accused a formal admission, summary, extract or edited version of the material;

- why the prosecutor contends that the public interest in withholding the material outweighs the public interest in disclosing it;

- where the material is the subject of a Type Two application, why it is considered inappropriate to inform the defence of the category of material into which the material falls; and

- where, exceptionally, the material is the subject of a Type Three application, why it is considered inappropriate to inform the defence at all.

8.34   Once the submissions have been provided to the court, the prosecutor should ascertain whether the judge wishes to view the material in advance of the hearing and, if so, make the necessary arrangements.[39]

---

38 CPS Disclosure Manual, para 13.14.
39 CPS Disclosure Manual, paras 13.19–13.21.

THE HEARING

8.35   The prosecutor and/or investigator should attend such applications.[40] Where a person claiming to have an interest in the sensitive material, and who shows that he was involved (whether alone or with others, directly or indirectly) in bringing the prosecutor's attention to the relevant material, he may apply to the court for the opportunity to be heard at the application.[41]

8.36   The public interest immunity hearing will be in private unless the court otherwise directs and, if the court so directs, the hearing may take place wholly or in part in the accused's absence.[42] In a case involving type one or type two material the defence will have the opportunity to make submissions on the material. As explained in *R v H & C* at para 20:

'In [type one cases], comprising most of the cases in which a PII issue arises, the prosecution must give notice to the defence that they are applying for a ruling of the court, and must indicate to the defence at least the category of the material they hold (that is, the broad ground upon which PII is claimed), and the defence must have the opportunity to make representations to the court. There is thus an inter partes hearing conducted in open court with reference to at least the category of the material in question. [In type two cases] in which the prosecution contend that the public interest would be injured if disclosure were made even of the category of the material. ... the prosecution must still notify the defence that an application to the court is to be made, but the category of the material need not be specified: the defence will still have an opportunity to address the court on the procedure to be adopted but the application will be made to the court in the absence of the defendant or anyone representing him. If the court considers that the application falls within the first class, it will order that procedure to be followed. Otherwise it will rule.'

8.37   The importance of involving the defence, where possible, was emphasised in *R v H & C* at para 37:[43]

'Throughout his or her consideration of any disclosure issue ... the judge should involve the defence to the maximum extent possible without disclosing that which the general interest requires to be protected but taking full account

---

40   Attorney General's Guidelines on Disclosure (2013), para 67.
41   Criminal Procedure and Investigation Act 1996, s16.
42   CrimPR 2015, r 15.3(6).
43   [2004] UKHL 3, per Lord Bingham CJ.

of the specific defence which is relied on. There will be very few cases indeed in which some measure of disclosure to the defence will not be possible, even if this is confined to the fact that an ex parte application is to be made. If even that information is withheld and if the material to be withheld is of significant help to the defendant, there must be a very serious question whether the prosecution should proceed, since special counsel, even if appointed, cannot then receive any instructions from the defence at all.'

8.38   Defence submissions that the accused can only have a fair trial if sensitive material is disclosed will be more credible if founded on a detailed defence statement supported by tailored and reasoned representations demonstrating, for example, why the location of the observation point or the existence of or identity of an informant would satisfy the prosecution disclosure test. The defence run the risk, in the absence of such detail, of being suspected by the court of manoeuvring the prosecution into deciding between disclosure or offering no evidence on groundless tactical bases.

8.39   As a general rule when the accused is present, the court will hear firstly from the prosecutor and any other interested party served with the application; secondly, from the defence in the presence of the other parties; and thirdly, from the prosecutor and any such other person in the accused's absence.[44]

8.40   The hearing should be before the trial judge. Even where the trial is to be conducted by the judge alone under the Criminal Justice Act 2003, s 44 this did not necessarily mean that the same judge should not carry out the PII hearing. The judge should proceed as normal, until and unless they required the assistance of special counsel (see **8.52** below). It is doubtful that procedure allows for the appointment of a 'disclosure judge'.[45] The court must study the material in question.[46] The court must address the questions set out in paragraph 36 of *R v H & C* (below). The application should be recorded and the judge should give a short statement of reasons, often on a document-by-document basis.[47]

8.41   The court may only determine the application if satisfied that it has been able to take adequate account of such rights of confidentiality as apply to the material and the accused's rights to a fair trial.[48] Duties of confidentiality are placed on the court officer who must not give notice to anyone other than the

---

44 Crim PR 2015, r 15.3(7)(a).
45 *R v Twomey* (No. 2) [2011] 1 Cr. App. R. 29 at para 51.
46 *R v Brown* [1995] 1 Cr. App. R. 191.
47 Judicial Protocol on the Disclosure of Unused Material in Criminal Cases, December 2013, paras 54, 55(e).
48 CrimPR 2015, r 15.3(8).

prosecutor of the hearing of an application (unless the prosecutor has served the application on that person) or the court's decision, unless directed to do so by the court.[49]

LEGAL PRINCIPLES TO BE APPLIED

8.42   The principles to be applied were set out by Lord Bingham CJ at paragraph 36 of *R v H & C*[50] in a series of questions:

> 'When any issue of derogation from the golden rule of full disclosure comes before it the court must address a series of points:
>
> (1)   What is the material which the Crown seek to withhold? This must be considered by the court in detail.
>
> (2)   Is the material such as may weaken the prosecution case or strengthen that of the defence? If No, disclosure should not be ordered. If Yes, full disclosure should (subject to (3), (4) and (5) below) be ordered.
>
> (3)   Is there a real risk of serious prejudice to an important public interest (and, if so what) if full disclosure of the material is ordered? If No, full disclosure should be ordered.
>
> (4)   If the answer to (2) and (3) is Yes, can the defendant's interest be protected without disclosure or disclosure be ordered to an extent or in a way which will give adequate protection to the public interest in question and also afford adequate protection to the interests of the defence?
>
> This question requires the court to consider, with specific reference to the material which the prosecution seek to withhold and the facts of the case and the defence as disclosed, whether the prosecution should formally admit what the defence seek to establish or whether disclosure short of full disclosure may be ordered. This may be done in appropriate cases by the preparation of summaries or extracts of evidence, or the provision of documents in an edited or anonymised form, provided the documents supplied are in each instance approved by the judge ...
>
> (5)   Do the measures proposed in answer to (4) represent the minimum derogation necessary to protect the public interest in question? If No, the court should order such greater disclosure as will represent the minimum derogation from the golden rule of full disclosure.

---

49   CrimPR 2015, r 15.3(9).
50   At para 36.

(6)   If limited disclosure is ordered pursuant to (4) or (5), may the effect be to render the trial process, viewed as a whole, unfair to the defendant? If Yes, then fuller disclosure should be ordered even if that leads or may lead the prosecution to discontinue the proceedings so as to avoid having to make disclosure.

(7)   If the answer to (6) when first given is No, does that remain the correct answer as the trial unfolds, evidence is adduced and the defence advanced?

It is important that the answer to (6) should not be treated as a final, once-and-for-all answer but as a provisional answer which the court must keep under review.'

8.43   These principles should be rigorously applied firstly by the prosecutor and then by the court to ensure that the procedure for examination of material in the absence of the accused is compliant with the ECHR, Article 6.[51]

REVIEW AND APPEAL

8.44   The Crown Court of its own motion must keep its decision not to disclose material on the grounds of public interest under review.[52] In both summary and Crown Court proceedings, the defence may apply to the court for a review of an earlier decision to withhold material.[53]

8.45   Under the CrimPR 2015 15.6(2), where the accused seeks a review they must serve an application on the prosecution and court officer describing:

•   the material he wants the prosecution to disclose; and

•   explain why it is no longer in the public interest for the prosecution not to disclose it.

8.46   The prosecution must serve the application on any person who would be directly affected if the material were disclosed and may be directed to do so by the court.[54] The prosecutor and any person directly affected must serve any representations on the court officer, the accused (unless to do so would reveal something that ought not to be disclosed) and may be directed by the court to do so.[55]

---

51 Attorney General's Guidelines on Disclosure (20135), para 68.
52 CPIA 1996, s 15(3) – there is no such obligation in the magistrates' court.
53 CPIA 1996, s 15(4).
54 CrimPR 2015, r 15.6(3), (5)(a).
55 CrimPR 2015, r 15.6(4), (5)(b).

8.47   The court may only conclude a review if satisfied that it has been able to take adequate account of such rights of confidentiality as apply to the material and the accused's rights to a fair trial.[56]

8.48   Where the judge's conduct of a PII hearing is raised as an issue in an appeal, the principles to be followed are:[57]

1.   The approach should be the same whether the ex parte PII hearing before the trial judge was or was not on notice. The principles in relation to the appointment of special counsel, or the need for the judge to recuse himself or herself are the same in both cases.

2.   The Court of Appeal (Criminal Division) will have to review ex parte with the prosecution present all the material which was before the trial judge. A prosecution summary will not usually suffice, but is always desirable and, in a complex case, essential.

3.   It will be necessary for that review to be carried out by the same constitution which is to hear the appeal.

4.   The review will have to take place sufficiently in advance of the substantive appeal hearing to permit, in those exceptional cases where this is necessary, special counsel to be appointed and suitably prepared.

5.   In the majority of cases, where the PII material can be read in an hour or two, this should present no listing difficulty and the PII hearing can take place, as frequently happens now, in the first week of a constitution sitting with the appeal being heard in the third week.

6.   In the minority of cases, where the PII material is unusually voluminous, special listing arrangements will have to be made over a longer time scale.

8.49   Where no PII application was made at the Crown Court, and the exercise is being conducted for the first time in relation to post-trial disclosure, it is not generally necessary for that review to be carried out by the same constitution which is to hear the appeal: the Full Court, Single Judge or the Registrar may direct that a Single Judge should consider the application. The Single Judge generally might, but does not have to be, part of the constitution which will hear any appeal.[58]

---

56   CrimPR 2015, r 3(8).
57   *R v McDonald* [2004] EWCA Crim 2614 at para 25.
58   *R v Clarke* [2017] EWCA Crim 37 at para 32 and 35.

CONSEQUENCES OF AN ORDER FOR DISCLOSURE

8.50   Where the court orders disclosure, it will be necessary for the prosecution to disclose the material in question if the case is to proceed. In appropriate cases disclosure may be by the preparation of summaries, extracts of evidence or the provision of documents in an edited or anonymised form, provided the documents supplied are approved by the judge. The prosecution may also formally admit what the defence seek to establish under the Criminal Justice Act 1967, s 10.[59]

8.51   An order by the court that the prosecution disclose material may lead to discontinuance of the case to avoid having to make this disclosure.[60] This situation is anticipated by the Attorney General's Guidelines on Disclosure (2015), para 69 which states:

> If prosecutors conclude that a fair trial cannot take place because material which satisfies the test for disclosure cannot be disclosed, and that this cannot be remedied by the above procedure ... they should not continue with the case

SPECIAL COUNSEL

8.52   The House of Lords in *R v H & C*[61] approved the use of special counsel in public interest immunity hearings in exceptional circumstances to protect the accused's right to a fair trial. Special counsel are appointed by the Attorney General on request from the trial judge.

8.53   Special counsel are intended to protect the interests of an accused against whom an adverse order may be made and who cannot (either personally or through his legal representative), for security reasons, be fully informed of all the material relied on against him.[62] As the accused's lawyers are unable to make informed submissions on his behalf, special counsel become necessary to ensure that the contentions of the prosecution are tested and the interests of the accused are protected.[63]

8.54   The judge has to be satisfied that no other course will adequately meet the overriding requirement of fairness to the accused.[64] The appointment

---

59 *R v H & C* [2004] UKHL 3, per Lord Bingham CJ, para 36; CPIA Code, para 10.5.
60 *R v H & C* [2004] UKHL 3, per Lord Bingham CJ, para 36, point (6).
61 [2004] UKHL 3 para 22.
62 *R v H & C* [2004] UKHL 3, per Lord Bingham CJ, para 21.
63 *R v H & C* [2004] UKHL 3, per Lord Bingham CJ, para 36, point (4).
64 *R v H & C* [2004] UKHL 3, per Lord Bingham CJ, para 22.

of special counsel will always be exceptional and a matter of last, and never first, resort. There has to be something that a special advocate can do which cannot properly be done by the judge.[65] A potential example is provided in the unusual circumstances of *R v Austin*[66] in which the defendant had previously had a conviction for drug smuggling quashed by the Court of Appeal who gave both open and closed judgments. In the course of a subsequent prosecution for money laundering, the defence mounted an abuse of process argument and sought disclosure of the material which had led to his previous conviction being quashed. In ruling that the defence were not entitled to any disclosure and that there was no abuse of process the judge revealed that he had viewed the closed Court of Appeal judgments. The Court of Appeal held that the judge should have informed the parties beforehand of the course he proposed to take and that in any event he should have accepted prosecution counsel's assurance that there was no material which passed the test for disclosure. It would also have been open to him, but not essential, to appoint special counsel to deal with the issue of disclosure. The Court of Appeal left open the question as to whether it would have been proper for special counsel to become involved in the substantive abuse of process issue.

8.55 Special counsel may be instructed only to deal with a single aspect of a case such as bail. The reasons may be more compelling for the appointment of special counsel where a decision has an immediate consequence upon the liberty of the accused.[67]

8.56 Special counsel should always see the material which is the subject of the public interest immunity application. Where the public interest immunity application is on notice, special counsel may obtain information from the defence.

---

65 *Chief Constable and AA v K* [2010] EWHC 2438 (Fam), per Sir Nicholas Wall P, para 92.
66 [2013] 2 Cr. App. R. 33.
67 *R (on the application of S) v Northampton Crown Court* [2010] EWHC 723 (Admin), per Langstaff J, paras 23–25, 28.

Chapter 9

Third party material

INTRODUCTION

9.01   Third party material is material, within the UK or outside the UK, held by a person, organisation or government department other than the investigator or prosecutor.[1] Investigators, disclosure officers and prosecutors cannot be regarded to be in constructive possession of material held by Government departments or Crown bodies simply by virtue of their status as Government departments or Crown bodies.[2] Material that is in the possession of a third party falls outside the CPIA 1996.[3]

9.02   Third parties are generally under no obligation to reveal material to the police or the prosecutor, nor need they retain material that may be relevant to a criminal investigation. The CPIA Code and the Attorney General's Guidelines do impose, however, obligations upon the investigator, disclosure officer and prosecutor to take appropriate steps to obtain material from third parties.

9.03   This chapter deals with:

• duties of police and prosecution	**9.04–9.11**
• methods of obtaining third party material	
– child abuse protocol and good practice model	**9.12–9.14**
– voluntary disclosure	**9.15–9.20**
– witness summons	**9.21–9.30**
• procedure for witness summons	**9.31–9.36**
• specific issues	**9.37–9.39**

---

1   Attorney General's Guidelines on Disclosure (2013): Supplementary Guidelines on Digitally Stored Material, para A53.
2   Attorney General's Guidelines on Disclosure (2013), para 54.
3   Attorney General's Guidelines on Disclosure (2013): Supplementary Guidelines on Digitally Stored Material, para A56.

DUTIES OF POLICE AND PROSECUTION

9.04   The CPIA Code, para 3.5 provides that an investigator should pursue all reasonable lines of enquiry, whether these point towards or away from the suspect. Reasonable lines of enquiry will include enquiries of third parties. What is reasonable will depend on the particular circumstances.

9.05   The CPIA Code, para 3.6 requires that where:

'... the officer in charge of an investigation believes that other persons may be in possession of material that may be relevant to the investigation, and if this has not been obtained under paragraph 3.5 above, he should ask the disclosure officer to inform them of the existence of the investigation and to invite them to retain the material in case they receive a request for its disclosure. The disclosure officer should inform the prosecutor that they may have such material ...'

9.06   The Attorney General's Guidelines on Disclosure (2013) place the burden upon the prosecutor, if necessary by a witness summons, to obtain material which satisfies the prosecution disclosure test.[4] The guidelines state at para. 56:

'There may be cases where the investigator, disclosure officer or prosecutor believes that a third party (for example, a local authority, a social services department, a hospital, a doctor, a school, a provider of forensic services) has material or information which might be relevant to the prosecution case. In such cases, investigators, disclosure officers and prosecutors should take reasonable steps to identify, secure and consider material held by any third party where it appears to the investigator, disclosure officer or prosecutor that (a) such material exists and (b) that it may be relevant to an issue in the case.'

9.07   A different approach is taken where government departments or other crown bodies may hold relevant material. The investigator, disclosure officer and prosecutor should inform the department or body of the nature of the case and the issues involved in respect of which it may hold material and ask whether it has such material.[5]

9.08   Where, after reasonable steps have been taken, access is still denied, consideration must be given as to what further steps might be taken to obtain the material or the defence should be informed.[6]

---

4   i.e. any prosecution material which might reasonably be considered capable of undermining the case for the prosecution against the accused or of assisting the case for the accused.
5   Attorney General's Guidelines on Disclosure (2013), para 53; Disclosure Protocol, para 50.
6   Attorney General's Guidelines on Disclosure (2013), para 55 and 57.

9.09   The obligation on the investigator and prosecutor to pursue all reasonable lines of enquiry applies to material held outside the United Kingdom.[7] Where it appears that there is relevant material held overseas, the prosecution must take reasonable steps to obtain it, either informally or under the Crime (International Co-operation) Act 2003 and any European Union or other international conventions.[8]

9.10   There may be cases where a foreign state or court refuses to make the material available or, though willing for the material to be inspected, does not allow notes or copies to be made.[9] It is for these reasons that there is no absolute duty on the prosecutor to disclose material held by overseas entities not subject to the jurisdiction of courts in England and Wales.[10] There will be no breach by the prosecution of its duty of disclosure by its failure to obtain material overseas provided the police and prosecution have taken reasonable steps to do so. It is ultimately for the court to judge in each case whether the prosecution have complied with its duty.[11] Investigators should therefore record and set out such information as they are able to clearly in writing, including any inability to inspect or retrieve any material that potentially ought to be disclosed, along with the steps that have been taken.

9.11   Although the Prosecution must be alive to their duties, they enjoy a 'margin of consideration' as to what steps they regard appropriate in a particular case. They will only be in breach of their obligations in relation to obtaining third party material if it can be shown that they did not act within the limits afforded by the Guidelines.[12]

METHODS OF OBTAINING THIRD PARTY MATERIAL

Child abuse protocol and good practice model

9.12   In cases involving alleged child abuse there is a Protocol and Good Practice Model for disclosure of information where there are linked criminal and

---

7   Attorney General's Guidelines on Disclosure (2013), para 59.
8   Attorney General's Guidelines on Disclosure (2013), para 60.
9   Attorney General's Guidelines on Disclosure (2013), para 61.
10   Attorney General's Guidelines on Disclosure (2013), para 62.
11   Attorney General's Guidelines on Disclosure (2013), para 63.
12   *R v Alibhai* [2004] EWCA Crim 681, per Longmore LJ, paras 62–63. But see *R v Flook* [2010] 1 Cr. App. R. 30, per Thomas LJ, para 37 where the court declined to decide whether the crown any longer has the margin of consideration referred to in *Alibhai*. The Attorney General's Guidelines on Disclosure (2013) still state, at para 63, that there is a margin of consideration.

care proceedings.[13] The protocol provides a framework within which the CPS, police and local authorities can co-operate voluntarily to share and exchange information. The protocol has been signed by the Senior Presiding Judge for England and Wales, the President of the Family Division and Director of Public Prosecutions and supported by the Association of Chief Police Officers and Local Government Association amongst others.

9.13   The procedure by which the police will request disclosure from the local authority under this protocol is set out at Parts 9 to 10. In summary:

• the police will send the relevant form to the Local Authority 'Single Point of Contact' (SPOC);

• the form includes details of the investigation and prosecution if commenced. Requests for material are set out and must be as prescriptive and detailed as possible and necessary for the pursuit of reasonable lines of enquiry;

• the form will include reasonable timescales for the police to be given access to relevant material, but the presumption will be that the Local Authority will deal with any request from the police as expeditiously as possible so as to not to jeopardise the criminal investigation;

• the SPOC will liaise with relevant departments in order to identify and collate relevant material from the Children's Services or other files as appropriate;

• the Local Authority will either identify the school(s) attended by the child/children subject to the investigation to enable the police to approach the school directly or, if practicable, will obtain and collate relevant educational files for police examination;

• where there are documents relating to Family Court proceedings, the Local Authority will provide a list of that material without describing what it is, in order for the police and/or the CPS, if appropriate, to apply to the Family Court for disclosure.

• the Local Authority can disclose to the police documents which are lodged at court, or used in the proceedings, which already existed (eg pre-existing medical reports). Similarly, the text or summary of a judgment given in the Family Court proceedings can be included in the files to be examined by the police;

---

13 The model protocol is available online at http://www.cps.gov.uk/publications/docs/third_party_protocol_2013.pdf.

- the police will examine and review the material and may make notes and/ or take copies of it but it will not be disclosed to the defence without further consultation with the Local Authority or order of the court; and

- where further relevant material comes to light after the police examination the Local Authority will contact the police and/or the CPS to arrange an examination of the new material. Similarly, where new issues arise in the criminal case the police will submit a further Form requesting access to material not previously examined.

9.14   For further detail as to how such material is then dealt with under the protocol and further detail in relation to disclosure between criminal and family proceedings see **Chapter 10.**

Voluntary disclosure

9.15   Third parties may, in some circumstances, provide disclosure voluntarily and the CPS Disclosure Manual, para 4.19 suggests that it may be appropriate for the prosecution, in the absence of any relevant protocol, to make a disclosure request directly to the third party concerned. Any formal request for the voluntary disclosure by the third party should explain:

- what material or information it is thought that the third party holds;

- the reasons why access to the material is sought;

- the known or suspected issues in the case;

- what will happen to the material if it is released;

- that views are invited from the third party on whether the material is considered sensitive; and

- what will happen if the material is not released.[14]

9.16   The third party should also be asked to list any additional material held in relation to the case, whether inspection of that material is permitted (and if not, why) and to retain such material.[15]

9.17   Sufficient time should be given for a third party to voluntarily respond to any request for disclosure before making an application for a witness summons.[16]

---

14 See CPS Disclosure Manual, Annex B1 'Specimen letter B1 – Letter to third parties'.
15 CPS Disclosure Manual, Annex B1 for 'Specimen letter B1 – Letter to third parties'.
16 CPS Disclosure Manual, para 4.20.

If sufficient time is not allowed, the summons may be set aside and may attract a wasted costs order.

9.18   Relevant information which comes to the knowledge of investigators or prosecutors as a result of liaison with third parties, such as information conveyed verbally, should be recorded in a durable or retrievable form, eg relevant information revealed in discussions at a child protection conference attended by police officers.[17]

9.19   Where material is disclosed voluntarily to the prosecution, consultation with the third party should take place before disclosure is made as there may be public interest immunity issues that would require the issue of disclosure to be placed before the court.[18] Where a person claiming to have an interest in that material applies to be heard and shows that he was involved in bringing the material to the prosecutor's attention, the court must not make an order without giving him an opportunity to be heard.[19]

9.20   The Data Protection Act 1998 gives individuals the right, subject to exceptions, to access their own personal data. Generally, provided the persons who are the subject of the data concerned give their consent, information relating to them such as their medical records, may be obtained by written request upon payment of the appropriate fee.[20]

Witness summons

9.21   Although no specific procedure exists for the recovery of material from a third party, a witness summons may be used to effect such disclosure. The Attorney General's Guidelines on Disclosure (2013), para 57 provides:

> 'If the investigator, disclosure officer or prosecutor seeks access to the material or information but the third party declines or refuses to allow access to it, the matter should not be left. If despite any reasons offered by the third party it is still believed that it is reasonable to seek production of the material or information, and the requirements of section 2 of the Criminal Procedure (Attendance of Witnesses) Act 1965 or as appropriate section 97 of the Magistrates Courts Act 1980 are satisfied (or any other relevant power), then

---

17 CPIA Code, para 4.1.
18 Attorney General's Guidelines on Disclosure (2013), para 58; Disclosure Protocol, para 44; CPS Disclosure Manual, para 4.9.
19 CPIA 1996, s 16.
20 The Data Protection Act 1998 contains exceptions to this general principle.

the prosecutor or investigator should apply for a witness summons causing a representative of the third party to produce the material to the court.'

9.22   Where the third party declines to allow inspection of the material or requires the prosecution to obtain an order before handing over copies of the material, the prosecutor will need to consider whether it is appropriate to issue a witness summons.[21]

9.23   Where the prosecution do not consider it appropriate to seek such a summons, the defence should consider doing so. The defence must not sit back and expect the prosecution to make the running.[22] To ensure that third party issues are identified at an early stage, the judge at the Plea and Trial Preparation Hearing should specifically enquire whether enquiries with a third party are likely to be appropriate and, if so, identify who is going to make the request, what material is to be sought, from whom the material is to be sought and within what timescale the matter is to be resolved.[23]

9.24   The Criminal Procedure (Attendance of Witnesses) Act 1965, s 2(1) provides that a witness summons may be issued where the Crown Court is satisfied that:

'(a)   a person is likely to be able to give evidence likely to be material evidence, or produce any document or thing likely to be material evidence, for the purposes of any criminal proceedings before the Crown Court, and

(b)   it is in the interests of justice to issue a summons under this section to secure the attendance of that person to give evidence or to produce the document or thing.'[24]

9.25   Material evidence needs to be evidence that is admissible per se. Documents, such as social services or medical records, may be material admissible *per se* if they can be said to be business records within the Criminal Justice Act 2003, s 117.[25] Evidence that is merely likely to afford or assist a

---

21 Disclosure Protocol, para 46.
22 Disclosure Protocol, para 44 and 48.
23 Disclosure Protocol, paras 9 and 47, and see CrimPR 2015, r 3.2 (the duty of the court to actively manage a case).
24 Similar provisions apply in the magistrates' court by virtue of Magistrates Court Act 1980, s 97.
25 *R v M* (unreported, 5 November 1999) (N 98/03990/Y4), per Rose LJ: *'Not only would the [social services records] have provided highly relevant and potentially damaging material for cross examination ... but the records would have been admissible under sections 23 and 24 Criminal Justice Act 1988.'* See also *R v Clowes* (1992) 95 Cr App R 440, per Phillips J; *R v Humphris* [2005] 169 JP 441, CA per Lord Woolf and *Wellington v DPP* 171 JP 497, QBD in relation to business records.

relevant line of enquiry or challenge or which may simply be useful in cross-examination is not admissible per se and cannot be extracted from third parties by the use of witness summonses.[26] In *R v Reading Justices ex p Berkshire County Council* documentation that was requested merely for the purposes of cross-examination was held not to be material evidence.[27] Simon Brown LJ in giving judgment considered a number of authorities and stated:

'The central principles to be derived from these authorities are as follows:

i.   to be material evidence documents must be not only relevant to issues arising in the criminal proceedings, but also documents admissible as such in evidence;

ii.   documents which are desired merely for the purpose of possible cross-examination are not admissible in evidence and, thus, are not material for the purposes of s.97;

iii.   whoever seeks production of documents must satisfy the justices with some material that the documents are "likely to be material" in the sense indicated, likelihood for this purpose involving a real possibility, although not necessarily a probability;

iv.   it is not sufficient that the applicant merely wants to find out whether or not the third party has such material documents. This procedure must not be used as a disguised attempt to obtain discovery.'

9.26   A witness summons requiring a person to produce a document or thing issued by the Crown Court may also require him to produce it for inspection before adducing it in evidence.[28] This gives the applicant the opportunity to decide not to adduce the material should it be unhelpful. In *R v Clowes* Phillips J stated:[29]

'It does not seem to me to offend against the letter or the spirit of section 2 of the 1965 Act to issue a witness summons for the production of documents which are admissible in evidence with the motive both of discovering the precise nature of the contents of the documents and, if these are helpful, adducing them in evidence.'

---

26 *R v H (L)* [1997] 1 Cr App R 176, per Sedley J.
27 (1996) 1 Cr App R 239. See also *R v Azmy* (1996) 7 Med LR 415 – counselling records were for cross examination only and not admissible per se. Note: it is arguable that counselling records are business documents and not just an aide memoire.
28 Criminal Procedure (Attendance of Witnesses) Act 1965, s 2A.
29 [1992] 95 Cr App R 440, p 448.

9.27 The Crown Court may issue a summons of its own motion requiring a person to give evidence or produce a thing or document.[30] A person who, without just excuse, disobeys a witness summons shall be in contempt of court.[31] Commercial confidentiality does not permit a third party to withhold material.[32]

9.28 'Fishing' exercises must not be embarked upon and a speculative challenge to a refusal to disclose, in the hope that something might emerge 'might well amount to an "improper, unreasonable or negligent act" capable of attracting a wasted costs order'.[33] It is clear, however, that injustice may occur where third parties are in possession of material, unbeknown to the defence, that is relevant and that the defence have no means of becoming aware of its existence.

9.29 The failure of the CPIA 1996 to directly address the disclosure of material in the hands of a third party is unsatisfactory. A witness summons to produce a 'document or thing' will not elicit information and cannot be issued to a person outside the jurisdiction.[34] Further, the test to be applied for a witness summons – that a person is likely to be able to give material evidence or produce any document or thing likely to be material evidence – is more restrictive than the prosecution disclosure test under the CPIA 1996.

9.30 Ultimately, a court may not have the power to order the disclosure of material which would otherwise be disclosable if it were in the hands of the prosecution. This may occur where the criteria for issuing a witness summons are not satisfied or an overseas third party refuses to make the material available. In the absence of such material, the defence may wish to consider making an abuse of process application.

PROCEDURE FOR WITNESS SUMMONS

9.31 An application for a witness summons which requires the proposed witness to produce in evidence a document or thing or to give evidence about information apparently held in confidence must be in writing and in the required form unless the court allows an oral application. A party wishing to make an oral

---

30 Criminal Procedure (Attendance of Witnesses) Act 1965, s 2D.
31 Criminal Procedure (Attendance of Witnesses) Act 1965, s 3.
32 *R v Alibhai* [2004] EWCA Crim 681, per Longmore LJ, para 107.
33 *R v Mildenhall Justices ex parte Graham* (unreported, 22 January 1987), QBD; *R v H (L)* 1997 1 Cr App R, per Sedley J, p 176; Disclosure Protocol, para 44.
34 *R v Alibhai* [2004] EWCA Crim 681, per Longmore LJ, para 34.

application must give as much notice as possible to those who would otherwise have received a written application and explain the reasons for wanting the court to consider the application orally.[35]

9.32   A party seeking the witness summons must apply as soon as practicable after becoming aware of the grounds for doing so. He must identify the proposed witness and explain:

- what evidence the proposed witness can give or produce;

- why it is likely to be material evidence; and

- why it would be in the interests of justice to issue.[36]

9.33   Care must be taken to ensure that the witness summons is not defective either in form or content and that good grounds can be shown for its issue.[37] Before the court can issue a summons, all persons to whom the application relates must have had 14 days' notice in which to make representations (unless the court shortens or extends the time period allowed) and the court must be satisfied that it has been able to take adequate account of the duties and rights, including rights of confidentiality, of the proposed witness and of any person to whom the proposed evidence relates.[38] The hearing must be in private, unless the court otherwise directs.[39]

9.34   The party making the application must serve it on the court officer and the proposed witness (unless the court otherwise directs). The court may direct that it is also served on a person to whom the evidence relates and/or another party.[40] In *R (on the application of B) v Stafford Combined Court* it was held that a patient should be given notice of an application for a witness summons to disclose his medical records and have the opportunity to make representations before any order is made.[41] Where confidential information is sought the court will usually direct that the application be served on the person to whom the information relates.[42]

---

35 CrimPR 2015, rr 17.3-17.5 and 17.8(2).
36 CrimPR 2015, r 17.3(2).
37 Barristers (Wasted Costs Order: Criminal Proceedings) (No. 5 of 1997).
38 CrimPR 2015, rr 17.5(4) and 17.8(1).
39 CrimPR 2015, r 17.2(2).
40 CrimPR 2015, r 17.4 and 17.5(3).
41 [2006] 2 Cr App R 34.
42 *R v Stafford Crown Court* [2006] 2 Cr App R 34, per May LJ, paras 22–28.

9.35 The CrimPR 2015 17.7 provides that a witness or any person to whom the evidence relates can apply in writing for the summons to be withdrawn on the grounds that:

- he was not aware of any application for it; and

- he cannot give or produce evidence likely to be material evidence; or

- even if he can, his duties or rights, including rights of confidentiality, or those of any person to whom the evidence relates, outweigh the reasons for the issue of the summons.

9.36 The application to set the witness summons aside should be made as soon as practicable after becoming aware of the grounds for the application. The court may withdraw a witness summons if the party who applied for it no longer needs it.[43]

SPECIFIC ISSUES

9.37 Where material relevant to the defence case is in the hands of the alleged victims, it is important that alleged victims are not only willing to disclose relevant material comprehensively and promptly, but also that they take all proper and efficient steps to bring about that disclosure.[44]

9.38 Although CCTV footage frequently causes difficulties, it should be treated as any other category of unused material and when potentially relevant CCTV footage is not in the possession of the police, the guidance in relation to third party material will apply. The police remain under a duty to pursue all reasonable lines of inquiry, including those leading away from a suspect, whether or not defence requests are made.[45]

9.39 In a case where pivotal evidence comes from a man with a known prison record, the Crown should at an early stage in its preparation equip itself with his prison records 'for all the obvious reasons'.[46]

---

43 CrimPR 2015, r 17.7(1)(a).
44 *R v Alibhai* [2004] EWCA Crim 681, per Longmore LJ, para 107.
45 Disclosure Protocol, para 35.
46 *R v McCartney and others* [2003] EWCA Crim 1372.

Chapter 10

Disclosure from family proceedings relating to children

INTRODUCTION

10.01   Cases involving the sexual and physical abuse of children may give rise to criminal and family proceedings. There is an overlap between the two jurisdictions as the same or similar factual issues, involving the same witnesses, are often before both courts. Any family proceedings in existence at the time of an associated criminal case can therefore provide an important source of material for the parties involved in criminal proceedings.

10.02   This chapter deals with:

• prohibition against publishing information	**10.03–10.06**
• permitted disclosure	**10.07–10.10**
• disclosure to investigation authorities	**10.11–10.15**
– Protocol and Good Practice Model for Disclosure of Information in Cases of Alleged Child Abuse and Linked Criminal and Care Directions Hearings	**10.16–10.20**
• disclosure to criminal defence lawyers	**10.21–10.26**
• defence application for disclosure	**10.27–10.34**
• protection from self-incrimination	**10.35–10.37**

PROHIBITION AGAINST PUBLISHING INFORMATION

10.03   Family proceedings are normally held in private[1] and are therefore confidential. The Administration of Justice Act 1960, s 12(1)(a) provides that where proceedings:

•   relate to the exercise of the inherent jurisdiction of the High Court with respect to minors;

---
1   FPR 2010, r 27.10.

- are brought under the Children Act 1989 or the Adoption and Children Act 2002; or

- otherwise relate wholly or mainly to the maintenance or upbringing of a minor;

it will be a contempt of court to publish 'information relating to the proceedings' except:

- where it is disclosed in accordance with the Family Procedure Rules 2010 (FPR 2010), Part 12 and its associated Practice Direction;[2] or

- with the permission of the Family Court.[3]

10.04 The prohibition applies to publishing 'information relating to the proceedings' which includes:

(a) accounts of what has taken place in front of the judge sitting in private;

(b) documents such as affidavits, witness statements, reports, position statements, skeleton arguments or other documents filed in the proceedings, transcripts or notes of evidence or submissions, and transcripts or notes of the judgment (this list is not necessarily exhaustive);

(c) extracts or quotations from such documents;

(d) summaries of such documents; and

(e) information, even if not reduced into writing, which has emerged during the course of information gathering for the purpose of proceedings already commenced.[4]

10.05 The prohibition applies whether or not the information or the document being published has been anonymised.[5]

10.06 Disclosure of information *not* relating to proceedings is allowed, although may still be subject to public interest immunity or other provisions.[6] The prohibition will not apply to documents (or the information contained in documents) prepared for purposes other than the above family proceedings. This will be the case even if the documents are lodged with the court - or referred to in,

---

2 FPR 2010 Practice Direction 12G, Communication of Information.
3 FPR 2010, r 12.73.
4 *In the Matter of W* [2010] EWHC 16 (Fam), per Munby J, paras 76, 112.
5 *In the Matter of W* [2010] EWHC 16 (Fam), per Munby J, para 76.
6 See Children Act 1989, s 97(5) which prohibits the publication of material which is likely to identify a child involved in such proceedings, their home or school, to the public at large.

or annexed to, a witness statement or report - unless the document or information is published in such a way to link it with proceedings so that it can sensibly be said that what is published is 'information relating to the proceedings'.[7]

PERMITTED DISCLOSURE

10.07   The FPR 2010, rule 12.73 provides for information to be disclosed to certain prescribed persons without the need for a court order. These include:

- the legal representative of the party;

- a professional legal advisor; and

- a professional acting in furtherance of the protection of children.

10.08   Family Procedure Rules, Practice Direction 12G permits disclosure by any party of:

- the text or summary of the whole or part of a judgment given in the proceedings to a police officer; and

- the text or summary of the whole or part of a judgment given in the proceedings to the Crown Prosecution Service.

10.09   Disclosure of information to the public at large or any section of it is not permitted[8] nor is the disclosure of any unapproved judgment handed down by the court.[9]

10.10   An important distinction is made between the disclosure of information and the disclosure of documents. The FPR 2010 only allows for the disclosure of information. Once the information is disclosed in accordance with the FPR 2010 it can be used, but the documents from which the information comes cannot be used without the express permission of the court.[10]

DISCLOSURE TO INVESTIGATING AUTHORITIES

10.11   Where a police officer is a 'professional acting in furtherance of the protection of children',[11] information relating to the proceedings can be disclosed

---

7   *In the Matter of W* [2010] EWHC 16 (Fam), per Munby J, para 112.
8   FPR 2010, r 12.73(2).
9   FPR 2010, r 12.73(3).
10   *Reading Borough Council v D (Angela)* [2006] EWHC 1465 (Fam), per Sumner J, para 70.
11   FPR 2010, r 12.73.

to him without the permission of the court. This information can thereafter be used for the investigation of criminal offences involving children.[12] A police officer is a 'professional acting in furtherance of the protection of children' where:

- he is exercising powers under the Children Act 1989, s 46 (removal and accommodation of children in cases of emergency); or

- he is serving in a child protection unit or paedophile unit of a police force.[13]

10.12 If a police officer does not meet the above criteria, no information can be disclosed to him, other than the court judgment, without permission of the court and he will need to make the necessary application.[14]

10.13 The distinction between 'information' - which may be disclosed and used without the permission of the court - and 'documentation' - which requires the express permission of the court before it can be used - creates difficulties because information is often disclosed in the form of documentation.[15] Once a document is disclosed into the possession of the prosecution, disclosure is governed by their obligations under the CPIA 1996. The documentation may still attract public interest immunity, but the issue of whether or not it should be disclosed to the defence will be a matter for the judge in the criminal proceedings and, to all intents and purposes, not under the control of the Family Court.

10.14 Although there are no guidelines on the distinction between using information and using a document, using a short quote from a document is unlikely to be regarded as using the document.[16]

10.15 Applications by the police to use documents, if unopposed, can be dealt with as a paper application or sought by the local authority on a directions hearing. The court can require an oral hearing if that appears advisable.[17] Practitioners must pay heed to the fact that many police authorities have developed their own protocols with their designated family judge which set out the procedures to be adopted when disclosure is sought and the information to be provided.

---

12 *Reading Borough Council v D (Angela)* [2006] EWHC 1465 (Fam), per Sumner J, para 73. For an alternative approach see *In A District Council v M* (2008) 2 FLR 390, per Baron J, para 21.
13 FPR 2010, r 2.3.
14 *Re B (A Child: Disclosure of Evidence in Care Proceedings)* [2012] 1 FLR 142.
15 *Reading Borough Council v D (Angela)* [2006] EWHC 1465 (Fam), per Sumner J, para 69 where this method of disclosure was considered to be perfectly proper.
16 *Reading Borough Council v D (Angela)* [2006] EWHC 1465 (Fam), per Sumner J, para 88.
17 *Reading Borough Council v D (Angela)* [2006] EWHC 1465 (Fam), per Sumner J, para 90.

Protocol and Good Practice Model for Disclosure of Information in Cases of Alleged Child Abuse and Linked Criminal and Care Directions Hearings

10.16   There is also a Protocol and Good Practice Model for Disclosure of Information in Cases of Alleged Child Abuse and Linked Criminal and Care Directions Hearings.[18] For the procedure relating to disclosure from local authorities to the police or CPS, see **Chapter 9.**

10.17   Part 11 of the protocol deals with applications to the family courts to disclose material to the police or CPS. Applications by the police must contain details of the named officer to whom release is sought. All applications should be made on a specific form and must:

- specify the purpose and use to which the material is intended to be put;

- seek leave where appropriate to disclose the material to the CPS or police;

- seek leave where appropriate to disclose the material to the criminal defence solicitors; and

- seek leave where appropriate, and subject to the Children Act 1989, s 98(2), to use the material in evidence at the criminal proceedings.

The application must be served on all parties to the Family Proceedings. The application will be determined at a hearing at the Family Court. Police and the CPS will not attend the hearing unless directed to do so by the Family Court.

10.18   Where it is practicable to seek prior written consent to disclosure from all parties to the Family Proceedings, the police or the CPS should do so. Application should then be made in writing to the Family Court seeking a consent order.

Alternatively, whenever possible, the police and/or the CPS should ask the Local Authority to request that the Family Court considers the issue of disclosure at the next hearing. The Local Authority will then put the other parties to the proceedings on notice and will provide the court with details of the officer to whom disclosure is to be made and the purpose for which it is to be made.

10.19   Under Part 12 of the protocol, the Local Authority will forward to the CPS copies of relevant Family Court judgments (and summaries thereof) in the

---

18 The model protocol is available online at http://www.cps.gov.uk/publications/docs/third_party_protocol_2013.pdf.

possession of the Local Authority. The judgments may be redacted appropriately. If the Local Authority is not in possession of a judgment which appears to be relevant to the concurrent criminal proceedings, it will notify the CPS accordingly. The CPS can then obtain the judgment directly from the Family Court. No formal application for disclosure is necessary in these circumstances as the CPS can simply request release of the judgment under Practice Direction 12G. Where it appears to the Local Authority that the judgment will be relevant to the criminal proceedings, the Local Authority should request that the Family Court expedites the preparation of the judgment for release to the CPS (and if possible at public expense).

10.20   Part 13 of the protocol deals with the treatment of material obtained.

- All material obtained, and the lists of material not disclosed, from the Local Authority will be listed by the police on the sensitive disclosure schedule MG6D.

- Material obtained by an officer on the basis that they are a 'professional acting in furtherance of the protection of children' in accordance with FPR, rule 12.73 must not be disclosed to the CPS. The police should reveal the existence of the material on the MG6D without describing it and the CPS will need to seek the permission of the Family Court to access the material if it considers it appropriate to do so.

- Where the police have obtained material following an application by the police to the Family Court, the police must indicate whether the Family Court has given permission for the material to be shared with the CPS and with the defence.

- Where a Local Authority document is not made available to the police on the basis of confidentiality (eg consent has not been obtained from the person to whom the document relates), the CPS will consider whether it is appropriate to seek access to such material by means of a witness summons in the criminal court. The CPS will serve any such application on the criminal court and the Local Authority, identifying the Local Authority point of contact as the person who is required to produce the document(s). Where the Crown Court so directs, the CPS will also serve the application on the person to whom the confidential document relates.

DISCLOSURE TO CRIMINAL DEFENCE LAWYERS

10.21   There is conflicting authority as to whether or not a criminal defence lawyer is a 'professional legal advisor' for the purposes of the FPR 2010, rule 12.73. If they are, then information can be disclosed to them without the permission of the court.

10.22 A 'professional legal advisor' is defined as including a barrister, solicitor or solicitor's employee 'who is providing advice to a party but is not instructed to represent that party in the proceedings'.[19] In *Reading Borough Council v D* Sumner J considered that the term 'professional legal advisor' did not cover a criminal defence lawyer because 'the language... is not apt to cover advice to someone who is, or may become a defendant in criminal proceedings rather than a party'.[20] By contrast in *Re B (A Child: Disclosure of Evidence in Care Proceedings)* Bodey J held that a defence solicitor was a 'professional legal advisor' for the purposes of the FPR 2010.[21]

10.23 Nothing in the FPR 2010 permits the disclosure of documents relating to the proceedings. Defence lawyers are best advised to seek the permission of the family court before receiving any disclosure, be it information or documentation, to ensure that they do not, albeit inadvertently, place themselves in contempt of court.

10.24 If, without the permission of the family court, a defence lawyer while in a conference with a criminal client receives information relating to family proceedings which assists his criminal case, he must apply to the family court before any document relating to the family proceedings is disclosed to him. The application to the family court must be made irrespective of whether the source of the document is the lay client or the solicitor.

10.25 If the defence lawyer intends to use the information (as opposed to the document) he has received without the permission of the family court in criminal proceedings, he should raise that matter with the prosecution and the trial judge, in chambers if necessary, so that any objections can be aired. The prosecution may want to seek their own disclosure from the family court to satisfy themselves that the information being put forward is accurate or to rebut it.

10.26 Where the CPS have obtained material from a Local Authority under the protocol, the CPS will review it in accordance with its statutory duties and under the Disclosure Guidelines. There will in no circumstances be 'blanket' disclosure to the defence. Under Part 13 of the protocol, where any such material falls within the CPIA disclosure test:

- the CPS will write to the Local Authority Single Point of Contact on the prescribed form and within 2 working days of review whenever possible,

---

19 FPR 2010, r 2.3.
20 *Reading Borough Council v D (Angela)* [2006] EWHC 1465 (Fam), per Sumner J, paras 92–94. Although Sumner J was referring to the FLR 2005, the definition is identical for the FLR 2010.
21 [2012] 1 FLR 142; *Reading Borough Council v D (Angela)* [2006] EWHC 1465 (Fam) does not appear to have been cited before the court.

setting out the reasons why the material falls to be disclosed and informing them of that decision;

- within 5 working days of receipt of that notification, the Local Authority shall be given an opportunity to make any representations in writing to the CPS on the issues of disclosure, including objections to disclosure on the basis that the person to whom the material relates has not consented; and

- disclosure of documentation which has been created under the auspices, and for the purposes, of the Local Safeguarding Children Board (LSCB), can only be made with the prior consent of the LSCB Chair.

DEFENCE APPLICATION FOR DISCLOSURE

10.27   There is no prescribed form for making an application for disclosure from the family court. Having regard to *Reading Borough Council v D*[22] and the procedure set out in the protocol above it is suggested that the following approach is taken:

- the application may be made through a party to the family proceedings where possible;

- the application should be in writing and served on all parties (including the guardian *ad litem*) in advance of any hearing at the court centre where the proceedings are listed;

- any application should identify the material being sought with an explanation as to why it is sought; and

- any application should be accompanied by the defence statement and any other material that would assist the court in determining whether or not disclosure should be ordered.

10.28   The Family Court has to carry out a balancing exercise when considering disclosure. In *Re L* Sir Thomas Bingham MR stated:

'It is plain that the public interest in the fair administration of justice, and the right of a criminal defendant to defend himself, are accepted as potent reasons for disclosure. If, on the other hand, it could be shown that disclosure would, for some reason, be unfair or oppressive to a party, to the wardship or Children Act proceedings,that would weigh against an order for disclosure.'[23]

---

22 [2006] EWHC 1465 (Fam), per Sumner J, paras 95–96.
23 [1996] 1 FCR 419. Approved by Hale LJ in *Re R (Children)* [2003] 1 FCR 193. See also *Reading Borough Council v D (Angela)* [2006] EWHC 1465 (Fam) and *In the Matter of the X Children* [2008] EWHC 242.

10.29   In *Re A (Criminal Proceedings: Disclosure)* Butler-Sloss LJ, in considering the balancing exercise which the court had to perform, said that it was between:

'... the importance of maintaining confidentiality in family cases and the public interest in making available material for the purposes of a criminal trial. Factors to take into account include the purpose for which information was required, the weight and significance of the information, the importance of the witness and the gravity of the offence.'[24]

10.30   In *Re C (A Minor) (Care Proceedings: Disclosure)* the Court listed ten factors which should be amongst those a judge considered when deciding whether to order disclosure. These are not in any order of importance, because the importance varies from case to case:

(1) The welfare and interests of the child or children concerned in the care proceedings. If the child is likely to be adversely affected by the order in any serious way, this will be a very important factor.

(2) The welfare and interests of other children generally.

(3) The maintenance of confidentiality in children cases.

(4) The importance of encouraging frankness in children's cases. This is likely to be of particular importance in a case to which section 98(2) applies. The underlying purpose of section 98 is to encourage people to tell the truth in cases concerning children, and the incentive is that any admission will not be admissible in evidence in a criminal trial. However, the added incentive of guaranteed confidentiality is not given by the words of the section and cannot be given.

(5) The public interest in the administration of justice. Barriers should not be erected between one branch of the judicature and another because this may be inimical to the overall interests of justice.

(6) The public interest in the prosecution of serious crime and the punishment of offenders, including the public interest in convicting those who have been guilty of violent or sexual offences against children. There is a strong public interest in making available material to the police which is relevant to a criminal trial. In many cases, this is likely to be a very important factor.

(7) The gravity of the alleged offence and the relevance of the evidence to it. If the evidence has little or no bearing on the investigation or the trial, this will militate against a disclosure order.

---

24 [1996] 1 FLR 221.

(8) The desirability of co-operation between various agencies concerned with the welfare of children, including the social services departments, the police service, medical practitioners, health visitors, schools, etc. This is particularly important in cases concerning children.

(9) In a case to which section 98(2) [of the Children Act 1989] applies, the terms of the section itself, namely that the witness was not excused from answering incriminating questions, and that any statement of admission would not be admissible against him in criminal proceedings. Fairness to the person who has incriminated himself and any others affected by the incriminating statement and any danger of oppression would also be relevant considerations.

(10) Any other material disclosure which has already taken place.[25]

10.31   Where an accused facing criminal charges has concurrent proceedings in the family jurisdiction, it is essential that there should be close liaison between the local authority and the Crown Prosecution Service.[26] Similarly, the judge in each jurisdiction must be fully informed.[27] Were the same judge to deal with both sets of proceedings, at least at the preliminary hearings, he would be able to keep abreast of disclosable family material. In *Re W*, Wall LJ said:

> '... there can be no excuse for either the profession or the judiciary not knowing about or following what is – or should be – a well established protocol particularly when, as here ... the Care Centre and the Crown Court are in the same building and there are many judges who have what has become known in the profession as both care and serious crime "tickets".'[28]

10.32   It is submitted that a judge would still be able to preside over the accused's criminal jury trial to its conclusion and thereafter properly conduct a 'finding of fact' hearing in family proceedings involving the same accused (but not vice versa). In a jury trial it is the jury and not the judge who makes findings of fact and therefore no issue of bias arises. In *R v K*,[29] Judge Lea simultaneously presided over a criminal jury trial and a fact-finding hearing in care proceedings in which the issues to be decided were the same, namely, had the accused sexually

---

25 [1997] 2 WLR 322.

26 *Re W (Children) (Care Order: Sexual Abuse)* [2009] EWCA Civ 644, per Wall LJ, para 73. Some areas, such as Greater London, have issued a Practice Statement setting out a scheme for the purpose of identifying cases where difficulties are likely to arise and providing for linked directions hearings to take place in the Crown Court to which the criminal case has been committed.

27 *Re W (Children) (Care Order: Sexual Abuse)* [2009] EWCA Civ 644, per Wall LJ, para 45.

28 *Re W (Children) (Care Order: Sexual Abuse)* [2009] EWCA Civ 644, per Wall LJ, paras 43 and 45.

29 (Unreported) Nottingham Crown Court, 15–22 October 2012.

abused the complainant. Upon the conclusion of the criminal trial (conviction and sentence), the court constituted itself as a family court to hear submissions from the family lawyers, who had been present throughout the criminal trial as noting briefs, as to what (if any) fact-finding issues remained.

10.33   If the application for disclosure is unopposed, it can be considered as a paper application but the court will always reserve the right to hear argument from the defence lawyer.[30]

10.34   Alternatively, the defence can:

•   draft a consent order;

•   secure the written consent of all parties to the proceedings; and

•   submit it to the court for approval.

PROTECTION FROM SELF-INCRIMINATION

10.35   The Children Act 1989, s 98, which removes the privilege against self-incrimination in care, supervision and protection of children cases, provides:

'(1)   In any proceedings in which a court is hearing an application for an order under Part IV [Care and Supervision] or V [Protection of Children], no person shall be excused from –

(a)   giving evidence on any matter; or

(b)   answering any question put to him in the course of his giving evidence,

on the ground that doing so might incriminate him or his spouse or civil partner of an offence.

(2)   A statement or admission made in such proceedings shall not be admissible in evidence against the person making it or his spouse or civil partner in proceedings for an offence other than perjury.'

10.36   The prohibition, preventing a statement or admission being used against its maker in criminal proceedings, does not extend to a police investigation and makes no provision for the giving of a guarantee for all time as to confidentiality.[31]

---

30 *Reading Borough Council v D (Angela)* [2006] EWHC 1465 (Fam), per Sumner J, para 96.
31 *Re C (A Minor) (Care Proceedings: Disclosure)* (1997) 2 WLR 322, per Swinton Thomas LJ.

10.37   The following legal principles can be identified:

- A judge hearing civil proceedings can compel a party to explain the circumstances in which a child has been injured and, by virtue of the Children Act 1989, s 98(1), that person cannot refuse to answer questions which might incriminate him.[32]

- The proceedings under the Children Act 1989, Parts IV and V are confidential, but that is subject to the FPR 2010 and the power of the judge, in appropriate circumstances, to order disclosure. Nothing in the Children Act 1989, s 98 detracts from that power and witnesses should be advised accordingly.[33]

- Questions involving disclosure to the police of information and documents connected with private family cases are of importance. Difficulties arise from the conflict between two principles, namely –

  - the need for confidentiality in children cases, to protect the child and promote frankness; and

  - the need to investigate and, where warranted, prosecute those criminally involved with children.[34]

- There is nothing to prevent a statement or admission being put to an accused during his police interview. It will be for the trial judge in the criminal proceedings to decide whether or not to admit into evidence any further admission made to the police in interview resulting from admissions made in care proceedings having regard to the provisions of the Children Act 1989, s 98 and any warning given to the accused person during the care proceedings.[35]

- Putting inconsistent statements to a witness in order to challenge his evidence or attack his credibility does not amount to using those statements against him within the meaning of the Children Act 1989, s 98(2)[36] and the prosecution can use the material to challenge any account he seeks to put forward which is inconsistent with his evidence in the family proceedings.[37]

---

32   *Re Y and K (Split hearing: Evidence)* [2003] EWCA (Civ) 699.
33   *Re C (A Minor) (Care Proceedings: Disclosure)* (1997) 2 WLR 322, per Swinton Thomas LJ.
34   *Reading Borough Council v D (Angela)* [2006] EWHC 1465 (Fam), per Sumner J, paras 35–37.
35   *Re C (A Minor) (Care Proceedings: Disclosure)* (1997) 2 WLR 322, per Swinton Thomas LJ.
36   *Re L (Care: Confidentiality)* [1999] 1 FLR 165.
37   *In the matter of X* [2008] EWHC 242.

Chapter 11

Consequences of non-disclosure

INTRODUCTION

11.01   The disclosure regime set out in the CPIA 1996 and the CPIA Code must be scrupulously followed by the police and prosecutors.[1] Where disclosure fails to take place in accordance with those obligations, or as directed by the court, various consequences may follow.[2]

11.02   This chapter deals with:

• discontinuance	**11.03–11.04**
• staying the proceedings	**11.05–11.16**
• refusing to extend custody time limits	**11.17–11.24**
• orders for costs	**11.25–11.31**
• exclusion of evidence	**11.32–11.34**
• acquittal against the weight of the evidence	**11.35**
• successful appeal	**11.36**

DISCONTINUANCE

11.03   There may be circumstances where it is not in the public interest to disclose material to the defence notwithstanding that the material satisfies the prosecution disclosure test.[3] The prosecution will have to decide whether to discontinue the case or make a public interest immunity application to withhold material from the defence. If they make an application and disclosure is ordered

---

1   Attorney General's Guidelines on Disclosure (2013), para 68; CPS Disclosure Manual, para 1.11.
2   CPR 2011, r 3.5(6) allows a court to, inter alia, cancel or adjourn a hearing, make a costs order or impose such other sanctions as 'may be appropriate'.
3   i.e. any prosecution material which might reasonably be considered capable of undermining the case for the prosecution against the accused or of assisting the case for the accused.

by the court, the prosecution will have to consider their position in the light of their obligations under the Attorney General's Guidelines on Disclosure (2013), para 69 which states:

> 69. If prosecutors conclude that a fair trial cannot take place because material which satisfies the test for disclosure cannot be disclosed, and that this cannot be remedied by the above procedure; how the case is presented; or by any other means, they should not continue with the case.

11.04   The prosecution cannot disobey an order of the court.[4] If disclosure is ordered by the court, the prosecutor can disclose the material, discontinue the case or appeal against what is, in effect, a terminatory ruling. The prosecutor may not appeal against a terminatory ruling unless he agrees, in respect of each offence which is the subject of the appeal, that the accused should be acquitted if the appeal fails or is abandoned.[5]

STAYING THE PROCEEDINGS

11.05   Lack of disclosure can give rise to an abuse of process argument which may result in the proceedings being stayed. However an abuse of process should not be necessary or appropriate where the Crown have failed to comply with their disclosure obligations and an application to adjourn is refused. In those circumstances, the Crown should offer no evidence.[6]

11.06   Two main strands of abuse were identified by Lord Dyson in *R v Maxwell*:[7]

> 'It is well established that the court has the power to stay proceedings in two categories of case, namely (i) where it will be impossible to give the accused a fair trial, and (ii) where it offends the court's sense of justice and propriety to be asked to try the accused in the particular circumstances of the case. In the first category of case, if the court concludes that an accused cannot receive a fair trial, it will stay the proceedings without more. No question of the balancing of competing interests arises. In the second category of case, the court is concerned to protect the integrity of the criminal justice system. Here a stay will be granted where the court concludes that in all the

---

4   *R v LR* [2010] EWCA Crim 924, per Judge LJ, para 16.
5   Criminal Justice Act 2003, s 58(8); see CPS Disclosure Manual, para 13.24.
6   Magistrates' Court Disclosure Review (May 2014) para. 148. However see *DPP v Petrie* [2015] EWHC 48 (Admin).
7   [2010] UKSC 48 at para 13.

circumstances a trial will "offend the court's sense of justice and propriety" (per Lord Lowry in R v Horseferry Road Magistrates' Court, Ex p Bennett [1994] 1 AC 42, 74G) or will "undermine public confidence in the criminal justice system and bring it into disrepute" (per Lord Steyn in R v Latif and Shahzad [1996] 1 WLR 104, 112F).'

11.07   In relation to the second category of case, Lord Dyson stated in *Curtis Francis Warren v Her Majesty's Attorney General of Jersey*:[8]

'... the balance must always be struck between the public interest in ensuring that those who are accused of serious crimes should be tried and the competing public interest in ensuring that executive misconduct does not undermine public confidence in the criminal justice system and bring it into disrepute.'

11.08   A stay should only be imposed in exceptional circumstances.[9] In considering whether to allow an abuse argument for lack of disclosure,[10] the court should consider a series of steps identified in *R (on the application of Ebrahim) v Feltham Magistrates' Court*:[11]

1   Determine what the nature and extent of the duty of the investigating authority and the prosecutor was, if any, to obtain and/or retain the material in question having regard to the Code and Attorney General's Guidelines.[12]

2   If in all the circumstances there were no duties to obtain and/or retain the material before the defence first sought its retention, there can be no question of the subsequent trial being unfair on that ground.[13]

3   Where the material was not obtained and/or retained, in breach of the obligations set out in the CPIA Code and the Attorney General's Guidelines, the ultimate objective is to ensure that there should be a fair trial according to the law. That involves fairness to both the accused and the prosecution. The trial process itself is equipped to deal with the bulk of the complaints on which applications for a stay are founded.[14]

4   A stay will only be imposed, subject to point 6 below, if the defence can show, on a balance of probabilities, that owing to the failure of the

---

8 [2011] UKPC 10 at para 26.
9 Attorney General's Reference (No. 1 of 1990) [1992] 3 WLR 9.
10 Different considerations apply where material has been lost or destroyed.
11 [2001] EWHC Admin 130.
12 *R v Feltham Magistrates' Court* [2001] EWHC Admin 130, per Brooke LJ, para 16.
13 *R v Feltham Magistrates' Court* [2001] EWHC Admin 130, per Brooke LJ, para 16.
14 *R v Feltham Magistrates' Court* [2001] EWHC Admin 130, per Brooke LJ, para 25.

police or the prosecution to obtain and/or retain the material the accused will suffer serious prejudice to the extent that no fair trial can be held, ie that the continuance of the prosecution would amount to a misuse of the powers of the court.[15]

5   Where, apart from the missing evidence,[16] there is sufficient credible evidence, which, if believed, would justify a safe conviction, a trial should proceed.[17]

6   If point 4 above does not apply but the behaviour of the prosecution has been so very bad that it is not fair for the accused to be tried, the proceedings will be stayed on that ground. For a stay to be granted in such circumstances it is likely that there must be –

    (a)   an element of bad faith on the part of the police or the prosecution authorities; or

    (b)   at the very least some serious fault on their part.[18]

11.09   The reference to fairness in point 6 (above) must be read in conjunction with the judgment of Lord Kerr in *Curtis Francis Warren v Her Majesty's Attorney General of Jersey* in which he stated:[19]

'For my part, I think that there is much to be said for discarding the notion of fairness when considering the second category of stay cases. Fairness to the accused, although not irrelevant in the assessment of whether it is fair to allow the trial to continue, is subsumed in the decision whether to grant a stay in second category cases based on the primary consideration of whether the stay is necessary to protect the integrity of the criminal justice system.'

11.10   The late disclosure of material is less likely to give rise to a stay of proceedings on the grounds of abuse than non-disclosure of material.[20]

---

15 *R v Feltham Magistrates' Court* [2001] EWHC Admin 130, per Brooke LJ, para 16 and para 24. The importance of the evidence rather than fault is the key issue, *Clay v Clerk to the Justices* [2014] EWHC 321 (Admin) paras. 46–48. See also *Khalid Ali v CPS, West Midlands* [2007] EWCA Crim 691, *DPP v Cooper* [2008] EWHC 507 (Admin) and *DPP v Fell* [2013] EWHC 562 (Admin).

16 Such as fingerprint or scientific evidence.

17 *R v Feltham Magistrates' Court* [2001] EWHC Admin 130, per Brooke LJ, para 27; approved in *Ali, Altaf v CPS* [2007] EWCA Crim 691 by Moses LJ, para 30 (although the test was met in that case and the prosecution appeal against the stay allowed).

18 *R v Feltham Magistrates' Court* [2001] EWHC Admin 130, per Brooke LJ, paras 23, 74.

19 [2011] UKPC 10, para 84.

20 See *R v O* [2007] EWCA Crim 3483 and *R v MO* [2011] EWCA Crim 2854 for cases concerned with the staying of proceedings for late disclosure by the prosecution.

11.11   On an application to stay proceedings, the trial judge should be invited to conduct a close analysis of the history of the case and should approach the issue of disclosure through the confines of the CPIA 1996.[21]

11.12   In *R v Salt*, the Court of Appeal allowed a prosecution appeal against a stay in a case involving sexual offences.[22] The Court balanced the following factors:

* the gravity of the charges;

* the denial of justice to the complainants;

* the importance of disclosure in sexual offences;

* the necessity for proper attention to be paid to disclosure;

* the nature and materiality of the failures;

* the failures by the defence lawyers:

* the waste of court resources and the effect on the jury; and

* the availability of other sanctions.

Whilst the conduct of the CPS and the police had been 'reprehensible' and the sanctions which the court could impose were inadequate, there was a very strong public interest in the grave offences in question being tried, the documents that were not disclosed were of the limited materiality and a fair trial was still possible.

11.13   In *R v R*, the court held that where failures in disclosure had led to delay but had not caused the defendants prejudice other than personal inconvenience and distress, that any breach of the 'reasonable time' requirement in the European Convention on Human Rights, Article 6 could be cured by a reduction at the sentencing stage and a stay was not necessary.[23] The court considered that, in addressing the need for public confidence in the system whilst there would be cases of gross misconduct which the criminal justice system could not approbate, on the other hand, it was 'important that conduct or results that may merely be the result of state incompetence or negligence should not necessarily justify the abandonment of a trial of serious allegations'.[24]

---

21 *R v O* [2007] EWCA Crim 3483, per Hooper LJ, para 42. This will normally require the defence to make an application for disclosure under CPIA 1996, s 8.
22 [2015] 2 Cr. App. R. 27.
23 [2016] 1 Cr. App. R. 20.
24 [2016] 1 Cr. App. R. 20, para 72.

11.14   The procedure to apply to stay an indictment on the grounds of abuse of process application is set out in the Consolidated Criminal Practice Directions, para IV.36 as follows:

IV.36.1   In all cases where a defendant in the Crown Court proposes to make an application to stay an indictment on the grounds of abuse of process, written notice of such application must be given to the prosecuting authority and to any co-defendant not later than 14 days before the date fixed or warned for trial ("the relevant date"). Such notice must:

(a)   give the name of the case and the indictment number;

(b)   state the fixed date or the warned date as appropriate;

(c)   specify the nature of the application;

(d)   set out in numbered sub-paragraphs the grounds upon which the application is to be made;

(e)   be copied to the chief listing officer at the court centre where the case is due to be heard.

IV.36.2   Any co-defendant who wishes to make a like application must give a like notice not later than seven days before the relevant date, setting out any additional grounds relied upon.

IV.36.3   In relation to such applications, the following automatic directions shall apply:

(a)   the advocate for the applicant(s) must lodge with the court and serve on all other parties a skeleton argument in support of the application, at least five clear working days before the relevant date. If reference is to be made to any document not in the existing trial documents, a paginated and indexed bundle of such documents is to be provided with the skeleton argument;

(b)   the advocate for the prosecution must lodge with the court and serve on all other parties a responsive skeleton argument at least two clear working days before the relevant date, together with a supplementary bundle if appropriate.

IV.36.4   All skeleton arguments must specify any propositions of law to be advanced (together with the authorities relied upon in support, with page references to passages relied upon) and, where appropriate, include a chronology of events and a list of dramatis personae. In all instances where reference is made to a document, the reference in the trial documents or supplementary bundle is to be given.

IV.36.5   The above time limits are minimum time limits. In appropriate cases the court will order longer lead times. To this end in all cases where defence advocates are, at the time of the plea and directions hearing, considering the possibility of an abuse of process application, this must be raised with the judge dealing with the matter, who will order a different timetable if appropriate, and may wish, in any event, to give additional directions about the conduct of the application.

11.15   In addition, Crim PR 3.20 provides that:

(1)   This rule applies where a defendant wants the Crown Court to stay the case on the grounds that the proceedings are an abuse of the court, or otherwise unfair.

(2)   Such a defendant must—

   (a)   apply in writing—

      (i)   as soon as practicable after becoming aware of the grounds for doing so,

      (ii)   at a pre-trial hearing, unless the grounds for the application do not arise until trial, and

      (iii)   in any event, before the defendant pleads guilty or the jury (if there is one) retires to consider its verdict at trial;

   (b)   serve the application on—

      (i)   the court officer, and

      (ii)   each other party; and

   (c)   in the application—

      (i)   explain the grounds on which it is made,

      (ii)   include, attach or identify all supporting material,

      (iii)   specify relevant events, dates and propositions of law, and

      (iv)   identify any witness the applicant wants to call to give evidence in person.

(3)   A party who wants to make representations in response to the application must serve the representations on—

   (a)   the court officer; and

   (b)   each other party, not more than 14 days after service of the application.

11.16   The point at which an abuse of process application may be made was dealt with by Lord Judge CJ in *R v F*:[25]

> 'An application to stay for an abuse of process ought ordinarily to be heard and determined at the outset of the case, and before any evidence is heard, unless there is a specific reason to defer it because the question of prejudice and fair trial can be better determined at a later stage.'

REFUSING TO EXTEND CUSTODY TIME LIMITS

11.17   A court may refuse to extend custody time limits where the prosecution has not complied with its disclosure obligations.

11.18   Where an application is made to extend the accused's custody time limits, it is for the prosecution to prove on a balance of probabilities that the two limbs of the Prosecution of Offences Act 1985, s 22(3) are satisfied, namely:

(a)   that the need for the extension is due to –

    (i)   the illness or absence of the accused, a necessary witness, a judge or a magistrate;

    (ii)   a postponement which is occasioned by the ordering by the court of separate trials in the case of two or more accused or two or more offences; or

    (iii)   some other good and sufficient cause; and

(b)   that the prosecution has acted with all due diligence and expedition.

11.19   If the court is not so satisfied, the custody time limits cannot be extended[26] and the accused is immediately entitled to bail subject to the Criminal Justice and Public Order Act 1994, s 25(1).[27]

11.20   It will be open for the defence to argue that the late disclosure of the prosecution papers or the late/non-disclosure of material that satisfies the

---

25   *R v F* [2011] EWCA Crim 1844, per Lord Judge CJ at para 48v.

26   *R v Manchester Crown Court ex parte McDonald* [1999] 1 Cr App R 409, per Lord Bingham CJ, p 413.

27   CJPO 1994, s 25 excludes the grant of bail to an accused charged with or convicted of homicide or rape with a previous conviction of such offences, save in exceptional circumstances. See *R (O) v Crown Court at Harrow* [2006] UKHL 42, per Lord Brown for the approach to be taken to this section.

prosecution disclosure test indicates that the prosecution have not acted with all due diligence and expedition.[28]

11.21   The prosecution are required to show such diligence and expedition as would be shown by a competent prosecutor, conscious of his duty to bring the case to trial as quickly, reasonably and fairly as possible.[29] They are not expected to be able to show that every action has been completed as quickly and efficiently as is humanly possible, nor should the history be approached on the unreal assumption that all involved on the prosecution side have been able to give the case their undivided attention.[30]

11.22   In a complex case the prosecutor cannot be expected to have detailed knowledge of every part of the investigation. Where the defence intend to criticize a particular part of the investigation in order to challenge an application to extend a custody time limit, reasonable notice should be given so that the prosecutor can respond appropriately.[31] In the absence of such notice, the court may decide that, at least for the time being, more general information from the prosecutor will suffice.[32]

11.23   While the prosecution cannot be responsible for the failures of third parties from whom they are seeking evidence, such as forensic science laboratories,[33] they do have an obligation to do all they can within their power to ensure that the evidence is available within the relevant custody time limit.[34] This would include notifying third parties of all the relevant dates and time limits, notifying them of the accused's remand status and maintaining good lines of communication.[35]

11.24   The CPS Casework Quality Standards require prosecutors to continually review the remand status of defendants, and ensuring that custody time limit cases are dealt with in accordance with the national standard.[36]

---

28 Prosecution of Offences Act 1985, s 22(3)(b).
29 *R v Manchester Crown Court ex parte McDonald* [1999] 1 Cr App R 409, per Lord Bingham CJ, p 414.
30 *R v Manchester Crown Court ex parte McDonald* [1999] 1 Cr App R 409, per Lord Bingham CJ, p 414.
31 *R v Manchester Crown Court ex parte McDonald* [1999] 1 Cr App R 409, per Lord Bingham CJ, p 414.
32 *R v Woolwich Crown Court ex parte Smith* [2002] EWHC 995 (Admin).
33 Forensic Science laboratories do not form part of the prosecution for the purposes of Prosecution of Offences Act 1985, s 22.
34 *R v Central Criminal Court ex parte Johnson* [1999] 2 Cr App R 51, per Collins J.
35 In *R (Holland) v Leeds Crown Court* [2002] EWHC 1862 (Admin), per Bell J the extension of custody time limits, caused by the late service of prosecution expert scientific evidence, was refused as the prosecution had not acted with all due diligence.
36 CPS Casework Quality Standards, Standard 3: Casework preparation.

ORDERS FOR COSTS

11.25   Costs may be an effective remedy where a hearing is adjourned or cancelled or a trial is aborted because of the late or non-disclosure of material by either the defence or prosecution. Where an adjournment is applied for, there is a duty on the advocate to be frank with the court as to the reasons why.[37] The power of the court to make a costs order is specifically provided for in CrimPR 2015 3.5(6) which states:

> 'If a party fails to comply with a rule or a direction, the court may –
>
> (a)   fix, postpone, bring forward, extend, cancel or adjourn a hearing;
>
> (b)   exercise its power to make a costs order; and
>
> (c)   impose such other sanctions as may be appropriate.'

11.26   The court can order one party in criminal proceedings to pay the other party's costs where they have been incurred as a result of 'an unnecessary or improper act or omission'.[38] The CPS is a party to the proceedings for these purposes.

11.27   The procedure to be followed where one party may be liable to pay another party's costs is set out at the CrimPR 2015 45.8 and the Practice Direction (Costs in Criminal Proceedings) (October 2015).[39] The Practice Direction suggests that the courts may find it helpful to adopt a three-stage approach:

(a)   Has there been an unnecessary improper act or omission?

(b)   As a result, have any costs been incurred by another party?

(c)   If the answers to (a) and (b) are 'yes', should the court exercise its discretion to order the party responsible to meet the whole or any part of the relevant costs, and if so what specific sum is involved?

11.28   The power of the court to order one party to pay the other's costs is to be distinguished from a 'wasted costs' order against a legal representative. The court can order a legal representative (which includes the crown prosecutor and prosecution advocate) to pay such costs or prohibit the payment of costs to him where a party has incurred costs:

•   as a result of any improper, unreasonable or negligent act or omission by a legal or other representative (or employee); or

---

37 *R v McDonagh* [2011] EWCA Crim 3238, per Thomas LJ, para 25.

38 Prosecution of Offences Act 1985, s 19; Costs in Criminal Cases (General) Regulations 1986 (SI 1986/1335), reg 3(1).

39 para 4.1.1.

• which it has become unreasonable for that party to pay because of such an act or omission occurring after those costs were incurred.[40]

11.29   The procedure to be followed where a judge is considering 'wasted costs' is set out at the CrimPR 2015 45.9, and the Practice Direction (Costs in Criminal Proceedings) (October 2015).[41] The Practice Direction again recommends that the courts use a similar three-stage approach to that set out above:

(a)   Has there been an unnecessary improper act or omission?

(b)   As a result, have any costs been incurred by another party?

(c)   If the answers to (a) and (b) are 'yes', should the court exercise its discretion to disallow or order the representative to meet the whole or any part of the relevant costs, and if so what specific sum is involved?

11.30   Costs payable under a costs order are limited to costs actually incurred under the graduated fee scheme, no matter how vital the work. The court has no power to make a costs order in respect of sums not claimable by the accused himself or those liable for his costs or the Legal Services Commission.[42]

11.31   Before any costs order is made in respect of either a party or legal representative, the court must hear from the parties and is entitled to take such an order into account when making any other costs order.

EXCLUSION OF EVIDENCE

11.32   The late or non-disclosure of material by the prosecution may lead to the exclusion of evidence. The Police and Criminal Evidence Act 1984 (PACE 1984), s 78(1) states:

'In any proceedings the court may refuse to allow evidence on which the prosecution proposes to rely to be given if it appears to the court that, having regard to all the circumstances, including the circumstances in which the evidence was obtained, the admission of the evidence would have such an adverse effect on the fairness of the proceedings that the court ought not to admit it.'

---

40 Prosecution of Offences Act 1985, s 19A; Costs in Criminal Cases (General) Regulations 1986, reg 3B (SI 1986/1335); CrimPR 2015, r 45.9.
41 Para 4.2.4.
42 *R v Fitzgerald* [2012] 3 Costs LR 437, per His Honour Judge Gordon, para 17 (Central Criminal Court).

11.33   All cases are fact specific. Where the prosecution discloses material which satisfies the prosecution disclosure test shortly before trial, there may be insufficient time for the defence to investigate the material properly. The prejudice caused to the defence may lead the trial judge to exclude the prosecution evidence to which the material relates. The judge is more likely to do this where there is no good reason for the late disclosure and there has been a breach of court orders. Evidence served late was excluded in *R v Boardman* which resulted in the Crown having to offer no evidence.[43] The court identified:

i)   whilst it is acknowledged the CPS are under pressure of resources, this cannot excuse late service as it would render case management ineffective.[44] The defence are also under pressure from fixed fees;[45]

ii)   there is responsibility on the defence to make appropriate requests and bring matters to the attention of the court; and[46]

iii)   although the defence cannot specify disclosure in a particular format, reasonable requests should be entertained.[47]

The Court added that:

> 'it should not be thought that this decision can be used to create a trap for the prosecution generally or the CPS in particular by the over-zealous pursuit of inconsequential material which does not go to the issue, all in the hope that the CPS will fall down and that an application can be made which has the effect of bringing the prosecution to an end. Such conduct is itself an abuse of the process of the court and judges will be assiduous to identify it and impose sanctions on those who seek to manipulate the system.'[48]

11.34   Evidence, even of substantial probative value, may on rare occasions be excluded where the PACE 1984, s 78 does not apply, but there has been a failure to comply with the Criminal Procedures Rules.[49]

---

43   [2015] EWCA Crim 175. See *R v Salt* [2015] 2 Cr. App. R. 27 for application of Boardman principles to abuse of process.
44   At paras. 35 and 38.
45   At para. 36.
46   At para. 28 and 40.
47   At para. 29.
48   At para. 42.
49   *R v Musone* [2007] EWCA Crim 1237: An accused intentionally sought to ambush a co-accused in breach of the Criminal Procedure Rules. Moses LJ, para 56 stated '... the judge was entitled to exclude that evidence in circumstances where he concluded the appellant had deliberately manipulated the trial process so as to give his co-defendant no opportunity of dealing properly with the allegation.' Note: Police and Criminal Evidence Act 1984, s 78 did not apply because it was not evidence upon which the prosecution proposed to rely. There was also no express power to exclude the evidence under Criminal Justice Act 2003, s 101(e) (bad character relating to a co-accused).

ACQUITTAL AGAINST THE WEIGHT OF THE EVIDENCE

11.35   Where the prosecution fail to comply with their disclosure obligations such failures may be highlighted in the closing speech of the defence advocate. A failure to disclose relevant material may give rise to a reasonable doubt about the integrity of the prosecution as a whole and may impact on a jury's view of the reliability of other evidence.

SUCCESSFUL APPEAL

11.36   In order for an appeal on the grounds of non-disclosure to succeed, it is not always necessary to demonstrate that disclosure of material would have affected the outcome of the proceedings because, even with the benefit of hindsight, it will often be difficult to say whether or not an undisclosed item of evidence might have shifted the balance or opened up a new line of defence.[50] In many cases, it would suffice for an accused to show a failure on the part of the prosecutor to meet disclosure obligations so that it is reasonable to suppose such failure might have affected the outcome of the trial.[51] Where there has been a failure on the part of the prosecution to make disclosure, the court will not regard a conviction as unsafe if the non-disclosure can properly be said to be of 'insignificance in regard to any real issue'.[52]

---

50   *R v Alibhai* [2004] EWCA Crim 681, per Longmore LJ, para 57; *R v Ward* [1993] 96 Cr App R 1, p 22.
51   *R v Alibhai* [2004] EWCA Crim 681, per Longmore LJ, para 57.
52   *R v Alibhai* [2004] EWCA Crim 681, per Longmore LJ, para 57; *R v Maguire* [1992] 94 Cr App R 133, p 148. However see also *Macklin v HM Advocate* [2015] UKSC 77 and *R v Asiedu* [2015] 2 Cr. App. R. 8.

Chapter 12

Post-conviction disclosure and review

INTRODUCTION

12.01   It is clear from the CPIA 1996, s 7A that the prosecution's statutory duty of continuing disclosure ceases upon conviction, acquittal or when the prosecution decides not to proceed with the case. A limited duty of disclosure still remains to disclose material which might cast doubt on the safety of the conviction.[1]

12.02   The general duty of the police and CPS to investigate also ceases on conviction. The common law duty of disclosure 'was not devised in order to equip convicted persons ... with a continuing right to indefinite re-investigation of their cases, and the fact that some such persons assert that their convictions were miscarriages of justice does not mean that it was'.[2] Further, '... after conviction there is no indefinitely continuing duty on the police or prosecutor either in the same form as existed pre-trial or to respond to whatever inquiries the defendant may make for access to the case materials to allow re-investigation'.[3]

12.03   This chapter deals with:

• post-conviction disclosure	**12.04–12.10**
• post-conviction review	**12.11–12.13**
• role of the courts	**12.14–12.15**
• role of the CCRC	**12.16–12.17**

---

1   *Nunn v Chief Constable of the Suffolk Constabulary* [2015] UKSC 37; [2015] AC 225, per Lord Hughes, paras 30, 42.
2   Ibid. para 31.
3   Ibid. para 42.

POST-CONVICTION DISCLOSURE

12.04   There is no statutory right to post-conviction disclosure.[4] Although the common law duty of disclosure remains, it does not extend as far as it would pre-conviction:

> 'There is no doubt that [the] principle of fairness informs the duty of disclosure at all stages of the criminal process. It does not, however, follow, that fairness requires the same level of disclosure at every stage ...
>
> The common law developed the duty as an incident of the trial process, to ensure that that process was fair to defendants. It was designed to avoid trials creating miscarriages of justice, not as a means of investigating alleged miscarriages after a proper trial process has been completed ...
>
> The defendant on trial must have the right to defend himself in any proper way he wishes, and to make full answer to the charge. The convicted defendant has had this opportunity. The public interest until conviction is in the trial process being as full and fair as it properly can be made to be.'[5]

12.05   The extent of the common law duty of disclosure post-conviction is not clear:

> '... but plainly it extends in principle to any material which is relevant to an identified ground of appeal and which might assist the appellant. Ordinarily this will arise only in relation to material which comes into the possession of the Crown after trial, for anything else relevant should have been disclosed beforehand under the Act. But if there has been a failure, for whatever reason, of disclosure at trial then the duty after trial will extend to pre-existing material which is relevant to the appeal.'[6]

Furthermore:

> 'There can be no doubt that if the police or prosecution come into possession, after the appellate process is exhausted, of something new which might afford arguable grounds for contending that the conviction was unsafe, it is their duty to disclose it to the convicted defendant. Simple examples might include a new (and credible) confession by someone else, or the discovery, incidentally to a different investigation, of a pattern, or of evidence, which throws doubt on the original conviction.'[7]

---

4   Ibid. para 2.
5   Ibid. para 22, 31 and 32.
6   Ibid. para 25.
7   Ibid. para 35.

12.06   For the purposes of an appeal, that burden does not extend to facilitating a re-investigation by the appellant or a general duty on police forces to respond to every request for further inquiry made by those doubting the safety of their convictions. The pressure on limited public resources would be significant if such a duty to investigate extended post-conviction and post-appeal and there was a considerable benefit to finality in proceedings.[8] The Supreme Court in *Nunn* found that the appropriate avenue for considering the merits of requests for further investigation is by application to the CCRC and that finality of first instance and appellate proceedings was an important factor in its decision making.[9]

12.07   However, the court did encourage the defence, the CPS and the police to cooperate holding that if 'there appears to be a real prospect that further inquiry will uncover something which may affect the safety of the conviction, then there should be co-operation in making it. It is in nobody's interests to resist all inquiry unless and until the CCRC directs it.'[10]

12.08   Where material comes to light post-conviction that may materially cast doubt upon the safety of a conviction, the prosecution has a duty to consider disclosure. This is embodied in the Attorney General's Guidelines on Disclosure (2013), para 72 which state:

> Where, after the conclusion of the proceedings, material comes to light, that might cast doubt upon the safety of the conviction, the prosecutor must consider disclosure of such material.

This was interpreted in *Nunn* to mean that not only should disclosure of such material be considered, but it should be made unless there is good reason why not.[11] The Supreme Court confirmed that:

> 'There can be no doubt that if the police or prosecution come into possession, after the appellate process is exhausted, of something new which might afford arguable grounds for contending that the conviction was unsafe, it is their duty to disclose it to the convicted defendant'.[12]

12.09   The CPS Disclosure Manual advises that the disclosure test to be applied post-conviction is as set out in the Attorney General's Guidelines, para 72 above. The defence case should be assessed as that advanced at trial or, if matters are

---

8   Ibid. para 31 and 38.
9   Ibid. para 39.
10   Ibid. para 41.
11   Ibid. para 30.
12   Ibid. para 35.

raised on appeal which were not raised during the trial process, set out in the appellant's grounds of appeal.[13] The CPS guidance confirms that the interests of justice dictate that, where material comes to light after a defendant's conviction that might cast doubt on the safety of conviction, a duty to consider disclosure remains. Further CPS guidance provides that the police and prosecutors can, in their discretion, choose to provide material to those making enquiries on behalf of convicted defendants, that they should exercise sensible judgment in relation to such representations and that such defence requests should be made in writing to the CPS and police.[14] Each case will be considered on a case-by-case basis. The CPS suggest that requests for case papers should usually be made to the original defence representatives before further inquiry is made with the Crown for these documents.

12.10   As a general rule, non-disclosure will not prevent an accused's guilty plea being regarded as safe. Where, however, the accused's decision to plead guilty is taken on the basis of information which was materially deficient due to the prosecution's failure to comply with its duty of disclosure, an appeal against conviction may succeed. In *R v Early*, B's conviction was quashed after he had pleaded guilty and the prosecution's failure to make proper disclosure had prevented him from pursuing an abuse of process argument. Rose LJ stated:[15]

'… a defendant who pleads guilty at an early stage should not, if inadequate disclosure has not been made by then, be in any worse position than a defendant who, as the consequence of an argument to stay proceedings as an abuse, has the benefit of further disclosure which leads to the abandonment of the proceedings against him.'

POST-CONVICTION REVIEW

12.11   The CPS may be required to review the safety of convictions as a consequence of a trigger event and conduct an assessment as to whether justice is served by allowing such convictions to stand.[16]

12.12   Triggers for potential CPS reviews of past convictions include:[17]

* where the competence and/or credibility or methodology of an expert witness is in doubt;

---

13 CPS Disclosure Manual, paras 2.10, 2.13, 2.14.
14 CPS Legal Guidance: Disclosure of Material to Third Parties, Post-Conviction.
15 [2002] EWCA Crim 1904, para 74 and applied in *R v Matthew Smith* [2004] EWCA Crim 2212.
16 CPS Legal Guidance, Reviewing Previously Finalised Cases – CPS Policy.
17 CPS Legal Guidance, Reviewing Previously Finalised Cases – CPS Policy, para 6.

- where a police officer's evidence is discredited;

- new scientific breakthroughs;

- developments of the law which affect the offence/defence;

- where the CPS guidance relied upon is legally incorrect;

- systemic failings in the disclosure process; and

- where a flaw has occurred in the trial process, eg a defective indictment.[18]

12.13   In order for the police and CPS to carry out a review, it will be necessary to show that there is something which may cast doubt upon the safety of the conviction. This may arise, for example, where scientific advances enable tests unavailable at the time of trial to be carried out which might reasonably be anticipated to affect the safety of a conviction.[19] In deciding whether to carry out a review into a conviction, the CPS must ask itself a number of questions and go through a number of stages. In summary, the procedure is as follows.[20]

- Is there likely to be injustice or significant damage to public confidence if no action is taken?

- If so, would disclosure of information or material to the defence be sufficient and appropriate action?

- If not, consider informing third parties including the Law Society, the Attorney General's Office, the CCRC and any other prosecutors or Government departments that may be affected.

- Where custodial sentences are still being served or ancillary orders are still outstanding, an urgent review should be set up.

- Where the review affects other cases (both finalised and ongoing) consideration should be given to notifying Areas and Casework Divisions and issuing appropriate guidance about how to handle the reviews.

ROLE OF THE COURTS

12.14   Where the claimant believes he has a proper case for further disclosure or the re-testing of items, he should write to the CPS setting out the grounds and

---

18 CPS Legal Guidance, Reviewing Previously Finalised Cases – CPS Policy, para 6.
19 See CPS Legal Guidance, Reviewing Previously Finalised Cases – CPS Policy, paras A–E for potential actions available to the CPS.
20 CPS Legal Guidance, Reviewing Previously Finalised Cases – CPS Policy, para 11 for questions to consider in deciding whether to review a conviction.

reasons supporting his claim. The courts have the power to intervene following the refusal of the CPS or the police to disclose material in appellate proceedings.

12.15   The argument that post-conviction disclosure should only be ordered if the police or CPS have acted irrationally has been expressly rejected in favour of a more pro-active approach by the courts.[21] The Criminal Appeal Act 1968 (CAA 1968), s 23(1) provides the Court of Appeal with the power to consider, where it is necessary or expedient in the interests of justice, to order the production or disclosure of a document, exhibit or item connected to a case if it is necessary for the determination of the case. Further, the Court of Appeal can order any compellable witness to attend court and receive any evidence not adduced in the original proceedings. The Court of Appeal can also direct the CCRC to carry out any investigation in order to assist with an appeal.[22] These are vital safeguards in correcting and guarding against miscarriages of justice.

ROLE OF THE CCRC

12.16   It is clear that the CCRC is an important organisation in dealing with post-conviction material and investigating the safety of convictions and a safety net for a convicted person seeking post-conviction disclosure.[23] The Criminal Appeal Act 1995 (CAA 1995), s 17 provides a power for the CCRC to require any public body to produce any document or information relevant to an application under consideration by the CCRC. The CCRC also has a power pursuant to CAA 1995, s 18A to apply to the Crown Court to compel any person, including private bodies, to allow the CCRC access to a document or material in that person's possession if the material may assist the CCRC. These are vital safeguards in light of the limited common law duty of disclosure that exists following the Supreme Court decision in *Nunn*.

12.17   Whilst the CCRC cannot necessarily disclose all the information and evidence it obtains,[24] it is required to disclose to its applicants sufficient information to allow the applicant to properly present their best possible case.[25]

---

21 *R v Clarke* [2007] EWCA Crim 37 dealing with the Court of Appeal's power to order disclosure.
22 Section 23A of the Criminal Appeal Act 1968 together with section 15 of the Criminal Appeal Act 1995.
23 *Nunn v Chief Constable of the Suffolk Constabulary* [2015] UKSC 37; [2015] AC 225, per Lord Hughes, para 39.
24 Sections 23 and 24 of the Criminal Appeal Act 1995.
25 *R v Secretary of State for the Home Department ex parte Hickey & Ors* (No.2) [1995] 1 All ER 489.

Chapter 13

Interception of communications

INTRODUCTION

13.01   The main purpose of the Regulation of Investigatory Powers Act 2000 (RIPA 2000) is to ensure that relevant investigatory powers are used in accordance with a person's human rights.[1] The golden rule of full disclosure, namely, that any material which satisfies the prosecution disclosure test must be disclosed to the defence,[2] is subject to the exception that the material must not be disclosed to the extent that its disclosure is prohibited by the RIPA 2000, s17.[3]

13.02   This chapter deals with:

• types of intercept requiring a warrant	**13.03–13.08**
• protections for the accused	**13.09–13.21**
• types of intercept not requiring a warrant	**13.22–13.27**
• private telecommunications	**13.28–13.30**

TYPES OF INTERCEPT REQUIRING A WARRANT

13.03   The RIPA 2000, s 1 provides that it is an offence for a person intentionally, and without lawful authority, to intercept any communication in the course of its transmission by means of:

•   a public postal service; or

•   a public telecommunications system.

---

1   See RIPA 2000, Explanatory Notes, para 3. See the Interception of Communications Code of Practice, published January 2016.
2   *R v H & C* [2004] UKHL 3, per Lord Bingham CJ, paras 14, 18, 36.
3   CPIA 1996, ss 3(7), 7A(9), 8(6) – these sections deal with the duties of initial disclosure, continuing disclosure and the application by the accused for disclosure respectively.

13.04   This will include, inter alia:

- any communications made via a public postal service;

- telephone calls through a landline or mobile phone network;

- text messages sent through a mobile phone network; and

- e-mail communications via the internet.

13.05   The offence arises where the intercept is made in the 'course of its transmission' and will not apply to messages stored once the transmission has ceased, eg recordings stored on answer machines.

13.06   An interception will have lawful authority where a warrant has been issued. The RIPA 2000, s 5(3) allows an interception warrant to be issued:

'If it is necessary –

(a)   in the interests of national security;

(b)   for the purpose of preventing or detecting serious crime;

(c)   for the purpose of safeguarding the economic well-being of the United Kingdom; or

(d)   for the purposes of ... any international mutual assistance agreement.'

13.07   Where a warrant is obtained for the intercept of a public postal or telecommunications system in the UK, all information relating to it is excluded from the public domain and cannot be disclosed to the defence or used in evidence. The RIPA 2000, s 17(1), provides that:

Subject to section 18, no evidence shall be adduced, question asked, assertion or disclosure made or other thing done in, for the purposes of or in connection with any legal proceedings which (in any manner) –

(a) discloses any of the contents of an intercepted communication or any related communications data, in circumstances from which its origin in anything falling within subsection (2) may be inferred; or

(b) tends (apart from any such disclosure) to suggest that anything falling within subsection (2) has or may have occurred or be going to occur.

13.08   Subsection 2 includes:

- unlawful interception of communications by, amongst others, police or HMRC which was or would be an offence under the RIPA 2000, s 1(1) or (2);

- the issue of an interception warrant;

- the making of an application by any person for an interception warrant; and

- the imposition of any requirement on any person to provide assistance with giving effect to an interception warrant.

PROTECTION FOR THE ACCUSED

13.09   The use of intercepted material is restricted to the minimum necessary for 'authorised purposes' and must be destroyed as soon as it is not required for any such 'authorised purpose'.[4] One of the authorised purposes is to 'ensure that a person conducting a criminal prosecution has the information he needs to determine what is required of him by his duty to secure the fairness of the prosecution'.[5]

13.10   Prosecutors may therefore have communicated to them intercept evidence which satisfies the prosecution disclosure test but is not disclosed to the accused because of the prohibition imposed by the RIPA 2000, s 17.

13.11   The issuing of a warrant for the purpose of preventing or detecting serious crime under s 5(3)(b) does not extend to gathering information for the purpose of a prosecution and therefore intercepted material may not survive to the prosecution stage.[6] If intercepted material is in existence after the commencement of a prosecution, it should only be because a conscious decision has been made to retain it for an authorised purpose.[7] The RIPA 2000, s 18(7) permits disclosure to a prosecutor for certain limited purposes including 'for the purpose only of enabling that person to determine what is required of him by his duty to secure the fairness of the prosecution ...'

13.12   This exception to the prohibition against disclosure does not mean that intercepted material should be retained against a remote possibility that it might be relevant to future proceedings, nor does it provide for any disclosure to the defence. The normal expectation is still for the intercepted material to be destroyed in accordance with the general safeguards provided by the RIPA 2000, s 15.[8]

---

4   RIPA 2000, s 15(2) and (3).
5   RIPA 2000, s 15(4)(d).
6   See RIPA 2000, s 5(3)(b); Interception of Communications Code of Practice, para 7, pursuant to RIPA 2000, s 71.
7   Interception of Communications Code of Practice, para 7.8.
8   Interception of Communications Code of Practice, para 7.7.

13.13 If intercepted material is not in existence at the commencement of a prosecution, it cannot be revealed to the prosecutor. There is no duty on investigators to brief prosecutors where there has been an interception and no product remains. As a matter of good practice, the police should draw the attention of the prosecutor to the fact of the interception and provide an assurance that, to the best of their knowledge, the destroyed product contained nothing that would affect the fairness of the trial.[9] If there is material which the officer recalls which may have a bearing on the fairness of the trial, the prosecutor should treat the officer's recollection as a document to be reviewed in accordance with RIPA 2000.

13.14 The Attorney General has issued guidelines on the approach to be taken in the application of the RIPA 2000, s 18.[10] If protected information is disclosed to a prosecutor under section 18, the prosecutor's first step should be to review any information from an interception that remains extant at the time he has conduct of the case. In reviewing it, the prosecutor should seek to identify any information whose existence, if the Crown took no action, might result in unfairness. For example, if the jury may otherwise draw an inference which the intercepted material shows to be wrong and to leave this uncorrected would disadvantage the accused.[11]

13.15 Where the prosecutor's view is that to take no action would render the proceedings unfair, the prosecutor should, after consulting with the relevant prosecution agency, take such steps as are available to secure the fairness of the proceedings provided these steps do not contravene the section 17 prohibition.[12]

13.16 The Attorney General's Section 18 RIPA Prosecutors Intercept Guidelines (RIPA Guidelines) state that steps which the prosecutor could take include:

'(i) putting the prosecution case in such a way that the misleading inference is not drawn by the jury; or

(ii) not relying upon the evidence which makes the information relevant; or

---

9 CPS Disclosure Manual, para 27.20.
10 Attorney General's Section 18 RIPA Prosecutors Intercept Guidelines England and Wales are set out in **Appendix 14**.
11 RIPA Guidelines, para 5.
12 RIPA 2000, s 18(9) and (10); RIPA Guidelines, para 6.

(iii)   discontinuing that part of the prosecution case in relation to which the protected material is relevant, by amending a charge or count or offering no evidence on such a charge or count; or

(iv)   making an admission of fact [provided that it does not contravene section 17, RIPA 2000, by revealing the existence of an interception warrant].'[13]

13.17   There is no requirement for the prosecutor to notify the judge of the action he has taken or proposes to take.

13.18   Where the prosecutor considers that he cannot secure the fairness of the proceedings without assistance from the relevant judge, the prosecutor can invite the judge to order disclosure of the protected material to him alone.[14] A judge must not order disclosure to himself unless he is satisfied that the exceptional circumstances of the case make that disclosure essential in the interests of justice.[15] Any application must be made ex parte.[16]

13.19   The RIPA Guidelines, para 8 suggest that there are two situations which would justify any disclosure to a judge:

•   where the judge's assistance is necessary to ensure the fairness of the trial through summing up, giving appropriate directions or requiring the Crown to make an admission of fact;[17] and

•   where the judge requires knowledge of the protected material for some other purpose, such as to properly assess the significance of public interest immunity material, or in order to ensure that the RIPA 2000, s 17(1) is not contravened during cross-examination.

13.20   Where no action can be taken by the prosecutor and/or the judge to prevent the continuation of the proceedings being unfair, the prosecutor will have 'no option but to offer no evidence on the charge in question, or to discontinue the proceedings in their entirety'.[18]

---

13   RIPA Guidelines, para 6. A breach of RIPA 2000, s 17 might occur not only from the factual content of the admission, but also from the circumstances in which it is made.
14   RIPA 2000, s 18(7)(b).
15   RIPA 2000, s 18(8).
16   RIPA Guidelines, para 11.
17   RIPA 2000, s 18(9).
18   RIPA Guidelines, para 9.

13.21 If a prosecutor is asked, by the court or by the defence, whether interception has taken place or whether protected information exists then, whether or not it has taken place or protected information exists, an answer along the following lines should be given:

'I am not in a position to answer that, but I am aware of sections 17 and 18 of the Regulation of Investigatory Powers Act 2000 and the Attorney General's Guidelines on the Disclosure of Information in Exceptional Circumstances under section 18.'[19]

TYPES OF INTERCEPT NOT REQUIRING A WARRANT

13.22 There is no prohibition on the evidential use of material obtained by lawful interception without the use of a warrant and therefore no prohibition on disclosure where it is sought to investigate the lawfulness of any interception. If the intercept is unlawful, it may be excluded from evidence.

13.23 The RIPA 2000, s 1(5) permits lawful interception without a warrant where:

- it is authorised under s 3 or 4 of the Act; and

- it is in the exercise, in relation to any stored communication, of some other statutory power exercised for the purpose of obtaining information or of taking possession of any document or other property.

13.24 Under the RIPA 2000, ss 3 and 4 the circumstances in which the intercept is lawful include where:

- both the sender and the intended recipient of a communication have consented to its interception;

- either the sender or intended recipient of a communication has consented to its interception and directed surveillance by means of that interception has been authorised under the RIPA 2000, Part II;[20] or

- where the conduct takes place in a prison '... if it is conduct in exercise of any power conferred by or under any rules made the Prison Act 1952, s 47 ...'[21] In brief, it is generally not unlawful to record all telephone

---

19 RIPA Guidelines, paras 10.
20 Part II deals with surveillance and covert human intelligence sources.
21 Section 4(4) RIPA 2000. Prison Act 1952, s 47 allows the Secretary of State to make rules for the regulation and management of prisons. In 1996 the Secretary of State directed that the PIN system, a system for recording calls, should be 'rolled out', pursuant to which it was rolled out to Category A and B prisons.

calls of prison inmates with their family, friends and others.[22] Similar provisions apply under s 4 in relation to secure psychiatric hospitals.

13.25   Under Prison Rules 1999, rule 35C a governor may not disclose intercepted material to a third party unless he considers that such disclosure is necessary and proportionate to what is sought to be achieved by disclosure, or the parties consent. Under rule 35A(4) the grounds considered necessary and proportionate for disclosure are:

(a)   the interests of national security;

(b)   the prevention, detection, investigation or prosecution of crime;

(c)   the interests of public safety;

(d)   securing or maintaining prison security or good order and discipline in prison;

(e)   the protection of health or morals; or

(f)   the protection of the rights and freedoms of any person.'

13.26   Even if a judge has decided that the intercept is lawful, it is still open for the defence to argue its admissibility under the Police and Criminal Evidence Act 1984, ss 76 and 78.

13.27   Where one party to a telephone conversation tape records the call, that does not amount to an interception. Hughes LJ in *R v Hardy*[23] stated at para 30:

'It is exactly the same as the undercover officer secreting a tape recorder in his pocket or briefcase whilst meeting the suspect face-to-face … it is surveillance and requires regulation. The Act provides for it, but it is not interception.'

PRIVATE TELECOMMUNICATIONS

13.28   Under the RIPA 2000, s 1(2) it is an offence for a person intentionally, and without lawful authority, to intercept any communication in the course of its communication by means of a private telecommunications system[24] unless

---

22 *R v Abiodun* [2005] EWCA Crim 9, para 55. In *Abiodun*, Clarke LJ gave detailed consideration to the system of recording prison calls. A policy of blanket interception and recording of calls was held not to be unlawful in *R v Mahmood* [2014] 1 Cr. App. R. 31.

23 [2003] 1 Cr. App. R. 30.

24 A private telecommunications system is any telecommunication system which is not a public telecommunications system but is attached to such a system.

the conduct is excluded from criminal liability under s 1(6). Such conduct is excluded from criminal liability under s 1(6) if the person intercepting:

- is a person with a right to control the operation or the use of the system; or

- has the express or implied consent of such a person to make the interception.

13.29   A person has a right to control the operation or the use of the system if he has the right to 'authorise or forbid the operation or the use of the system'.[25] Merely having the right to access or operate the system without restriction will not suffice. This will include the private communications network of an employer or organisation that is linked to a public telecommunications system by a private exchange.

13.30   There is no prohibition on the evidential use of material obtained by lawful interception of a private telecommunications system and therefore no prohibition on disclosure where it is sought in order to investigate the lawfulness of any interception made. If the interception is unlawful, it may be excluded from evidence.

---

25 *R v Stanford* [2006] 2 Cr. App. R. 5, per Lord Phillips CJ.

Criminal Procedure and Investigations Act 1996, Parts I and II (as amended)

PART I DISCLOSURE

Introduction

1.– Application of this Part.

(1)   This Part applies where –

    (a)   a person is charged with a summary offence in respect of which a court proceeds to summary trial and in respect of which he pleads not guilty,

    (b)   a person who has attained the age of 18 is charged with an offence which is triable either way, in respect of which a court proceeds to summary trial and in respect of which he pleads not guilty, or

    (c)   a person under the age of 18 is charged with an indictable offence in respect of which a court proceeds to summary trial and in respect of which he pleads not guilty.

(2)   This Part also applies where –

    [(a)   ...

    (b)   ...

    (c)   ...]^1

    [(cc)   a person is charged with an offence for which he is sent for trial [...]^2,]^3

    (d)   a count charging a person with a summary offence is included in an indictment under the authority of section 40 of the Criminal Justice Act 1988 (common assault etc.), or

    (e)   a bill of indictment charging a person with an indictable offence is preferred under the authority of section 2(2)(b) of the Administration of Justice (Miscellaneous Provisions) Act 1933 (bill preferred by direction of Court of Appeal, or by direction or with consent of a judge)[, or]^4

[(f)   a bill of indictment charging a person with an indictable offence is preferred under section 22B(3)(a) of the Prosecution of Offences Act 1985]⁴[, or]⁵

[(g)   following the preferment of a bill of indictment charging a person with an indictable offence under the authority of section 2(2)(ba) of the Administration of Justice (Miscellaneous Provisions) Act 1933 (bill of indictment preferred with consent of Crown Court judge following approval of deferred prosecution agreement), the suspension of the proceedings against the person under paragraph 2(2) of Schedule 17 to the Crime and Courts Act 2013 is lifted under paragraph 2(3) of that Schedule.]⁵

(3)   This Part applies in relation to alleged offences into which no criminal investigation has begun before the appointed day.

(4)   For the purposes of this section a criminal investigation is an investigation which police officers or other persons have a duty to conduct with a view to it being ascertained –

(a)   whether a person should be charged with an offence, or

(b)   whether a charged with an offence is guilty of it.

(5)   The reference in subsection (3) to the appointed day is to such day as is appointed for the purposes of this Part by the Secretary of State by order.

[(6)   *In this Part—*

(a)   subsections (3) to (5) of section 3 (in their application for the purposes of section 3, 7 or 9), and

(b)   sections 17 and 18,

have effect subject to subsections (2) and (3) of section 9 of the Sexual Offences (Protected Material) Act 1997 (by virtue of which those provisions of this Act do not apply in relation to disclosures regulated by that Act).]⁶

Notes

1   Repealed by Criminal Justice Act 2003, ss 41, 332, Sch 3, para 66(1), (2)(a), Sch 37, Pt 4 (18 June 2012 in relation to certain local justice areas specified in SI 2012/1320, art 4(2) and for purposes specified in SI 2012/1320, art 4(3) subject to savings specified in SI 2012/1320, art 5; 5 November 2012 in relation to certain local justice areas specified in SI 2012/2574, art 2(2), Schedule and for purposes specified in SI 2012/2574, art 2(3) subject to saving provisions specified in SI 2012/2574, arts 3, 4; 28 May 2013 in relation to the remaining local justice areas and purposes specified in SI 2013/1103, art 2(3) subject to savings specified in SI 2013/1103, arts 3, 4 otherwise).

2   Words repealed by Criminal Justice Act 2003, ss 41, 332, Sch 3, para 66(1), (2)(b), Sch 37, Pt 4 (9 May 2005 in relation to cases sent for trial under Crime and Disorder Act 1998, ss 51 or 51A(3)(d); 18 June 2012 in relation to certain local justice areas specified in

SI 2012/1320, art 4(2) and for purposes specified in SI 2012/1320, art 4(3) subject to savings specified in SI 2012/1320, art 5; 5 November 2012 in relation to certain local justice areas specified in SI 2012/2574, art 2(2), Schedule and for purposes specified in SI 2012/2574, art 2(3) subject to saving provisions specified in SI 2012/2574, arts 3, 4; 28 May 2013 in relation to the remaining local justice areas and purposes specified in SI 2013/1103, art 2(3) subject to savings specified in SI 2013/1103, arts 3, 4 otherwise).

3   Inserted by Crime and Disorder Act 1998, s 119, Sch 8, para 125(a) (4 January 1999 for purposes specified in SI 1998/2327, art 4(2) and Sch 2; 15 January 2001 subject to savings specified in SI 2000/3283, art 3 otherwise).

4   Inserted by Crime and Disorder Act 1998, s 119, Sch 8, para 125(b) (1 June 1999).

5   Inserted by Crime and Courts Act 2013, s 45, Sch 17, para 37(1), (2) (24 February 2014 subject to transitional provisions and savings specified in Crime and Courts Act 2013, s 15, Sch 8, Sch 17, para 39).

6   Inserted by Sexual Offences (Protected Material) Act 1997, s 9(4) (date to be appointed).

Commencement

Pt I, s 1(1)–(5): 4 July 1996 (1 April 1997 in relation to England and Wales; 1 January 1998 otherwise).

Extent

Pt I, s. 1(1)–(6)(b): England, Wales, Northern Ireland.

2.– General interpretation.

(1)   References to the accused are to the person mentioned in section 1(1) or (2).

(2)   Where there is more than one accused in any proceedings this Part applies separately in relation to each of the accused.

(3)   References to the prosecutor are to any person acting as prosecutor, whether an individual or a body.

(4)   References to material are to material of all kinds, and in particular include references to –

>   (a)   information, and

>   (b)   objects of all descriptions.

(5)   References to recording information are to putting it in a durable or retrievable form (such as writing or tape).

(6)   This section applies for the purposes of this Part.

Commencement

Pt I, s 2(1)–(6): 4 July 1996 (1 April 1997 in relation to England and Wales; 1 January 1998 otherwise).

Extent

Pt I, s 2(1)–(6): England, Wales, Northern Ireland.

The main provisions

3.– [Initial duty of prosecutor to disclose][1].

(1)   The prosecutor must –

>   (a)   disclose to the accused any prosecution material which has not previously been disclosed to the accused and which [might reasonably be considered capable of undermining][2] the case for the prosecution against the accused [or of assisting the case for the accused][3], or

>   (b)   give to the accused a written statement that there is no material of a description mentioned in paragraph (a).

(2)   For the purposes of this section prosecution material is material –

>   (a)   which is in the prosecutor's possession, and came into his possession in connection with the case for the prosecution against the accused, or

>   (b)   which, in pursuance of a code operative under Part II, he has inspected in connection with the case for the prosecution against the accused.

(3)   Where material consists of information which has been recorded in any form the prosecutor discloses it for the purposes of this section –

>   (a)   by securing that a copy is made of it and that the copy is given to the accused, or

>   (b)   if in the prosecutor's opinion that is not practicable or not desirable, by allowing the accused to inspect it at a reasonable time and a reasonable place or by taking steps to secure that he is allowed to do so;

and a copy may be in such form as the prosecutor thinks fit and need not be in the same form as that in which the information has already been recorded.

(4)   Where material consists of information which has not been recorded the prosecutor discloses it for the purposes of this section by securing that it is recorded in such form as he thinks fit and –

>   (a)   by securing that a copy is made of it and that the copy is given to the accused, or

>   (b)   if in the prosecutor's opinion that is not practicable or not desirable, by allowing the accused to inspect it at a reasonable time and a reasonable place or by taking steps to secure that he is allowed to do so.

(5)   Where material does not consist of information the prosecutor discloses it for the purposes of this section by allowing the accused to inspect it at a reasonable time and a reasonable place or by taking steps to secure that he is allowed to do so.

(6)   Material must not be disclosed under this section to the extent that the court, on an application by the prosecutor, concludes it is not in the public interest to disclose it and orders accordingly.

(7)   Material must not be disclosed under this section to the extent that [it is material the disclosure of which is prohibited by section 17 of the Regulation of Investigatory Powers Act 2000.]⁴

(8)   The prosecutor must act under this section during the period which, by virtue of section 12, is the relevant period for this section.

Notes

1   Words substituted by Criminal Justice Act 2003, s 331, Sch 36, paras 20, 21 (4 April 2005 in relation to England and Wales subject to savings specified in SI 2005/950, arts 2, 4, Sch 2, para 2; 15 July 2005 in relation to Northern Ireland subject to savings specified in SI 2005/1817, art 3).

2   Words substituted by Criminal Justice Act 2003, s 32(a) (4 April 2005 in relation to England and Wales subject to savings specified in SI 2005/950, arts 2, 4, Sch 2, para 2; 15 July 2005 in relation to Northern Ireland subject to savings specified in SI 2005/1817, art 3).

3   Words inserted by Criminal Justice Act 2003, s 32(b) (4 April 2005 in relation to England and Wales subject to savings specified in SI 2005/950, arts 2, 4, Sch 2, para 2; 15 July 2005 in relation to Northern Ireland subject to savings specified in SI 2005/1817, art 3).

4   Words substituted by Regulation of Investigatory Powers Act 2000, s 82, Sch 4, para 7(1) (2 October 2000 subject to transitional provisions specified in SI 2000/2543, art 5).

Commencement

Pt I, s 3(1)–(8): 4 July 1996 (1 April 1997 in relation to England and Wales; 1 January 1998 otherwise).

Extent

Pt I, s 3(1)–(8): England, Wales, Northern Ireland.

4.– [Initial duty to disclose]¹: further provisions.

(1)   This section applies where –

    (a)   the prosecutor acts under section 3, and

    (b)   before so doing he was given a document in pursuance of provision included, by virtue of section 24(3), in a code operative under Part II.

(2)   In such a case the prosecutor must give the document to the accused at the same time as the prosecutor acts under section 3.

Notes

1   Words substituted by Criminal Justice Act 2003, s 331, Sch 36, paras 20, 22 (4 April 2005 in relation to England and Wales subject to savings specified in SI 2005/950, arts 2, 4, Sch 2, para 2; 15 July 2005 in relation to Northern Ireland subject to savings specified in SI 2005/1817, art 3).

Commencement

Pt I, s 4(1)–(2): 4 July 1996 (1 April 1997 in relation to England and Wales; 1 January 1998 otherwise).

Extent

Pt I, s 4(1)–(2): England, Wales, Northern Ireland.

5.– Compulsory disclosure by accused.

(1)   Subject to subsections [(3A) and]¹ (4) this section applies where –

    (a)   this Part applies by virtue of section 1(2), and

    (b)   the prosecutor complies with section 3 or purports to comply with it.

[(2)   ...

(3)   ...]²

[(3A) Where this Part applies by virtue of section 1(2)(cc), this section does not apply unless–

    (a)   copies of the documents containing the evidence have been served on the accused under regulations made under paragraph 1 of Schedule 3 to the Crime and Disorder Act 1998; and

    (b)   a copy of the notice under [subsection (1) of section 51D]³ of that Act has been served on him under that subsection.]⁴

(4)   Where this part applies by virtue of section 1(2)(e), this section does not apply unless the prosecutor has served on the accused a copy of the indictment and a copy of the set of documents containing the evidence which is the basis of the charge.

(5)   Where this section applies, the accused must give a defence statement to the court and the prosecutor.

[(5A)   Where there are other accused in the proceedings and the court so orders, the accused must also give a defence statement to each other accused specified by the court.

(5B)   The court may make an order under subsection (5A) either of its own motion or on the application of any party.

(5C)   A defence statement that has to be given to the court and the prosecutor (under subsection (5)) must be given during the period which, by virtue of section 12, is the relevant period for this section.

(5D)   A defence statement that has to be given to a co-accused (under subsection (5A)) must be given within such period as the court may specify.]^5

[(6)   ...

(7)   ...

(8)   ...

(9)   ...]^6

Notes

1   Words substituted by Criminal Justice Act 2003, s 41, Sch 3, para 66(1), (3)(a) (18 June 2012 in relation to certain local justice areas specified in SI 2012/1320, art 4(2) and for purposes specified in SI 2012/1320, art 4(3) subject to savings specified in SI 2012/1320, art 5; 5 November 2012 in relation to certain local justice areas specified in SI 2012/2574, art 2(2), Schedule and for purposes specified in SI 2012/2574, art 2(3) subject to saving provisions specified in SI 2012/2574, arts 3, 4; 28 May 2013 in relation to the remaining local justice areas and purposes specified in SI 2013/1103, art 2(3) subject to savings specified in SI 2013/1103, arts 3, 4 otherwise).

2   Repealed by Criminal Justice Act 2003, ss 41, 332, Sch 3, para 66(1), (3)(b), Sch 37, Pt 4 (18 June 2012 in relation to certain local justice areas specified in SI 2012/1320, art 4(2) and for purposes specified in SI 2012/1320, art 4(3) subject to savings specified in SI 2012/1320, art 5; 5 November 2012 in relation to certain local justice areas specified in SI 2012/2574, art 2(2), Schedule and for purposes specified in SI 2012/2574, art 2(3) subject to saving provisions specified in SI 2012/2574, arts 3, 4; 28 May 2013 in relation to the remaining local justice areas and purposes specified in SI 2013/1103, art 2(3) subject to savings specified in SI 2013/1103, arts 3, 4 otherwise).

3   Words substituted by Criminal Justice Act 2003, s 41, Sch 3, para 66(3)(c) (9 May 2005 in relation to cases sent for trial under Crime and Disorder Act 1998, s 51A(3)(d); 18 June 2012 in relation to certain local justice areas specified in SI 2012/1320, art 4(2) and for purposes specified in SI 2012/1320, art 4(3) subject to savings specified in SI 2012/1320, art 5; 5 November 2012 in relation to certain local justice areas specified in SI 2012/2574, art 2(2), Schedule and for purposes specified in SI 2012/2574, art 2(3) subject to saving provisions specified in SI 2012/2574, arts 3, 4; 28 May 2013 in relation to the remaining local justice areas and purposes specified in SI 2013/1103, art 2(3) subject to savings specified in SI 2013/1103, arts 3, 4 otherwise).

4   Inserted by Crime and Disorder Act 1998, s 119, Sch 8, para 126 (4 January 1999 for purposes specified in SI 1998/2327, art 4(2) and Sch 2; 15 January 2001 subject to savings specified in SI 2000/3283, art 3 otherwise).

5   Inserted by Criminal Justice Act 2003, s 33(1) (24 July 2006 in relation to sub-s (5C) subject to transitional provisions specified in SI 2006/1835, art 3; not yet in force otherwise).

6   Repealed by Criminal Justice Act 2003, ss 331, 332, Sch 36, paras 20, 23, Sch 37, Pt 3 (4 April 2005 in relation to England and Wales subject to savings specified in SI 2005/950, arts 2, 4, Sch 2, para 2; 15 July 2005 in relation to Northern Ireland subject to savings specified in SI 2005/1817, art 3).

Commencement

Pt I, s. 5(1)–(9): 4 July 1996 (1 April 1997 in relation to England and Wales; 1 January 1998 otherwise).

Extent

Pt I, s 5(1)–(9): England, Wales, Northern Ireland.

6.– Voluntary disclosure by accused.

(1)   This section applies where –

      (a)   this Part applies by virtue of section 1(1), and

      (b)   the prosecutor complies with section 3 or purports to comply with it.

(2)   The accused –

      (a)   may give a defence statement to the prosecutor, and

      (b)   if he does so, must also give such a statement to the court.

[(3)   ...]¹

(4)   If the accused gives a defence statement under this section he must give it during the period which, by virtue of section 12 is the relevant period for this section.

Notes

1   Repealed by Criminal Justice Act 2003, ss 331, 332, Sch 36, paras 20, 24, Sch 37, Pt 3 (4 April 2005 in relation to England and Wales subject to savings specified in SI 2005/950, arts 2, 4, Sch 2, para 2; 15 July 2005 in relation to Northern Ireland subject to savings specified in SI 2005/1817, art 3).

Commencement

Pt I, s 6(1)–(4): 4 July 1996 (1 April 1997 in relation to England and Wales; 1 January 1998 otherwise).

Extent

Pt I, s 6(1)–(4): England, Wales, Northern Ireland.

[6A.– Contents of defence statement

(1)   For the purposes of this Part a defence statement is a written statement –

      (a)   setting out the nature of the accused's defence, including any particular defences on which he intends to rely,

      (b)   indicating the matters of fact on which he takes issue with the prosecution,

      (c)   setting out, in the case of each such matter, why he takes issue with the prosecution,

      [(ca)   setting out particulars of the matters of fact on which he intends to rely for the purposes of his defence,]¹ and

      (d)   indicating any point of law (including any point as to the admissibility of evidence or an abuse of process) which he wishes

169

to take, and any authority on which he intends to rely for that purpose.

(2)   A defence statement that discloses an alibi must give particulars of it, including –

(a)   the name, address and date of birth of any witness the accused believes is able to give evidence in support of the alibi, or as many of those details as are known to the accused when the statement is given;

(b)   any information in the accused's possession which might be of material assistance in identifying or finding any such witness in whose case any of the details mentioned in paragraph (a) are not known to the accused when the statement is given.

(3)   For the purposes of this section evidence in support of an alibi is evidence tending to show that by reason of the presence of the accused at a particular place or in a particular area at a particular time he was not, or was unlikely to have been, at the place where the offence is alleged to have been committed at the time of its alleged commission.

(4)   The Secretary of State may by regulations make provision as to the details of the matters that, by virtue of subsection (1), are to be included in defence statements.]²

Notes

1   Inserted by Criminal Justice and Immigration Act 2008, s 60(1) (3 November 2008 subject to savings and transitional provisions specified in SI 2008/2712, art 3).

2   Inserted by Criminal Justice Act 2003, s 33(2) (4 April 2005 in relation to England and Wales subject to savings specified in SI 2005/950, arts 2, 4, Sch 2, para 2; 15 July 2005 in relation to Northern Ireland subject to savings specified in SI 2005/1817, art 3).

Extent

Pt I, s 6A(1)–(4): England, Wales, Northern Ireland.

[6B.– Updated disclosure by accused

(1)   Where the accused has, before the beginning of the relevant period for this section, given a defence statement under section 5 or 6, he must during that period give to the court and the prosecutor either –

(a)   a defence statement under this section (an 'updated defence statement'), or

(b)   a statement of the kind mentioned in subsection (4).

(2)   The relevant period for this section is determined under section 12.

(3)   An updated defence statement must comply with the requirements imposed by or under section 6A by reference to the state of affairs at the time when the statement is given.

(4)   Instead of an updated defence statement the accused may give a written statement stating that he has no changes to make to the defence statement which was given under section 5 or 6.

(5)   Where there are other accused in the proceedings and the court so orders, the accused must also give either an updated defence statement or a statement of the kind mentioned in subsection (4), within such period as may be specified by the court, to each other accused so specified.

(6)   The court may make an order under subsection (5) either of its own motion or on the application of any party.][1]

Notes

1   Inserted by Criminal Justice Act 2003, s 33(3) (date to be appointed).

Extent

Pt I, s 68(1)–(6): England, Wales, Northern Ireland.

[6C.– Notification of intention to call defence witnesses

(1)   The accused must give to the court and the prosecutor a notice indicating whether he intends to call any persons (other than himself) as witnesses at his trial and, if so –

(a)   giving the name, address and date of birth of each such proposed witness, or as many of those details as are known to the accused when the notice is given;

(b)   providing any information in the accused's possession which might be of material assistance in identifying or finding any such proposed witness in whose case any of the details mentioned in paragraph (a) are not known to the accused when the notice is given.

(2)   Details do not have to be given under this section to the extent that they have already been given under section 6A(2).

(3)   The accused must give a notice under this section during the period which, by virtue of section 12, is the relevant period for this section.

(4)   If, following the giving of a notice under this section, the accused –

(a)   decides to call a person (other than himself) who is not included in the notice as a proposed witness, or decides not to call a person who is so included, or

(b)   discovers any information which, under subsection (1), he would have had to include in the notice if he had been aware of it when giving the notice,

he must give an appropriately amended notice to the court and the prosecutor.][1]

Notes

1   Inserted by Criminal Justice Act 2003, s 34 (1 May 2010 in relation to England and Wales subject to transitional provisions specified in SI 2010/1183, art 4(2); not yet in force otherwise).

Extent

Pt I, s 6C(1)–(4)(b): England, Wales, Northern Ireland.

[6D.– Notification of names of experts instructed by accused

(1)   If the accused instructs a person with a view to his providing any expert opinion for possible use as evidence at the trial of the accused, he must give to the court and the prosecutor a notice specifying the person's name and address.

(2)   A notice does not have to be given under this section specifying the name and address of a person whose name and address have already been given under section 6C.

(3)   A notice under this section must be given during the period which, by virtue of section 12, is the relevant period for this section.][1]

Notes

1   Inserted by Criminal Justice Act 2003, s 35 (date to be appointed).

Extent

Pt I, s 6D(1)–(3): England, Wales, Northern Ireland.

[6E.– Disclosure by accused: further provisions

(1)   Where an accused's solicitor purports to give on behalf of the accused –

(a)   a defence statement under section 5, 6 or 6B, or

(b)   a statement of the kind mentioned in section 6B(4),

the statement shall, unless the contrary is proved, be deemed to be given with the authority of the accused.

(2)   If it appears to the judge at a pre-trial hearing that an accused has failed to comply fully with section 5, 6B or 6C, so that there is a possibility of comment being made or inferences drawn under section 11(5), he shall warn the accused accordingly.

(3)   In subsection (2) 'pre-trial hearing' has the same meaning as in Part 4 (see section 39).

(4)   The judge in a trial before a judge and jury –

(a)   may direct that the jury be given a copy of any defence statement, and

(b)   if he does so, may direct that it be edited so as not to include references to matters evidence of which would be inadmissible.

(5)   A direction under subsection (4) –

(a)   may be made either of the judge's own motion or on the application of any party;

(b)   may be made only if the judge is of the opinion that seeing a copy of the defence statement would help the jury to understand the case or to resolve any issue in the case.

(6)   The reference in subsection (4) to a defence statement is a reference –

(a)   where the accused has given only an initial defence statement (that is, a defence statement given under section 5 or 6), to that statement;

(b)   where he has given both an initial defence statement and an updated defence statement (that is, a defence statement given under section 6B), to the updated defence statement;

(c)   where he has given both an initial defence statement and a statement of the kind mentioned in section 6B(4), to the initial defence statement.][1]

Notes

1   Inserted by Criminal Justice Act 2003, s 36 (4 April 2005 in relation to England and Wales subject to savings specified in SI 2005/950, arts 2, 4, Sch 2, para 2; 15 July 2005 in relation to Northern Ireland subject to savings specified in SI 2005/1817, art 3).

Extent

Pt I, s 6E(1)–(6)(c): England, Wales, Northern Ireland.

[7.– ...

...][1]

Notes

1   Repealed by Criminal Justice Act 2003, ss 331, 332, Sch 36, paras 20, 25, Sch 37, Pt 3 (4 April 2005 in relation to England and Wales subject to savings specified in SI 2005/950, arts 2, 4, Sch 2, para 2; 15 July 2005 in relation to Northern Ireland subject to savings specified in SI 2005/1817, art 3).

[7A.– Continuing duty of prosecutor to disclose

(1)   This section applies at all times –

    (a)   after the prosecutor has complied with section 3 or purported to comply with it, and

    (b)   before the accused is acquitted or convicted or the prosecutor decides not to proceed with the case concerned.

(2)   The prosecutor must keep under review the question whether at any given time (and, in particular, following the giving of a defence statement) there is prosecution material which –

    (a)   might reasonably be considered capable of undermining the case for the prosecution against the accused or of assisting the case for the accused, and

    (b)   has not been disclosed to the accused.

(3)   If at any time there is any such material as is mentioned in subsection (2) the prosecutor must disclose it to the accused as soon as is reasonably practicable (or within the period mentioned in subsection (5)(a) where that applies).

(4)   In applying subsection (2) by reference to any given time the state of affairs at that time (including the case for the prosecution as it stands at that time) must be taken into account.

(5)   Where the accused gives a defence statement under section 5, 6 or 6B –

    (a)   if as a result of that statement the prosecutor is required by this section to make any disclosure, or further disclosure, he must do so during the period which, by virtue of section 12, is the relevant period for this section;

    (b)   if the prosecutor considers that he is not so required, he must during that period give to the accused a written statement to that effect.

(6)   For the purposes of this section prosecution material is material –

    (a)   which is in the prosecutor's possession and came into his possession in connection with the case for the prosecution against the accused, or

    (b)   which, in pursuance of a code operative under Part 2, he has inspected in connection with the case for the prosecution against the accused.

(7)   Subsections (3) to (5) of section 3 (method by which prosecutor discloses) apply for the purposes of this section as they apply for the purposes of that.

(8)   Material must not be disclosed under this section to the extent that the court, on an application by the prosecutor, concludes it is not in the public interest to disclose it and orders accordingly.

(9)   Material must not be disclosed under this section to the extent that it is material the disclosure of which is prohibited by section 17 of the Regulation of Investigatory Powers Act 2000 (c. 23).][1]

Notes

1   Inserted by Criminal Justice Act 2003, s 37 (4 April 2005 in relation to England and Wales subject to savings specified in SI 2005/950, arts 2, 4, Sch 2, para 2; 15 July 2005 in relation to Northern Ireland subject to savings specified in SI 2005/1817, art 3).

Extent

Pt I, s 7A(1)–(9): England, Wales, Northern Ireland.

8.– Application by accused for disclosure.

[(1)   This section applies where the accused has given a defence statement under section 5, 6 or 6B and the prosecutor has complied with section 7A(5) or has purported to comply with it or has failed to comply with it.

(2)   If the accused has at any time reasonable cause to believe that there is prosecution material which is required by section 7A to be disclosed to him and has not been he may apply to the court for an order requiring the prosecutor to disclose it to him.][1]

(3)   For the purposes of this section prosecution material is material –

    (a)   which is in the prosecutor's possession and came into his possession in connection with the case for the prosecution against the accused,

    (b)   which, in pursuance of a code operative under Part II, he has inspected in connection with the case for the prosecution against the accused, or

    (c)   which falls within subsection (4).

(4)   Material falls within this subsection if in pursuance of a code operative under Part II the prosecutor must, if he asks for the material, be given a copy of it or be allowed to inspect it in connection with the case for the prosecution against the accused.

(5)   Material must not be disclosed under this section to the extent that the court, on an application by the prosecutor, concludes it is not in the public interest to disclose it and orders accordingly.

(6)   Material must not be disclosed under this section to the extent that [it is material the disclosure of which is prohibited by section 17 of the Regulation of Investigatory Powers Act 2000.]²

Notes

1   Substituted by Criminal Justice Act 2003, s 38 (4 April 2005 in relation to England and Wales subject to savings specified in SI 2005/950, arts 2, 4, Sch 2, para 2; 15 July 2005 in relation to Northern Ireland subject to savings specified in SI 2005/1817, art 3).

2   Words substituted by Regulation of Investigatory Powers Act 2000, s 82, Sch 4, para 7(1) (2 October 2000 subject to transitional provisions specified in SI 2000/2543, art 5).

Commencement

Pt I, s 8(1)–(6)(b): 4 July 1996 (1 April 1997 in relation to England and Wales; 1 January 1998 otherwise).

Extent

Pt I, s 8(1)–(6)(b): England, Wales, Northern Ireland.

[9.– ...

...]¹

Notes

1   Repealed by Criminal Justice Act 2003, ss 331, 332, Sch 36, paras 20, 26, Sch 37, Pt 3 (4 April 2005 in relation to England and Wales subject to savings specified in SI 2005/950, arts 2, 4, Sch 2, para 2; 15 July 2005 in relation to Northern Ireland subject to savings specified in SI 2005/1817, art 3).

10.– Prosecutor's failure to observe time limits.

(1)   This section applies if the prosecutor –

(a)   purports to act under section 3 after the end of the period which, by virtue of section 12, is the relevant period for section 3, or

[(b)   purports to act under section 7A(5) after the end of the period which, by virtue of section 12, is the relevant period for section 7A.]¹

(2)   Subject to subsection (3) the failure to act during the period concerned does not on its own constitute grounds for staying the proceedings for abuse of process.

(3)   Subsection (2) does not prevent the failure constituting such grounds if it involves such delay by the prosecutor that the accused is denied a fair trial.

Notes

1   Substituted by Criminal Justice Act 2003, s 331, Sch 36, paras 20, 27 (4 April 2005 in relation to England and Wales subject to savings specified in SI 2005/950, arts 2, 4,

Sch 2, para 2; 15 July 2005 in relation to Northern Ireland subject to savings specified in SI 2005/1817, art 3).

Commencement

Pt I, s 10(1)–(3): 4 July 1996 (1 April 1997 in relation to England and Wales; 1 January 1998 otherwise).

Extent

Pt I, s 10(1)–(3): England, Wales, Northern Ireland.

11.– Faults in disclosure by accused.

The text of this provision varies depending on jurisdiction or other application.

Northern Ireland

[(1)   This section applies in the three cases set out in subsections (2), (3) and (4).

(2)   The first case is where section 5 applies and the accused –

    (a)   fails to give an initial defence statement,

    (b)   gives an initial defence statement but does so after the end of the period which, by virtue of section 12, is the relevant period for section 5,

    (c)   is required by section 6B to give either an updated defence statement or a statement of the kind mentioned in subsection (4) of that section but fails to do so,

    (d)   gives an updated defence statement or a statement of the kind mentioned in section 6B(4) but does so after the end of the period which, by virtue of section 12, is the relevant period for section 6B,

    (e)   sets out inconsistent defences in his defence statement, or

    (f)   at his trial –

        (i)   puts forward a defence which was not mentioned in his defence statement or is different from any defence set out in that statement,

        (ii)   relies on a matter [(or any particular of any matter of fact)] which, in breach of the requirements imposed by or under section 6A, was not mentioned in his defence statement,

        (iii)   adduces evidence in support of an alibi without having given particulars of the alibi in his defence statement, or

        (iv)   calls a witness to give evidence in support of an alibi without having complied with section 6A(2)(a) or (b) as regards the witness in his defence statement.

(3)   The second case is where section 6 applies, the accused gives an initial defence statement, and the accused –

(a)   gives the initial defence statement after the end of the period which, by virtue of section 12, is the relevant period for section 6, or

(b)   does any of the things mentioned in paragraphs (c) to (f) of subsection (2).][1]

(4)   Where the accused puts forward a defence which is different from any defence set out in a defence statement given under section 5 or 6, in doing anything under subsection (3) or in deciding whether to do anything under it the court shall have regard –

(a)   to the extent of the difference in the defences, and

(b)   to whether there is any justification for it.

[(5)   Where this section applies –

(a)   the court or any other party may make such comment as appears appropriate;

(b)   the court or jury may draw such inferences as appear proper in deciding whether the accused is guilty of the offence concerned.

(6)   Where –

(a)   this section applies by virtue of subsection (2)(f)(ii) (including that provision as it applies by virtue of subsection (3)(b)), and

(b)   the matter which was not mentioned is a point of law (including any point as to the admissibility of evidence or an abuse of process) or an authority,

comment by another party under subsection (5)(a) may be made only with the leave of the court.][1]

[(8)   Where the accused puts forward a defence which is different from any defence set out in his defence statement, in doing anything under subsection (5) or in deciding whether to do anything under it the court shall have regard –

(a)   to the extent of the differences in the defences, and

(b)   to whether there is any justification for it.

(9)   Where the accused calls a witness whom he has failed to include, or to identify adequately, in a witness notice, in doing anything under subsection (5) or in deciding whether to do anything under it the court shall have regard to whether there is any justification for the failure.

(10)   A person shall not be convicted of an offence solely on an inference drawn under subsection (5).][1]

[(12) In this section –

   (a) 'initial defence statement' means a defence statement given under section 5 or 6;

   (b) 'updated defence statement' means a defence statement given under section 6B;

   (c) a reference simply to an accused's 'defence statement' is a reference –

      (i) where he has given only an initial defence statement, to that statement;

      (ii) where he has given both an initial and an updated defence statement, to the updated defence statement;

      (iii) where he has given both an initial defence statement and a statement of the kind mentioned in section 6B(4), to the initial defence statement;

   (d) a reference to evidence in support of an alibi shall be construed in accordance with section 6A(3);

   (e) 'witness notice' means a notice given under section 6C.][1]

Notes

1   Substituted by Criminal Justice Act 2003, s 38 (15 July 2005 in relation to Northern Ireland subject to savings specified in SI 2005/1817, art 3).

England and Wales

[(1) This section applies in the three cases set out in subsections (2), (3) and (4).

(2) The first case is where section 5 applies and the accused –

   (a) fails to give an initial defence statement,

   (b) gives an initial defence statement but does so after the end of the period which, by virtue of section 12, is the relevant period for section 5,

   (c) is required by section 6B to give either an updated defence statement or a statement of the kind mentioned in subsection (4) of that section but fails to do so,

   (d) gives an updated defence statement or a statement of the kind mentioned in section 6B(4) but does so after the end of the period which, by virtue of section 12, is the relevant period for section 6B,

   (e) sets out inconsistent defences in his defence statement, or

(f)   at his trial –

   (i)   puts forward a defence which was not mentioned in his defence statement or is different from any defence set out in that statement,

   (ii)   relies on a matter (or any particular of any matter of fact) which, in breach of the requirements imposed by or under section 6A, was not mentioned in his defence statement,

   (iii)   adduces evidence in support of an alibi without having given particulars of the alibi in his defence statement, or

   (iv)   calls a witness to give evidence in support of an alibi without having complied with section 6A(2)(a) or (b) as regards the witness in his defence statement.

(3)   The second case is where section 6 applies, the accused gives an initial defence statement, and the accused –

   (a)   gives the initial defence statement after the end of the period which, by virtue of section 12, is the relevant period for section 6, or

   (b)   does any of the things mentioned in paragraphs (c) to (f) of subsection (2).][1]

[(4)   The third case is where the accused –

   (a)   gives a witness notice but does so after the end of the period which, by virtue of section 12, is the relevant period for section 6C, or

   (b)   at his trial calls a witness (other than himself) not included, or not adequately identified, in a witness notice.][2]

[(5)   Where this section applies –

   (a)   the court or any other party may make such comment as appears appropriate;

   (b)   the court or jury may draw such inferences as appear proper in deciding whether the accused is guilty of the offence concerned.

(6)   Where –

   (a)   this section applies by virtue of subsection (2)(f)(ii) (including that provision as it applies by virtue of subsection (3)(b)), and

   (b)   the matter which was not mentioned is a point of law (including any point as to the admissibility of evidence or an abuse of process) or an authority,

comment by another party under subsection (5)(a) may be made only with the leave of the court.][1]

[(7)   Where this section applies by virtue of subsection (4), comment by another party under subsection (5)(a) may be made only with the leave of the court.]²

[(8)   Where the accused puts forward a defence which is different from any defence set out in his defence statement, in doing anything under subsection (5) or in deciding whether to do anything under it the court shall have regard –

  (a)   to the extent of the differences in the defences, and

  (b)   to whether there is any justification for it.

(9)   Where the accused calls a witness whom he has failed to include, or to identify adequately, in a witness notice, in doing anything under subsection (5) or in deciding whether to do anything under it the court shall have regard to whether there is any justification for the failure.

(10)   A person shall not be convicted of an offence solely on an inference drawn under subsection (5).]

[(12) In this section –

  (a)   'initial defence statement' means a defence statement given under section 5 or 6;

  (b)   'updated defence statement' means a defence statement given under section 6B;

  (c)   a reference simply to an accused's 'defence statement' is a reference –

    (i)   where he has given only an initial defence statement, to that statement;

    (ii)   where he has given both an initial and an updated defence statement, to the updated defence statement;

    (iii)   where he has given both an initial defence statement and a statement of the kind mentioned in section 6B(4), to the initial defence statement;

  (d)   a reference to evidence in support of an alibi shall be construed in accordance with section 6A(3);

  (e)   'witness notice' means a notice given under section 6C.]¹

Notes

1   Substituted by Criminal Justice Act 2003, s 38 (4 April 2005 in relation to England and Wales subject to savings specified in SI 2005/950, arts 2, 4, Sch 2, para 2).

2   Substituted by Criminal Justice Act 2003, s 38 (1 May 2010 in relation to England and Wales subject to transitional provisions specified in SI 2010/1183, art 4(2)).

Commencement

Pt I, s 11(1)–(6): 4 July 1996 (1 April 1997 in relation to England and Wales; 1 January 1998 otherwise).

Extent

Pt I, s. 11(1)–(12)(e): England. Wales, Northern Ireland.

Time limits

12.– Time limits.

(1)   This section has effect for the purpose of determining the relevant period for sections 3, 5, 6[, 6B, 6C and 7A(5)][1].

(2)   Subject to subsection (3), the relevant period is a period beginning and ending with such days as the Secretary of State prescribes by regulations for the purposes of the section concerned.

(3)   The regulations may do one or more of the following –

  (a)   provide that the relevant period for any section shall if the court so orders be extended (or further extended) by so many days as the court specifies;

  (b)   provide that the court may only make such an order if an application is made by a prescribed person and if any other prescribed conditions are fulfilled;

  (c)   provide that an application may only be made if prescribed conditions are fulfilled;

  (d)   provide that the number of days by which a period may be extended shall be entirely at the court's discretion;

  (e)   provide that the number of days by which a period may be extended shall not exceed a prescribed number;

  (f)   provide that there shall be no limit on the number of applications that may be made to extend a period;

  (g)   provide that no more than a prescribed number of applications may be made to extend a period;

and references to the relevant period for a section shall be construed accordingly.

(4)   Conditions mentioned in subsection (3) may be framed by reference to such factors as the Secretary of State thinks fit.

(5)   Without prejudice to the generality of subsection (4), so far as the relevant period for section 3 or [7A(5)][1] is concerned –

(a)   conditions may be framed by reference to the nature or volume of the material concerned;

(b)   the nature of material may be defined by reference to the prosecutor's belief that the question of non-disclosure on grounds of public interest may arise.

(6)   In subsection (3) 'prescribed' means prescribed by regulations under this section.

Notes

1   Substituted by Criminal Justice Act 2003, s 331, Sch 36, paras 20, 28 (4 April 2005 in relation to England and Wales subject to savings specified in SI 2005/950, arts 2, 4, Sch 2, para 2; 15 July 2005 in relation to Northern Ireland subject to savings specified in SI 2005/1817, art 3).

Commencement

Pt I, s 12(1)–(6): 4 July 1996 (1 April 1997 in relation to England and Wales; 1 January 1998 otherwise).

Extent

Pt I, s 12(1)–(6): England, Wales, Northern Ireland.

13.– Time limits: transitional.

(1)   As regards a case in relation to which no regulations under section 12 have come into force for the purposes of section 3, section 3(8) shall have effect as if it read –

'(8) The prosecutor must act under this section as soon as is reasonably practicable after –

[(a)   ...

(b)   ...

(c)   ...]¹

[(ca)   copies of the documents containing the evidence on which the charge or charges are based are served on the accused (where this Part applies by virtue of section 1(2)(cc)),]²

(d)   the count is included in the indictment (where this Part applies by virtue of section 1(2)(d)), or

(e)   the bill of indictment is preferred (where this Part applies by virtue of [section 1(2)(e) or (f)]³).'

[(2)   As regards a case in relation to which no regulations under section 12 have come into force for the purposes of section 7A, section 7A(5) shall have effect as if –

(a)   in paragraph (a) for the words from 'during the period' to the end, and

(b)   in paragraph (b) for 'during that period',

there were substituted 'as soon as is reasonably practicable after the accused gives the statement in question'.][4]

Notes

1   Repealed by Criminal Justice Act 2003, ss 41, 332, Sch 3, para 66(1), (4), Sch 37, Pt 4 (18 June 2012 in relation to certain local justice areas specified in SI 2012/1320, art 4(2) and for purposes specified in SI 2012/1320, art 4(3) subject to savings specified in SI 2012/1320, art 5; 5 November 2012 in relation to certain local justice areas specified in SI 2012/2574, art 2(2), Schedule and for purposes specified in SI 2012/2574, art 2(3) subject to saving provisions specified in SI 2012/2574, arts 3, 4; 28 May 2013 in relation to the remaining local justice areas and purposes specified in SI 2013/1103, art 2(3) subject to savings specified in SI 2013/1103, arts 3, 4 otherwise).

2   Inserted by Access to Justice Act 1999, s 67(2) (27 September 1999 in relation to petty sessions areas specified in SI 1999/2657, Sch 1; 8 January 2001 otherwise).

3   Words inserted by Crime and Disorder Act 1998, s 119, Sch 8, para 127(b) (1 June 1999).

4   Substituted by Criminal Justice Act 2003, s 331, Sch 36, paras 20, 29 (4 April 2005 in relation to England and Wales subject to savings specified in SI 2005/950, arts 2, 4, Sch 2, para 2; 15 July 2005 in relation to Northern Ireland subject to savings specified in SI 2005/1817, art 3).

Commencement

Pt I, s 13(1)–(2): 4 July 1996 (1 April 1997 in relation to England and Wales; 1 January 1998 otherwise).

Extent

Pt I, s 13(1)–(2)(b): England, Wales, Northern Ireland.

Public interest

14.– Public interest: review for summary trials.

(1)   This section applies where this Part applies by virtue of section 1(1).

(2)   At any time –

(a)   after a court makes an order under section 3(6), [7A(8) or 8(5)][1] and

(b)   before the accused is acquitted or convicted or the prosecutor decides not to proceed with the case concerned,

the accused may apply to the court for a review of the question whether it is still not in the public interest to disclose material affected by its order.

(3)   In such a case the court must review that question, and if it concludes that it is in the public interest to disclose material to any extent –

    (a)   it shall so order, and

    (b)   it shall take such steps as are reasonable to inform the prosecutor of its order.

(4)   Where the prosecutor is informed of an order made under subsection (3) he must act accordingly having regard to the provisions of this Part (unless he decides not to proceed with the case concerned).

Notes

1   Words substituted by Criminal Justice Act 2003, s 331, Sch 36, paras 20, 30 (4 April 2005 in relation to England and Wales subject to savings specified in SI 2005/950, arts 2, 4, Sch 2, para 2; 15 July 2005 in relation to Northern Ireland subject to savings specified in SI 2005/1817, art 3).

Commencement

Pt I, s 14(1)–(4): 4 July 1996 (1 April 1997 in relation to England and Wales; 1 January 1998 otherwise).

Extent

Pt I, s 14(1)–(4): England, Wales. Northern Ireland.

15.– Public interest: review in other cases.

(1)   This section applies where this Part applies by virtue of section 1(2).

(2)   This section applies at all times –

    (a)   after a court makes an order under section 3(6), [7A(8) or 8(5)][1], and

    (b)   before the accused is acquitted or convicted or the prosecutor decides not to proceed with the case concerned.

(3)   The court must keep under review the question whether at any given time it is still not in the public interest to disclose material affected by its order.

(4)   The court must keep the question mentioned in subsection (3) under review without the need for an application; but the accused may apply to the court for a review of that question.

(5)   If the court at any time concludes that it is in the public interest to disclose material to any extent –

    (a)   it shall so order, and

    (b)   it shall take such steps as are reasonable to inform the prosecutor of its order.

(6)   Where the prosecutor is informed of an order made under subsection (5) he must act accordingly having regard to the provisions of this Part (unless he decides not to proceed with the case concerned).

Notes

1   Words substituted by Criminal Justice Act 2003, s 331, Sch 36, paras 20, 31 (4 April 2005 in relation to England and Wales subject to savings specified in SI 2005/950, arts 2, 4, Sch 2, para 2; 15 July 2005 in relation to Northern Ireland subject to savings specified in SI 2005/1817, art 3).

Commencement

Pt I, s 15(1)–(6): 4 July 1996 (1 April 1997 in relation to England and Wales; 1 January 1998 otherwise).

Extent

Pt I, s 15(1)–(6): England, Wales, Northern Ireland.

16.– Applications: opportunity to be heard.

Where –

(a)   an application is made under section 3(6), [7A(8), 8(5)]^1, 14(2) or 15(4),

(b)   a person claiming to have an interest in the material applies to be heard by the court, and

(c)   he shows that he was involved (whether alone or with others and whether directly or indirectly) in the prosecutor's attention being brought to the material,

the court must not make an order under section 3(6), [7A(8), 8(5)]^1, 14(3) or 15(5) (as the case may be) unless the person applying under paragraph (b) has been given an opportunity to be heard.

Notes

1   Words substituted by Criminal Justice Act 2003, s 331, Sch 36, paras 20, 32 (4 April 2005 in relation to England and Wales subject to savings specified in SI 2005/950, arts 2, 4, Sch 2, para 2; 15 July 2005 in relation to Northern Ireland subject to savings specified in SI 2005/1817, art 3).

Commencement

Pt I, s 16(a)–(c): 4 July 1996 (1 April 1997 in relation to England and Wales; 1 January 1998 otherwise).

Extent

Pt I, s 16(a)–(c): England, Wales, Northern Ireland.

Confidentiality

17.– Confidentiality of disclosed information.

(1)   If the accused is given or allowed to inspect a document or other object under –

(a)   section 3, 4, [7A]¹, 14 or 15, or

(b)   an order under section 8,

then, subject to subsections (2) to (4), he must not use or disclose it or any information recorded in it.

(2)   The accused may use or disclose the object or information –

(a)   in connection with the proceedings for whose purposes he was given the object or allowed to inspect it,

(b)   with a view to the taking of further criminal proceedings (for instance, by way of appeal) with regard to the matter giving rise to the proceedings mentioned in paragraph (a), or

(c)   in connection with the proceedings first mentioned in paragraph (b).

(3)   The accused may use or disclose –

(a)   the object to the extent that it has been displayed to the public in open court, or

(b)   the information to the extent that it has been communicated to the public in open court;

but the preceding provisions of this subsection do not apply if the object is displayed or the information is communicated in proceedings to deal with a contempt of court under section 18.

(4)   If –

(a)   the accused applies to the court for an order granting permission to use or disclose the object or information, and

(b)   the court makes such an order,

the accused may use or disclose the object or information for the purpose and to the extent specified by the court.

(5)   An application under subsection (4) may be made and dealt with at any time, and in particular after the accused has been acquitted or convicted or the prosecutor has decided not to proceed with the case concerned: but this is subject to rules made by virtue of section 19(2).

(6)   Where –

   (a)   an application is made under subsection (4), and

   (b)   the prosecutor or a person claiming to have an interest in the object or information applies to be heard by the court,

the court must not make an order granting permission unless the person applying under paragraph (b) has been given an opportunity to be heard.

(7)   References in this section to the court are to –

   (a)   a magistrates' court, where this Part applies by virtue of section 1(1);

   (b)   the Crown Court, where this Part applies by virtue of section 1(2).

(8)   Nothing in this section affects any other restriction or prohibition on the use or disclosure of an object or information, whether the restriction or prohibition arises under an enactment (whenever passed) or otherwise.

Notes

1   Words substituted by Criminal Justice Act 2003, s 331, Sch 36, paras 20, 33 (4 April 2005 in relation to England and Wales subject to savings specified in SI 2005/950, arts 2, 4, Sch 2, para 2; 15 July 2005 in relation to Northern Ireland subject to savings specified in SI 2005/1817, art 3).

Commencement

Pt I, s 17(1)–(8): 4 July 1996 (1 April 1997 in relation to England and Wales; 1 January 1998 otherwise).

Extent

Pt I, s 17(1)–(8): England, Wales, Northern Ireland.

18.– Confidentiality: contravention.

(1)   It is a contempt of court for a person knowingly to use or disclose an object or information recorded in it if the use or disclosure is in contravention of section 17.

(2)   The following courts have jurisdiction to deal with a person who is guilty of a contempt under this section –

   (a)   a magistrates' court, where this Part applies by virtue of section 1(1),

   (b)   the Crown Court, where this Part applies by virtue of section 1(2).

(3)   A person who is guilty of a contempt under this section may be dealt with as follows –

   (a)   a magistrates' court may commit him to custody for a specified period not exceeding six months or impose on him a fine not exceeding £5,000 or both;

(b)   the Crown Court may commit him to custody for a specified period not exceeding two years or impose a fine on him or both.

(4)   If –

(a)   a person is guilty of a contempt under this section, and

(b)   the object concerned is in his possession,

the court finding him guilty may order that the object shall be forfeited and dealt with in such manner as the court may order.

(5)   The power of the court under subsection (4) includes power to order the object to be destroyed or to be given to the prosecutor or to be placed in his custody for such period as the court may specify.

(6)   If –

(a)   the court proposes to make an order under subsection (4), and

(b)   the person found guilty, or any other person claiming to have an interest in the object, applies to be heard by the court,

the court must not make the order unless the applicant has been given an opportunity to be heard.

(7)   If –

(a)   a person is guilty of a contempt under this section and

(b)   a copy of the object concerned is in his possession,

the court finding him guilty may order that the copy shall be forfeited and dealt with in such manner as the court may order.

(8)   Subsections (5) and (6) apply for the purposes of subsection (7) as they apply for the purposes of subsection (4), but as if references to the object were references to the copy.

(9)   An object or information shall be inadmissible as evidence in civil proceedings if to adduce it would in the opinion of the court be likely to constitute a contempt under this section and 'the court' here means the court before which the civil proceedings are being taken.

(10)   The powers of a magistrates' court under this section may be exercised either of the court's own motion or by order on complaint.

Commencement

Pt I, s 18(1)–(10): 4 July 1996 (1 April 1997 in relation to England and Wales; 1 January 1998 otherwise).

Extent

Pt I, s 18(1)–(10): England, Wales, Northern Ireland.

Other provisions

19.– Rules of court.

(1)   [The power to make Criminal Procedure Rules][1] includes power to make provision mentioned in subsection (2).

(2)   The provision is provision as to the practice and procedure to be followed in relation to –

> (a)   proceedings to deal with a contempt of court under section 18;
>
> (b)   an application under section 3(6), [5(5B), 6B(6), 6E(5), 7A(8), 8(2) or (5)][2], 14(2), 15(4), 16(b), 17(4), or (6)(b) or 18(6);
>
> (c)   an application under regulations made under section 12;
>
> (d)   an order under section 3(6), [5(5B), 6B(6), 6E(5), 7A(8), 8(2) or (5)][2], 14(3), 17(4) or 18(4) or (7);
>
> (e)   an order under section 15(5) (whether or not an application is made under section 15(4);
>
> (f)   an order under regulations made under section 12.

(3)   [Criminal Procedure Rules made][3] by virtue of subsection (2)(a) above may contain or include provision equivalent to Schedule 3 to the Contempt of Court Act 1981 (proceedings for disobeying magistrates' court order) [or such provision with modifications][3].

(4)   Rules made by virtue of subsection (2)(b) in relation to an application under section 17(4) may include provision –

> (a)   that an application to a magistrates' court must be made to a particular magistrates' court;
>
> (b)   that an application to the Crown Court must be made to the Crown Court sitting at a particular place;
>
> (c)   requiring persons to be notified of an application.

(5)   Rules made by virtue of this section may make different provision for different cases or classes of case.

Notes

1   Words substituted by Courts Act 2003, s 109(1), Sch 8, para 377 (1 September 2004 subject to saving specified in SI 2004/2066, art 3).

2   Substituted by Criminal Justice Act 2003, s 331, Sch 36, paras 20, 34 (4 April 2005 in relation to England and Wales subject to savings specified in SI 2005/950, arts 2, 4, Sch 2, para 2; 15 July 2005 in relation to Northern Ireland subject to savings specified in SI 2005/1817, art 3).

3 Words substituted by Constitutional Reform Act 2005, s 15(1), Sch 4, para 251 (3 April 2006).

Commencement

Pt I, s 19(1)–(5): 4 July 1996 (1 April 1997 in relation to England and Wales; 1 January 1998 otherwise).

Extent

Pt I, s 19(1)–(5): England, Wales, Northern Ireland.

20.– Other statutory rules as to disclosure.

(1) A duty under any of the disclosure provisions shall not affect or be affected by any duty arising under any other enactment with regard to material to be provided to or by the accused or a person representing him; but this is subject to subsection (2).

[(2) ...]¹

(3) [The power to make Criminal Procedure Rules]² includes power to make, with regard to any proceedings before a magistrates' court which relate to an alleged offence, provision for –

>   (a) requiring any party to the proceedings to disclose to the other party or parties any expert evidence which he proposes to adduce in the proceedings;

>   (b) prohibiting a party who fails to comply in respect of any evidence with any requirement imposed by virtue of paragraph (a) from adducing that evidence without the leave of the court.

(4) Rules made by virtue of subsection (3) –

>   (a) may specify the kinds of expert evidence to which they apply;

>   (b) may exempt facts or matters of any description specified in the rules.

(5) For the purposes of this section –

>   (a) the disclosure provisions are [sections 3 to 8]³;

>   (b) 'enactment'' includes an enactment comprised in subordinate legislation (which here has the same meaning as in the Interpretation Act 1978).

Notes

1 Repealed by Criminal Justice Act 2003, ss 331, 332, Sch 36, paras 20, 35(a), Sch 37, Pt 3 (4 April 2005 in relation to England and Wales subject to savings specified in SI 2005/950, arts 2, 4, Sch 2, para 2; 15 July 2005 in relation to Northern Ireland subject to savings specified in SI 2005/1817, art 3).

2   Words substituted by Courts Act 2003, s 109(1), Sch 8, para 378 (1 September 2004 subject
         to saving specified in SI 2004/2066, art 3).

3   Words substituted by Criminal Justice Act 2003, s 331, Sch 36, paras 20, 35(b) (4 April 2005
         in relation to England and Wales subject to savings specified in SI 2005/950, arts 2, 4,
         Sch 2, para 2; 15 July 2005 in relation to Northern Ireland subject to savings specified in SI
         2005/1817, art 3).

Commencement

Pt I, s 20(1)–(5)(b): 4 July 1996 (1 April 1997 in relation to England and Wales; 1 January 1998
otherwise).

Extent

Pt I, s 20(1)–(5)(b): England, Wales, Northern Ireland.

21.– Common law rules as to disclosure.

(1)   Where this Part applies as regards things falling to be done after the
relevant time in relation to an alleged offence, the rules of common law which –

    (a)   were effective immediately before the appointed day, and

    (b)   relate to the disclosure of material by the prosecutor,

do not apply as regards things falling to be done after that time in relation to the
alleged offence.

(2)   Subsection (1) does not affect the rules of common law as to whether
disclosure is in the public interest.

(3)   References in subsection (1) to the relevant time are to the time when –

    (a)   the accused pleads not guilty (where this Part applies by virtue of
        section 1(1)),

    [(b)   the accused is sent for trial (where this Part applies by virtue of
        section 1(2)(cc)),][1]

    (d)   the count is included in the indictment (where this Part applies by
        virtue of section 1(2)(d), or

    (e)   the bill of indictment is preferred (where this Part applies by virtue
        of section 1(2)(e)).

(4)   The reference in subsection (1) to the appointed day is to the day appointed
under section 1(5).

Notes

1   Substituted for s 21(3)(b) and (c) by Criminal Justice Act 2003, s 41, Sch 3, para 66(1),
         (5) (18 June 2012 in relation to certain local justice areas specified in SI 2012/1320, art
         4(2) and for purposes specified in SI 2012/1320, art 4(3) subject to savings specified in
         SI 2012/1320, art 5; 5 November 2012 in relation to certain local justice areas specified
         in SI 2012/2574, art 2(2), Schedule and for purposes specified in SI 2012/2574, art 2(3)

subject to saving provisions specified in SI 2012/2574, arts 3, 4; 28 May 2013 in relation to the remaining local justice areas and purposes specified in SI 2013/1103, art 2(3) subject to savings specified in SI 2013/1103, arts 3, 4 otherwise).

Commencement

Pt I, s 21(1)–(4): 4 July 1996 (1 April 1997 in relation to England and Wales; 1 January 1998 otherwise).

Extent

Pt I, s 21(1)–(4): England, Wales, Northern Ireland.

[21A.– Code of practice for police interviews of witnesses notified by accused.

(1)   The Secretary of State shall prepare a code of practice which gives guidance to police officers, and other persons charged with the duty of investigating offences, in relation to the arranging and conducting of interviews of persons –

(a)   particulars of whom are given in a defence statement in accordance with section 6A(2), or

(b)   who are included as proposed witnesses in a notice given under section 6C.

(2)   The code must include (in particular) guidance in relation to –

(a)   information that should be provided to the interviewee and the accused in relation to such an interview;

(b)   the notification of the accused's solicitor of such an interview;

(c)   the attendance of the interviewee's solicitor at such an interview;

(d)   the attendance of the accused's solicitor at such an interview;

(e)   the attendance of any other appropriate person at such an interview taking into account the interviewee's age or any disability of the interviewee.

(3)   Any police officer or other person charged with the duty of investigating offences who arranges or conducts such an interview shall have regard to the code.

(4)   In preparing the code, the Secretary of State shall consult –

[(za)   [the National Police Chiefs' Council]¹;]²

(a)   to the extent the code applies to England and Wales –

(i)   [...]³

(ii)   the General Council of the Bar;

          (iii)   the Law Society of England and Wales;

          (iv)   the Institute of Legal Executives;

  (b)   to the extent the code applies to Northern Ireland –

          (i)   the Chief Constable of the Police Service of Northern Ireland;

          (ii)   the General Council of the Bar of Northern Ireland;

          (iii)   the Law Society of Northern Ireland;

  (c)   such other persons as he thinks fit.

(5)   The code shall not come into operation until the Secretary of State by order so provides.

(6)   The Secretary of State may from time to time revise the code and subsections (4) and (5) shall apply to a revised code as they apply to the code as first prepared.

(7)   An order bringing the code into operation may not be made unless a draft of the order has been laid before each House of Parliament and approved by a resolution of each House.

(8)   An order bringing a revised code into operation shall be laid before each House of Parliament if the order has been made without a draft having been so laid and approved by a resolution of each House.

(9)   When an order or a draft of an order is laid in accordance with subsection (7) or (8), the code to which it relates shall also be laid.

(10)   No order or draft of an order may be laid until the consultation required by subsection (4) has taken place.

(11)   A failure by a person mentioned in subsection (3) to have regard to any provision of a code for the time being in operation by virtue of an order under this section shall not in itself render him liable to any criminal or civil proceedings.

(12)   In all criminal and civil proceedings a code in operation at any time by virtue of an order under this section shall be admissible in evidence.

(13)   If it appears to a court or tribunal conducting criminal or civil proceedings that –

  (a)   any provision of a code in operation at any time by virtue of an order under this section, or

  (b)   any failure mentioned in subsection (11),

is relevant to any question arising in the proceedings, the provision or failure shall be taken into account in deciding the question.][4]

Notes

1   Repealed by Police and Justice Act 2006, ss 6(1), 52, Sch 4, para 9(b), Sch 15, Pt 1(B) (1 April 2007).

2   Inserted by Police and Justice Act 2006, s 6(1), Sch 4, para 9(a) (1 April 2007).

3   Words substituted by Policing and Crime Act 2017, s 51, Sch 14, paras 4, 5 (3 April 2017).

4   Inserted by Criminal Justice Act 2003, s 40 (5 April 2004 in relation to England and Wales).

Extent

Pt I, s 21A(1)–(13)(b): England, Wales, Northern Ireland.

PART II CRIMINAL INVESTIGATIONS

22.– Introduction.

(1)   For the purposes of this Part a criminal investigation is an investigation conducted by police officers with a view to it being ascertained –

     (a)   whether a person should be charged with an offence, or

     (b)   whether a person charged with an offence is guilty of it.

(2)   In this Part references to material are to material of all kinds, and in particular include references to –

     (a)   information, and

     (b)   objects of all descriptions.

(3)   In this Part references to recording information are to putting it in a durable or retrievable form (such as writing or tape).

Commencement

Pt II, s 22(1)–(3): 4 July 1996.

Extent

Pt II, s 22(1)–(3); England, Wales, Northern Ireland.

23.– Code of practice.

(1)   The Secretary of State shall prepare a code of practice containing provisions designed to secure –

     (a)   that where a criminal investigation is conducted all reasonable steps are taken for the purposes of the investigation and, in particular, all reasonable lines of inquiry are pursued;

     (b)   that information which is obtained in the course of a criminal investigation and may be relevant to the investigation is recorded;

(c)   that any record of such information is retained;

(d)   that any other material which is obtained in the course of a criminal investigation and may be relevant to the investigation is retained;

(e)   that information falling within paragraph (b) and material falling within paragraph (d) is revealed to a person who is involved in the prosecution of criminal proceedings arising out of or relating to the investigation and who is identified in accordance with prescribed provisions;

(f)   that where such a person inspects information or other material in pursuance of a requirement that it be revealed to him, and he requests that it be disclosed to the accused, the accused is allowed to inspect it or is given a copy of it;

(g)   that where such a person is given a document indicating the nature of information or other material in pursuance of a requirement that it be revealed to him, and he requests that it be disclosed to the accused, the accused is allowed to inspect it or is given a copy of it;

(h)   that the person who is to allow the accused to inspect information or other material or to give him a copy of it shall decide which of those (inspecting or giving a copy) is appropriate;

(i)   that where the accused is allowed to inspect material as mentioned in paragraph (f) or (g) and he requests a copy, he is given one unless the person allowing the inspection is of opinion that it is not practicable or not desirable to give him one;

(j)   that a person mentioned in paragraph (e) is given a written statement that prescribed activities which the code requires have been carried out.

(2)   The code may include provision –

(a)   that a police officer identified in accordance with prescribed provisions must carry out a prescribed activity which the code requires;

(b)   that a police officer so identified must take steps to secure the carrying out by a person (whether or not a police officer) of a prescribed activity which the code requires;

(c)   that a duty must be discharged by different people in succession in prescribed circumstances (as where a person dies or retires).

(3)   The code may include provision about the form in which information is to be recorded.

(4)   The code may include provision about the manner in which and the period for which –

 (a)   a record of information is to be retained, and

 (b)   any other material is to be retained;

and if a person is charged with an offence the period may extend beyond a conviction or an acquittal.

(5)   The code may include provision about the time when, the form in which, the way in which, and the extent to which, information or any other material is to be revealed to the person mentioned in subsection (1)(c).

(6)   The code must be so framed that it does not apply to material intercepted in obedience to a warrant issued under section 2 of the Interception of Communications Act 1985 [or under the authority of an interception warrant under section 5 of the Regulation of Investigatory Powers Act 2000.][1]

(7)   The code may –

 (a)   make different provision in relation to different cases or descriptions of case;

 (b)   contain exceptions as regards prescribed cases or descriptions of case.

(8)   In this section 'prescribed' means prescribed by the code.

Notes

1 Words inserted by Regulation of Investigatory Powers Act 2000, s 82, Sch 4, para 7(2) (2 October 2000 subject to transitional provisions specified in SI 2000/2543, art 5).

Commencement

Pt II, s 23(1)–(8): 4 July 1996.

Extent

Pt II, s 23(1)–(8); England, Wales, Northern Ireland.

24.– Examples of disclosure provisions.

(1)   This section gives examples of the kinds of provision that may be included in the code by virtue of section 23(5).

(2)   The code may provide that if the person required to reveal material has possession of material which he believes is sensitive he must give a document which –

 (a)   indicates the nature of that material, and

 (b)   states that he so believes.

(3)   The code may provide that if the person required to reveal material has possession of material which is of a description prescribed under this subsection and which he does not believe is sensitive he must give a document which –

(a)   indicates the nature of that material, and

(b)   states that he does not so believe.

(4)   The code may provide that if –

(a)   a document is given in pursuance of provision contained in the code by virtue of subsection (2), and

(b)   a person identified in accordance with prescribed provisions asks for any of the material,

the person giving the document must give a copy of the material asked for to the person asking for it or (depending on the circumstances) must allow him to inspect it.

(5)   The code may provide that if –

(a)   a document is given in pursuance of provision contained in the code by virtue of subsection (3),

(b)   all or any of the material is of a description prescribed under this subsection, and

(c)   a person is identified in accordance with prescribed provisions as entitled to material of that description,

the person giving the document must give a copy of the material of that description to the person so identified or (depending on the circumstances) must allow him to inspect it.

(6)   The code may provide that if –

(a)   a document is given in pursuance of provision contained in the code by virtue of subsection (3),

(b)   all or any of the material is not of a description prescribed under subsection (5), and

(c)   a person identified in accordance with prescribed provisions asks for any of the material not of that description,

the person giving the document must give a copy of the material asked for to the person asking for it or (depending on the circumstances) must allow him to inspect it.

(7)   The code may provide that if the person required to reveal material has possession of material which he believes is sensitive and of such a nature that

provision contained in the code by virtue of subsection (2) should not apply with regard to it –

    (a)   that provision shall not apply with regard to the material,

    (b)   he must notify a person identified in accordance with prescribed provisions of the existence of the material, and

    (c)   he must allow the person so notified to inspect the material.

(8)   For the purposes of this section material is sensitive to the extent that its disclosure under Part I would be contrary to the public interest.

(9)   In this section 'prescribed' means prescribed by the code.

Commencement

Pt II, s 24(1)–(9): 4 July 1996.

Extent

Pt II, s 24(1)–(9): England, Wales, Northern Ireland.

25.– Operation and revision of code.

(1)   When the Secretary of State has prepared a code under section 23 –

    (a)   he shall publish it in the form of a draft,

    (b)   he shall consider any representations made to him about the draft, and

    (c)   he may modify the draft accordingly.

(2)   When the Secretary of State has acted under subsection (1) he shall lay the code before each House of Parliament, and when he has done so he may bring it into operation on such day as he may appoint by order.

(3)   A code brought into operation under this section shall apply in relation to suspected or alleged offences into which no criminal investigation has begun before the day so appointed.

(4)   The Secretary of State may from time to time revise a code previously brought into operation under this section; and the preceding provisions of this section shall apply to a revised code as they apply to the code as first prepared.

Commencement

Pt II, s 25(1)–(4): 4 July 1996.

Extent

Pt II, s 25(1)–(4): England, Wales, Northern Ireland.

26.– Effect of code.

(1)   A person other than a police officer who is charged with the duty of conducting an investigation with a view to it being ascertained –

    (a)   whether a person should be charged with an offence, or

    (b)   whether a person charged with an offence is guilty of it,

shall in discharging that duty have regard to any relevant provision of a code which would apply if the investigation were conducted by police officers.

(2)   A failure –

    (a)   by a police officer to comply with any provision of a code for the time being in operation by virtue of an order under section 25, or

    (b)   by a person to comply with subsection (1),

shall not in itself render him liable to any criminal or civil proceedings.

(3)   In all criminal and civil proceedings a code in operation at any time by virtue of an order under section 25 shall be admissible in evidence.

(4)   If it appears to a court or tribunal conducting criminal or civil proceedings that –

    (a)   any provision of a code in operation at any time by virtue of an order under section 25, or

    (b)   any failure mentioned in subsection (2)(a) or (b),

is relevant to any question arising in the proceedings, the provision or failure shall be taken into account in deciding the question.

Commencement

Pt II, s 26(1)–(4)(b): 4 July 1996.

Extent

Pt II, s 26(1)–(4)(b): England, Wales, Northern Ireland.

27.– Common law rules as to criminal investigations.

(1)   Where a code prepared under section 23 and brought into operation under section 25 applies in relation to a suspected or alleged offence, the rules of common law which –

    (a)   were effective immediately before the appointed day, and

    (b)   relate to the matter mentioned in subsection (2),

shall not apply in relation to the suspected or alleged offence.

(2)   The matter is the revealing of material –

(a)   by a police officer or other person charged with the duty of conducting an investigation with a view to it being ascertained whether a person should be charged with an offence or whether a person charged with an offence is guilty of it;

(b)   to a person involved in the prosecution of criminal proceedings.

(3)   In subsection (1) 'the appointed day' means the day appointed under section 25 with regard to the code as first prepared.

Commencement

Pt II, s 27(1)–(3): 4 July 1996.

Extent

Pt II, s 27(1)–(3): England, Wales, Northern Ireland.

Criminal Procedure and Investigations Act 1996 (section 23(1)) Code of Practice

Revised in accordance with section 25(4) of the Criminal Procedure and Investigations Act 1996

March 2015

CONTENTS

Criminal Procedure and Investigations Act 1996 Code of Practice under Part II

PREAMBLE

This code of practice is issued under Part II of the Criminal Procedure and Investigations Act 1996 ('the Act'). It sets out the manner in which police officers are to record, retain and reveal to the prosecutor material obtained in a criminal investigation and which may be relevant to the investigation, and related matters.

1.   INTRODUCTION

1.1   This code of practice applies in respect of criminal investigations conducted by police officers which begin on or after the day on which this code comes into effect. Persons other than police officers who are charged with the duty of conducting an investigation as defined in the Act are to have regard to the relevant provisions of the code, and should take these into account in applying their own operating procedures.

1.2   This code does not apply to persons who are not charged with the duty of conducting an investigation as defined in the Act.

1.3   Nothing in this code applies to material intercepted in obedience to a warrant issued under section 2 of the Interception of Communications Act 1985 or section 5 of the Regulation of Investigatory Powers Act 2000, or to any copy of that material as defined in section 10 of the 1985 Act or section 15 of the 2000 Act.

1.4   This code extends only to England and Wales.

2.   DEFINITIONS

2.1   In this code:

*   *a criminal investigation* is an investigation conducted by police officers with a view to it being ascertained whether a person should be charged with an offence, or whether a person charged with an offence is guilty of it. This will include:

    *   investigations into crimes that have been committed;

- • investigations whose purpose is to ascertain whether a crime has been committed, with a view to the possible institution of criminal proceedings; and

- • investigations which begin in the belief that a crime may be committed, for example when the police keep premises or individuals under observation for a period of time, with a view to the possible institution of criminal proceedings;

- charging a person with an offence includes prosecution by way of summons or postal requisition;

- *an investigator* is any police officer involved in the conduct of a criminal investigation. All investigators have a responsibility for carrying out the duties imposed on them under this code, including in particular recording information, and retaining records of information and other material;

- the *officer in charge of an investigation* is the police officer responsible for directing a criminal investigation. He is also responsible for ensuring that proper procedures are in place for recording information, and retaining records of information and other material, in the investigation;

- the *disclosure officer* is the person responsible for examining material retained by the police during the investigation; revealing material to the prosecutor during the investigation and any criminal proceedings resulting from it, and certifying that he has done this; and disclosing material to the accused at the request of the prosecutor;

- the *prosecutor* is the authority responsible for the conduct, on behalf of the Crown, of criminal proceedings resulting from a specific criminal investigation;

- *material* is material of any kind, including information and objects, which is obtained or inspected in the course of a criminal investigation and which may be relevant to the investigation. This includes not only material coming into the possession of the investigator (such as documents seized in the course of searching premises) but also material generated by him (such as interview records);

- material may be *relevant to an investigation* if it appears to an investigator, or to the officer in charge of an investigation, or to the disclosure officer, that it has some bearing on any offence under investigation or any person being investigated, or on the surrounding circumstances of the case, unless it is incapable of having any impact on the case;

- *sensitive material* is material, the disclosure of which, the disclosure officer believes, would give rise to a real risk of serious prejudice to an important public interest;

- references to *prosecution disclosure* are to the duty of the prosecutor under sections 3 and 7A of the Act to disclose material which is in his possession or which he has inspected in pursuance of this code, and which might reasonably be considered capable of undermining the case against the accused, or of assisting the case for the accused;

- references to the disclosure of material to a person accused of an offence include references to the disclosure of material to his legal representative;

- references to police officers and to the chief officer of police include those employed in a police force as defined in section 3(3) of the Prosecution of Offences Act 1985.

3.   GENERAL RESPONSIBILITIES

3.1   The functions of the investigator, the officer in charge of an investigation and the disclosure officer are separate. Whether they are undertaken by one, two or more persons will depend on the complexity of the case and the administrative arrangements within each police force. Where they are undertaken by more than one person, close consultation between them is essential to the effective performance of the duties imposed by this code.

3.2   In any criminal investigation, one or more deputy disclosure officers may be appointed to assist the disclosure officer, and a deputy disclosure officer may perform any function of a disclosure officer as defined in paragraph 2.1.

3.3   The chief officer of police for each police force is responsible for putting in place arrangements to ensure that in every investigation the identity of the officer in charge of an investigation and the disclosure officer is recorded. The chief officer of police for each police force shall ensure that disclosure officers and deputy disclosure officers have sufficient skills and authority, commensurate with the complexity of the investigation, to discharge their functions effectively. An individual must not be appointed as disclosure officer, or continue in that role, if that is likely to result in a conflict of interest, for instance, if the disclosure officer is the victim of the alleged crime which is the subject of the investigation. The advice of a more senior officer must always be sought if there is doubt as to whether a conflict of interest precludes an individual acting as disclosure officer. If thereafter the doubt remains, the advice of a prosecutor should be sought.

3.4   The officer in charge of an investigation may delegate tasks to another investigator, to civilians employed by the police force, or to other persons participating in the investigation under arrangements for joint investigations, but he remains responsible for ensuring that these have been carried out and for accounting for any general policies followed in the investigation. In particular, it is an essential part of his duties to ensure that all material which may be relevant to an investigation is retained, and either made available to the disclosure officer or (in exceptional circumstances) revealed directly to the prosecutor.

3.5   In conducting an investigation, the investigator should pursue all reasonable lines of inquiry, whether these point towards or away from the suspect. What is reasonable in each case will depend on the particular circumstances. For example, where material is held on computer, it is a matter for the investigator to decide which material on the computer it is reasonable to inquire into, and in what manner.

3.6   If the officer in charge of an investigation believes that other persons may be in possession of material that may be relevant to the investigation, and if this has not been obtained under paragraph 3.5 above, he should ask the disclosure officer to inform them of the existence of the investigation and to invite them to retain the material in case they receive a request for its disclosure. The disclosure officer should inform the prosecutor that they may have such material. However, the officer in charge of an investigation is not required to make speculative enquiries of other persons; there must be some reason to believe that they may have relevant material. That reason may come from information provided to the police by the accused or from other inquiries made or from some other source.

3.7   If, during a criminal investigation, the officer in charge of an investigation or disclosure officer for any reason no longer has responsibility for the functions falling to him, either his supervisor or the police officer in charge of criminal investigations for the police force concerned must assign someone else to assume that responsibility. That person's identity must be recorded, as with those initially responsible for these functions in each investigation.

4.   RECORDING OF INFORMATION

4.1   If material which may be relevant to the investigation consists of information which is not recorded in any form, the officer in charge of an investigation must ensure that it is recorded in a durable or retrievable form (whether in writing, on video or audio tape, or on computer disk).

4.2   Where it is not practicable to retain the initial record of information because it forms part of a larger record which is to be destroyed, its contents should be transferred as a true record to a durable and more easily-stored form before that happens.

4.3   Negative information is often relevant to an investigation. If it may be relevant it must be recorded. An example might be a number of people present in a particular place at a particular time who state that they saw nothing unusual.

4.4   Where information which may be relevant is obtained, it must be recorded at the time it is obtained or as soon as practicable after that time. This includes, for example, information obtained in house-to-house enquiries, although the requirement to record information promptly does not require an investigator to take a statement from a potential witness where it would not otherwise be taken.

5.   RETENTION OF MATERIAL

(a)   Duty to retain material

5.1   The investigator must retain material obtained in a criminal investigation which may be relevant to the investigation. Material may be photographed, video-recorded, captured digitally or otherwise retained in the form of a copy rather than the original at any time, if the original is perishable; the original was supplied to the investigator rather than generated by him and is to be returned to its owner; or the retention of a copy rather than the original is reasonable in all the circumstances.

5.2   Where material has been seized in the exercise of the powers of seizure conferred by the Police and Criminal Evidence Act 1984, the duty to retain it under this code is subject to the provisions on the retention of seized material in section 22 of that Act.

5.3   If the officer in charge of an investigation becomes aware as a result of developments in the case that material previously examined but not retained (because it was not thought to be relevant) may now be relevant to the investigation, he should, wherever practicable, take steps to obtain it or ensure that it is retained for further inspection or for production in court if required.

5.4   The duty to retain material includes in particular the duty to retain material falling into the following categories, where it may be relevant to the investigation:

   •   crime reports (including crime report forms, relevant parts of incident report books or police officers' notebooks);

   •   custody records;

- records which are derived from tapes of telephone messages (for example, 999 calls) containing descriptions of an alleged offence or offender;

- final versions of witness statements (and draft versions where their content differs from the final version), including any exhibits mentioned (unless these have been returned to their owner on the understanding that they will be produced in court if required);

- interview records (written records, or audio or video tapes, of interviews with actual or potential witnesses or suspects);

- communications between the police and experts such as forensic scientists, reports of work carried out by experts, and schedules of scientific material prepared by the expert for the investigator, for the purposes of criminal proceedings;

- records of the first description of a suspect by each potential witness who purports to identify or describe the suspect, whether or not the description differs from that of subsequent descriptions by that or other witnesses;

- any material casting doubt on the reliability of a witness.

5.5   The duty to retain material, where it may be relevant to the investigation, also includes in particular the duty to retain material which may satisfy the test for prosecution disclosure in the Act, such as:

- information provided by an accused person which indicates an explanation for the offence with which he has been charged;

- any material casting doubt on the reliability of a confession;

- any material casting doubt on the reliability of a prosecution witness.

5.6   The duty to retain material falling into these categories does not extend to items which are purely ancillary to such material and possess no independent significance (for example, duplicate copies of records or reports).

(b) Length of time for which material is to be retained

5.7   All material which may be relevant to the investigation must be retained until a decision is taken whether to institute proceedings against a person for an offence.

5.8   If a criminal investigation results in proceedings being instituted, all material which may be relevant must be retained at least until the accused is acquitted or convicted or the prosecutor decides not to proceed with the case.

5.9   Where the accused is convicted, all material which may be relevant must be retained at least until:

- the convicted person is released from custody, or discharged from hospital, in cases where the court imposes a custodial sentence or a hospital order;

- six months from the date of conviction, in all other cases.

If the court imposes a custodial sentence or hospital order and the convicted person is released from custody or discharged from hospital earlier than six months from the date of conviction, all material which may be relevant must be retained at least until six months from the date of conviction.

5.10   If an appeal against conviction is in progress when the release or discharge occurs, or at the end of the period of six months specified in paragraph 5.9, all material which may be relevant must be retained until the appeal is determined. Similarly, if the Criminal Cases Review Commission is considering an application at that point in time, all material which may be relevant must be retained at least until the Commission decides not to refer the case to the Court.

6.   PREPARATION OF MATERIAL FOR PROSECUTOR

(a)   *Introduction*

6.1   The officer in charge of the investigation, the disclosure officer or an investigator may seek advice from the prosecutor about whether any particular item of material may be relevant to the investigation.

6.2   Material which may be relevant to an investigation, which has been retained in accordance with this code, and which the disclosure officer believes will not form part of the prosecution case, must be listed on a schedule. This process will differ depending on whether the case is likely to be heard in the magistrates' court or the Crown Court.

(b)   *Magistrates' Court*

Anticipated Guilty pleas

6.3   If the accused is charged with a summary offence or an either-way offence that is likely to remain in the magistrates' court, and it is considered that he is likely to plead guilty (e.g. because he has admitted the offence), a schedule or streamlined disclosure certificate is not required.

However, the Common Law duty to disclose material which may assist the defence at bail hearings or in the early preparation of their case remains, and where there is such material the certification on the Police Report (MG5/SDF) must be completed. Where there is no such material, a certificate to that effect must be completed in like form to that attached at the Annex.

6.4   If, contrary to the expectation of a guilty plea being entered, the accused pleads not guilty at the first hearing, the disclosure officer must ensure that the streamlined disclosure certificate is prepared and submitted as soon as is reasonably practicable after that happens.

Anticipated Not Guilty pleas

6.5   If the accused is charged with a summary offence or an either-way offence that is likely to remain in the magistrates' court, and it is considered that he is likely to plead not guilty, a streamlined disclosure certificate must be completed in like form to that attached at the Annex.

Material which may assist the defence

6.6   In every case, irrespective of the anticipated plea, if there is material known to the disclosure officer that might assist the defence with the early preparation of their case or at a bail hearing (for example, a key prosecution witness has relevant previous convictions or a witness has withdrawn his or her statement), a note must be made on the MG5 (or other format agreed under the National File Standards). The material must be disclosed to the prosecutor who will disclose it to the defence if he thinks it meets this Common Law test.

No undermining or assisting material and sensitive material – magistrates' court cases

6.7   If there is no material which might fall to be disclosed as undermining the prosecution case or assisting the defence, the officer should complete the appropriate entry on the streamlined disclosure certificate. If there is any sensitive unused material the officer should complete a sensitive material schedule (MG6D or similar) and attach it to the prosecution file. In exceptional circumstances, when its existence is so sensitive that it cannot be listed, it should be revealed to the prosecutor separately.

(c) *Crown Court*

6.8 For cases to be held in the Crown Court, the unused material schedules (MG6 series) are used.

6.9 The disclosure officer must ensure that a schedule is prepared in the following circumstances:

- the accused is charged with an offence which is triable only on indictment;

- the accused is charged with an offence which is triable either way, and it is considered that the case is likely to be tried on indictment.

6.10 Material which the disclosure officer does not believe is sensitive must be listed on a schedule of non-sensitive material. The schedule must include a statement that the disclosure officer does not believe the material is sensitive.

Way in which material is to be listed on schedule

6.11 For indictable only cases or either-way cases sent to the Crown Court, schedules MG6 C, D and E should be completed to facilitate service of the MG6C with the prosecution case, wherever possible. The disclosure officer should ensure that each item of material is listed separately on the schedule, and is numbered consecutively. The description of each item should make clear the nature of the item and should contain sufficient detail to enable the prosecutor to decide whether he needs to inspect the material before deciding whether or not it should be disclosed.

6.12 In some enquiries it may not be practicable to list each item of material separately. For example, there may be many items of a similar or repetitive nature. These may be listed in a block and described by quantity and generic title.

6.13 Even if some material is listed in a block, the disclosure officer must ensure that any items among that material which might satisfy the test for prosecution disclosure are listed and described individually.

(d) *Sensitive material – Crown Court*

6.14 Any material which is believed to be sensitive either must be listed on a schedule of sensitive material or, in exceptional circumstances where its existence is so sensitive that it cannot be listed, it should be revealed to the prosecutor separately. If there is no sensitive material, the disclosure officer must record this fact on a schedule of sensitive material, or otherwise so indicate.

6.15 Subject to paragraph 6.16 below, the disclosure officer must list on a sensitive schedule any material the disclosure of which he believes would give rise to a real risk of serious prejudice to an important public interest, and the reason for that belief. The schedule must include a statement that the disclosure officer believes the material is sensitive. Depending on the circumstances, examples of such material may include the following among others:

- material relating to national security;

- material received from the intelligence and security agencies;

- material relating to intelligence from foreign sources which reveals sensitive intelligence gathering methods;

- material given in confidence;

- material relating to the identity or activities of informants, or undercover police officers, or witnesses, or other persons supplying information to the police who may be in danger if their identities are revealed;

- material revealing the location of any premises or other place used for police surveillance, or the identity of any person allowing a police officer to use them for surveillance;

- material revealing, either directly or indirectly, techniques and methods relied upon by a police officer in the course of a criminal investigation, for example covert surveillance techniques, or other methods of detecting crime;

- material whose disclosure might facilitate the commission of other offences or hinder the prevention and detection of crime;

- material upon the strength of which search warrants were obtained;

- material containing details of persons taking part in identification parades;

- material supplied to an investigator during a criminal investigation which has been generated by an official of a body concerned with the regulation or supervision of bodies corporate or of persons engaged in financial activities, or which has been generated by a person retained by such a body;

- material supplied to an investigator during a criminal investigation which relates to a child or young person and which has been

213

generated by a local authority social services department, an Area Child Protection Committee or other party contacted by an investigator during the investigation;

- material relating to the private life of a witness.

6.16   In exceptional circumstances, where an investigator considers that material is so sensitive that its revelation to the prosecutor by means of an entry on the sensitive schedule is inappropriate, the existence of the material must be revealed to the prosecutor separately. This will apply only where compromising the material would be likely to lead directly to the loss of life, or directly threaten national security.

6.17   In such circumstances, the responsibility for informing the prosecutor lies with the investigator who knows the detail of the sensitive material. The investigator should act as soon as is reasonably practicable after the file containing the prosecution case is sent to the prosecutor. The investigator must also ensure that the prosecutor is able to inspect the material so that he can assess whether it is disclosable and, if so, whether it needs to be brought before a court for a ruling on disclosure.

7.   REVELATION OF MATERIAL TO PROSECUTOR

7.1   Certain unused material must be disclosed to the accused at Common Law if it would assist the defence with the early preparation of their case or at a bail hearing. This material may consist of items such as a previous relevant conviction of a key prosecution witness or the withdrawal of support for the prosecution by a witness. This material must be revealed to the prosecutor for service on the defence with the initial details of the prosecution case.

7.1A   In anticipated not guilty plea cases for hearing in the magistrates' court the disclosure officer must give the streamlined disclosure certificate to the prosecutor at the same time as he gives the prosecutor the file containing the material for the prosecution case.

7.1B   In cases sent to the Crown Court, wherever possible, the disclosure officer should give the schedules concerning unused material to the prosecutor at the same time as the prosecution file in preparation for the first hearing and any case management that the judge may wish to conduct at that stage.

7.2   The disclosure officer should draw the attention of the prosecutor to any material an investigator has retained (including material to which paragraph 6.16 applies) which may satisfy the test for prosecution disclosure in the Act, and should explain why he has come to that view.

7.3   At the same time as complying with the duties in paragraphs 7.1 and 7.2, the disclosure officer must give the prosecutor a copy of any material which falls into the following categories (unless such material has already been given to the prosecutor as part of the file containing the material for the prosecution case):

- information provided by an accused person which indicates an explanation for the offence with which he has been charged;

- any material casting doubt on the reliability of a confession;

- any material casting doubt on the reliability of a prosecution witness;

- any other material which the investigator believes may satisfy the test for prosecution disclosure in the Act.

7.4   If the prosecutor asks to inspect material which has not already been copied to him, the disclosure officer must allow him to inspect it. If the prosecutor asks for a copy of material which has not already been copied to him, the disclosure officer must give him a copy. However, this does not apply where the disclosure officer believes, having consulted the officer in charge of the investigation, that the material is too sensitive to be copied and can only be inspected.

7.5   If material consists of information which is recorded other than in writing, whether it should be given to the prosecutor in its original form as a whole, or by way of relevant extracts recorded in the same form, or in the form of a transcript, is a matter for agreement between the disclosure officer and the prosecutor.

8.   SUBSEQUENT ACTION BY DISCLOSURE OFFICER

8.1   At the time when a streamlined disclosure certificate is prepared for magistrates' court cases, or a schedule of non-sensitive material is prepared for Crown Court cases, the disclosure officer may not know exactly what material will form the case against the accused. In addition, the prosecutor may not have given advice about the likely relevance of particular items of material. Once these matters have been determined, the disclosure officer must give the prosecutor, where necessary, an amended certificate or schedule listing any additional material:

- which may be relevant to the investigation,

- which does not form part of the case against the accused,

- which is not already listed on the schedule, and

- which he believes is not sensitive,

unless he is informed in writing by the prosecutor that the prosecutor intends to disclose the material to the defence.

8.2 Section 7A of the Act imposes a continuing duty on the prosecutor, for the duration of criminal proceedings against the accused, to disclose material which satisfies the test for disclosure (subject to public interest considerations). To enable him to do this, any new material coming to light should be treated in the same way as the earlier material.

8.3 In particular, after a defence statement has been given, or details of the issues in dispute have been recorded on the effective trial preparation form, the disclosure officer must look again at the material which has been retained and must draw the attention of the prosecutor to any material which might reasonably be considered capable of undermining the case for the prosecution against the accused or of assisting the case for the accused; and he must reveal it to him in accordance with paragraphs 7.4 and 7.5 above.

9. CERTIFICATION BY DISCLOSURE OFFICER

9.1 The disclosure officer must certify to the prosecutor that, to the best of his knowledge and belief, all relevant material which has been retained and made available to him has been revealed to the prosecutor in accordance with this code. He must sign and date the certificate. It will be necessary to certify not only at the time when the schedule and accompanying material is submitted to the prosecutor, and when relevant material which has been retained is reconsidered after the accused has given a defence statement, but also whenever a schedule is otherwise given or material is otherwise revealed to the prosecutor.

10. DISCLOSURE OF MATERIAL TO ACCUSED

10.1 Other than early disclosure under Common Law, in the magistrates' court the streamlined certificate at the Annex (and any relevant unused material to be disclosed under it) must be disclosed to the accused either:

- at the hearing where a not guilty plea is entered, or

- as soon as possible following a formal indication from the accused or representative that a not guilty plea will be entered at the hearing.

10.1A   If material has not already been copied to the prosecutor, and he requests its disclosure to the accused on the ground that:

- it satisfies the test for prosecution disclosure, **or**

- the court has ordered its disclosure after considering an application from the accused,

the disclosure officer must disclose it to the accused.

10.2   If material has been copied to the prosecutor, and it is to be disclosed, whether it is disclosed by the prosecutor or the disclosure officer is a matter of agreement between the two of them.

10.3   The disclosure officer must disclose material to the accused either by giving him a copy or by allowing him to inspect it. If the accused person asks for a copy of any material which he has been allowed to inspect, the disclosure officer must give it to him, unless in the opinion of the disclosure officer that is either not practicable (for example because the material consists of an object which cannot be copied, or because the volume of material is so great), or not desirable (for example because the material is a statement by a child witness in relation to a sexual offence).

10.4   If material which the accused has been allowed to inspect consists of information which is recorded other than in writing, whether it should be given to the accused in its original form or in the form of a transcript is a matter for the discretion of the disclosure officer. If the material is transcribed, the disclosure officer must ensure that the transcript is certified to the accused as a true record of the material which has been transcribed.

10.5   If a court concludes that an item of sensitive material satisfies the prosecution disclosure test and that the interests of the defence outweigh the public interest in withholding disclosure, it will be necessary to disclose the material if the case is to proceed. This does not mean that sensitive documents must always be disclosed in their original form: for example, the court may agree that sensitive details still requiring protection should be blocked out, or that documents may be summarised, or that the prosecutor may make an admission about the substance of the material under section 10 of the Criminal Justice Act 1967.

ANNEX

1.   FOR USE IN GAP CASES AT 1ST HEARING WHERE THERE IS NOTHING TO DISCLOSE PURSUANT TO R v DPP *ex parte* LEE

URN: Defendant: First Name Last Name

Reporting Officer's Certification
In accordance with Common Law I certify that to the best of my knowledge and belief there is no relevant unused material that might reasonably assist the defence with the early preparation of their case or at a bail hearing.
Reporting Officer Name
SIGNATURE
Date

2. FOR USE IN ALL NGAP CASES AT 1ST HEARING WHERE THERE IS NOTHING TO DISCLOSE

URN: Defendant: First Name Last Name

	SCHEDULE OF NON-SENSITIVE UNUSED MATERIAL – NOT FOR DISCLOSURE	
No.	Police use (Brief description of materials)	CPS use
1		Having applied the disclosure tests set out in the CPIA 1996, I am satisfied from the descriptions listed in this schedule that the items in question are clearly not disclosable.
2		
3		
4		
5		
6		
7		
8		
9		
10		
Disclosure Officer's Certification I certify – • that any relevant unused material has been recorded and retained in accordance with the CPIA 1996 Code of Practice (as amended), • that such material as is non-sensitive is shown on the schedule above, • and that to the best of my knowledge and belief there are no items shown in the schedule that might reasonably undermine the prosecution case, or, so far as it is apparent, assist the defence with the early preparation of their case or at a bail hearing. Disclosure Officer Name SIGNATURE:		CPS Prosecutor Name SIGNATURE:
Date		Date

3.   FOR USE IN ALL NGAP CASES AT 1ST HEARING WHERE THERE ARE SOME ITEMS TO DISCLOSE

URN: Defendant: First Name Last Name

	SCHEDULE OF NON-SENSITIVE UNUSED MATERIAL	
No.	**Police use**	**CPS use**
	(Brief description of materials including those falling under para.7.3 of the Code)	(Against each item insert **D** for disclose; **I** for inspect; **CND** for clearly not disclosable)
1		
2		
3		
4		
5		
6		
7		
8		
9		
10		

DISCLOSURE OFFICER'S CERTIFICATION

I certify –

- that any relevant unused material has been recorded and retained in accordance with the CPIA 1996 Code of Practice (as amended)

- that such material as is non-sensitive is shown on the schedule above,

- and that to the best of my knowledge and belief items ...

- in the schedule might reasonably undermine the prosecution case, or assist the defence with the early preparation of their case or at a bail hearing, because ....

Disclosure Officer Name   CPS Prosecutor Name

SIGNATURE: SIGNATURE:

Date   Date

Criminal Procedure Rules (CrimPR), Parts 1–4

Part 1
The Overriding Objective

Contents of this Part

The overriding objective

1.1.—(1) The overriding objective of this procedural code is that criminal cases be dealt with justly.

(2) Dealing with a criminal case justly includes—

    (a) acquitting the innocent and convicting the guilty;

    (b) dealing with the prosecution and the defence fairly;

    (c) recognising the rights of a defendant, particularly those under Article 6 of the European Convention on Human Rights;

    (d) respecting the interests of witnesses, victims and jurors and keeping them informed of the progress of the case;

    (e) dealing with the case efficiently and expeditiously;

    (f) ensuring that appropriate information is available to the court when bail and sentence are considered; and

    (g) dealing with the case in ways that take into account—

        (i) the gravity of the offence alleged,

        (ii) the complexity of what is in issue,

(iii)   the severity of the consequences for the defendant and others affected, and

(iv)   the needs of other cases.

The duty of the participants in a criminal case

1.2.—(1)   Each participant, in the conduct of each case, must—

(a)   prepare and conduct the case in accordance with the overriding objective;

(b)   comply with these Rules, practice directions and directions made by the court; and

(c)   at once inform the court and all parties of any significant failure (whether or not that participant is responsible for that failure) to take any procedural step required by these Rules, any practice direction or any direction of the court. A failure is significant if it might hinder the court in furthering the overriding objective.

(2)   Anyone involved in any way with a criminal case is a participant in its conduct for the purposes of this rule.

The application by the court of the overriding objective

1.3.—The court must further the overriding objective in particular when—

(a)   exercising any power given to it by legislation (including these Rules);

(b)   applying any practice direction; or

(c)   interpreting any rule or practice direction.

Part 2
Understanding and Applying the Rules

Contents of this Part

When the Rules apply

2.1.—(1)   In general, Criminal Procedure Rules apply—

(a)   in all criminal cases in magistrates' courts and in the Crown Court;

(b) in extradition cases in the High Court; and

(c) in all cases in the criminal division of the Court of Appeal.

(2) If a rule applies only in one or some of those courts, the rule makes that clear.

(3) These Rules apply on and after 5th October, 2015, but—

(a) unless the court otherwise directs, they do not affect a right or duty existing under the Criminal Procedure Rules 2014; and

(b) unless the High Court otherwise directs, Section 3 of Part 50 (Extradition – appeal to the High Court) does not apply to a case in which notice of an appeal was given before 6th October, 2014.

(4) In a case in which a request for extradition was received by a relevant authority in the United Kingdom on or before 31st December, 2003—

(a) the rules in Part 50 (Extradition) do not apply; and

(b) the rules in Part 17 of the Criminal Procedure Rules 2012 (Extradition) continue to apply as if those rules had not been revoked.

[Note. The rules replaced by the first Criminal Procedure Rules (the Criminal Procedure Rules 2005) were revoked when those Rules came into force by provisions of the Courts Act 2003, the Courts Act 2003 (Consequential Amendments) Order 2004 and the Courts Act 2003 (Commencement No. 6 and Savings) Order 2004. The first Criminal Procedure Rules reproduced the substance of all the rules they replaced.

The rules in Part 17 of the Criminal Procedure Rules 2012 applied to extradition proceedings under the Backing of Warrants (Republic of Ireland) Act 1965 or under the Extradition Act 1989. By section 218 of the Extradition Act 2003, the 1965 and 1989 Acts ceased to have effect when the 2003 Act came into force. By article 2 of the Extradition Act 2003 (Commencement and Savings) Order 2003, the 2003 Act came into force on 1st January, 2004. However, article 3 of that Order provided that the coming into force of the Act did not apply for the purposes of any request for extradition, whether made under any of the provisions of the Extradition Act 1989 or of the Backing of Warrants (Republic of Ireland) Act 1965 or otherwise, which was received by the relevant authority in the United Kingdom on or before 31st December, 2003.]

Definitions

2.2.—(1) In these Rules, unless the context makes it clear that something different is meant:

'advocate' means a person who is entitled to exercise a right of audience in the court under section 13 of the Legal Services Act 2007;

'business day' means any day except Saturday, Sunday, Christmas Day, Boxing Day, Good Friday, Easter Monday or a bank holiday;

'court' means a tribunal with jurisdiction over criminal cases. It includes a judge, recorder, District Judge (Magistrates' Court), lay justice and, when exercising their judicial powers, the Registrar of Criminal Appeals, a justices' clerk or assistant clerk;

'court officer' means the appropriate member of the staff of a court;

'justices' legal adviser' means a justices' clerk or an assistant to a justices' clerk;

'legal representative' means:

(i)   the person for the time being named as a party's representative in any legal aid representation order made under section 16 of the Legal Aid, Sentencing and Punishment of Offenders Act 2012, or

(ii) subject to that, the person named as a party's representative in any notice for the time being given under rule 46.2 (Notice of appointment or change of legal representative), provided that person is entitled to conduct litigation in the court under section 13 of the Legal Services Act 2007;

'live link' means an arrangement by which a person can see and hear, and be seen and heard by, the court when that person is not in the courtroom;

'Practice Direction' means the Lord Chief Justice's Criminal Practice Directions, as amended, and 'Criminal Costs Practice Direction' means the Lord Chief Justice's Practice Direction (Costs in Criminal Proceedings), as amended;

'public interest ruling' means a ruling about whether it is in the public interest to disclose prosecution material under sections 3(6), 7A(8) or 8(5) of the Criminal Procedure and Investigations Act 1996; and

'Registrar' means the Registrar of Criminal Appeals or a court officer acting with the Registrar's authority.

(2)   Definitions of some other expressions are in the rules in which they apply.

[Note. The glossary at the end of the Rules is a guide to the meaning of certain legal expressions used in them.]

References to legislation, including these Rules

2.3.—(1)   In these Rules, where a rule refers to an Act of Parliament or to subordinate legislation by title and year, subsequent references to that Act or to that legislation in the rule are shortened: so, for example, after a reference to the Criminal Procedure and Investigations Act 1996 that Act is called 'the 1996 Act'; and after a reference to the Criminal Procedure and Investigations Act 1996 (Defence Disclosure Time Limits) Regulations 2011 those Regulations are called 'the 2011 Regulations'.

(2)   In the courts to which these Rules apply—

(a)   unless the context makes it clear that something different is meant, a reference to the Criminal Procedure Rules, without reference to a year, is a reference to the Criminal Procedure Rules in force at the date on which the event concerned occurs or occurred;

(b)   a reference to the Criminal Procedure Rules may be abbreviated to 'CrimPR'; and

(c)   a reference to a Part or rule in the Criminal Procedure Rules may be abbreviated to, for example, 'CrimPR Part 3' or 'CrimPR 3.5'.

Part 3

Case Management

Contents of this Part

General rules

Preparation for trial in the Crown Court

General Rules

When this Part applies

3.1.—(1)   Rules 3.1 to 3.12 apply to the management of each case in a magistrates' court and in the Crown Court (including an appeal to the Crown Court) until the conclusion of that case.

(2)   Rules 3.13 to 3.26 apply where—

(a)   the defendant is sent to the Crown Court for trial;

(b)   a High Court or Crown Court judge gives permission to serve a draft indictment; or

(c)   the Court of Appeal orders a retrial.

[Note. Rules that apply to procedure in the Court of Appeal are in Parts 36 to 42 of these Rules.

A magistrates' court may send a defendant for trial in the Crown Court under section 51 or 51A of the Crime and Disorder Act 1998. See Part 9 for the procedure on allocation and sending for trial.

Under paragraph 2(1) of Schedule 17 to the Crime and Courts Act 2013 and section 2 of the Administration of Justice (Miscellaneous Provisions) Act 1933, the Crown Court may give permission to serve a draft indictment where it approves a deferred prosecution agreement. See Part 11 for the rules about that procedure and Part 10 for the rules about indictments.

The procedure for applying for the permission of a High Court judge to serve a draft indictment is in rules 6 to 10 of the Indictments (Procedure) Rules 1971. See also the Practice Direction.

The Court of Appeal may order a retrial under section 8 of the Criminal Appeal Act 1968 (on a defendant's appeal against conviction) or under section 77 of the Criminal Justice Act 2003 (on a prosecutor's application for the retrial of a serious offence after acquittal). Section 8 of the 1968 Act, section 84 of the 2003 Act and rules 27.6 and 39.14 require the arraignment of a defendant within 2 months.]

The duty of the court

3.2.—(1)   The court must further the overriding objective by actively managing the case.

(2)   Active case management includes—

(a)   the early identification of the real issues;

(b)   the early identification of the needs of witnesses;

(c)   achieving certainty as to what must be done, by whom, and when, in particular by the early setting of a timetable for the progress of the case;

(d)   monitoring the progress of the case and compliance with directions;

(e)   ensuring that evidence, whether disputed or not, is presented in the shortest and clearest way;

(f)   discouraging delay, dealing with as many aspects of the case as possible on the same occasion, and avoiding unnecessary hearings;

(g)   encouraging the participants to co-operate in the progression of the case; and

(h)   making use of technology.

(3)   The court must actively manage the case by giving any direction appropriate to the needs of that case as early as possible.

(4)   Where appropriate live links are available, making use of technology for the purposes of this rule includes directing the use of such facilities, whether an application for such a direction is made or not—

(a)   for the conduct of a pre-trial hearing, including a pre-trial case management hearing;

(b)   for the defendant's attendance at such a hearing—

(i)   where the defendant is in custody, or where the defendant is not in custody and wants to attend by live link, but

(ii)   only if the court is satisfied that the defendant can participate effectively by such means, having regard to all the circumstances including whether the defendant is represented or not; and

(c)   for receiving evidence under one of the powers to which the rules in Part 18 apply (Measures to assist a witness or defendant to give evidence).

(5)   Where appropriate telephone facilities are available, making use of technology for the purposes of this rule includes directing the use of such facilities, whether an application for such a direction is made or not, for the conduct of a pre-trial case management hearing—

(a)   if telephone facilities are more convenient for that purpose than live links;

(b)   unless at that hearing the court expects to take the defendant's plea; and

(c)   only if—

   (i)   the defendant is represented, or

   (ii)   exceptionally, the court is satisfied that the defendant can participate effectively by such means without a representative.

[Note. In relation to the defendant's attendance by live link at a pre-trial hearing, see sections 46ZA and 47 of the Police and Criminal Evidence Act 1984 and sections 57A to 57D and 57F of the Crime and Disorder Act 1998.

In relation to the giving of evidence by a witness and the giving of evidence by the defendant, see section 32 of the Criminal Justice Act 1988, sections 19, 24 and 33A of the Youth Justice and Criminal Evidence Act 1999 and section 51 of the Criminal Justice Act 2003. Part 18 (Measures to assist a witness or defendant to give evidence) contains relevant rules.]

The duty of the parties

3.3.—(1)   Each party must—

   (a)   actively assist the court in fulfilling its duty under rule 3.2, without or if necessary with a direction; and

   (b)   apply for a direction if needed to further the overriding objective.

(2)   Active assistance for the purposes of this rule includes—

   (a)   at the beginning of the case, communication between the prosecutor and the defendant at the first available opportunity and in any event no later than the beginning of the day of the first hearing;

   (b)   after that, communication between the parties and with the court officer until the conclusion of the case;

   (c)   by such communication establishing, among other things—

      (i)   whether the defendant is likely to plead guilty or not guilty,

      (ii)   what is agreed and what is likely to be disputed,

      (iii)   what information, or other material, is required by one party of another, and why, and

      (iv)   what is to be done, by whom, and when (without or if necessary with a direction);

   (d)   reporting on that communication to the court—

      (i)   at the first hearing, and

      (ii)   after that, as directed by the court; and

   (e)   alerting the court to any reason why—

(i)   a direction should not be made in any of the circumstances listed in rule 3.2(4) or (5) (The duty of the court: use of live link or telephone facilities), or

(ii)   such a direction should be varied or revoked.

Case progression officers and their duties

3.4.—(1)   At the beginning of the case each party must, unless the court otherwise directs—

(a)   nominate someone responsible for progressing that case; and

(b)   tell other parties and the court who that is and how to contact that person.

(2)   In fulfilling its duty under rule 3.2, the court must where appropriate—

(a)   nominate a court officer responsible for progressing the case; and

(b)   make sure the parties know who that is and how to contact that court officer.

(3)   In this Part a person nominated under this rule is called a case progression officer.

(4)   A case progression officer must—

(a)   monitor compliance with directions;

(b)   make sure that the court is kept informed of events that may affect the progress of that case;

(c)   make sure that he or she can be contacted promptly about the case during ordinary business hours;

(d)   act promptly and reasonably in response to communications about the case; and

(e)   if he or she will be unavailable, appoint a substitute to fulfil his or her duties and inform the other case progression officers.

The court's case management powers

3.5.—(1)   In fulfilling its duty under rule 3.2 the court may give any direction and take any step actively to manage a case unless that direction or step would be inconsistent with legislation, including these Rules.

(2)   In particular, the court may—

(a)   nominate a judge, magistrate or justices' legal adviser to manage the case;

(b)   give a direction on its own initiative or on application by a party;

(c)   ask or allow a party to propose a direction;

(d)   receive applications, notices, representations and information by letter, by telephone, by live link, by email or by any other means of electronic communication, and conduct a hearing by live link, telephone or other such electronic means;

(e)   give a direction—

   (i)   at a hearing, in public or in private, or

   (ii)   without a hearing;

(f)   fix, postpone, bring forward, extend, cancel or adjourn a hearing;

(g)   shorten or extend (even after it has expired) a time limit fixed by a direction;

(h)   require that issues in the case should be—

   (i)   identified in writing,

   (ii)   determined separately, and decide in what order they will be determined; and

(i)   specify the consequences of failing to comply with a direction.

(3)   A magistrates' court may give a direction that will apply in the Crown Court if the case is to continue there.

(4)   The Crown Court may give a direction that will apply in a magistrates' court if the case is to continue there.

(5)   Any power to give a direction under this Part includes a power to vary or revoke that direction.

(6)   If a party fails to comply with a rule or a direction, the court may—

(a)   fix, postpone, bring forward, extend, cancel or adjourn a hearing;

(b)   exercise its powers to make a costs order; and

(c)   impose such other sanction as may be appropriate.

[Note. Depending upon the nature of a case and the stage that it has reached, its progress may be affected by other Criminal Procedure Rules and by other legislation. The note at the end of this Part lists other rules and legislation that may apply.

See also rule 3.9 (Case preparation and progression).

The court may make a costs order under—

   (a)   section 19 of the Prosecution of Offences Act 1985, where the court decides that one party to criminal proceedings has incurred costs as a result of an unnecessary or improper act or omission by, or on behalf of, another party;

(b)   *section 19A of that Act, where the court decides that a party has incurred costs as a result of an improper, unreasonable or negligent act or omission on the part of a legal representative;*

(c)   *section 19B of that Act, where the court decides that there has been serious misconduct by a person who is not a party.*

Under some other legislation, including Parts 19, 20 and 21 of these Rules, if a party fails to comply with a rule or a direction then in some circumstances—

(a)   *the court may refuse to allow that party to introduce evidence;*

(b)   *evidence that that party wants to introduce may not be admissible;*

(c)   *the court may draw adverse inferences from the late introduction of an issue or evidence.*

See also—

(a)   *section 81(1) of the Police and Criminal Evidence Act 1984 and section 20(3) of the Criminal Procedure and Investigations Act 1996 (advance disclosure of expert evidence);*

(b)   *section 11(5) of the Criminal Procedure and Investigations Act 1996 (faults in disclosure by accused);*

(c)   *section 132(5) of the Criminal Justice Act 2003 (failure to give notice of hearsay evidence).]*

Application to vary a direction

3.6.—(1)   A party may apply to vary a direction if—

(a)   the court gave it without a hearing;

(b)   the court gave it at a hearing in that party's absence; or

(c)   circumstances have changed.

(2)   A party who applies to vary a direction must—

(a)   apply as soon as practicable after becoming aware of the grounds for doing so; and

(b)   give as much notice to the other parties as the nature and urgency of the application permits.

Agreement to vary a time limit fixed by a direction

3.7.—(1)   The parties may agree to vary a time limit fixed by a direction, but only if—

(a)   the variation will not—

(i)   affect the date of any hearing that has been fixed, or

           (ii)   significantly affect the progress of the case in any other way;

   (b)   the court has not prohibited variation by agreement; and

   (c)   the court's case progression officer is promptly informed.

(2)   The court's case progression officer must refer the agreement to the court if in doubt that the condition in paragraph (1)(a) is satisfied.

Court's power to vary requirements under this Part

3.8.—(1)   The court may—

   (a)   shorten or extend (even after it has expired) a time limit set by this Part; and

   (b)   allow an application or representations to be made orally.

(2)   A person who wants an extension of time must—

   (a)   apply when serving the application or representations for which it is needed; and

   (b)   explain the delay.

Case preparation and progression

3.9.—(1) At every hearing, if a case cannot be concluded there and then the court must give directions so that it can be concluded at the next hearing or as soon as possible after that.

(2)   At every hearing the court must, where relevant—

   (a)   if the defendant is absent, decide whether to proceed nonetheless;

   (b)   take the defendant's plea (unless already done) or if no plea can be taken then find out whether the defendant is likely to plead guilty or not guilty;

   (c)   set, follow or revise a timetable for the progress of the case, which may include a timetable for any hearing including the trial or (in the Crown Court) the appeal;

   (d)   in giving directions, ensure continuity in relation to the court and to the parties' representatives where that is appropriate and practicable; and

   (e)   where a direction has not been complied with, find out why, identify who was responsible, and take appropriate action.

(3)   In order to prepare for the trial, the court must take every reasonable step—

(a)   to encourage and to facilitate the attendance of witnesses when they are needed; and

(b)   to facilitate the participation of any person, including the defendant.

(4)   Facilitating the participation of the defendant includes finding out whether the defendant needs interpretation because—

(a)   the defendant does not speak or understand English; or

(b)   the defendant has a hearing or speech impediment.

(5)   Where the defendant needs interpretation—

(a)   the court officer must arrange for interpretation to be provided at every hearing which the defendant is due to attend;

(b)   interpretation may be by an intermediary where the defendant has a speech impediment, without the need for a defendant's evidence direction;

(c)   on application or on its own initiative, the court may require a written translation to be provided for the defendant of any document or part of a document, unless—

(i)   translation of that document, or part, is not needed to explain the case against the defendant, or

(ii)   the defendant agrees to do without and the court is satisfied that the agreement is clear and voluntary and that the defendant has had legal advice or otherwise understands the consequences;

(d)   on application by the defendant, the court must give any direction which the court thinks appropriate, including a direction for interpretation by a different interpreter, where—

(i)   no interpretation is provided,

(ii)   no translation is ordered or provided in response to a previous application by the defendant, or

(iii)   the defendant complains about the quality of interpretation or of any translation.

(6)   Facilitating the participation of any person includes giving directions for the appropriate treatment and questioning of a witness or the defendant,

especially where the court directs that such questioning is to be conducted through an intermediary.

(7)   Where directions for appropriate treatment and questioning are required, the court must—

    (a)   invite representations by the parties and by any intermediary; and

    (b)   set ground rules for the conduct of the questioning, which rules may include—

        (i)   a direction relieving a party of any duty to put that party's case to a witness or a defendant in its entirety,

        (ii)   directions about the manner of questioning,

        (iii)   directions about the duration of questioning,

        (iv)   if necessary, directions about the questions that may or may not be asked,

        (v)   where there is more than one defendant, the allocation among them of the topics about which a witness may be asked, and

        (vi)   directions about the use of models, plans, body maps or similar aids to help communicate a question or an answer.

[Note. Part 18 (Measures to assist a witness or defendant to give evidence) contains rules about an application for a defendant's evidence direction under (among other provisions) sections 33BA and 33BB of the Youth Justice and Criminal Evidence Act 1999.

See also Directive 2010/64/EU of the European Parliament and of the Council of 20th October, 2010, on the right to interpretation and translation in criminal proceedings.

Where a trial in the Crown Court will take place in Wales and a participant wishes to use the Welsh language, see rule 3.26. Where a trial in a magistrates' court will take place in Wales, a participant may use the Welsh language: see rule 24.14.]

Readiness for trial or appeal

3.10.—(1)   This rule applies to a party's preparation for trial or appeal, and in this rule and rule 3.11 'trial' includes any hearing at which evidence will be introduced.

(2)   In fulfilling the duty under rule 3.3, each party must—

    (a)   comply with directions given by the court;

    (b)   take every reasonable step to make sure that party's witnesses will attend when they are needed;

    (c)   make appropriate arrangements to present any written or other material; and

(d)   promptly inform the court and the other parties of anything that may—

(i)   affect the date or duration of the trial or appeal, or

(ii)   significantly affect the progress of the case in any other way.

(3)   The court may require a party to give a certificate of readiness.

Conduct of a trial or an appeal

3.11.   In order to manage a trial or an appeal, the court—

(a)   must establish, with the active assistance of the parties, what are the disputed issues;

(b)   must consider setting a timetable that—

(i)   takes account of those issues and of any timetable proposed by a party, and

(ii)   may limit the duration of any stage of the hearing;

(c)   may require a party to identify—

(i)   which witnesses that party wants to give evidence in person,

(ii)   the order in which that party wants those witnesses to give their evidence,

(iii)   whether that party requires an order compelling the attendance of a witness,

(iv)   what arrangements are desirable to facilitate the giving of evidence by a witness,

(v)   what arrangements are desirable to facilitate the participation of any other person, including the defendant,

(vi)   what written evidence that party intends to introduce,

(vii)   what other material, if any, that person intends to make available to the court in the presentation of the case, and

(viii)   whether that party intends to raise any point of law that could affect the conduct of the trial or appeal; and

(d)   may limit—

(i)   the examination, cross-examination or re-examination of a witness, and

(ii)   the duration of any stage of the hearing.

[Note. See also rules 3.5 (The court's case management powers) and 3.9 (Case preparation and progression).]

Duty of court officer

3.12.   The court officer must—

(a)   where a person is entitled or required to attend a hearing, give as much notice as reasonably practicable to—

(i)   that person, and

(ii)   that person's custodian (if any);

(b)   where the court gives directions, promptly make a record available to the parties.

[Note. See also rule 5.7 (Supply to a party of information or documents from records or case materials).]

Preparation for Trial in the Crown Court
Pre-trial hearings: general rules

3.13.—(1)   The Crown Court—

(a)   may, and in some cases must, conduct a preparatory hearing where rule 3.14 applies;

(b)   must conduct a plea and trial preparation hearing;

(c)   may conduct a further pre-trial case management hearing (and if necessary more than one such hearing) only where—

(i)   the court anticipates a guilty plea,

(ii)   it is necessary to conduct such a hearing in order to give directions for an effective trial, or

(iii)   such a hearing is required to set ground rules for the conduct of the questioning of a witness or defendant.

(2)   A pre-trial case management hearing—

(a)   must be in public, as a general rule, but all or part of the hearing may be in private if the court so directs; and

(b)   must be recorded, in accordance with rule 5.5 (Recording and transcription of proceedings in the Crown Court).

(3)   Where the court determines a pre-trial application in private, it must announce its decision in public.

[Note. See also the general rules in the first section of this Part (rules 3.1 to 3.12) and the other rules in this section.

The Practice Direction lists the circumstances in which a further pre-trial case management hearing is likely to be needed in order to give directions for an effective trial.

There are rules relevant to applications which may be made at a pre-trial hearing in Part 6 (Reporting, etc. restrictions), Part 14 (Bail and custody time limits), Part 15 (Disclosure), Part 17 (Witness summonses, warrants and orders), Part 18 (Measures to assist a witness or defendant to give evidence), Part 19 (Expert evidence), Part 20 (Hearsay evidence), Part 21 (Evidence of bad character), Part 22 (Evidence of a complainant's previous sexual behaviour) and Part 23 (Restriction on cross-examination by a defendant).

On an application to which Part 14 (Bail and custody time limits) applies, rule 14.2 (exercise of court's powers under that Part) may require the defendant's presence, which may be by live link. Where rule 14.10 applies (Consideration of bail in a murder case), the court officer must arrange for the Crown Court to consider bail within 2 business days of the first hearing in the magistrates' court.

Under section 40 of the Criminal Procedure and Investigations Act 1996, a pre-trial ruling about the admissibility of evidence or any other question of law is binding unless it later appears to the court in the interests of justice to discharge or vary that ruling.]

Preparatory hearing

3.14.—(1) This rule applies where the Crown Court—

    (a)   can order a preparatory hearing, under—

        (i)   section 7 of the Criminal Justice Act 1987 (cases of serious or complex fraud), or

        (ii)   section 29 of the Criminal Procedure and Investigations Act 1996 (other complex, serious or lengthy cases);

    (b)   must order such a hearing, to determine an application for a trial without a jury, under—

        (i)   section 44 of the Criminal Justice Act 2003 (danger of jury tampering), or

        (ii)   section 17 of the Domestic Violence, Crime and Victims Act 2004 (trial of sample counts by jury, and others by judge alone);

    (c)   must order such a hearing, under section 29 of the 1996 Act, where section 29(1B) or (1C) applies (cases in which a terrorism offence is charged, or other serious cases with a terrorist connection).

(2)   The court may decide whether to order a preparatory hearing—

    (a)   on an application or on its own initiative;

    (b)   at a hearing (in public or in private), or without a hearing;

    (c)   in a party's absence, if that party—

        (i)   applied for the order, or

        (ii)   has had at least 14 days in which to make representations.

[Note. See also section 45(2) of the Criminal Justice Act 2003 and section 18(1) of the Domestic Violence, Crime and Victims Act 2004.

At a preparatory hearing, the court may—

(a)   *require the prosecution to set out its case in a written statement, to arrange its evidence in a form that will be easiest for the jury (if there is one) to understand, to prepare a list of agreed facts, and to amend the case statement following representations from the defence (section 9(4) of the 1987 Act, section 31(4) of the 1996 Act); and*

(b)   *require the defence to give notice of any objection to the prosecution case statement, and to give notice stating the extent of agreement with the prosecution as to documents and other matters and the reason for any disagreement (section 9(5) of the 1987 Act, section 31(6), (7), (9) of the 1996 Act).*

Under section 10 of the 1987 Act, and under section 34 of the 1996 Act, if either party later departs from the case or objections disclosed by that party, then the court, or another party, may comment on that, and the court may draw such inferences as appear proper.]

Application for preparatory hearing

3.15.—(1)   A party who wants the court to order a preparatory hearing must—

(a)   apply in writing—

(i)   as soon as reasonably practicable, and in any event

(ii)   not more than 14 days after the defendant pleads not guilty;

(b)   serve the application on—

(i)   the court officer, and

(ii)   each other party.

(2)   The applicant must—

(a)   if relevant, explain what legislation requires the court to order a preparatory hearing;

(b)   otherwise, explain—

(i)   what makes the case complex or serious, or makes the trial likely to be long,

(ii)   why a substantial benefit will accrue from a preparatory hearing, and

(iii)   why the court's ordinary powers of case management are not adequate.

(3)   A prosecutor who wants the court to order a trial without a jury must explain—

(a)   where the prosecutor alleges a danger of jury tampering—

(i)   what evidence there is of a real and present danger that jury tampering would take place,

238

(ii)   what steps, if any, reasonably might be taken to prevent jury tampering, and

(iii)   why, notwithstanding such steps, the likelihood of jury tampering is so substantial as to make it necessary in the interests of justice to order such a trial; or

(b)   where the prosecutor proposes trial without a jury on some counts on the indictment—

(i)   why a trial by jury involving all the counts would be impracticable,

(ii)   how the counts proposed for jury trial can be regarded as samples of the others, and

(iii)   why it would be in the interests of justice to order such a trial.

Application for non-jury trial containing information withheld from a defendant

3.16.—(1)   This rule applies where—

(a)   the prosecutor applies for an order for a trial without a jury because of a danger of jury tampering; and

(b)   the application includes information that the prosecutor thinks ought not be revealed to a defendant.

(2)   The prosecutor must—

(a)   omit that information from the part of the application that is served on that defendant;

(b)   mark the other part to show that, unless the court otherwise directs, it is only for the court; and

(c)   in that other part, explain why the prosecutor has withheld that information from that defendant.

(3)   The hearing of an application to which this rule applies—

(a)   must be in private, unless the court otherwise directs; and

(b)   if the court so directs, may be, wholly or in part, in the absence of a defendant from whom information has been withheld.

(4)   At the hearing of an application to which this rule applies—

    (a)   the general rule is that the court will receive, in the following sequence—

        (i)   representations first by the prosecutor and then by each defendant, in all the parties' presence, and then

        (ii)   further representations by the prosecutor, in the absence of a defendant from whom information has been withheld; but

    (b)   the court may direct other arrangements for the hearing.

(5)   Where, on an application to which this rule applies, the court orders a trial without a jury—

    (a)   the general rule is that the trial will be before a judge other than the judge who made the order; but

    (b)   the court may direct other arrangements.

Representations in response to application for preparatory hearing

3.17.—(1)   This rule applies where a party wants to make representations about—

    (a)   an application for a preparatory hearing;

    (b)   an application for a trial without a jury.

(2)   Such a party must—

    (a)   serve the representations on—

        (i)   the court officer, and

        (ii)   each other party;

    (b)   do so not more than 14 days after service of the application;

    (c)   ask for a hearing, if that party wants one, and explain why it is needed.

(3)   Where representations include information that the person making them thinks ought not be revealed to another party, that person must—

    (a)   omit that information from the representations served on that other party;

    (b)   mark the information to show that, unless the court otherwise directs, it is only for the court; and

    (c)   with that information include an explanation of why it has been withheld from that other party.

(4)   Representations against an application for an order must explain why the conditions for making it are not met.

Commencement of preparatory hearing

3.18. At the beginning of a preparatory hearing, the court must—

    (a)   announce that it is such a hearing; and

    (b)   take the defendant's plea under rule 3.24 (Arraigning the defendant on the indictment), unless already done.

[Note. See section 8 of the Criminal Justice Act 1987 and section 30 of the Criminal Procedure and Investigations Act 1996.]

Defence trial advocate

3.19.—(1) The defendant must notify the court officer of the identity of the intended defence trial advocate—

    (a)   as soon as practicable, and in any event no later than the day of the plea and trial preparation hearing;

    (b)   in writing, or orally at that hearing.

(2)   The defendant must notify the court officer in writing of any change in the identity of the intended defence trial advocate as soon as practicable, and in any event not more than 5 business days after that change.

Application to stay case for abuse of process

3.20.—(1) This rule applies where a defendant wants the Crown Court to stay the case on the grounds that the proceedings are an abuse of the court, or otherwise unfair.

(2)   Such a defendant must—

    (a)   apply in writing—

        (i)   as soon as practicable after becoming aware of the grounds for doing so,

        (ii)   at a pre-trial hearing, unless the grounds for the application do not arise until trial, and

        (iii)   in any event, before the defendant pleads guilty or the jury (if there is one) retires to consider its verdict at trial;

    (b)   serve the application on—

        (i)   the court officer, and

        (ii)   each other party; and

    (c)   in the application—

        (i)   explain the grounds on which it is made,

        (ii)   include, attach or identify all supporting material,

        (iii)   specify relevant events, dates and propositions of law, and

        (iv)   identify any witness the applicant wants to call to give evidence in person.

(3)   A party who wants to make representations in response to the application must serve the representations on—

    (a)   the court officer; and

    (b)   each other party,

not more than 14 days after service of the application.

Application for joint or separate trials, etc.

3.21.—(1) This rule applies where a party wants the Crown Court to order—

    (a)   the joint trial of—

        (i)   offences charged by separate indictments, or

        (ii)   defendants charged in separate indictments;

    (b)   separate trials of offences charged by the same indictment;

    (c)   separate trials of defendants charged in the same indictment; or

    (d)   the deletion of a count from an indictment.

(2)   Such a party must—

    (a)   apply in writing—

        (i)   as soon as practicable after becoming aware of the grounds for doing so, and

        (ii)   before the trial begins, unless the grounds for the application do not arise until trial;

    (b)   serve the application on—

        (i)   the court officer, and

        (ii)   each other party; and

    (c)   in the application—

        (i)   specify the order proposed, and

        (ii)   explain why it should be made.

(3)   A party who wants to make representations in response to the application must serve the representations on—

   (a)   the court officer; and

   (b)   each other party,

not more than 14 days after service of the application.

(4)   Where the same indictment charges more than one offence, the court—

   (a)   must exercise its power to order separate trials of those offences unless the offences to be tried together—

      (i)   are founded on the same facts, or

      (ii)   form or are part of a series of offences of the same or a similar character;

   (b)   may exercise its power to order separate trials of those offences if of the opinion that—

      (i)   the defendant otherwise may be prejudiced or embarrassed in his or her defence, or

      (ii)   for any other reason it is desirable that the defendant should be tried separately for any one or more of those offences.

[Note. See section 5 of the Indictments Act 1915. Rule 10.2 (The indictment: general rules) governs the form and content of an indictment.]

Order for joint or separate trials, or amendment of the indictment

3.22.—(1)   This rule applies where the Crown Court makes an order—

   (a)   on an application under rule 3.21 applies (Application for joint or separate trials, etc.); or

   (b)   amending an indictment in any other respect.

(2)   Unless the court otherwise directs, the court officer must endorse any paper copy of each affected indictment made for the court with—

   (a)   a note of the court's order; and

   (b)   the date of that order.

Application for indication of sentence

3.23.—(1)   This rule applies where a defendant wants the Crown Court to give an indication of the maximum sentence that would be passed if a guilty plea were entered when the indication is sought.

(2)   Such a defendant must—

   (a)   apply in writing as soon as practicable; and

    (b)   serve the application on—

        (i)   the court officer, and

        (ii)   the prosecutor.

(3)   The application must—

    (a)   specify—

        (i)   the offence or offences to which it would be a guilty plea, and

        (ii)   the facts on the basis of which that plea would be entered; and

    (b)   include the prosecutor's agreement to, or representations on, that proposed basis of plea.

(4)   The prosecutor must—

    (a)   provide information relevant to sentence, including—

        (i)   any previous conviction of the defendant, and the circumstances where relevant,

        (ii)   any statement of the effect of the offence on the victim, the victim's family or others; and

    (b)   identify any other matter relevant to sentence, including—

        (i)   the legislation applicable,

        (ii)   any sentencing guidelines, or guideline cases, and

        (iii)   aggravating and mitigating factors.

(5)   The hearing of the application—

    (a)   may take place in the absence of any other defendant;

    (b)   must be attended by—

        (i)   the applicant defendant's legal representatives (if any), and

        (ii)   the prosecution advocate.

Arraigning the defendant on the indictment

3.24.—(1)   In order to take the defendant's plea, the Crown Court must—

    (a)   obtain the prosecutor's confirmation, in writing or orally—

        (i)   that the indictment (or draft indictment, as the case may be) sets out a statement of each offence that the prosecutor wants the court to try and such particulars of the conduct

244

> constituting the commission of each such offence as the prosecutor relies upon to make clear what is alleged, and
>
> (ii) of the order in which the prosecutor wants the defendants' names to be listed in the indictment, if the prosecutor proposes that more than one defendant should be tried at the same time;

(b) ensure that the defendant is correctly identified by the indictment or draft indictment;

(c) in respect of each count—

> (i) read the count aloud to the defendant, or arrange for it to be read aloud or placed before the defendant in writing,
>
> (ii) ask whether the defendant pleads guilty or not guilty to the offence charged by that count, and
>
> (iii) take the defendant's plea.

(2) Where a count is read which is substantially the same as one already read aloud, then only the materially different details need be read aloud.

(3) Where a count is placed before the defendant in writing, the court must summarise its gist aloud.

(4) In respect of each count in the indictment—

(a) if the defendant declines to enter a plea, the court must treat that as a not guilty plea unless rule 25.11 applies (Defendant unfit to plead);

(b) if the defendant pleads not guilty to the offence charged by that count but guilty to another offence of which the court could convict on that count—

> (i) if the prosecutor and the court accept that plea, the court must treat the plea as one of guilty of that other offence, but
>
> (ii) otherwise, the court must treat the plea as one of not guilty;

(c) if the defendant pleads a previous acquittal or conviction of the offence charged by that count—

> (i) the defendant must identify that acquittal or conviction in writing, explaining the basis of that plea, and
>
> (ii) the court must exercise its power to decide whether that plea disposes of that count.

(5)   In a case in which a magistrates' court sends the defendant for trial, the Crown Court must take the defendant's plea—

(a)   not less than 2 weeks after the date on which that sending takes place, unless the parties otherwise agree; and

(b)   not more than 16 weeks after that date, unless the court otherwise directs (either before or after that period expires).

[Note. See section 6 of the Criminal Law Act 1967, section 77 of the Senior Courts Act 1981 and section 122 of the Criminal Justice Act 1988. Part 10 contains rules about indictments: see in particular rule 10.2 (The indictment: general rules).

Under section 6(2) of the 1967 Act, on an indictment for murder a defendant may instead be convicted of manslaughter or another offence specified by that provision. Under section 6(3) of that Act, on an indictment for an offence other than murder or treason a defendant may instead be convicted of another offence if—

(a)   the allegation in the indictment amounts to or includes an allegation of that other offence; and

(b)   the Crown Court has power to convict and sentence for that other offence.]

Place of trial

3.25.—(1)   Unless the court otherwise directs, the court officer must arrange for the trial to take place in a courtroom provided by the Lord Chancellor.

(2)   The court officer must arrange for the court and the jury (if there is one) to view any place required by the court.

[Note. See section 3 of the Courts Act 2003 and section 14 of the Juries Act 1974.

In some circumstances the court may conduct all or part of the hearing outside a courtroom.]

Use of Welsh language at trial

3.26.   Where the trial will take place in Wales and a participant wishes to use the Welsh language—

(a)   that participant must serve notice on the court officer, or arrange for such a notice to be served on that participant's behalf—

(i)   at or before the plea and trial preparation hearing, or

(ii)   in accordance with any direction given by the court; and

(b)   if such a notice is served, the court officer must arrange for an interpreter to attend.

[Note. See section 22 of the Welsh Language Act 1993.]

Other provisions affecting case management

Case management may be affected by the following other rules and legislation:

Criminal Procedure Rules

Part 8 Initial details of the prosecution case

Part 9 Allocation and sending for trial

Part 10 The indictment

Part 15 Disclosure

Parts 16–23: the rules that deal with evidence

Part 24 Trial and sentence in a magistrates' court

Part 25 Trial and sentence in the Crown Court

Regulations

The Prosecution of Offences (Custody Time Limits) Regulations 1987

The Crime and Disorder Act 1998 (Service of Prosecution Evidence) Regulations 2005

The Criminal Procedure and Investigations Act 1996 (Defence Disclosure Time Limits) Regulations 2011

Acts of Parliament

Sections 10 and 18, Magistrates' Courts Act 1980: powers to adjourn hearings

Sections 128 and 129, Magistrates' Courts Act 1980: remand in custody by magistrates' courts

Sections 19 and 24A, Magistrates' Courts Act 1980 and sections 51 and 51A, Crime and Disorder Act 1998: allocation and sending for trial

Section 2, Administration of Justice (Miscellaneous Provisions) Act 1933: procedural conditions for trial in the Crown Court

Sections 8A and 8B, Magistrates' Courts Act 1980: pre-trial hearings in magistrates' courts

Section 7, Criminal Justice Act 1987; Parts III and IV, Criminal Procedure and Investigations Act 1996: pre-trial and preparatory hearings in the Crown Court

Section 9, Criminal Justice Act 1967: proof by written witness statement

Part 1, Criminal Procedure and Investigations Act 1996: disclosure.]

Part 4
Service of Documents

Contents of this Part

When this Part applies

4.1.—(1)   The rules in this Part apply—

  (a)   to the service of every document in a case to which these Rules apply; and

  (b)   for the purposes of section 12 of the Road Traffic Offenders Act 1988, to the service of a requirement to which that section applies.

(2)   The rules apply subject to any special rules in other legislation (including other Parts of these Rules) or in the Practice Direction.

[Note. Section 12 of the Road Traffic Offenders Act 1988 allows the court to accept the documents to which it refers as evidence of a driver's identity where a requirement to state that identity has been served under section 172 of the Road Traffic Act 1988 or under section 112 of the Road Traffic Regulation Act 1984.]

Methods of service

4.2.—(1)   A document may be served by any of the methods described in rules 4.3 to 4.6 (subject to rules 4.7 and 4.10), or in rule 4.8.

(2)   Where a document may be served by electronic means under rule 4.6, the general rule is that the person serving it must use that method.

Service by handing over a document

4.3.—(1)   A document may be served on—

    (a)   an individual by handing it to him or her;

    (b)   a corporation by handing it to a person holding a senior position in that corporation;

    (c)   an individual or corporation who is legally represented in the case by handing it to that legal representative;

    (d)   the prosecution by handing it to the prosecutor or to the prosecution representative;

    (e)   the court officer by handing it to a court officer with authority to accept it at the relevant court office; and

    (f)   the Registrar of Criminal Appeals by handing it to a court officer with authority to accept it at the Criminal Appeal Office.

(2)   If an individual is under 18, a copy of a document served under paragraph (1)(a) must be handed to his or her parent, or another appropriate adult, unless no such person is readily available.

(3)   Unless the court otherwise directs, for the purposes of paragraph (1)(c) or (d) (service by handing a document to a party's representative) 'representative' includes an advocate appearing for that party at a hearing.

(4)   In this rule, 'the relevant court office' means—

    (a)   in relation to a case in a magistrates' court or in the Crown Court, the office at which that court's business is administered by court staff;

    (b)   in relation to an application to a High Court judge for permission to serve a draft indictment—

        (i)   in London, the Listing Office of the Queen's Bench Division of the High Court, and

        (ii)   elsewhere, the office at which court staff administer the business of any court then constituted of a High Court judge;

    (c)   in relation to an extradition appeal case in the High Court, the Administrative Court Office of the Queen's Bench Division of the High Court.

[Note. Some legislation treats a body that is not a corporation as if it were one for the purposes of rules about service of documents. See for example section 143 of the Adoption and Children Act 2002.]

Service by leaving or posting a document

4.4.—(1)   A document may be served by addressing it to the person to be served and leaving it at the appropriate address for service under this rule, or by sending it to that address by first class post or by the equivalent of first class post.

(2)   The address for service under this rule on—

    (a)   an individual is an address where it is reasonably believed that he or she will receive it;

    (b)   a corporation is its principal office, and if there is no readily identifiable principal office then any place where it carries on its activities or business;

    (c)   an individual or corporation who is legally represented in the case is that legal representative's office;

    (d)   the prosecution is the prosecutor's office;

    (e)   the court officer is the relevant court office; and

    (f)   the Registrar of Criminal Appeals is the Criminal Appeal Office, Royal Courts of Justice, Strand, London WC2A 2LL.

(3)   In this rule, 'the relevant court office' means—

    (a)   in relation to a case in a magistrates' court or in the Crown Court, the office at which that court's business is administered by court staff;

    (b)   in relation to an application to a High Court judge for permission to serve a draft indictment—

        (i)   in London, the Queen's Bench Listing Office, Royal Courts of Justice, Strand, London WC2A 2LL, and

        (ii)   elsewhere, the office at which court staff administer the business of any court then constituted of a High Court judge;

    (c)   in relation to an extradition appeal case in the High Court, the Administrative Court Office, Royal Courts of Justice, Strand, London WC2A 2LL.

[Note. In addition to service in England and Wales for which these rules provide, service outside England and Wales may be allowed under other legislation. See—

    (a)   section 39 of the Criminal Law Act 1977 (service of summons, etc. in Scotland and Northern Ireland);

(b)   *section 1139(4) of the Companies Act 2006 (service of copy summons, etc. on company's registered office in Scotland and Northern Ireland);*

(c)   *sections 3, 4, 4A and 4B of the Crime (International Co-operation) Act 2003 (service of summons, etc. outside the United Kingdom) and rules 49.1 and 49.2; and*

(d)   *section 1139(2) of the Companies Act 2006 (service on overseas company).]*

Service by document exchange

4.5.—(1)   This rule applies where—

(a)   the person to be served—

(i)   has given a document exchange (DX) box number, and

(ii)   has not refused to accept service by DX; or

(b)   the person to be served is legally represented in the case and the legal representative has given a DX box number.

(2)   A document may be served by—

(a)   addressing it to that person or legal representative, as appropriate, at that DX box number; and

(b)   leaving it at—

(i)   the document exchange at which the addressee has that DX box number, or

(ii)   a document exchange at which the person serving it has a DX box number.

Service by electronic means

4.6.—(1)   This rule applies where—

(a)   the person to be served—

(i)   has given an electronic address and has not refused to accept service at that address, or

(ii)   is given access to an electronic address at which a document may be deposited and has not refused to accept service by the deposit of a document at that address; or

(b)   the person to be served is legally represented in the case and the legal representative—

(i)   has given an electronic address, or

(ii)   is given access to an electronic address at which a document may be deposited.

(2)   A document may be served—

(a)   by sending it by electronic means to the address which the recipient has given; or

(b)   by depositing it at an address to which the recipient has been given access and—

(i)   in every case, making it possible for the recipient to read the document, or view or listen to its content, as the case may be,

(ii)   unless the court otherwise directs, making it possible for the recipient to make and keep an electronic copy of the document, and

(iii) notifying the recipient of the deposit of the document (which notice may be given by electronic means).

(3)   Where a document is served under this rule the person serving it need not provide a paper copy as well.

Documents that must be served by specified methods

4.7.—(1)   An application or written statement, and notice, under rule 48.9 alleging contempt of court may be served—

(a)   on an individual, only under rule 4.3(1)(a) (by handing it to him or her);

(b)   on a corporation, only under rule 4.3(1)(b) (by handing it to a person holding a senior position in that corporation).

(2)   For the purposes of section 12 of the Road Traffic Offenders Act 1988, a notice of a requirement under section 172 of the Road Traffic Act 1988 or under section 112 of the Road Traffic Regulation Act 1984 to identify the driver of a vehicle may be served—

(a)   on an individual, only by post under rule 4.4(1) and (2)(a);

(b)   on a corporation, only by post under rule 4.4(1) and (2)(b).

Service by person in custody

4.8.—(1)   A person in custody may serve a document by handing it to the custodian addressed to the person to be served.

(2)   The custodian must—

(a)   endorse it with the time and date of receipt;

(b)   record its receipt; and

(c)   forward it promptly to the addressee.

Service by another method

4.9.—(1)   The court may allow service of a document by a method—

(a)   other than those described in rules 4.3 to 4.6 and in rule 4.8;

(b)   other than one specified by rule 4.7, where that rule applies.

(2)   An order allowing service by another method must specify—

(a)   the method to be used; and

(b)   the date on which the document will be served.

Documents that may not be served on a legal representative

4.10.   Unless the court otherwise directs, service on a party's legal representative of any of the following documents is not service of that document on that party—

(a)   a summons, requisition, single justice procedure notice or witness summons;

(b)   notice of an order under section 25 of the Road Traffic Offenders Act 1988;

(c)   a notice of registration under section 71(6) of that Act;

(d)   notice of a hearing to review the postponement of the issue of a warrant of detention or imprisonment under section 77(6) of the Magistrates' Courts Act 1980;

(e)   notice under section 86 of that Act of a revised date to attend a means inquiry;

(f)   any notice or document served under Part 14 (Bail and custody time limits);

(g)   notice under rule 24.16(a) of when and where an adjourned hearing will resume;

(h)   notice under rule 28.5(3) of an application to vary or discharge a compensation order;

(i)   notice under rule 28.10(2)(c) of the location of the sentencing or enforcing court;

(j)   a collection order, or notice requiring payment, served under rule 30.2(a); or

(k)   an application or written statement, and notice, under rule 48.9 alleging contempt of court.

Date of service

4.11.—(1)   A document served under rule 4.3 or rule 4.8 is served on the day it is handed over.

(2)   Unless something different is shown, a document served on a person by any other method is served—

(a)   in the case of a document left at an address, on the next business day after the day on which it was left;

(b)   in the case of a document sent by first class post or by the equivalent of first class post, on the second business day after the day on which it was posted or despatched;

(c)   in the case of a document served by document exchange, on the second business day after the day on which it was left at a document exchange allowed by rule 4.5;

(d)   in the case of a document served by electronic means—

(i)   on the day on which it is sent under rule 4.6(2)(a), if that day is a business day and if it is sent by no later than 2.30pm that day,

(ii)   on the day on which notice of its deposit is given under rule 4.6(2)(b), if that day is a business day and if that notice is given by no later than 2.30pm that day, or

(iii)   otherwise, on the next business day after it was sent or such notice was given; and

(e)   in any case, on the day on which the addressee responds to it, if that is earlier.

(3)   Unless something different is shown, a document produced by a computer system for dispatch by post is to be taken as having been sent by first class post, or by the equivalent of first class post, to the addressee on the business day after the day on which it was produced.

(4)   Where a document is served on or by the court officer, 'business day' does not include a day on which the court office is closed.

Proof of service

4.12.   The person who serves a document may prove that by signing a certificate explaining how and when it was served.

Court's power to give directions about service

4.13.—(1)   The court may specify the time as well as the date by which a document must be—

(a)   served under rule 4.3 (Service by handing over a document) or rule 4.8 (Service by person in custody); or

(b)   sent or deposited by electronic means, if it is served under rule 4.6.

(2)   The court may treat a document as served if the addressee responds to it even if it was not served in accordance with the rules in this Part.

Appendix 4

Criminal Procedure Rules (CrimPR), Part 15
DISCLOSURE

Contents of this Part

WHEN THIS PART APPLIES

15.1.—This Part applies—

(a)   in a magistrates' court and in the Crown Court;

(b)   where Parts I and II of the Criminal Procedure and Investigations Act 1996 apply.

[Note. A summary of the disclosure requirements of the Criminal Procedure and Investigations Act 1996 is at the end of this Part.]

PROSECUTION DISCLOSURE

15.2.—(1) This rule applies where, under section 3 of the Criminal Procedure and Investigations Act 1996, the prosecutor—

   (a)   discloses prosecution material to the defendant; or

   (b)   serves on the defendant a written statement that there is no such material to disclose. (2) The prosecutor must at the same time so inform the court officer.

[Note. See section 3 of the Criminal Procedure and Investigations Act 1996 and paragraph 10 of the Code of Practice accompanying the Criminal Procedure and Investigations Act 1996 (Code of Practice) Order 2015.]

PROSECUTOR'S APPLICATION FOR PUBLIC INTEREST RULING

15.3.—(1) This rule applies where—

   (a)   without a court order, the prosecutor would have to disclose material; and

   (b)   the prosecutor wants the court to decide whether it would be in the public interest to disclose it.

(2)   The prosecutor must—

   (a)   apply in writing for such a decision; and

   (b)   serve the application on—

      (i)   the court officer,

      (ii)   any person who the prosecutor thinks would be directly affected by disclosure of the material, and

      (iii)   the defendant, but only to the extent that serving it on the defendant would not disclose what the prosecutor thinks ought not be disclosed.

(3)   The application must—

   (a)   describe the material, and explain why the prosecutor thinks that—

      (i)   it is material that the prosecutor would have to disclose,

      (ii)   it would not be in the public interest to disclose that material, and

       (iii)   no measure such as the prosecutor's admission of any fact, or disclosure by summary, extract or edited copy, adequately would protect both the public interest and the defendant's right to a fair trial;

    (b)   omit from any part of the application that is served on the defendant anything that would disclose what the prosecutor thinks ought not be disclosed (in which case, paragraph (4) of this rule applies); and

    (c)   explain why, if no part of the application is served on the defendant.

(4)   Where the prosecutor serves only part of the application on the defendant, the prosecutor must—

    (a)   mark the other part, to show that it is only for the court; and

    (b)   in that other part, explain why the prosecutor has withheld it from the defendant.

(5)   Unless already done, the court may direct the prosecutor to serve an application on—

    (a)   the defendant;

    (b)   any other person who the court considers would be directly affected by the disclosure of the material.

(6)   The court must determine the application at a hearing which—

    (a)   must be in private, unless the court otherwise directs; and

    (b)   if the court so directs, may take place, wholly or in part, in the defendant's absence.

(7)   At a hearing at which the defendant is present—

    (a)   the general rule is that the court must consider, in the following sequence—

       (i)   representations first by the prosecutor and any other person served with the application, and then by the defendant, in the presence of them all, and then

       (ii)   further representations by the prosecutor and any such other person in the defendant's absence; but

    (b)   the court may direct other arrangements for the hearing.

(8)   The court may only determine the application if satisfied that it has been able to take adequate account of—

    (a)   such rights of confidentiality as apply to the material; and

    (b)   the defendant's right to a fair trial.

(9)   Unless the court otherwise directs, the court officer—

    (a)   must not give notice to anyone other than the prosecutor—

        (i)   of the hearing of an application under this rule, unless the prosecutor served the application on that person, or

        (ii)   of the court's decision on the application;

    (b)   may—

        (i)   keep a written application or representations, or

        (ii)   arrange for the whole or any part to be kept by some other appropriate person, subject to any conditions that the court may impose.

[Note. The court's power to order that it is not in the public interest to disclose material is provided for by sections 3(6), 7(6) (where the investigation began between 1st April, 1997 and 3rd April, 2005) and 7A(8) (where the investigation began on or after 4th April, 2005) of the Criminal Procedure and Investigations Act 1996.

See also sections 16 and 19 of the 1996 Act.]

DEFENCE DISCLOSURE

15.4.—(1) This rule applies where—

    (a)   under section 5 or 6 of the Criminal Procedure and Investigations Act 1996, the defendant gives a defence statement;

    (b)   under section 6C of the 1996 Act, the defendant gives a defence witness notice.

(2)   The defendant must serve such a statement or notice on—

    (a)   the court officer; and

    (b)   the prosecutor.

[Note. The Practice Direction sets out forms of—

    (a)   defence statement; and

    (b)   defence witness notice.

Under section 5 of the 1996 Act, in the Crown Court the defendant must give a defence statement. Under section 6 of the Act, in a magistrates' court the defendant may give such a statement but need not do so.

Under section 6C of the 1996 Act, in the Crown Court and in magistrates' courts the defendant must give a defence witness notice indicating whether he or she intends to call any witnesses (other than him or herself) and, if so, identifying them.]

DEFENDANT'S APPLICATION FOR PROSECUTION DISCLOSURE

15.5.—(1) This rule applies where the defendant—

    (a)   has served a defence statement given under the Criminal Procedure and Investigations Act 1996; and

    (b)   wants the court to require the prosecutor to disclose material.

(2)   The defendant must serve an application on—

    (a)   the court officer; and

    (b)   the prosecutor.

(3)   The application must—

    (a)   describe the material that the defendant wants the prosecutor to disclose;

    (b)   explain why the defendant thinks there is reasonable cause to believe that—

        (i)   the prosecutor has that material, and

        (ii)   it is material that the Criminal Procedure and Investigations Act 1996 requires the prosecutor to disclose; and

    (c)   ask for a hearing, if the defendant wants one, and explain why it is needed.

(4)   The court may determine an application under this rule—

    (a)   at a hearing, in public or in private; or

    (b)   without a hearing.

(5)   The court must not require the prosecutor to disclose material unless the prosecutor—

    (a)   is present; or

    (b)   has had at least 14 days in which to make representations.

[Note. The Practice Direction sets out a form of application for use in connection with this rule.

Under section 8 of the Criminal Procedure and Investigations Act 1996, a defendant may apply for prosecution disclosure only if the defendant has given a defence statement.]

REVIEW OF PUBLIC INTEREST RULING

15.6.—(1) This rule applies where the court has ordered that it is not in the public interest to disclose material that the prosecutor otherwise would have to disclose, and—

    (a)   the defendant wants the court to review that decision; or

    (b)   the Crown Court reviews that decision on its own initiative.

(2)   Where the defendant wants the court to review that decision, the defendant must—

    (a)   serve an application on—

        (i)   the court officer, and

        (ii)   the prosecutor; and

    (b)   in the application—

        (i)   describe the material that the defendant wants the prosecutor to disclose, and

        (ii)   explain why the defendant thinks it is no longer in the public interest for the prosecutor not to disclose it.

(3)   The prosecutor must serve any such application on any person who the prosecutor thinks would be directly affected if that material were disclosed.

(4)   The prosecutor, and any such person, must serve any representations on—

    (a)   the court officer; and

    (b)   the defendant, unless to do so would in effect reveal something that either thinks ought not be disclosed.

(5)   The court may direct—

    (a)   the prosecutor to serve any such application on any person who the court considers would be directly affected if that material were disclosed;

    (b)   the prosecutor and any such person to serve any representations on the defendant.

(6)   The court must review a decision to which this rule applies at a hearing which—

    (a)   must be in private, unless the court otherwise directs; and

    (b)   if the court so directs, may take place, wholly or in part, in the defendant's absence.

(7)   At a hearing at which the defendant is present—

    (a)   the general rule is that the court must consider, in the following sequence—

        (i)   representations first by the defendant, and then by the prosecutor and any other person served with the application, in the presence of them all, and then

        (ii)   further representations by the prosecutor and any such other person in the defendant's absence; but

    (b)   the court may direct other arrangements for the hearing.

(8)   The court may only conclude a review if satisfied that it has been able to take adequate account of—

    (a)   such rights of confidentiality as apply to the material; and

    (b)   the defendant's right to a fair trial.

[Note. The court's power to review a public interest ruling is provided for by sections 14 and 15 of the Criminal Procedure and Investigations Act 1996. Under section 14 of the Act, a magistrates' court may reconsider an order for non-disclosure only if a defendant applies. Under section 15, the Crown Court may do so on an application, or on its own initiative.

See also sections 16 and 19 of the 1996 Act.]

DEFENDANT'S APPLICATION TO USE DISCLOSED MATERIAL

15.7.—(1) This rule applies where a defendant wants the court's permission to use disclosed prosecution material—

    (a)   otherwise than in connection with the case in which it was disclosed; or

    (b)   beyond the extent to which it was displayed or communicated publicly at a hearing.

(2)   The defendant must serve an application on—

    (a)   the court officer; and

    (b)   the prosecutor.

(3)   The application must—

    (a)   specify what the defendant wants to use or disclose; and

    (b)   explain why.

(4)   The court may determine an application under this rule—

(a)   at a hearing, in public or in private; or

(b)   without a hearing.

(5)   The court must not permit the use of such material unless—

(a)   the prosecutor has had at least 28 days in which to make representations; and

(b)   the court is satisfied that it has been able to take adequate account of any rights of confidentiality that may apply to the material.

[Note. The court's power to allow a defendant to use disclosed material is provided for by section 17 of the Criminal Procedure and Investigations Act 1996.

See also section 19 of the 1996 Act.]

UNAUTHORISED USE OF DISCLOSED MATERIAL

15.8.—(1) This rule applies where a person is accused of using disclosed prosecution material in contravention of section 17 of the Criminal Procedure and Investigations Act 1996.

(2)   A party who wants the court to exercise its power to punish that person for contempt of court must comply with the rules in Part 48 (Contempt of court).

(3)   The court must not exercise its power to forfeit material used in contempt of court unless—

(a)   the prosecutor; and

(b)   any other person directly affected by the disclosure of the material,

is present, or has had at least 14 days in which to make representations.

[Note. Under section 17 of the Criminal Procedure and Investigations Act 1996, a defendant may use disclosed prosecution material—

(a)   in connection with the case in which it was disclosed, including on an appeal;

(b)   to the extent to which it was displayed or communicated publicly at a hearing in public; or

(c)   with the court's permission.

Under section 18 of the 1996 Act, the court can punish for contempt of court any other use of disclosed prosecution material. See also section 19 of the 1996 Act.]

COURT'S POWER TO VARY REQUIREMENTS UNDER THIS PART

15.9. The court may—

(a) shorten or extend (even after it has expired) a time limit under this Part;

(b) allow a defence statement, or a defence witness notice, to be in a different written form to one set out in the Practice Direction, as long as it contains what the Criminal Procedure and Investigations Act 1996 requires;

(c) allow an application under this Part to be in a different form to one set out in the Practice Direction, or to be presented orally; and

(d) specify the period within which—

(i) any application under this Part must be made, or

(ii) any material must be disclosed, on an application to which rule 15.5 applies (Defendant's application for prosecution disclosure).

Summary of disclosure requirements of Criminal Procedure and Investigations Act 1996

The Criminal Procedure and Investigations Act 1996 came into force on 1st April, 1997. It does not apply where the investigation began before that date. With effect from 4th April, 2005, the Criminal Justice Act 2003 made changes to the 1996 Act that do not apply where the investigation began before that date.

In some circumstances, the prosecutor may be required to disclose material to which the 1996 Act does not apply: see sections 1 and 21.

Part I of the 1996 Act contains sections 1 to 21A. Part II, which contains sections 22 to 27, requires an investigator to record information relevant to an investigation that is obtained during its course. See also the Criminal Procedure and Investigations Act 1996 (Code of Practice) (No. 2) Order 1997, the Criminal Procedure and Investigations Act 1996 (Code of Practice) Order 2005 and the Criminal Procedure and Investigations Act 1996 (Code of Practice) Order 2015 issued under sections 23 to 25 of the 1996 Act.

Prosecution disclosure

Where the investigation began between 1st April, 1997, and 3rd April, 2005, sections 3 and 7 of the 1996 Act require the prosecutor—

(a) to disclose material not previously disclosed that in the prosecutor's opinion might undermine the case for the prosecution against the defendant—

(i) in a magistrates' court, as soon as is reasonably practicable after the defendant pleads not guilty, and

(ii) in the Crown Court, as soon as is reasonably practicable after the case is committed or transferred for trial, or after the evidence is served where the case is sent for trial; and

264

(b)   *as soon as is reasonably practicable after service of the defence statement, to disclose material not previously disclosed that might be reasonably expected to assist the defendant's case as disclosed by that defence statement; or in either event*

(c)   *if there is no such material, then to give the defendant a written statement to that effect.*

Where the investigation began on or after 4th April, 2005, sections 3 and 7A of the 1996 Act require the prosecutor—

(a)   *to disclose prosecution material not previously disclosed that might reasonably be considered capable of undermining the case for the prosecution against the defendant or of assisting the case for the defendant—*

    (i)   *in a magistrates' court, as soon as is reasonably practicable after the defendant pleads not guilty, or*

    (ii)   *in the Crown Court, as soon as is reasonably practicable after the case is committed or transferred for trial, or after the evidence is served where the case is sent for trial, or after a count is added to the indictment; and in either case*

(b)   *if there is no such material, then to give the defendant a written statement to that effect; and after that*

(c)   *in either court, to disclose any such material—*

    (i)   *whenever there is any, until the court reaches its verdict or the prosecutor decides not to proceed with the case, and*

    (ii)   *in particular, after the service of the defence statement.*

Sections 2 and 3 of the 1996 Act define material, and prescribe how it must be disclosed.

In some circumstances, disclosure is prohibited by section 17 of the Regulation of Investigatory Powers Act 2000.

The prosecutor must not disclose material that the court orders it would not be in the public interest to disclose: see sections 3(6), 7(6) and 7A(8) of the 1996 Act.

Sections 12 and 13 of the 1996 Act prescribe the time for prosecution disclosure. Under paragraph 10 of the Code of Practice accompanying the Criminal Procedure and Investigations Act 1996 (Code of Practice) Order 2015, in a magistrates' court the prosecutor must disclose any material due to be disclosed at the hearing where a not guilty plea is entered, or as soon as possible following a formal indication from the accused or representative that a not guilty plea will be entered at that hearing.

See also sections 1, 4 and 10 of the 1996 Act.

Defence disclosure

Under section 5 of the 1996 Act, in the Crown Court the defendant must give a defence statement. Under section 6 of the Act, in a magistrates' court the defendant may give such a statement but need not do so.

Under section 6C of the 1996 Act, in the Crown Court and in magistrates' courts the defendant must give a defence witness notice indicating whether he or she intends to call any witnesses (other than him or herself) and, if so, identifying them.

Appendix 4 *Criminal Procedure Rules (CrimPR), Part 15*

The time for service of a defence statement is prescribed by section 12 of the 1996 Act(c) and by the Criminal Procedure and Investigations Act 1996 (Defence Disclosure Time Limits) Regulations 2011. It is—

    (a)   in a magistrates' court, not more than 14 days after the prosecutor—

        (i)   discloses material under section 3 of the 1996 Act, or

        (ii)   serves notice that there is no such material to disclose;

    (b)   in the Crown Court, not more than 28 days after either of those events, if the prosecution evidence has been served on the defendant.

The requirements for the content of a defence statement are set out in—

    (a)   section 5 of the 1996 Act, where the investigation began between 1ˢᵗ April, 1997 and 3ʳᵈ April, 2005;

    (b)   section 6A of the 1996 Act, where the investigation began on or after 4ᵗʰ April, 2005. See also section 6E of the Act.

Where the investigation began between 1ˢᵗ April, 1997 and 3ʳᵈ April, 2005, the defence statement must—

    (a)   set out in general terms the nature of the defence;

    (b)   indicate the matters on which the defendant takes issue with the prosecutor, and, in respect of each, explain why;

    (c)   if the defence statement discloses an alibi, give particulars, including—

        (i)   the name and address of any witness whom the defendant believes can give evidence in support (that is, evidence that the defendant was in a place, at a time, inconsistent with having committed the offence),

        (ii)   where the defendant does not know the name or address, any information that might help identify or find that witness.

Where the investigation began on or after 4ᵗʰ April, 2005, the defence statement must—

    (a)   set out the nature of the defence, including any particular defences on which the defendant intends to rely;

    (b)   indicate the matters of fact on which the defendant takes issue with the prosecutor, and, in respect of each, explain why;

    (c)   set out particulars of the matters of fact on which the defendant intends to rely for the purposes of the defence;

    (d)   indicate any point of law that the defendant wants to raise, including any point about the admissibility of evidence or about abuse of process, and any authority relied on; and

    (e)   if the defence statement discloses an alibi, give particulars, including—

        (i)   the name, address and date of birth of any witness whom the defendant believes can give evidence in support (that is, evidence that the defendant was in a place, at a time, inconsistent with having committed the offence),

        (ii)   where the defendant does not know any of those details, any information that might help identify or find that witness.

The time for service of a defence witness notice is prescribed by section 12 of the 1996 Act and by the Criminal Procedure and Investigations Act 1996 (Defence Disclosure Time Limits) Regulations 2011. The time limits are the same as those for a defence statement.

A defence witness notice that identifies any proposed defence witness (other than the defendant) must—

    (a)   give the name, address and date of birth of each such witness, or as many of those details as are known to the defendant when the notice is given;

    (b)   provide any information in the defendant's possession which might be of material assistance in identifying or finding any such witness in whose case any of the details mentioned in paragraph (a) are not known to the defendant when the notice is given; and

    (c)   amend any earlier such notice, if the defendant—

        (i)   decides to call a person not included in an earlier notice as a proposed witness,

        (ii)   decides not to call a person so included, or

        (iii)   discovers any information which the defendant would have had to include in an earlier notice, if then aware of it.

Under section 11 of the 1996 Act, if a defendant—

    (a)   fails to disclose what the Act requires;

    (b)   fails to do so within the time prescribed;

    (c)   at trial, relies on a defence, or facts, not mentioned in the defence statement;

    (d)   at trial, introduces alibi evidence without having given in the defence statement—

        (i)   particulars of the alibi, or

        (ii)   the details of the alibi witness, or witnesses, required by the Act; or

    (e)   at trial, calls a witness not identified in a defence witness notice,

then the court or another party at trial may comment on that, and the court may draw such inferences as appear proper in deciding whether the defendant is guilty.

Under section 6E(2) of the 1996 Act, if before trial in the Crown Court it seems to the court that section 11 may apply, then the court must warn the defendant.

Attorney General's Guidelines on Disclosure
For investigators, prosecutors and defence practitioners

December 2013

CONTENTS

FOREWORD

We are pleased to publish a revised judicial protocol and revised guidance on the disclosure of unused material in criminal cases. Proper disclosure of unused material, made through a rigorous and carefully considered application of the law, remains a crucial part of a fair trial, and essential to avoiding miscarriages of justice. These new documents are intended to clarify the procedures to be followed and to encourage the active participation of all parties.

They have been prepared following the recommendations of Lord Justice Gross in his September 2011 'Review of Disclosure in Criminal Proceedings' and take account of Lord Justice Gross and Lord Justice Treacy's 'Further review of disclosure in criminal proceedings: sanctions for disclosure failure', published in November 2012.

There are important roles for the prosecution, the defence and the court in ensuring that disclosure is conducted properly, including on the part of the investigating, case progression and disclosure officers, as well as the lawyers and advocates. Lord Justice Gross particularly recommended that the guidance on disclosure of unused material in criminal cases should be consolidated and abbreviated. Given all of those involved in this process have separate constitutional roles, the judiciary and the Attorney-General have worked together to produce complementary guidance that is shorter than the previous iterations, but remains comprehensive. The two documents are similarly structured for ease of reference and should be read together.

The Rt. Hon. Dominic Grieve QC MP Attorney General

The Rt. Hon. The Lord Thomas Lord Chief Justice of England and Wales

INTRODUCTION

These Guidelines are issued by the Attorney General for investigators, prosecutors and defence practitioners on the application of the disclosure regime contained in the Criminal Procedure and Investigations Act 1996 ('CPIA'). The Guidelines emphasise the importance of prosecution-led disclosure and the importance of applying the CPIA regime in a "thinking manner", tailored, where appropriate, to the type of investigation or prosecution in question.

The Guidelines do not contain the detail of the disclosure regime; they outline the high level principles which should be followed when the disclosure regime is applied.

These Guidelines replace the existing Attorney General's Guidelines on Disclosure issued in 2005 and the Supplementary Guidelines on Digital Material issued in 2011, which is an annex to the general guidelines.

The Guidelines are intended to operate alongside the Judicial Protocol on the Disclosure of Unused Material in Criminal Cases. They are not designed to be an unequivocal statement of the law at any one time, nor are they a substitute for a thorough understanding of the relevant legislation, codes of practice, case law and procedure.

Readers should note that a review of disclosure in the magistrates' courts is currently being undertaken by HHJ Kinch QC and the Chief Magistrate, on behalf of Lord Justice Gross, the Senior Presiding Judge. Amendments may therefore be made to these documents following the recommendations of that review, and in accordance with other forthcoming changes to the criminal justice system.

THE IMPORTANCE OF DISCLOSURE

1. The statutory framework for criminal investigations and disclosure is contained in the Criminal Procedure and Investigations Act 1996 (the CPIA) and the CPIA Code of Practice. The CPIA aims to ensure that criminal investigations are conducted in a fair, objective and thorough manner, and requires prosecutors to disclose to the defence material which has not previously been disclosed to the accused and which might reasonably be considered capable of undermining the case for the prosecution against the accused or of assisting the case for the accused. The CPIA requires a timely dialogue between the prosecution, defence and the court to enable the prosecution properly to identify such material.

2. Every accused person has a right to a fair trial, a right long embodied in our law and guaranteed by Article 6 of the European Convention on Human Rights (ECHR). A fair trial is the proper object and expectation of all participants in the trial process. Fair disclosure to the accused is an inseparable part of a fair trial. A fair trial should not require consideration of irrelevant material and should not involve spurious applications or arguments which serve to divert the trial process from examining the real issues before the court.

3. Properly applied, the CPIA should ensure that material is not disclosed which overburdens the participants in the trial process, diverts attention from the relevant issues, leads to unjustifiable delay, and is wasteful of resources. Consideration of disclosure issues should be an integral part of a good investigation and not something that exists separately.

DISCLOSURE: GENERAL PRINCIPLES

4. Disclosure refers to providing the defence with copies of, or access to, any prosecution material which might reasonably be considered capable of undermining the case for the prosecution against the accused, or of assisting the case for the accused, and which has not previously been disclosed (section 3 CPIA).

5. Prosecutors will only be expected to anticipate what material might undermine their case or strengthen the defence in the light of information available at the time of the disclosure decision, and they may take into account information revealed during questioning.

6. In deciding whether material satisfies the disclosure test, consideration should be given amongst other things to:

    a. the use that might be made of it in cross-examination;

      b.   its capacity to support submissions that could lead to:

           (i)   the exclusion of evidence;

           (ii)   a stay of proceedings, where the material is required to allow a proper application to be made;

           (iii)   a court or tribunal finding that any public authority had acted incompatibly with the accused's rights under the ECHR;

      c.   its capacity to suggest an explanation or partial explanation of the accused's actions;

      d.   the capacity of the material to have a bearing on scientific or medical evidence in the case.

7.   It should also be borne in mind that while items of material viewed in isolation may not be reasonably considered to be capable of undermining the prosecution case or assisting the accused, several items together can have that effect.

8.   Material relating to the accused's mental or physical health, intellectual capacity, or to any ill treatment which the accused may have suffered when in the investigator's custody is likely to fall within the test for disclosure set out in paragraph 4 above.

9.   Disclosure must not be an open-ended trawl of unused material. A critical element to fair and proper disclosure is that the defence play their role to ensure that the prosecution are directed to material which might reasonably be considered capable of undermining the prosecution case or assisting the case for the accused. This process is key to ensuring prosecutors make informed determinations about disclosure of unused material. The defence statement is important in identifying the issues in the case and why it is suggested that the material meets the test for disclosure.

10.   Disclosure should be conducted in a thinking manner and never be reduced to a box-ticking exercise[1]; at all stages of the process, there should be consideration of **why** the CPIA disclosure regime requires a particular course of action and what should be done to achieve that aim.

11.   There will always be a number of participants in prosecutions and investigations: senior investigation officers, disclosure officers, investigation officers, reviewing prosecutors, leading counsel, junior counsel, and sometimes disclosure counsel. Communication within the "prosecution

---

1   R v Olu, Wilson and Brooks [2010] EWCA Crim 2975 at paragraph 42.

team" is vital to ensure that all matters which could have a bearing on disclosure issues are given sufficient attention by the right person. This is especially so given many reviewing lawyers will be unable to sit behind the trial advocate throughout the trial. In practice, this is likely to mean that a full log of disclosure decisions (with reasons) must be kept on the file and made available as appropriate to the prosecution team.

12.   The role of the reviewing lawyer will be central to ensuring all members of the prosecution team are aware of, and carry out, their duties and role(s). Where this involves counsel or more than one reviewing lawyer, this should be done by giving clear written instructions and record keeping.

13.   The centrality of the reviewing lawyer does not mean that he or she has to do all the work personally; on the contrary, it will often mean effective delegation. Where the conduct of a prosecution is assigned to more than one prosecutor, steps must be taken to ensure that all involved in the case properly record their decisions. Subsequent prosecutors must be able to see and understand previous disclosure decisions before carrying out their continuous review function.

14.   Investigators must always be alive to the potential need to reveal and prosecutors to the potential need to disclose material, in the interests of justice and fairness in the particular circumstances of any case, after the commencement of proceedings but before their duty arises under the Act. For instance, disclosure ought to be made of significant information that might affect a bail decision. This is likely to depend on what the defence chooses to reveal at that stage.

INVESTIGATORS AND DISCLOSURE OFFICERS

15.   Investigators and disclosure officers must be fair and objective and must work together with prosecutors to ensure that disclosure obligations are met. Investigators and disclosure officers should be familiar with the CPIA Code of Practice, in particular their obligations to **retain** and **record** relevant material, to **review** it and to **reveal** it to the prosecutor.

16.   Whether a case is a summary only matter or a long and complex trial on indictment, it is important that investigators and disclosure officers should approach their duties in a "thinking manner" and not as a box ticking exercise. Where necessary, the reviewing lawyer should be consulted. It is important that investigators and disclosure officers are deployed on cases which are commensurate with their training, skills and experience. The conduct of an investigation provides the foundation for the entire case, and may even impact the conduct of linked cases. It is vital that

there is always consideration of disclosure matters at the outset of an investigation, regardless of its size.

17.   A fair investigation involves the pursuit of material following all reasonable lines of enquiry, whether they point towards or away from the suspect. What is 'reasonable' will depend on the context of the case. A fair investigation does not mean an endless investigation: investigators and disclosure officers must give thought to defining, and thereby limiting, the scope of their investigations, seeking the guidance of the prosecutor where appropriate

18.   Where there are a number of disclosure officers assigned to a case, there should be a lead disclosure officer who is the focus for enquiries and whose responsibility it is to ensure that the investigator's disclosure obligations are complied with. Where appropriate, regular case conferences and other meetings should be held to ensure prosecutors are apprised of all relevant developments in investigations. Full records should be kept of such meetings.

19.   The CPIA Code of Practice encourages investigators and disclosure officers to seek advice from prosecutors about whether any particular item of material may be relevant to the investigation, and if so, how. Investigators and disclosure officers should record key decisions taken on these matters and be prepared to account for their actions later. An identical approach is not called for in each and every case.

20.   Investigators are to approach their task seeking to establish what actually happened. They are to be fair and objective.

21.   Disclosure officers (or their deputies) must inspect, view, listen to or search all relevant material that has been retained by the investigator and the disclosure officer must provide a personal declaration to the effect that this task has been undertaken. In some cases, a detailed examination of all material seized may be required. In others, however, a detailed examination of every item of material seized would be virtually impossible: see the **Annex**.

22.   Prosecutors only have knowledge of matters which are revealed to them by investigators and disclosure officers, and the schedules are the written means by which that revelation takes place. Whatever the approach taken by investigators or disclosure officers to examining the material gathered or generated in the course of an investigation, it is crucial that disclosure officers record their reasons for a particular approach in writing.

23.   In meeting the obligations in paragraph 6.9 and 8.1 of the Code, schedules must be completed in a form which not only reveals sufficient information to the prosecutor, but which demonstrates a transparent and

thinking approach to the disclosure exercise, to command the confidence of the defence and the court. Descriptions on non-sensitive schedules must be clear and accurate, and must contain sufficient detail to enable the prosecutor to make an informed decision on disclosure. The use of abbreviations and acronyms can be problematic and lead to difficulties in appreciating the significance of the material.

24.   Sensitive schedules must contain sufficiently clear descriptions to enable the prosecutor to make an informed decision as to whether or not the material itself should be viewed, to the extent possible without compromising the confidentiality of the information.

25.   It may become apparent to an investigator that some material obtained in the course of an investigation, either because it was considered to be potentially relevant, or because it was inextricably linked to material that was relevant, is, in fact, incapable of impact. It is not necessary to retain such material, although the investigator should err on the side of caution in reaching that conclusion and should be particularly mindful of the fact that some investigations continue over some time and that what is incapable of impact may change over time. The advice of the prosecutor should be sought where appropriate.

26.   Disclosure officers must specifically draw material to the attention of the prosecutor for consideration where they have any doubt as to whether it might reasonably be considered capable of undermining the prosecution case or of assisting the case for the accused.

27.   Disclosure officers must seek the advice and assistance of prosecutors when in doubt as to their responsibility as early as possible. They must deal expeditiously with requests by the prosecutor for further information on material, which may lead to disclosure.

PROSECUTORS

28.   Prosecutors are responsible for making proper disclosure in consultation with the disclosure officer. The duty of disclosure is a continuing one and disclosure should be kept under review. In addition, prosecutors should ensure that advocates in court are properly instructed as to disclosure issues. Prosecutors must also be alert to the need to provide advice to, and where necessary probe actions taken by, disclosure officers to ensure that disclosure obligations are met. There should be no aspects of an investigation about which prosecutors are unable to ask probing questions.

29.   Prosecutors must review schedules prepared by disclosure officers thoroughly and must be alert to the possibility that relevant material may

exist which has not been revealed to them or material included which should not have been. If no schedules have been provided, or there are apparent omissions from the schedules, or documents or other items are inadequately described or are unclear, the prosecutor must at once take action to obtain properly completed schedules. Likewise schedules should be returned for amendment if irrelevant items are included. If prosecutors remain dissatisfied with the quality or content of the schedules they must raise the matter with a senior investigator to resolve the matter satisfactorily.

30.   Where prosecutors have reason to believe that the disclosure officer has not discharged the obligation in paragraph 21 to inspect, view, listen to or search relevant material, they must at once raise the matter with the disclosure officer and request that it be done. Where appropriate the matter should be raised with the officer in the case or a senior officer.

31.   Prosecutors should copy the defence statement to the disclosure officer and investigator as soon as reasonably practicable and prosecutors should advise the investigator if, in their view, reasonable and relevant lines of further enquiry should be pursued. If the defence statement does point to other reasonable lines of enquiry, further investigation is required and evidence obtained as a result of these enquiries may be used as part of the prosecution case or to rebut the defence.

32.   It is vital that prosecutors consider defence statements thoroughly. Prosecutors cannot comment upon, or invite inferences to be drawn from, failures in defence disclosure otherwise than in accordance with section 11 of the CPIA. Prosecutors may cross-examine the accused on differences between the defence case put at trial and that set out in his or her defence statement. In doing so, it may be appropriate to apply to the judge under section 6E of the CPIA for copies of the statement to be given to a jury, edited if necessary to remove inadmissible material. Prosecutors should examine the defence statement to see whether it points to other lines of enquiry.

33.   Prosecutors should challenge the lack of, or inadequate, defence statements in writing, copying the document to the court and the defence and seeking directions from the court to require the provision of an adequate statement from the defence.

34.   If the material does not fulfil the disclosure test there is no requirement to disclose it. For this purpose, the parties' respective cases should not be restrictively analysed but must be carefully analysed to ascertain the specific facts the prosecution seek to establish and the specific grounds on which the charges are resisted.

PROSECUTION ADVOCATES

35.   Prosecution advocates should ensure that all material which ought to be disclosed under the Act is disclosed to the defence. However, prosecution advocates cannot be expected to disclose material if they are not aware of its existence. As far as is possible, prosecution advocates must place themselves in a fully informed position to enable them to make decisions on disclosure.

36.   Upon receipt of instructions, prosecution advocates should consider as a priority all the information provided regarding disclosure of material. Prosecution advocates should consider, in every case, whether they can be satisfied that they are in possession of all relevant documentation and that they have been fully instructed regarding disclosure matters. If as a result the advocate considers that further information or action is required, written advice should promptly be provided setting out the aspects that need clarification or action.

37.   The prosecution advocate must keep decisions regarding disclosure under review until the conclusion of the trial, whenever possible in consultation with the reviewing prosecutor. The prosecution advocate must in every case specifically consider whether he or she can satisfactorily discharge the duty of continuing review on the basis of the material supplied already, or whether it is necessary to inspect further material or to reconsider material already inspected. Prosecution advocates must not abrogate their responsibility under the CPIA by disclosing material which does not pass the test for disclosure, set out in paragraph 4, above.

38.   There remains no basis in practice or law for counsel to counsel disclosure.

DEFENCE

39.   Defence engagement must be early and meaningful for the CPIA regime to function as intended. Defence statements are an integral part of this and are intended to help focus the attention of the prosecutor, court and co-defendants on the relevant issues in order to identify exculpatory unused material. Defence statements should be drafted in accordance with the relevant provisions of the CPIA.

40.   Defence requests for further disclosure should ordinarily only be answered by the prosecution if the request is relevant to and directed to an issue identified in the defence statement. If it is not, then a further or amended defence statement should be sought by the prosecutor and obtained before considering the request for further disclosure.

41.   In some cases that involve extensive unused material that is within the knowledge of a defendant, the defence will be expected to provide the prosecution and the court with assistance in identifying material which is suggested to pass the test for disclosure.

42.   The prosecution's continuing duty to keep disclosure under review is crucial, and particular attention must be paid to understanding the significance of developments in the case on the unused material and earlier disclosure decisions. Meaningful defence engagement will help the prosecution to keep disclosure under review. The continuing duty of review for prosecutors is less likely to require the disclosure of further material to the defence if the defence have clarified and articulated their case, as required by the CPIA.

43.   In the magistrates' courts, where the provision of a defence statement is not mandatory, early identification of the material issues by the defence, whether through a defence statement, case management form or otherwise, will help the prosecution to focus its preparation of the case and allow any defence disclosure queries to be dealt with promptly and accurately.

MAGISTRATES' COURTS (INCLUDING THE YOUTH COURT)

44.   The majority of criminal cases are heard in the magistrates' court. The requirement for the prosecution to provide initial disclosure only arises after a not guilty plea has been entered but prosecutors should be alert to the possibility that material may exist which should be disclosed to the defendant prior to the CPIA requirements applying to the case[2].

45.   Where a not guilty plea is entered in the magistrates' court, prosecutors should ensure that any issues of dispute which are raised are noted on the file. They should also seek to obtain a copy of any Magistrates' Court Trial Preparation Form. Consideration of the issues raised in court and on the Trial Preparation Form will assist in deciding what material undermines the prosecution case or assists the defendant.

46.   Where a matter is set down for trial in the magistrates' court, prosecutors should ensure that the investigator is requested to supply any outstanding disclosure schedules as a matter of urgency. Prosecutors should serve initial disclosure in sufficient time to ensure that the trial date is effective.

---

2   See for example *R v DPP ex parte Lee [1999] 2 All ER 737.*

47.   There is no requirement for a defence statement to be served in the magistrates' court but it should be noted that if none is given the court has no power to hear an application for further prosecution disclosure under section 8 of the CPIA and the Criminal Procedure Rules.

CASES IN THE CROWN COURT

48.   The exponential increase in the use of technology in society means that many routine Crown Court cases are increasingly likely to have to engage with digital material of some form. It is not only in large and complex cases that there may be large quantities of such material. Where such investigations involve digital material, it will be virtually impossible for investigators (or prosecutors) to examine every item of such material individually and there should be no expectation that such material will be so examined. Having consulted with the prosecution as appropriate, disclosure officers should determine what their approach should be to the examination of the material. Investigators or disclosure officers should decide how best to pursue a reasonable line of enquiry in relation to the relevant digital material, and ensure that the extent and manner of the examination are commensurate with the issues in the case.

49.   Consideration should be given to any local or national agreements in relation to disclosure in 'Early Guilty Plea Scheme' cases.

LARGE AND COMPLEX CASES IN THE CROWN COURT

50.   The particular challenges presented by large and complex criminal prosecutions require an approach to disclosure which is specifically tailored to the needs of such cases. In these cases more than any other is the need for careful thought to be given to prosecution-led disclosure matters from the very earliest stage. It is essential that the prosecution takes a grip on the case and its disclosure requirements from the very outset of the investigation, which must continue throughout all aspects of the case preparation.

DISCLOSURE MANAGEMENT DOCUMENTS

51.   Accordingly, investigations and prosecutions of large and complex cases should be carefully defined and accompanied by a clear investigation and prosecution strategy. The approach to disclosure in such cases

should be outlined in a document which should be served on the defence and the court at an early stage. Such documents, sometimes known as Disclosure Management Documents, will require careful preparation and presentation, tailored to the individual case. They may include:

a.   Where prosecutors and investigators operate in an integrated office, an explanation as to how the disclosure responsibilities have been managed;

b.   A brief summary of the prosecution case and a statement outlining how the prosecutor's general approach will comply with the CPIA regime, these Guidelines and the Judicial Protocol on the Disclosure of Unused Material in Criminal Cases;

c.   The prosecutor's understanding of the defence case, including information revealed during interview;

d.   An outline of the prosecution's general approach to disclosure, which may include detail relating to:

   (i)   Digital material: explaining the method and extent of examination, in accordance with the **Annex** to these Guidelines;

   (ii)   Video footage;

   (iii) Linked investigations: explaining the nexus between investigations, any memoranda of understanding or disclosure agreements between investigators;

   (iv)   Third party and foreign material, including steps taken to obtain the material;

   (v)   Reasonable lines of enquiry: a summary of the lines pursued, particularly those that point away from the suspect, or which may assist the defence;

   (vi)   Credibility of a witness: confirmation that witness checks, including those of professional witnesses have, or will be, carried out.

52.   Thereafter the prosecution should follow the Disclosure Management Document. They are living documents and should be amended in light of developments in the case; they should be kept up to date as the case progresses. Their use will assist the court in its own case management and will enable the defence to engage from an early stage with the prosecution's proposed approach to disclosure.

MATERIAL NOT HELD BY THE PROSECUTION

Involvement of other agencies: material held by other Government departments and third parties

53.　Where it appears to an investigator, disclosure officer or prosecutor that a Government department or other Crown body has material that may be relevant to an issue in the case, reasonable steps should be taken to identify and consider such material. Although what is reasonable will vary from case to case, the prosecution should inform the department or other body of the nature of its case and of relevant issues in the case in respect of which the department or body might possess material, and ask whether it has any such material.

54.　It should be remembered that investigators, disclosure officers and prosecutors cannot be regarded to be in constructive possession of material held by Government departments or Crown bodies simply by virtue of their status as Government departments or Crown bodies.

55.　Where, after reasonable steps have been taken to secure access to such material, access is denied, the investigator, disclosure officer or prosecutor should consider what if any further steps might be taken to obtain the material or inform the defence. The final decision on any further steps will be for the prosecutor.

Third party material: other domestic bodies

56.　There may be cases where the investigator, disclosure officer or prosecutor believes that a third party (for example, a local authority, a social services department, a hospital, a doctor, a school, a provider of forensic services) has material or information which might be relevant to the prosecution case. In such cases, investigators, disclosure officers and prosecutors should take reasonable steps to identify, secure and consider material held by any third party where it appears to the investigator, disclosure officer or prosecutor that (a) such material exists and (b) that it may be relevant to an issue in the case.

57.　If the investigator, disclosure officer or prosecutor seeks access to the material or information but the third party declines or refuses to allow access to it, the matter should not be left. If despite any reasons offered by the third party it is still believed that it is reasonable to seek production of the material or information, and the requirements of section 2 of the Criminal Procedure (Attendance of Witnesses) Act 1965 or as appropriate section 97 of the Magistrates Courts Act 1980 are satisfied (or any other relevant power), then the prosecutor or investigator should apply for a witness summons causing a representative of the third party to produce the material to the court.

58.   Sometimes, for example through multi-agency working arrangements, investigators, disclosure officers or prosecutors may become aware of the content or nature of material held by a third party. Consultation with the relevant third party must always take place before disclosure is made; there may be public interest reasons to apply to the Court for an order for non-disclosure in the public interest, in accordance with the procedure outlined in paragraph 65 and following.

INTERNATIONAL MATTERS

59.   The obligations under the CPIA Code to pursue all reasonable lines of enquiry apply to material held overseas.

60.   Where it appears that there is relevant material, the prosecutor must take reasonable steps to obtain it, either informally or making use of the powers contained in the Crime (International Co-operation) Act 2003 and any EU and international conventions. See CPS Guidance 'Obtaining Evidence and Information from Abroad'.

61.   There may be cases where a foreign state or a foreign court refuses to make the material available to the investigator or prosecutor. There may be other cases where the foreign state, though willing to show the material to investigators, will not allow the material to be copied or otherwise made available and the courts of the foreign state will not order its provision.

62.   It is for these reasons that there is no absolute duty on the prosecutor to disclose relevant material held overseas by entities not subject to the jurisdiction of the courts in England and Wales. However consideration should be given to whether the type of material believed to be held can be provided to the defence.

63.   The obligation on the investigator and prosecutor under the CPIA is to take reasonable steps. Where investigators are allowed to examine files of a foreign state but are not allowed to take copies or notes or list the documents held, there is no breach by the prosecution in its duty of disclosure by reason of its failure to obtain such material, provided reasonable steps have been taken to try and obtain the material. Prosecutors have a margin of consideration as to what steps are appropriate in the particular case but prosecutors must be alive to their duties and there may be some circumstances where these duties cannot be met. Whether the

prosecutor has taken reasonable steps is for the court to determine in each case if the matter is raised.

64. In these circumstances it is important that the position is clearly set out in writing so that the court and the defence know what the position is. Investigators and prosecutors must record and explain the situation and set out, insofar as they are permitted by the foreign state, such information as they can and the steps they have taken.

APPLICATIONS FOR NON-DISCLOSURE IN THE PUBLIC INTEREST

65. The CPIA allows prosecutors to apply to the court for an order to withhold material which would otherwise fall to be disclosed if disclosure would give rise to a real risk of serious prejudice to an important public interest. Before making such an application, prosecutors should aim to disclose as much of the material as they properly can (for example, by giving the defence redacted or edited copies or summaries). Neutral material or material damaging to the defendant need not be disclosed and there is no need to bring it to the attention of the court. Only in truly borderline cases should the prosecution seek a judicial ruling on whether material in its possession should be disclosed.

66. Prior to the hearing, the prosecutor and the prosecution advocate must examine all material which is the subject matter of the application and make any necessary enquiries of the investigator. The investigator must be frank with the prosecutor about the full extent of the sensitive material. Prior to or at the hearing, the court must be provided with full and accurate information about the material

67. The prosecutor (or representative) and/or investigator should attend such applications. Section 16 of the CPIA allows a person claiming to have an interest in the sensitive material to apply to the court for the opportunity to be heard at the application.

68. The principles set out at paragraph 36 of *R v H & C* [2004] 2 Cr. App. R. 10 [2004] UKHL 3 should be applied rigorously, firstly by the prosecutor and then by the court considering the material. It is essential that these principles are scrupulously adhered to, to ensure that the procedure for examination of material in the absence of the accused is compliant with Article 6.

69. If prosecutors conclude that a fair trial cannot take place because material which satisfies the test for disclosure cannot be disclosed, and that this

cannot be remedied by the above procedure; how the case is presented; or by any other means, they should not continue with the case.

OTHER DISCLOSURE

70.   Disclosure of any material that is made outside the ambit of CPIA will attract confidentiality by virtue of *Taylor v SFO* [1999] 2 AC 177.

Material relevant to sentence

71.   In all cases the prosecutor must consider disclosing in the interests of justice any material which is relevant to sentence (e.g. information which might mitigate the seriousness of the offence or assist the accused to lay blame in part upon a co-accused or another person).

Post-conviction

72.   Where, after the conclusion of the proceedings, material comes to light, that might cast doubt upon the safety of the conviction, the prosecutor must consider disclosure of such material.

Applicability of these Guidelines

73.   These Guidelines shall have immediate effect.

ANNEX: ATTORNEY GENERAL'S GUIDELINES ON DISCLOSURE: SUPPLEMENTARY GUIDELINES ON DIGITALLY STORED MATERIAL (2011)

A1.   The Guidelines are intended to supplement the Attorney General's Guidelines on Disclosure.

A2.   As a result of the number of cases now involving digitally stored material and the scale of the digital material that may be involved, more detailed guidance is considered to be needed. The objective of these Guidelines is to set out how material satisfying the tests for disclosure can best be identified and disclosed to the defence without imposing unrealistic or disproportionate demands on the investigator and prosecutor.

A3.   The approach set out in these Guidelines is in line with existing best practice, in that:

   a.   Investigating and prosecuting agencies, especially in large and complex cases, will apply their respective case management and disclosure strategies and policies and be transparent with the defence and the courts about how the prosecution has approached complying with its disclosure obligations in the context of the individual case; and,

   b.   The defence will be expected to play their part in defining the real issues in the case. In this context, the defence will be invited to participate in defining the scope of the reasonable searches that may be made of digitally stored material by the investigator to identify material that might reasonably be expected to undermine the prosecution case or assist the defence.

A4.   Only if this approach is followed can the courts be in a position to use their case management powers effectively and to determine applications for disclosure fairly.

A5.   The Attorney General's Guidelines are not detailed operational guidelines. They are intended to set out a common approach to be adopted in the context of digitally stored material.

TYPES OF DIGITAL MATERIAL

A6.   Digital material falls into two categories: the first category is material which is created natively within an electronic environment (e.g. email, office files, system files, digital photographs, audio etc.); the second category is material which has been digitised from an analogue form (e.g. scanned copy of a document, scanned photograph, a faxed document). Irrespective of the way in which technology changes, the categorisation of digital material will remain the same.

A7.   Digital material is usually held on one of the three types of media. Optical media (e.g. CD, DVD, Blu-ray) and Solid-State media (e.g. removable memory cards, solid state music players or mobile devices etc.) cater for usually lower volume storage. Magnetic media (e.g. disk drives and back up tapes) usually cater for high volume storage.

GENERAL PRINCIPLES FOR INVESTIGATORS

A8.   The general principles[3] to be followed by investigators in handling and examining digital material are:

   a.   No action taken by investigators or their agents should change data held on a computer or storage media which may subsequently be relied upon in court;

   b.   In circumstances where a person finds it necessary to access original data held on computer or storage media, that person must be competent to do so and be able to give evidence explaining the relevance and implications of their actions;

   c.   An audit trail or other record of all processes applied to computer-based electronic evidence should be created and preserved. An independent third party should be able to examine those processes (see further the sections headed Record keeping and Scheduling below); and,

   d.   The person in charge of the investigation has overall responsibility for ensuring that the law and these principles are followed.

A9.   Where an investigator has reasonable grounds for believing that digital material may contain material subject to legal professional privilege, very strong legal constraints apply. No digital material may be seized which an investigator has reasonable grounds for believing to be subject to legal privilege, other than where the provisions of the Criminal Justice and Police Act 2001 apply. Strict controls need to be applied where privileged material is seized. See the more detailed section on Legal Professional Privilege starting at paragraph A28, below.

---

3   Based on: <u>Association of Chief Police Officers: Good Practice Guide for Computer Based Electronic Evidence Version 0.1.4.</u>

SEIZURE, RELEVANCE AND RETENTION

A10. The legal obligations are to be found in a combination of the Police and Criminal Evidence Act 1984 (PACE), the Criminal Justice and Police Act 2001 (CJPA 2001) and the Criminal Procedure and Investigations Act 1996 (the CPIA 1996).

A11. These Guidelines also apply to digital material seized or imaged under other statutory provisions. For example, the Serious Fraud Office has distinct powers of seizure under warrant obtained under section 2(4) of the Criminal Justice Act 1987. In cases concerning indecent images of children and obscene material, special provisions apply to the handling, storage and copying of such material. Practitioners should refer to specific guidance on the application of those provisions.

SEIZURE

A12. Before searching a suspect's premises where digital evidence is likely to be found, consideration must be given to what sort of evidence is likely to be found and in what volume, whether it is likely to be possible to view and copy, if relevant, the material at the location (it is not uncommon with the advent of cloud computing for digital material to be hosted by a third party) and to what should be seized. Business and commercial premises will often have very substantial amounts of digital material stored on computers and other media. Investigators will need to consider the practicalities of seizing computer hard drives and other media, the effect this may have on the business and, where it is not feasible to obtain an image of digital material, the likely timescale for returning seized items.

A13. In deciding whether to seize and retain digital material it is important that the investigator either complies with the procedure under the relevant statutory authority, relying either on statutory powers or a search warrant, or obtains the owner's consent. In particular, investigators need to be aware of the constraints applying to legally privileged material.

A14. A computer hard drive or single item of media, such as a back up tape, is a single storage entity. This means that if any digital material found on the hard drive or other media can lawfully be seized the computer hard drive or single item of media may, if appropriate, be seized or imaged. In some circumstances investigators may wish to image specific folders, files or categories of data where it is feasible to do so without seizing the hard drive or other media, or instead of taking an image of all data on the hard drive or other media. In practice, the configuration of most systems means that data may be contained across a number of hard drives and more than one hard drive or item of media may be required in order to access the information sought.

A15. Digital material must not be seized if an investigator has reasonable grounds for believing it is subject to legal professional privilege, other than where sections 50 or 51 of the CJPA 2001 apply. If such material is seized it must be isolated from other seized material and any other investigation material in the possession of the investigating authority.

The Police and Criminal Evidence Act 1984

A16. PACE 1984 provides powers to seize and retain anything for which the search has been authorised or after arrest, other than items attracting legal professional privilege.[4] In addition, there is a general power to seize anything which is on the premises if there are reasonable grounds to believe that it has been obtained in the commission of an offence, or that it is evidence and that it is necessary to seize it to prevent it being concealed, lost, altered or destroyed.[5] There is another related power to require information which is stored in any electronic form and is accessible from the premises to be produced in a form in which it can be taken away and in which it is visible and legible or from which it can readily be produced in a visible and legible form.[6]

A17. An image (a forensically sound copy) of the digital material may be taken at the location of the search. Where the investigator makes an image of the digital material at the location, the original need not be seized. Alternatively, when originals are taken, investigators must be prepared to copy or image the material for the owners when reasonably practicable in accordance with PACE 1984 Code B 7.17.

A18. Where it is not possible or reasonably practicable to image the computer or hard drive, it will need to be removed from the location or premises for examination elsewhere. This allows the investigator to seize and sift material for the purpose of identifying that which meets the tests for retention in accordance with the 1984 PACE.[7]

---

4   By warrant under section 8 and Schedule 1 and section 18 of PACE.
5   Section 19 of PACE.
6   Section 20 of PACE.
7   Special provision exists for investigations conducted by Her Majesty's Revenue and Customs in the application of their powers under PACE – see section 114(2)(b) – and the CJPA 2001.

THE CRIMINAL JUSTICE AND POLICE ACT 2001

A19.   The additional powers of seizure in sections 50 and 51 of the CJPA 2001 Act only extend the scope of existing powers of search and seizure under the PACE and other specified statutory authorities[8] where the relevant conditions and circumstances apply.

A20.   Investigators must be careful only to exercise powers under the CJPA 2001 when it is necessary and not to remove any more material than is justified. The removal of large volumes of material, much of which may not ultimately be retainable, may have serious consequences for the owner of the material, particularly when they are involved in business or other commercial activities.

A21.   A written notice must be given to the occupier of the premises where items are seized under sections 50 and 51.[9]

A22.   Until material seized under the CJPA 2001 has been examined, it must be kept securely and separately from any material seized under other powers. Any such material must be examined as soon as reasonably practicable to determine which elements may be retained and which should be returned. Regard must be had to the desirability of allowing the person from whom the property was seized – or a person with an interest in the property – an opportunity of being present or represented at the examination.

RETENTION

A23.   Where material is seized under the powers conferred by PACE the duty to retain it under the Code of Practice issued under the CPIA is subject to the provisions on retention under section 22 of PACE. Material seized under sections 50 and 51 of the CJPA 2001 may be retained or returned in accordance with sections 53–58 of that Act.

A24.   Retention is limited to evidence and relevant material (as defined in the Code of Practice issued under the CPIA). Where either evidence or relevant material is inextricably linked to non-relevant material which is not reasonably practicable to separate, that material can also be retained. Inextricably linked material is material that is not reasonably practicable to separate from other linked material without prejudicing the use of that other material in any investigation or proceedings.

---

8   Schedule 1 of the CJPA 2001.
9   Section 52 of the CJPA 2001.

A25.   However, inextricably linked material must not be examined, imaged, copied or used for any purpose other than for providing the source of or the integrity of the linked material.

A26.   There are four categories of material that may be retained:

    a.   Material that is evidence or potential evidence in the case. Where material is retained for evidential purposes there will be a strong argument that the whole thing (or an authenticated image or copy) should be retained for the purpose of proving provenance and continuity;

    b.   Where evidential material has been retained, inextricably linked non-relevant material which is not reasonably practicable to separate can also be retained (PACE Code B paragraph 7);

    c.   An investigator should retain material that is relevant to the investigation and required to be scheduled as unused material. This is broader than but includes the duty to retain material which may satisfy the test for prosecution disclosure. The general duty to retain relevant material is set out in the CPIA Code at paragraph 5; or,

    d.   Material which is inextricably linked to relevant unused material which of itself may not be relevant material. Such material should be retained (PACE Code B paragraph 7).

A27.   The balance of any digital material should be returned in accordance with sections 53–55 of the CJPA 2001 if seized under that Act.

LEGAL PROFESSIONAL PRIVILEGE (LPP)

A28.   No digital material may be seized which an investigator has reasonable grounds for believing to be subject to LPP, other than under the additional powers of seizure in the CJPA 2001.

A29.   The CJPA 2001 enables an investigator to seize relevant items which contain LPP material where it is not reasonably practicable on the search premises to separate LPP material from non-LPP material.

A30.   Where LPP material or material suspected of containing LPP is seized, it must be isolated from the other material which has been seized in the investigation. The mechanics of securing property vary according to the circumstances; "bagging up", i.e. placing materials in sealed bags or containers, and strict subsequent control of access, is the appropriate procedure in many cases.

A31. Where material has been identified as potentially containing LPP it must be reviewed by a lawyer independent of the prosecuting authority. No member of the investigative or prosecution team involved in either the current investigation or, if the LPP material relates to other criminal proceedings, in those proceedings should have sight of or access to the LPP material.

A32. If the material is voluminous, search terms or other filters may have to be used to identify the LPP material. If so this will also have to be done by someone independent and not connected with the investigation.

A33. It is essential that anyone dealing with LPP material maintains proper records showing the way in which the material has been handled and those who have had access to it as well as decisions taken in relation to that material.

A34. LPP material can only be retained in specific circumstances in accordance with section 54 of the CJPA 2001 i.e. where the property which comprises the LPP material has been lawfully seized and it is not reasonably practicable for the item to be separated from the rest of the property without prejudicing the use of the rest of the property. LPP material which cannot be retained must be returned as soon as practicable after the seizure without waiting for the whole examination of the seized material.

EXCLUDED AND SPECIAL PROCEDURE MATERIAL

A35. Similar principles to those that apply to LPP material apply to excluded or special procedure material, as set out in section 55 of the CJPA 2001.[10]

ENCRYPTION

A36. Part III of the Regulation of Investigatory Powers Act 2000 (RIPA) and the Investigation of Protected Electronic Information Code of Practice govern encryption. See the CPS's Guidance RIPA Part III.

A37. RIPA enables specified law enforcement agencies to compel individuals or companies to provide passwords or encryption keys for the purpose of rendering protected material readable. Failure to comply with RIPA Part III orders is a criminal offence. The Code of Practice provides guidance when exercising powers under RIPA, to require disclosure of protected

---

10 Special provision exists for investigations conducted by Her Majesty's Revenue and Customs in the application of their powers under PACE – see section 114(2)(b) – and the CJPA.

electronic data in an intelligible form or to acquire the means by which protected electronic data may be accessed or put in an intelligible form.

SIFTING/EXAMINATION

A38. In complying with its duty of disclosure, the prosecution should follow the procedure as outlined below.

A39. Where digital material is examined, the extent and manner of inspecting, viewing or listening will depend on the nature of the material and its form.

A40. It is important for investigators and prosecutors to remember that the duty under the CPIA Code of Practice is to "pursue all reasonable lines of enquiry including those that point away from the suspect". Lines of enquiry, of whatever kind, should be pursued only if they are reasonable in the context of the individual case. It is not the duty of the prosecution to comb through all the material in its possession – e.g. every word or byte of computer material – on the look out for anything which might conceivably or speculatively assist the defence. The duty of the prosecution is to disclose material which might reasonably be considered capable of undermining its case or assisting the case for the accused which they become aware of, or to which their attention is drawn.

A41. In some cases the sift may be conducted by an investigator/disclosure officer manually assessing the content of the computer or other digital material from its directory and determining which files are relevant and should be retained for evidence or unused material.

A42. In other cases such an approach may not be feasible. Where there is an enormous volume of material it is perfectly proper for the investigator/disclosure officer to search it by sample, key words, or other appropriate search tools or analytical techniques to locate relevant passages, phrases and identifiers.

A43. In cases involving very large quantities of data, the person in charge of the investigation will develop a strategy setting out how the material should be analysed or searched to identify categories of data. Where search tools are used to examine digital material it will usually be appropriate to provide the accused and his or her legal representative with a copy of reasonable search terms used, or to be used, and invite them to suggest any further reasonable search terms. If search terms are suggested which the investigator or prosecutor believes will not be productive – for example because of the use of common words that are likely to identify a mass of irrelevant material, the investigator or prosecutor is entitled to open a dialogue with the defence representative with a view to agreeing sensible refinements. The purpose of this dialogue is to ensure that reasonable and proportionate searches can be carried out.

A44.   It may be necessary to carry out sampling and searches on more than one occasion, especially as there is a duty on the prosecutor to keep duties of disclosure under review. To comply with this duty it may be appropriate (and should be considered) where further evidence or unused material is obtained in the course of the investigation; the defence statement is served on the prosecutor; the defendant makes an application under section 8 of the CPIA for disclosure; or the defendant requests that further sampling or searches be carried out (provided it is a reasonable line of enquiry).

RECORD KEEPING

A45.   A record or log must be made of all digital material seized or imaged and subsequently retained as relevant to the investigation.

A46.   In cases involving very large quantities of data where the person in charge of the investigation has developed a strategy setting out how the material should be analysed or searched to identify categories of data, a record should be made of the strategy and the analytical techniques used to search the data. The record should include details of the person who has carried out the process and the date and time it was carried out. In such cases the strategy should record the reasons why certain categories have been searched for (such as names, companies, dates etc).

A47.   In any case it is important that any searching or analytical processing of digital material, as well as the data identified by that process, is properly recorded. So far as practicable, what is required is a record of the terms of the searches or processing that has been carried out. This means that in principle the following details may be recorded:

a.   A record of all searches carried out, including the date of each search and the person(s) who conducted it;

b.   A record of all search words or terms used on each search. However where it is impracticable to record each word or terms (such as where Boolean searches or search strings or conceptual searches are used) it will usually be sufficient to record each broad category of search;

c.   A log of the key judgements made while refining the search strategy in the light of what is found, or deciding not to carry out further searches; and,

> d.   Where material relating to a "hit" is not examined, the decision not
> to examine should be explained in the record of examination or in
> a statement. For instance, a large number of "hits" may be obtained
> in relation to a particular search word or term, but material relating
> to the "hits" is not examined because they do not appear to be
> relevant to the investigation. Any subsequent refinement of the
> search terms and further hits should also be noted and explained as
> above.

A48.   Just as it is not necessary for the investigator or prosecutor to produce
records of every search made of hard copy material, it is not necessary
to produce records of what may be many hundreds of searches or
analyses that have been carried out on digitally stored material, simply
to demonstrate that these have been done. It should be sufficient for the
prosecution to explain how the disclosure exercise has been approached
and to give the accused or suspect's legal representative an opportunity to
participate in defining the reasonable searches to be made, as described in
the section on sifting/examination.

SCHEDULING

A49.   The disclosure officer should ensure that scheduling of relevant material
is carried out in accordance with the CPIA Code of Practice. This requires
each item of unused material to be listed separately on the unused material
schedule and numbered consecutively. The description of each item
should make clear the nature of the item and should contain sufficient
detail to enable the prosecutor to decide whether he needs to inspect
the material before deciding whether or not it should be disclosed (see
paragraph A24).

A50.   In some enquiries it may not be practicable to list each item of material
separately. If so, these may be listed in a block and described by quantity
and generic title. Even if the material is listed in a block, the search terms
used and any items of material which might satisfy the disclosure test
are listed and described separately. In practical terms this will mean,
where appropriate, cross referencing the schedules to your disclosure
management document.

A51.   The remainder of any computer hard drive/media containing material
which is not responsive to search terms or other analytical technique
or not identified by any "hits", and material identified by "hits" but not
examined, is unused material and should be recorded (if appropriate by a
generic description) and retained.

A52. Where continuation sheets of the unused material schedule are used, or additional schedules are sent subsequently, the item numbering must be, where possible, sequential to all other items on earlier schedules.

THIRD PARTY MATERIAL

A53. Third party material is material held by a person, organisation, or government department other than the investigator and prosecutor within the UK or outside the UK.

WITHIN THE UK

A54. The CPIA Code and the AG's Guidelines make clear the obligation on the prosecution to pursue all reasonable lines of enquiry in relation to material held by third parties within the UK.

A55. If as a result of the duty to pursue all reasonable lines of enquiry, the investigator or prosecutor obtains or receives the material from the third party, then it must be dealt with in accordance with the CPIA i.e. the prosecutor must disclose material if it meets the disclosure tests, subject to any public interest immunity claim. The person who has an interest in the material (the third party) may make representations to the court concerning public interest immunity (see section 16 of the CPIA 1996).

A56. Material not in the possession of an investigator or prosecutor falls outside the CPIA. In such cases the Attorney General's Guidelines on Disclosure prescribe the approach to be taken to disclosure of material held by third parties as does the judicial disclosure protocol.

**Annexed to the revised Attorney General's Guidelines
on Disclosure December 2013**

Judicial Protocol on the Disclosure of Unused Material in Criminal Cases

December 2013

CONTENTS

FOREWORD

We are pleased to publish a revised judicial protocol and revised guidance on the disclosure of unused material in criminal cases. Proper disclosure of unused material, made through a rigorous and carefully considered application of the law, remains a crucial part of a fair trial, and essential to avoiding miscarriages of justice. These new documents are intended to clarify the procedures to be followed and to encourage the active participation of all parties.

They have been prepared following the recommendations of Lord Justice Gross in his September 2011 'Review of Disclosure in Criminal Proceedings' and take account of Lord Justice Gross and Lord Justice Treacy's 'Further review of disclosure in criminal proceedings: sanctions for disclosure failure', published in November 2012.

There are important roles for the prosecution, the defence and the court in ensuring that disclosure is conducted properly, including on the part of the investigating, case progression and disclosure officers, as well as the lawyers and advocates. Lord Justice Gross particularly recommended that the guidance on disclosure of unused material in criminal cases should be consolidated and abbreviated. Given all of those involved in this process have separate constitutional roles, the judiciary and the Attorney-General have worked together to produce complementary guidance that is shorter than the previous iterations, but remains comprehensive. The two documents are similarly structured for ease of reference and should be read together.

The Rt. Hon. The Lord Thomas Lord Chief Justice of England and Wales

The Rt. Hon. Dominic Grieve QC MP Attorney General

INTRODUCTION

This protocol is prescribed for use by CPD IV Disclosure 22A: Disclosure of Unused Material. It is applicable in all the criminal courts of England and Wales, including the Crown Court, the Court Martial[1] and the magistrates' courts. It replaces the previous judicial document 'Disclosure: a Protocol for the Control and Management of Unused Material in the Crown Court'[2] and it also replaces section 4 'Disclosure' of the Lord Chief Justice's Protocol on the Control and Management of Heavy Fraud and Other Complex Criminal Cases, dated 22 March 2005.[3]

This protocol is intended to provide a central source of guidance for the judiciary, although that produced by the Attorney General also requires attention.

In summary, this judicial protocol sets out the principles to be applied to, and the importance of, disclosure; the expectations of the court and its role in disclosure, in particular in relation to case management; and the consequences if there is a failure by the prosecution or defence to comply with their obligations.

Readers should note that a review of disclosure in the magistrates' courts is currently being undertaken by HHJ Kinch QC and the Chief Magistrate, on behalf of Lord Justice Gross, the Senior Presiding Judge. Amendments may therefore be made following the recommendations of that review, and in accordance with other forthcoming changes to the criminal justice system.

---

1   The timetables given here may vary in the Court Martial and reference should be made to the Criminal Procedure and Investigations Act 1996 (Application to the Armed Forces) Order 2009 and to any practice note issued by the Judge Advocate General.

2   The previous judicial protocol was endorsed by the Court of Appeal in *R v K* [2006] EWCA Crim 724; [2006] 2 All ER 552 (Note); [2006] Crim LR 1012.

3   This protocol also replaces the Protocol for the Provision of Advance Information, Prosecution Evidence and Disclosure of Unused Material in the Magistrates' Courts, dated 12 May 2006, which was adopted as part of the Stop Delaying Justice initiative.

THE IMPORTANCE OF DISCLOSURE FOR FAIR TRIALS

1. Disclosure remains one of the most important – as well as one of the most misunderstood and abused – of the procedures relating to criminal trials. Lord Justice Gross' review has re-emphasised the need for all those involved to understand the statutory requirements and to undertake their roles with rigour, in a timely manner.

2. The House of Lords stated in *R v H and C* [2004] UKHL 3; [2004] 2 AC 134; [2004] 2 Cr App R 10:

    > *"Fairness ordinarily requires that any material held by the prosecution which weakens its case or strengthens that of the defendant, if not relied on as part of its formal case against the defendant, should be disclosed to the defence. Bitter experience has shown that miscarriages of justice may occur where such material is withheld from disclosure. The golden rule is that full disclosure of such material should be made."* (*[2004] 2 AC 134, at 147*)

    The Criminal Cases Review Commission has recently noted that failure to disclose material to the defence to which they were entitled remains the biggest single cause of miscarriages of justice.

3. However, it is also essential that the trial process is not overburdened or diverted by erroneous and inappropriate disclosure of unused prosecution material or by misconceived applications. Although the drafters of the Criminal Procedure and Investigations Act 1996 ('CPIA 1996') cannot have anticipated the vast increase in the amount of electronic material that has been generated in recent years, nevertheless the principles of that Act still hold true. Applications by the parties or decisions by judges based on misconceptions of the law or a general laxity of approach (however well-intentioned) which result in an improper application of the disclosure regime have, time and again, proved unnecessarily costly and have obstructed justice. As Lord Justice Gross noted, the burden of disclosure must not be allowed to render the prosecution of cases impracticable.

4. The overarching principle is that unused prosecution material will fall to be disclosed if, and only if, it satisfies the test for disclosure applicable to the proceedings in question, subject to any overriding public interest considerations. The test for disclosure will depend on the date the criminal investigation in question commenced, as this will determine whether the common law disclosure regime applies, or either of the two disclosure regimes under the CPIA 1996.

5. The test for disclosure under section 3 of the CPIA 1996 as amended will be applicable in nearly every case and all those involved in the process will need to be familiar with it. Material fulfils the test if – but only if – it

'might reasonably be considered capable of undermining the case for the prosecution ... or of assisting the case for the accused.'

6. The disclosure process must be led by the prosecution so as to trigger comprehensive defence engagement, supported by robust judicial case management. Active participation by the court in the disclosure process is a critical means of ensuring that delays and adjournments are avoided, given failures by the parties to comply with their obligations may disrupt and (in some cases) frustrate the course of justice.

DISCLOSURE OF UNUSED MATERIAL
IN CRIMINAL CASES

7.　　The court should keep the timetable for prosecution and defence disclosure under review from the first hearing. Judges should as a matter of course ask the parties to identify the issues in the case, and invite the parties to indicate whether further disclosure is sought, and on what topics. For example, it is not enough for the judge to rely on the content of the PCMH form. Proper completion of the disclosure process is a vital part of case preparation, and it may well affect the progress of the case. The court will expect disclosure to have been considered from the outset; the prosecution and defence advocates need to be aware of any potential problems and substantive difficulties should be explained to the judge; and the parties should propose a sensible timetable. Realism is preferable to optimistic but unachievable deadlines which may dislocate the court schedule and imperil the date of trial. It follows that judges should not impose deadlines for service of the case papers or disclosure until they are confident that the prosecution advocate has taken instructions from the individuals who are best placed to evaluate the work to be undertaken.

8.　　The advocates – both prosecution and defence – must be kept fully informed throughout the course of the proceedings as to any difficulties which may prevent them from complying with their disclosure obligations. When problems arise or come to light after directions have been given, the advocates should notify the court and the other party (or parties) immediately rather than waiting until the date set by the court for the service of the material is imminent or has passed, and they must provide the court with a suggested timetable in order to resolve the problem. The progress of the disclosure process should be reviewed at every hearing. There remains no basis in practice or law for Counsel to Counsel disclosure.

9.　　If there is a preliminary hearing the judge should seize the opportunity to impose an early timetable for disclosure and to identify any likely problems including as regards third party material and material that will require an application to the Family Court. In an appropriate case the court should consider holding a Joint Criminal/Care Directions Hearing. See Material held by Third Parties, from paragraph 44 below.

10.　　For the PCMH to be effective, the defence must have a proper opportunity to review the case papers and consider initial disclosure, with a view to preparing a properly completed defence statement which will inform the judge's conduct of the PCMH, and inform the prosecution of the matters required by sections 5, 6A and 6C of the CPIA. As the Court of Appeal noted in *R v Newell* [2012] EWCA Crim 650; [2012] 2 Cr App R 10, "a typed defence statement must be provided before the PCMH. If there is no defence statement by the time of the PCMH, then a judge will usually require the trial advocate to see that such a statement is provided and not proceed with the PCMH until that is done. In the ordinary case the trial advocate will be required to do that at the court and the PCMH resumed later in the day to avoid delay". There may be some instances when there will be a well-founded defence application to extend the 28-day time limit for serving a proper defence statement. In a proper case (but never routinely), it may be appropriate to put the PCMH back by a week or more, to enable an appropriate defence statement to be filed.

11.   The defence statement can be admitted into evidence under section 6E(4) of the CPIA 1996. However, information included on the PCMH form (which is primarily an administrative form) will not usually be admitted in evidence when the defence advocate has complied with the letter and the spirit of the Criminal Procedure Rules.[4] Introducing the PCMH form (or part of it) during the trial is likely to be an exceptional event. The status of the trial preparation form in the magistrates' court is somewhat different, as discussed below.

12.   The court should not extend time lightly or as a matter of course. If an extension is sought, it ought to be accompanied by an appropriate explanation. For instance, it is not sufficient for the prosecutor merely to say that the investigator has delivered the papers late: the underlying reasons are to be provided to the court. The same applies if the defence statement is delayed. Whichever party is at fault, realistic proposals for service are to be set out.

13.   Judges should not allow the prosecution to avoid their statutory responsibility for reviewing the unused material by the expedient of permitting the defence to have access to (or providing the defence with copies of) the material listed in the schedules of non-sensitive unused prosecution material irrespective of whether it satisfies, wholly or in part, the relevant test for disclosure. Additionally, it is for the prosecutor to decide on the manner of disclosure, and it does not have to mirror the form in which the information was originally recorded. Rose LJ gave guidance on case management issues in this context in *R v CPS* (Interlocutory Application under sections 35/36 CPIA) [2005] EWCA Crim 2342. Allowing the defence to inspect items that fulfil the disclosure test is also a valid means of providing disclosure.

14.   The larger and more complex the case, the more important it is for the prosecution to adhere to the overarching principle and ensure that

---

4   *R v Newell* [2012] EWCA Crim 650; [2012] 2 Cr App R 10.

sufficient prosecution attention and resources are allocated to the task. Handing the defendant the "keys to the warehouse" has been the cause of many gross abuses in the past, resulting in considerable expenditure by the defence without any material benefit to the course of justice. The circumstances relating to large and complex cases are outlined below.

15.   The court will require the defence to engage and assist in the early identification of the real issues in the case and, particularly in the larger and more complex cases, to contribute to the search terms to be used for, and the parameters of, the review of any electronically held material (which can be very considerable). Any defence criticisms of the prosecution approach to disclosure should be timely and reasoned; there is no place for disclosure "ambushes" or for late or uninformative defence statements. Admissions should be used so far as possible to narrow the real issues in dispute.

16.   A constructive approach to disclosure is a necessary part of professional best practice, for the defence and prosecution. This does not undermine the defendant's legitimate interests, it accords with his or her obligations under the Rules and it ensures that all the relevant material is provided. Delays and failures by the prosecution and the defence are equally damaging to a timely, fair and efficient trial, and judges should be vigilant in preventing and addressing abuses. Accordingly, whenever there are potential failings by either the defence or the prosecution, judges, in exercising appropriate oversight of disclosure, should carefully investigate the suggested default and give timely directions.

17.   In the Crown Court, the defence statement is to be served within 28 days of the date when the prosecution complies with its duty of initial disclosure (or purports to do so) and whenever section 5(5) of the CPIA applies to the proceedings, and the defence statement must comply with section 6A of the CPIA. Service of the defence statement is a most important stage in the disclosure process, and timely service is necessary to facilitate proper consideration of the disclosure issues well in advance of the trial date. Judges expect a defence statement to contain a clear and detailed exposition of the issues of fact and law. Defence statements that merely rehearse the suggestion that the defendant is innocent do not comply with the requirements of the CPIA.

18.   The prosecutor should consider the defence statement carefully and promptly provide a copy to the disclosure officer, to assist the prosecution in its continuing disclosure obligations. The court expects the Crown to identify any suggested deficiencies in the defence statement, and to draw these to the attention of the defence and the court; in particular in large and complex cases, it will assist the court if this is in writing. Although the prosecution's ability to request, and the court's jurisdiction to give, an

adverse inference direction under section 11 of CPIA is not contingent on the prosecution having earlier identified any suggested deficiencies, nevertheless the prosecutor must provide a timely written explanation of its position.

19.   Judges should examine the defence statement with care to ensure that it complies with the formalities required by the CPIA. As stated in *R v H and C* (supra) (paragraph 35):

> *"If material does not weaken the prosecution case or strengthen that of the defendant, there is no requirement to disclose it. For this purpose the parties' respective cases should not be restrictively analysed. But they must be carefully analysed, to ascertain the specific facts the prosecution seek to establish and the specific grounds on which the charges are resisted. The trial process is not well served if the defence are permitted to make general and unspecified allegations and then seek far-reaching disclosure in the hope that material may turn up to make them good. Neutral material or material damaging to the defendant need not be disclosed and should not be brought to the attention of the court."*

20.   If no defence statement – or an inadequate defence statement – is served within the relevant time limits, the judge should investigate the position. At every PCMH where there is no defence statement, including those where an extension has been given, or the time for filing has not yet expired, the defence should be warned in appropriate terms that pursuant to section 6E(2) of the CPIA an adverse inference may be drawn during the trial, and this result is likely if there is no justification for the deficiency. The fact that a warning has been given should be noted.

21.   An adverse inference may be drawn under section 11 of the CPIA if the accused fails to discharge his or her disclosure obligations. Whenever the amended CPIA regime applies, the prosecution may comment on any failure in defence disclosure (except where the failure relates to a point of law) without leave of the court, but counsel should use a measure of judgment as to whether it is wise to embark on cross-examination about such a failure.[5] If the accused is cross-examined about discrepancies between his evidence and his defence statement, or if adverse comment is made, the judge must give appropriate guidance to the jury.[6]

22.   In order to secure a fair trial, it is vital that the prosecution is mindful of its continuing duty of disclosure. Once the defence statement has been received, the Crown must review disclosure in the light of the issues

---

5   *R v Essa* [2009] EWCA Crim 43, paragraph 22.
6   *R v Hanyes* [2011] EWCA Crim 3281.

identified in the defence statement. In cases of complexity, the following steps are then likely to be necessary:

i.   Service by the prosecution of any further material due to the defence following receipt of the defence statement.

ii. Any defence request to the prosecution for service of additional specific items. As discussed below, these requests must be justified by reference to the defence statement and they should be submitted on the section 8 form.

iii. Prosecution response to the defence request.

iv. If the defence considers that disclosable items are still outstanding, a section 8 application should be made using the appropriate form.

23. It follows that all requests by the defence to the prosecution for disclosure should be made on the section 8 application form, even if no hearing is sought in the first instance. Discussion and co-operation between the parties outside of court is encouraged in order to ensure that the court is only asked to issue a ruling when strictly necessary. However, use of the section 8 form will ensure that focussed requests are clearly set out in one place.

24. The judge should set a date as part of the timetabling exercise by which any application under section 8 is to be made, if this appears to be a likely eventuality.

25. The Court will require the section 8 application to be served on the prosecution well in advance of the hearing – indeed, prior to requesting the hearing – to enable the Crown to identify and serve any items that meet the test for disclosure.

26. Service of a defence statement is an essential precondition for an application under section 8, and applications should not be heard or directions for disclosure issued in the absence of a properly completed statement (see Part 22 of the Criminal Procedure Rules). In particular, blanket orders in this context are inconsistent with the statutory framework for disclosure laid down by the CPIA and the decision of the House of Lords in *R v H and C* (supra). It follows that defence requests for disclosure of particular pieces of unused prosecution material which are not referable to any issue in the case identified in the defence statement should be rejected.

27. Judges must ensure that defendants are not prejudiced on account of the failures of their lawyers, and, when necessary, the professions should be reminded that if justice is to be done, and if disclosure is to be dealt with fairly in accordance with the law, a full and careful defence statement and a reasoned approach to section 8 applications are essential. In

exploring the adequacy of the defence statement, a judge should always ask what the issues are and upon what matters of fact the defendant intends to rely[7] and on what matters of fact the defendant takes issue.

LISTING

28.   Sufficient time is necessary for the judge properly to undertake the PCMH, and this is a paramount consideration when listing cases. Unless the court is able to sit early, judges who are part heard on trials are probably not best placed to conduct PCMHs.

29.   Cases that raise particularly difficult issues of disclosure should be referred to the Resident Judge for directions (unless a trial judge has been allocated) and, for trials of real complexity, the trial judge should be identified at an early stage, prior to the PCMH if possible. Listing officers, working in consultation with the Resident Judge and, if allocated, the trial judge, should ensure that sufficient time is allowed for judges to prepare and deal with prosecution and defence applications relating to disclosure, particularly in the more complex cases.

MAGISTRATES' COURTS (INCLUDING THE YOUTH COURT)

30.   The principles relating to disclosure apply equally in the magistrates' courts. It follows that whilst disclosure of unused material in compliance with the statutory test is undoubtedly essential in order to achieve justice, it is critical that summary trials are not delayed or made over-complicated by misconceived applications for, or inappropriate disclosure of, prosecution material.

31.   Magistrates will rely on their legal advisers for guidance, and the latter should draw the attention of the parties and the court to the statutory provisions and the applicable case law. Cases raising disclosure issues of particular complexity should be referred to a District Judge (Magistrates' Courts), if available.

32.   Although service of a defence statement is voluntary for summary trials (section 6 CPIA), the defendant cannot make an application for specific disclosure under section 8 CPIA, and the court cannot make any orders in this regard, unless a proper defence statement has been provided.

---

7   *R v Rochford* [2010] EWCA Crim 1928; [2011] 1 Cr App R 11.

It follows that although providing a defence statement is not mandatory, it remains a critical stage in the disclosure process. If disclosure issues are to be raised by the defence, a defence statement must be served well in advance of the trial date. Any section 8 application must be made in strict compliance with the Rules.

33.   The case-management forms used in the magistrates' courts fulfil some of the functions of a defence statement, and the prosecution must take into account the information provided as to the defence case when conducting its on-going review of unused material. As the Court of Appeal noted in *R v Newell* (supra), admissions can be made in the Trial Preparation Form and the defence is able to identify the matters that are not in issue. Admissions made in these circumstances may be admissible during the trial. However, other information on the form that does not come within the section relating to admissions should be treated in the same way as the contents of a PCMH form in the Crown Court and it should not generally be introduced as part of the evidence at trial. However, the contents of the Trial Preparation Form do not replace the need to serve a defence statement if the defendant seeks to apply for disclosure under section 8 CPIA.

34.   The standard directions require that any defence statement is to be served within 14 days of the date upon which the prosecution has complied with, or purported to comply with, the duty to provide initial disclosure. There may be some instances when there will be a well-founded defence application to extend the 14-day time limit for serving the defence statement. These applications must be made in accordance with the Criminal Procedure Rules, in writing and before the time limit expires.

35.   Although CCTV footage frequently causes difficulties, it is to be treated as any other category of unused material and it should only be disclosed if the material meets the appropriate test for disclosure under the CPIA. The defence should either be provided with copies of the sections of the CCTV or afforded an opportunity to view them. If the prosecution refuses to disclose CCTV material that the defence considers to be discloseable, the courts should not make standard or general directions requiring the prosecutor to disclose material of this kind in the absence of an application under section 8. When potentially relevant CCTV footage is not in the possession of the police, the guidance in relation to third party material will apply, although the police remain under a duty to pursue all reasonable lines of inquiry, including those leading away from a suspect, whether or not defence requests are made.

36.   The previous convictions of witnesses and any disciplinary findings against officers in the case are frequently discloseable and care should be taken to disclose them as appropriate. Documents such as crime reports or records

of emergency calls should not be provided on a routine basis, for instance as part of a bundle of disclosed documents, irrespective of whether the material satisfies the appropriate test for disclosure. Defence advocates should not request this material in standard or routine correspondence, and instead focussed consideration should be given to the circumstances of the particular case. Unjustified requests for disclosure of material of this kind are routinely made, frequently leading to unnecessary delays and adjournments. The prosecution should always consider whether the request is properly made out.

37.   The supervisory role of the courts is critical in this context, and magistrates must guard against granting unnecessary adjournments and issuing unjustified directions.

LARGE AND COMPLEX CASES IN THE CROWN COURT

38.   Disclosure is a particular problem with the larger and more complex cases, which require a scrupulous approach by the parties and robust case management by the judiciary. If possible, the trial judge should be identified at the outset.

39.   The legal representatives need to fulfil their duties in this context with care and efficiency; they should co-operate with the other party (or parties) and the court; and the judge and the other party (or parties) are to be informed of any difficulties, as soon as they arise. The court should be provided with an up-to-date timetable for disclosure whenever there are material changes in this regard. A disclosure-management document, or similar, prepared by the prosecution will be of particular assistance to the court in large and complex cases.

40.   Judges should be prepared to give early guidance as to the prosecution's approach to disclosure, thereby ensuring early engagement by the defence.

41.   Cases of this nature frequently include large volumes of digitally stored material. The Attorney General's 2011 guidance (now included as an annex to the Attorney General's Guidelines on Disclosure 2013) is of particular relevance and assistance in this context.

42.   Applications for witness anonymity orders require particular attention; as the Court of Appeal noted in *R v Mayers and Others* [2008] EWCA Crim 2989; [2009] 1 Cr App R 30, in making such an application, the prosecution's obligations of disclosure "go much further than the ordinary duties of disclosure".

43.   If the judge considers that there are reasonable grounds to doubt the good faith of the investigation, he or she will be concerned to see that there has

been independent and effective appraisal of the documents contained in the disclosure schedule and that its contents are adequate. In appropriate cases where this issue has arisen and there are grounds which show there is a real issue, consideration should be given to receiving evidence on oath from the senior investigating officer at an early case management hearing.

MATERIAL HELD BY THIRD PARTIES

44.   Where material is held by a third party such as a local authority, a social services department, hospital or business, the investigators and the prosecution may need to make enquiries of the third party, with a view to inspecting the material and assessing whether the relevant test for disclosure is met and determining whether any or all of the material should be retained, recorded and, in due course, disclosed to the accused. If access by the prosecution is granted, the investigators and the prosecution will need to establish whether the custodian of the material intends to raise PII issues, as a result of which the material may have to be placed before the court for a decision. This does not obviate the need for the defence to conduct its own enquiries as appropriate. Speculative enquiries without any proper basis in relation to third party material – whether by the prosecution or the defence – are to be discouraged, and, in appropriate cases, the court will consider making an order for costs where an application is clearly unmeritorious and misconceived.

45.   The 2013 Protocol and Good Practice Model on Disclosure of Information in Cases of Alleged Child Abuse and Linked Criminal and Care Directions Hearings has recently been published. It provides a framework and timetable for the police and CPS to obtain discloseable material from local authorities, and for applications to be made to the Family Court. It is applicable to all cases of alleged child abuse where the child is aged 17 years or under. It is not binding on local authorities, but it does represent best practice and therefore should be consulted in all such cases. Delays in obtaining this type of material have led to unacceptable delays to trials involving particularly vulnerable witnesses and every effort must be made to ensure that all discloseable material is identified at an early stage so that any necessary applications can be made and the defence receive material to which they are entitled in good time.

46.   There is no specific procedure for disclosure of material held by third parties in criminal proceedings, although the procedure established under section 2 of the Criminal Procedure (Attendance of Witnesses) Act 1965 or section 97 of the Magistrates' Courts Act 1980 is often used for this purpose. Where the third party in question declines to allow inspection

of the material, or requires the prosecution to obtain an order before providing copies, the prosecutor will need to consider whether it is appropriate to obtain a witness summons under either section 2 of the Criminal Procedure (Attendance of Witnesses) Act 1965 or section 97 of the Magistrates' Court Act 1980. Part 28 of the Criminal Procedure Rules and paragraphs 3.5 and 3.6 of the Code of Practice under the CPIA 1996 should be followed.

47. Applications for third party disclosure must identify the documents that are sought and provide full details of why they are discloseable. This is particularly relevant when access is sought to the medical records of those who allege they are victims of crime. It should be appreciated that a duty to assert confidentiality may arise when a third party receives a request for disclosure, or the right to privacy may be claimed under article 8 of the ECHR (see in particular Crim PR Part 28.6). Victims do not waive the confidentiality of their medical records, or their right to privacy under article 8 of the ECHR, by making a complaint against the accused. The court, as a public authority, must ensure that any interference with the right to privacy under article 8 is in accordance with the law, and is necessary in pursuit of a legitimate public interest. General and unspecified requests to trawl through such records should be refused. Confidentiality rests with the subject of the material, not with the authority holding it. The subject is entitled to service of the application and has the right to make representations: Criminal Procedure Rule 22.3 and *R (on the application of B) v Stafford Combined Court* [2006] EWHC 1645 (Admin); [2006] 2 Cr App R 34. The 2013 Protocol and Good Practice Model at paragraph 13 should be followed. It is likely that the judge will need to issue directions when issues of this kind are raised (e.g. whether enquiries with the third party are likely to be appropriate; who is to make the request; what material is to be sought, and from whom; and a timetable should be set).

48. The judge should consider whether to take any steps if a third party fails, or refuses, to comply with a request for disclosure, including suggesting that either of the parties pursue the request and, if necessary, make an application for a witness summons. In these circumstances, the court will need to set an appropriate timetable for compliance with Part 28 of the Rules. Any failure to comply with the timetable must immediately be referred back to the court for further directions, although a hearing will not always be necessary. Generally, it may be appropriate for the defence to pursue requests of this kind when the prosecution, for good reason, decline to do so and the court will need to ensure that this procedure does not delay the trial.

49. There are very limited circumstances in which information relating to Family Court proceedings (e.g. where there have been care proceedings

in relation to a child who has complained to the police of mistreatment) may be communicated without a court order: see the Family Procedure Rules 12.73. Reference should be made to the 2013 Protocol and Good Practice Model. In most circumstances, a court order will be required and paragraph 11 of the Protocol which sets out how an application should be made should be followed.

Other Government Departments

50.   Material held by other government departments or other Crown agencies will not be prosecution material for the purposes of section 3(2) or section 8(4) of the CPIA if it has not been inspected, recorded and retained during the course of the relevant criminal investigation. The CPIA Code of Practice and the Attorney General's Guidelines on Disclosure, however, impose a duty upon the investigators and the prosecution to pursue all reasonable lines of inquiry and that may involve seeking disclosure from the relevant body.

INTERNATIONAL MATTERS

51.   The obligations of the Crown in relation to relevant third-party material held overseas are as set out in *R v Flook* [2009] EWCA Crim 682; [2010] 1 Cr App R 30: the Crown must pursue reasonable lines of enquiry and if it appears there is relevant material, all reasonable steps must be taken to obtain it, whether formally or otherwise. To a great extent, the success of these enquiries will depend on the laws of the country where the material is held and the facts of the individual case. It needs to be recognised that when the material is held in a country outside of the European Union, the power of the Crown and the courts of England and Wales to obtain third-party material may well be limited. If informal requests are unsuccessful, the avenues are limited to the Crime (International Co-operation) Act 2003 and any applicable international conventions. It cannot, in any sense, be guaranteed that a request to a foreign government, court or body will produce the material sought. Additionally, some foreign authorities may be prepared to show the material in question to the investigating officers, whilst refusing to allow the material to be copied or otherwise made available.

52.   As the Court of Appeal observed in *R v Khyam* [2008] EWCA Crim 1612; [2009] 1 Cr App R (S) 77:

> *"The prosecuting authorities in this jurisdiction simply cannot compel authorities in a foreign country to acknowledge, let alone comply with, our disclosure principles." ([2008] EWCA Crim 1612, at paragraph 37)*

The obligation is therefore to take reasonable steps. Whether the Crown has complied with that obligation is for the courts to judge in each case.

53.   It is, therefore, important that the prosecution sets out the position clearly in writing, including any inability to inspect or retrieve any material that potentially ought to be disclosed, along with the steps that have been taken.

APPLICATIONS FOR NON-DISCLOSURE IN THE PUBLIC INTEREST

54.   Applications in this context, whenever possible, should be considered by the trial judge. The House of Lords in *R v H and C* (supra) has provided useful guidance as to the proper approach to be applied (paragraph 36):

> *"When any issue of derogation from the golden rule of full disclosure comes before it, the court must address a series of questions:*
>
> *(1)   What is the material which the prosecution seek to withhold? This must be considered by the court in detail.*
>
> *(2)   Is the material such as may weaken the prosecution case or strengthen that of the defence? If No, disclosure should not be ordered. If Yes, full disclosure should (subject to (3), (4) and (5) below) be ordered.*
>
> *(3)   Is there a real risk of serious prejudice to an important public interest (and, if so, what) if full disclosure of the material is ordered? If No, full disclosure should be ordered.*
>
> *(4)   If the answer to (2) and (3) is Yes, can the defendant's interest be protected without disclosure or disclosure be ordered to an extent or in a way which will give adequate protection to the public interest in question and also afford adequate protection to the interests of the defence?*
>
> *This question requires the court to consider, with specific reference to the material which the prosecution seek to withhold and the facts of the case and the defence as disclosed, whether the prosecution should formally admit what the defence seek to establish or whether disclosure short of full disclosure may be ordered. This may be done in appropriate cases by the preparation of summaries or extracts of evidence, or the provision of documents in an edited or anonymised form, provided the documents supplied are in each instance approved by the judge. In appropriate cases the appointment of special*

counsel may be a necessary step to ensure that the contentions of the prosecution are tested and the interests of the defendant protected (see para 22 above). In cases of exceptional difficulty the court may require the appointment of special counsel to ensure a correct answer to questions (2) and (3) as well as (4).

(5)   *Do the measures proposed in answer to (4) represent the minimum derogation necessary to protect the public interest in question? If No, the court should order such greater disclosure as will represent the minimum derogation from the golden rule of full disclosure.*

(6)   *If limited disclosure is ordered pursuant to (4) or (5), may the effect be to render the trial process, viewed as a whole, unfair to the defendant? If Yes, then fuller disclosure should be ordered even if this leads or may lead the prosecution to discontinue the proceedings so as to avoid having to make disclosure.*

(7)   *If the answer to (6) when first given is No, does that remain the correct answer as the trial unfolds, evidence is adduced and the defence advanced?*

It is important that the answer to (6) should not be treated as a final, once-and for-all, answer but as a provisional answer which the court must keep under review." ([2004] 2 AC 134, at 155–156)

55.   In this context, the following matters are to be emphasised:

a.   The procedure for making applications to the court is set out in the Criminal Procedure Rules, Part 22;

b.   When the PII application is a Type 1 or Type 2 application, proper notice to the defence is necessary to enable the accused to make focused submissions to the court and the notice should be as specific as the nature of the material allows. It is appreciated that in some cases only the generic nature of the material can be identified. In some wholly exceptional cases (Type 3 cases) it may be justified to give no notice at all. The judge should always ask the prosecution to justify the form of notice (or the decision to give no notice at all).

c.   The prosecution should be alert to the possibility of disclosing a statement in a redacted form by, for example, simply removing personal details. This may obviate the need for a PII application, unless the redacted material satisfies the test for disclosure.

d.   Except when the material is very short (for instance only a few sheets), or for reasons of sensitivity, the prosecution should supply securely sealed copies to the judge in advance, together with a short statement explaining the relevance of each document, how it satisfies the disclosure test and why it is suggested that disclosure would result in a real risk of serious prejudice to an important public interest; in undertaking this task, the use of merely formulaic expressions is to be discouraged. In any case of complexity a schedule of the material should be provided, identifying the particular objection to disclosure in relation to each item, and leaving a space for the judge's decision.

e.   The application, even if held in private or in secret, should be recorded. The judge should give some short statement of reasons; this is often best done document by document as the hearing proceeds.

f.   The recording, copies of the judge's orders (and any copies of the material retained by the court) should be clearly identified, securely sealed and kept in the court building in a safe or locked cabinet consistent with its security classification, and there should be a proper register of the contents. Arrangements should be made for the return of the material to the prosecution once the case is concluded and the time for an appeal has elapsed.

CONCLUSION

56.   Historically, disclosure was viewed essentially as being a matter to be resolved between the parties, and the court only became engaged if a particular issue or complaint was raised. That perception is now wholly out of date. The regime established under the Criminal Justice Act 2003 and the Criminal Procedure Rules gives judges the power – indeed, it imposes a duty on the judiciary – actively to manage disclosure in every case. The efficient, effective and timely resolution of these issues is a critical element in meeting the overriding objective of the Criminal Procedure Rules of dealing with cases justly.

Appendix 7

Manual Guidance Form MG6C: Police Schedule of Non-Sensitive Unused Material

[Form reproduced overleaf.]

MG 6C

Page No .... of ....

RESTRICTED (when complete)

POLICE SCHEDULE OF NON-SENSITIVE UNUSED MATERIAL

R v ....

URN

Is there any material in this case which has not been examined by either the investigating or disclosure officer? Yes ☐ No ☐

If 'Yes' please attach MG11 (refer to the Manual of Guidance)

The Disclosure Officer believes that the following material, which does not form part of the prosecution case, is NOT SENSITIVE.

FOR CPS USE:
* Enter: D = Disclose to defence
  I = Defence may inspect
  CND = Clearly not disclosable

Item No.	DESCRIPTION AND RELEVANCE (Give sufficient detail for CPS to decide if material should be disclosed or requires more detailed examination)	LOCATION	*	COMMENT

Signature:

Date:

Name:

Reviewing lawyer signature:

Print name:

Date:

2004/05 (1)

318

Appendix 8

Manual Guidance Form MG6D: Police Schedule of Sensitive Material

[Form reproduced overleaf.]

Appendix 8 *Manual Guidance Form MG6D*

MG 6D

RESTRICTED/CONFIDENTIAL *–
FOR POLICE AND PROSECUTION ONLY (when complete)

*delete as applicable

POLICE SCHEDULE OF SENSITIVE MATERIAL

R v ....

Page No .... of ....

URN

The Disclosure Officer believes that the following material, which does not form part of the prosecution case, is SENSITIVE

*Tick if copy supplied to CPS

Item No.	Description	Reason for sensitivity	*

Signature:

Date:

Name:

FOR CPS USE

Agree sensitive Yes/No	Court application Yes/No	CPS views

Reviewing lawyer signature:

Print name:

Date:

2004/05 (1)

Appendix 9

Manual Guidance Form MG6E: Disclosure Officer's Report

[Form reproduced overleaf.]

MG 6E

RESTRICTED/CONFIDENTIAL* –
FOR POLICE AND PROSECUTION ONLY (when complete)

DISCLOSURE OFFICER'S REPORT

Page No .... of ....

R v ....   URN

The following items are listed on the schedule(s) for this case and might:

*undermine the prosecution case (primary disclosure) / *reasonably assist the defence (secondary disclosure) /
*are required to be supplied under paragraph 7.3 of the Code (see overleaf)   (*delete as applicable).

*Enter C or D to denote schedule MG6C or 6D and enter item no. from schedule

* Schedule	Item no.	Reason	Tick if attached

Certification in all cases:
I certify that, to the best of my knowledge and belief, all material which has been retained and made available to me has been inspected, viewed, or listened to (other than unexamined irrelevant material) and revealed to the prosecutor in accordance with the Criminal Procedure and Investigations Act 1996 Code of Practice, and the Attorney General's Guidelines 2000* and

*(Primary Disclosure only) – those items that might undermine the prosecution are listed above OR to the best of my knowledge and belief there are no items that might undermine the prosecution case.

*(Secondary Disclosure only) – items that might assist the defence in the light of the defence statement are listed above OR to the best of my knowledge and belief there are no items that might assist the defence in light of the defence statement.
(*Delete as appropriate)

Signature of Disclosure Officer: .... Date:...........................

Name of Disclosure Officer: ....

2004/05 (1)

322

Defence Statement Form

[Form reproduced overleaf.]

Appendix 10   *Defence Statement Form*

DEFENCE STATEMENT

(Criminal Procedure and Investigations Act 1996, section 5 & 6; Criminal Procedure and Investigations Act 1996 (Defence Disclosure Time Limits) Regulations 2011; Criminal Procedure Rules, rule 15.4)

Case details

Name of defendant:

Court:

Case reference number:

Charge(s):

When to use this form

If you are a defendant pleading not guilty:

(a) in a Crown Court case, you **must** give the information listed in Part 2 of this form;

(b) in a magistrates' court case, you **may** give that information but you do not have to do so.

The time limit for giving the information is:

14 days (in a magistrates' court case)

28 days (in a Crown Court case)

after initial prosecution disclosure (or notice from the prosecutor that there is no material to disclose).

How to use this form

1. Complete the case details box above, and Part 1 below.

2. Attach as many sheets as you need to give the information listed in Part 2.

3. Sign and date the completed form.

4. Send a copy of the completed form to:

(a) **the court, and**

(b) **the prosecutor**

before the time limit expires.

If you need more time, you **must** apply to the court **before** the time limit expires. You should apply in writing, but no special form is needed.

Part 1: Plea

I confirm that I intend to plead not guilty to [all the charges] [the following charges] against me:

Part 2: Nature of the defence

Attach as many sheets as you need to give the information required.

Under section 6A of the Criminal Procedure and Investigations Act 1996, you must:

(a) set out the nature of your defence, including any particular defences on which you intend to rely;

(b) indicate the matters of fact on which you take issue with the prosecutor, and in respect of each explain why;

(c) set out particulars of the matters of fact on which you intend to rely for the purposes of your defence;

(d) indicate any point of law that you wish to take, including any point about the admissibility of evidence or about abuse of process, and any authority relied on; and

(e) if your defence statement includes an alibi (i.e. an assertion that you were in a place, at a time, inconsistent with you having committed the offence), give particulars, including –

(i) the name, address and date of birth of any witness who you believe can give evidence in support of that alibi,

(ii) if you do not know all of those details, any information that might help identify or find that witness.

Signed: .... defendant / defendant's solicitor

Date: ....

WARNING: Under section 11 of the Criminal Procedure and Investigations Act 1996, **if you (a) do not disclose what the Act requires; (b) do not give a defence statement before the time limit expires; (c) at trial, rely on a defence, or facts, that you have not disclosed; or (d) at trial, call an alibi witness whom you have not identified in advance, then the court, the prosecutor or another defendant may comment on that, and the court may draw such inferences as it thinks proper in deciding whether you are guilty**.

Appendix 11

Defence Witness Notice

[Form reproduced on opposite page.]

DEFENCE WITNESS NOTICE

(Criminal Procedure and Investigations Act 1996, section 6C; Criminal Procedure and Investigations Act 1996 (Defence Disclosure Time Limits) Regulations 2011; Criminal Procedure Rules, rule 15.4)

Case details

Name of defendant:

Court:

Case reference number:

Charge(s):

When to use this form

Under section 6C of the Criminal Procedure and Investigations Act 1996, if you are a defendant pleading not guilty you must:

(a) let the court and the prosecutor know **whether you intend to call anyone other than yourself as a witness at your trial;**

(b) do so **not more than -**

> **14 days** (in a magistrates' court case)

> **28 days** (in a Crown Court case)

after initial prosecution disclosure (or notice from the prosecutor that there is no material to disclose);

(c) give as many details of each witness as you can (see the list below);

(d) let the court and the prosecutor know if you later -

> (i) decide to call a witness, other than yourself, whom you have not already identified in a defence witness notice,

> (ii) decide not to call a witness you have listed in a notice, or

> (iii) discover information which you should have included in a notice if you had known it then.

How to use this form

1. Complete the case details box above and give the details required below.

2. Sign and date the completed form.

3. Send a copy of the completed form to:

> **(a) the court, and**

> **(b) the prosecutor**

before the time limit expires.

If you need more time, you **must** apply to the court **before** the time limit expires. You should apply in writing, but no special form is needed.

List of intended defence witness(es)

1. Do you intend to call anyone other than yourself as a witness at your trial ?   No ☐   Yes ☐ If yes, give details below. If you use an electronic version of this form, the boxes will expand. If you use a paper version and need more space, you may attach extra sheets.

Name	Date of birth (if known)	Address, or any other contact or identifying details

2. Have you given a defence witness notice in this case before?
   No ☐   Yes ☐ If yes, give the date(s).

Signed: ....[defendant / defendant's solicitor]

Date: ....

WARNING: Under section 11 of the Criminal Procedure and Investigations Act 1996, if you (a) do not give a defence witness notice before the time limit expires, or (b) at trial, call a witness whom you have not identified in a witness notice then the court, the prosecutor or another defendant may comment on that, and the court may draw such inferences as it thinks proper in deciding whether you are guilty.

Appendix 12

Defendant's Application for Prosecution Disclosure Form for use with CPR 2012, Part 22 (section 8 application)

[Form reproduced overleaf.]

DEFENDANT'S APPLICATION FOR PROSECUTION DISCLOSURE

(Criminal Procedure and Investigations Act 1996, section 8;
Criminal Procedure Rules, rule 22.5)

Case details

Name of defendant:

Court:

Case reference number:

Charge(s):

Note: You <u>must</u> give a defence statement, and allow the prosecutor time to respond, <u>before</u> you can make an application for prosecution disclosure.

How to use this form

1. Complete the Case details box above and answer the questions set out in the boxes below. If you use an electronic version of this form, the boxes will expand. If you use a paper version and need more space, you may attach extra sheets.

2. Attach to this form:

   (a) a copy of your defence statement, and

   (b) copies of any correspondence with the prosecutor about disclosure.

3. Sign and date the completed form.

4. Send a copy of the completed form and everything attached to:

   (a) the court, and

   (b) the prosecutor.

1) What material do you want the prosecutor to disclose ?

2) Why do you think the prosecutor has that material ?

3) Why might that material:

    (a) undermine the prosecutor's case against you, or

    (b) assist your case ?

4) Do you want the court to arrange a hearing of this application ? YES / NO

If YES, explain why you think a hearing is needed. (If you do not ask for a hearing, the court may arrange one anyway.)

Signed: .... **defendant / defendant's solicitor**

Date: ....

Appendix 13

2013 Protocol and Good Practice Model Disclosure of information in cases of alleged child abuse and linked criminal and care directions hearings

October 2013

Association of Chief Police Officers

Association of Directors of Children Services

Association of Independent Local Safeguarding Children Board Chairs

Crown Prosecution Service

Department for Education

HM Courts & Tribunals Service

Local Government Association

President of the Family Division

Senior Presiding Judge for England and Wales

Welsh Government

CONTENTS

1. PARTIES

1.1.   The signatories to the 2013 Protocol and Good Practice Model (hereinafter the "2013 protocol") with the exception of the paragraphs listed at 1.4 below are the Senior Presiding Judge, the President of the Family Division, and the Director of Public Prosecutions on behalf of the Crown Prosecution Service (CPS).

1.2.   This 2013 protocol is issued with the support of the Association of Chief Police Officers (ACPO), HM Courts & Tribunals Service and the Association of Independent Local Safeguarding Children Board (LSCB) Chairs.

1.3.   The Department for Education (DfE), the Welsh Government (WG), Local Government Association (LGA) and Association of Directors of Children Services (ADCS) are not signatories to the 2013 protocol and the content of this document is not, nor does it seek to be binding on Local Authorities. However, the DfE, WG, LGA and ADCS support the content of this document and consider it to be a Good Practice Model, offered by way of assistance, and therefore urge all Local Authorities to adopt the disclosure practices described within the document, observance of which will improve timeliness and therefore achieve better outcomes for children and young people who are subject to the relevant proceedings.

1.4.   Paragraphs 7.1, 11.5, 11.7, 11.8, 16.1 to 16.7, 16.9, 16.10, 16.15 and all of 17 of this 2013 protocol are directed at the judiciary. The signatories to those paragraphs are the President of the Family Division and the Senior Presiding Judge.

2. SCOPE

2.1.   This 2013 protocol will apply to cases involving criminal investigations into alleged child abuse[1] (child victims who were aged 17 and under at the time of the alleged offending) and/or Family Court[2] proceedings concerning a child (aged 17 and under).

2.2.   This 2013 protocol will come into force on 1 January 2014.

3. AIMS AND OBJECTIVES

3.1.   To provide early notification to the Local Authority and to the Family Court that a criminal investigation has been commenced.

3.2.   To provide timely early notification to the Local Authority and to the Family Court of the details and timescale of criminal prosecution.

---

[1]   Child abuse includes both sexual abuse and non-sexual abuse.

[2]   Family Court means for the time being the Family Proceedings Court, the County Court (when exercising its family jurisdiction) and the Family Division of the High Court. Once the Family Court comes into existence it means the Family Court and the Family Division of the High Court.

3.3.   To facilitate timely and consistent disclosure of information and documents from the police, and the CPS, into the Family Justice System.

3.4.   To provide notification to the police and the CPS of an application to the Family Court for an order for the disclosure of prosecution material into the Family Justice System.

3.5.   Subject to the Family Procedure Rules 2010 (and relevant Practice Directions[3]) the Criminal Procedure Rules 2013 and the common law duty of confidentiality, to facilitate timely and consistent disclosure of information and documents from the Family Justice System to the police and/or the CPS.

3.6.   To provide a timely expeditious process for the Local Authority to respond to a request from the police for material held by the Local Authority which would assist a criminal investigation.

3.7.   To provide for timely consultation between the CPS and the Local Authority where Local Authority material satisfies the test in Criminal Procedure and Investigations Act 1996 for disclosure to the defence.

3.8.   To provide a streamlined and standard process for applications by the police and/or the CPS for the permission of the Family Court for disclosure of material relating to Family Court Proceedings.

3.9.   To specify a procedure for linked directions hearings in concurrent criminal and care proceedings.

Part A: Disclosure into the Family Justice System

4. LOCAL AUTHORITY REQUEST TO THE POLICE FOR DISCLOSURE

4.1.   As soon as reasonably practicable and in any event on issue of proceedings, the Local Authority will provide notice to the police of the contemplation or existence of Family Proceedings using the form at Annex D to this agreement. The form at Annex D also acts as a request for disclosure from the police (to include a reasonable timescale[4] not exceeding 14 days for the disclosure of the material). The form at Annex D will be sent to the police single point of contact (SPOC) attached at Annex A; (see paragraph 19.2 below).

4.2.   Where criminal proceedings have been commenced (or are contemplated), the police will immediately forward a copy of the form at Annex D to the CPS.

---

[3]   In particular, Practice Direction 12G.

[4]   In setting the appropriate reasonable timescale, the Local Authority will take account of the timetable of the Family Court proceedings, the requirement that care proceedings must be completed within 26 weeks of the date on which the application was issued, and the requirements of the revised Public Law Outline (PLO).

The CPS will give due priority to making charging decisions in cases involving Family Court Proceedings.

4.3.   Where the information or documents sought does not relate to a child abuse investigation, the police SPOC will forward the form at Annex D to the unit or units holding the information or documents and will take responsibility for liaison with those units and to ensure the provision of information to the Local Authority.

4.4.   It is to be understood by all Parties that the 2013 protocol should be used proportionately and is designed to facilitate only requests for material held by the police relevant to the central issues in the case. Requests for disclosure should not be drawn any wider than is absolutely necessary and only relevant material should be disclosed. The disclosure request to the police must be focussed identifying the documents which are really needed[5].

5. NOTIFICATION BY THE POLICE TO THE LOCAL AUTHORITY OF THE EXISTENCE AND STATUS OF CRIMINAL INVESTIGATION

5.1.   Within 5 working days of the commencement of the investigation, the police will provide to the Local Authority SPOC details of the criminal investigation using the form at Annex C to this Protocol (contact details for Local Authority SPOCs are listed at Annex B, see paragraph 19.3 below).

5.2.   The police will contact the Local Authority SPOC at the point of charge, providing details of offences, custody status of defendants, bail conditions and court timescales. The police will also provide to the Local Authority contact details for the CPS.

5.3.   In the event that the suspect(s) is/are not charged, the police in consultation with the CPS will provide the Local Authority with reasons why there will be no prosecution[6].

5.4.   Within 5 working days of each Case Management Hearing[7] in the Crown Court, the CPS will provide to the Local Authority SPOC (or Local Authority lawyer if known) details of the future timetable of the criminal proceedings and details of any directions relevant to the Local Authority or to concurrent Family Proceedings.

5.5.   Within 2 working days of receipt, the Local Authority will forward the details at paragraphs 5.1 to 5.4 above to the Family Court.

---

5   Re H-L (A child) [2013] EWCA Civ 655.
6   Decisions to prosecute are made in accordance with the Code for Crown Prosecutors (section 10 Prosecution of Offences Act 1985).
7   Case management hearings in the Crown Court will include Preliminary Hearings and Plea and Case Management Hearings.

6. VOLUNTARY DISCLOSURE BY POLICE/CPS TO LOCAL AUTHORITY AND INTO THE FAMILY JUSTICE SYSTEM

6.1.   Where criminal proceedings have been commenced (or are contemplated), the police should consult with the CPS before a decision is made on whether to disclose police material to the Local Authority. The timing of such consultation must take into account any reasonable timescale specified by the Local Authority at paragraph 4.1 above.

6.2.   Within the timescale specified by the Local Authority in Annex D (paragraph 4.1 above), the police will provide (via secure means, e.g. secure email) the requested material to the Local Authority. The police will complete and return the second part of the form at Annex D. The Local Authority agrees that the police material will only be disclosed to the professionals and Parties in the Family Proceedings (unless the permission of the court is obtained to disclose material to others).

6.3.   Visually recorded interviews (Achieving Best Evidence interviews) will not be released to the Local Authority except against a written undertaking from the Local Authority in order to prevent the unauthorised use of the evidence. The form of undertaking at Annex G should be used for this purpose.

6.4.   Unless disclosure is required to ensure the immediate safety of a child, the police will not disclose material where to do so might prejudice the investigation and/or prosecution (or where on the grounds of confidentiality it is necessary to obtain the consent of persons providing statements). However, redacted disclosure should be made wherever possible. The police will indicate on the form at Annex D the approximate date on which disclosure can be made. The police (in consultation with the CPS) must provide detailed reasons on Annex D as to why any material is being withheld.

6.5.   Alternatively, the police can indicate that disclosure will be made in the event that the Local Authority obtains a Family Court order stating that the material is not to be disclosed to named individual(s) (typically, suspects and/ or witnesses in the criminal proceedings). Such a court order should also be obtained where possible in the event that disclosure is made (as at paragraph 6.4 above) to ensure the immediate safety of a child.

6.6.   The Family Court may request disclosure from the Local Authority of material held by them and relating to the criminal case. Again, the Local Authority will notify the CPS (or the police if criminal proceedings have not commenced) as soon as reasonably practicable. Where the police and/or the CPS object to disclosure, they will make appropriate **and timely** representations to the Family Court explaining why such disclosure might be capable of prejudicing the criminal proceedings.

7. FAMILY COURT PROCEEDINGS: ORDERS FOR DISCLOSURE AGAINST THE POLICE AND/OR THE CPS

7.1.   The Local Authority shall notify (within 2 working days of the application being made) the police and the CPS of any application to the Family Court (whether by the Local Authority or any other party) for disclosure of prosecution material. The Local Authority shall notify the police and/or the CPS of the date and time of the Family Court hearing at which disclosure will be determined[8]. Any order by the Family Court for disclosure will be in the form at Annex H to this protocol (use of which by the Family Court is mandatory). Where appropriate, the police and/or the CPS will assist the Local Authority in drafting Directions.

7.2.   Where directed, the police and/or the CPS shall attend the Family Court hearing to explain the implications for a criminal trial when orders for disclosure are being considered by the court. In any event, the police and/or the CPS shall provide written representations to the Family Court and the Local Authority where disclosure is opposed (**explaining why** disclosure might reasonably be considered capable of prejudicing the investigation and/or prosecution).

7.3.   The Local Authority will ensure that any Order against the police and/or the CPS is served as soon as reasonably practicable (and in any event within 2 working days of the date of the order) on the police and/or the CPS.

7.4.   The police and the CPS will comply with any court order.

Part B: Disclosure from the Local Authority/ Family Justice System into the Criminal Justice System

8. NOTIFICATION BY LOCAL AUTHORITY TO THE POLICE OF THE EXISTENCE AND STATUS OF FAMILY PROCEEDINGS

8.1.   As soon as reasonably practicable and in any event on issue of proceedings, the Local Authority will provide notice to the police of the contemplation or existence of Family Proceedings using the form at Annex D to this 2013 protocol. Where Family Proceedings have commenced, details of all parties (and legal representatives) will be provided. Details of the allocated Local Authority lawyer will be provided. The form at Annex D will be sent to the police single point of contact (SPOC) attached at Annex A.

8.2.   Where the form at Annex D is sent to the police at a stage before details of all parties to the Family Proceedings are known, the Local Authority will

---

[8]   The Standard Directions Order, which is made by the Family Court in accordance with the PLO within 24 hours of care proceedings being issued, provides for any application for disclosure from any agency to be filed and served by a specified date *prior to* the Case Management Hearing (CMH) in the Family Court. Note that the PLO requires the CMH to be no later than 12 working days after the commencement of the care proceedings.

notify the police recipient of Annex D of the details of all parties (and legal representatives) to the Family Proceedings. The Local Authority will also provide details of the future timetable of the Family Proceedings. The police will forward the information to the CPS.

8.3.   Where criminal proceedings have been commenced (or are contemplated), the police will forward a copy of the form at Annex D to the CPS. The CPS will give due priority to making charging decisions in cases involving Family Court Proceedings.

9. POLICE REQUEST TO LOCAL AUTHORITY FOR DISCLOSURE

9.1.   Following the commencement of the investigation, the police will provide to the Local Authority SPOC the form at Annex C to this 2013 protocol. Details of the SPOC for each Local Authority are set out at Annex B (see paragraph 19.3 below).

9.2.   The Annex C form will include details of the investigation and prosecution if commenced (see paragraph 5.1 above). Requests for material **must** be as prescriptive and detailed as possible and necessary for the pursuit of reasonable lines of enquiry[9]. The form at Annex C will include reasonable timescales for the police to be given access to relevant material, but the presumption will be that the Local Authority will deal with any request from the police as expeditiously as possible so as to not to jeopardise the criminal investigation. Timescales will be case specific taking account of the stage/nature of the investigation and/or prosecution.

10. DISCLOSURE BY THE LOCAL AUTHORITY TO THE POLICE

10.1.   Upon receipt of the form at Annex C from the police, the Local Authority SPOC (or delegated officer) will identify and collate relevant material from the Children's Services or other files as appropriate, the SPOC (or delegated officer) will liaise with relevant departments within the Local Authority in the collation of such material for the police to assist the criminal investigation.

10.2.   The Local Authority will identify for the police the school(s) attended by the child/children subject to the investigation. This will enable the police to approach the school directly. Alternatively, if it is practicable to do so, the Local Authority will obtain and collate relevant educational files for police examination.

10.3.   Subject to paragraphs 10.4 and 10.5 below, the Local Authority will ensure that documents relating to Family Court proceedings[10] are not included in the files to be examined by the police. Where there are documents relating to Family Court proceedings, the Local Authority will provide a list (e.g. by providing a copy of redacted court index) of that material without describing

---

9   Paragraph 3.6 Code of Practice Criminal Procedure and Investigations Act 1996.
10   Section 12(1) Administration of Justice Act 1960 prohibits such communication.

what it is, in order for the police and/or the CPS, if appropriate, to apply to the Family Court for disclosure.

10.4. Importantly, the Local Authority can disclose to the police documents which are lodged at court, or used in the proceedings, which already existed[11] (e.g. pre-existing medical reports). Similarly, the text or summary of a judgment given in the Family Court proceedings can be included in the files to be examined by the police[12].

10.5. Paragraph 10.3 above does not prevent the Local Authority providing to the police documents or information relating to Family Court proceedings where (a) the police officer to whom disclosure is made is carrying out duties under section 46 Children Act 1989 or serving in a child protection or paedophile unit and (b) disclosure is for the purposes of child protection and not for the purposes of the criminal investigation[13].

10.6. Where material is disclosed in accordance with paragraph 10.5 above, the police cannot make onward disclosure of any documentation **or information** contained therein for the purpose of the investigation or prosecution without the express permission of the Family Court[14] (for the avoidance of doubt, this will include disclosure to the CPS).

10.7. Where, in exceptional circumstances[15], the Local Authority is not able to include other material (not relating to Family Court proceedings) in the files to be examined by the police, the Local Authority will notify the police in writing of the existence of this material; indicating the reason why the material is not being made available to the police. Such a course should be exceptional because the Local Authority recognises that the material will be regarded as sensitive by the police and the CPS. It will not be disclosed to the defence without further consultation with the Local Authority or order of the court (see paragraph 13.9 to 14.3 below).

10.8. Within the timescales set out in the Annex C request (or otherwise agreed between the Local Authority and the police), the police will examine and review the material collated by the Local Authority. The review will usually take place on Local Authority premises but may be elsewhere by agreement. The police may make notes and/or take copies of the material. The material will not be

---

[11] Re Ward (A Child) [2010] EWHC 16 (Fam); [2010] 1 FLR 1497.

[12] Rule 12.73(1)(c) Family Procedure Rules 2010 and Practice Direction 12G.

[13] Rule 12.73(1)(a)(viii) Family Procedure Rules 2010.

[14] A District Council (Applicant) v M (Respondent) & West Yorkshire Police (Interveners) [2007] EWHC 3471 (Fam); [2008] 2 FLR 390.

[15] The law permits the disclosure of confidential information where a countervailing public interest can be identified. Such a public interest will include the administration of justice, the prevention of wrongdoing and enabling another public body to perform its public duty (R v Chief Constable of North Wales Police ex parte Thorpe [1996] QB 396). In these circumstances, the exchange of relevant material with the police and CPS is not restricted under Data Protection Act 1998.

disclosed to the defence without further consultation with the Local Authority or order of the court (see paragraph 13.9 to 14.3 below).

10.9.   Where further relevant Local Authority material comes to light after the police examination of the material at paragraph 10.8 above, the Local Authority will contact the police and/or the CPS to arrange an examination of the new material by the police.

10.10. Similarly, where new issues arise in the criminal case (e.g. following the receipt of the defence case statement), the police will submit a further Annex C form requesting access to material not previously examined.

11. APPLICATIONS BY POLICE AND THE CPS TO THE FAMILY COURT FOR DISCLOSURE OF MATERIAL RELATING TO FAMILY PROCEEDINGS

11.1.   At the stage prior to service of prosecution papers pursuant to section 51 of the Crime and Disorder Act 1998, applications will be generally made by the police. After this stage, applications will generally be made by the CPS.

11.2.   Applications by the police for disclosure must contain details of the named officer to whom release is sought[16] and must specify the purpose and use to which the material is intended to be put. Applications should seek leave (where appropriate) to disclose the material to the CPS, to disclose the material to the criminal defence solicitors[17] and (subject to section 98(2) of the Children Act 1989[18]) to use the material in evidence at the criminal proceedings.

11.3.   Applications by the CPS must specify the purpose and use to which the material is intended to be put and should seek leave to share the material with the police and with the defence and (subject to section 98(2) Children Act 1989) to use the material in evidence at the criminal proceedings.

11.4.   Applications shall be made on Form C2. The application must be served by police or the CPS on all Parties to the Family Proceedings (The Local Authority having informed the police of details of all parties to Family Proceedings as per paragraphs 8.1 and 8.2 of this protocol).

11.5.   The application will be determined at a hearing at the Family Court. Police and the CPS will not attend the hearing unless directed to do so by the Family Court.

11.6.   Where it is practicable to seek prior written consent to disclosure from **all Parties** to the Family Proceedings, the police or the CPS should do so. Application should then be made in writing to the Family Court seeking a consent order.

---

[16]   Re H (Children) [2009] EWCA Civ. 704; [2009] 1 FLR 1531.
[17]   Where required under section 3 or section 7A Criminal Procedure and Investigations Act 1996.
[18]   Section 98(2) provides that statements and admissions in Family Court proceedings are not admissible in criminal proceedings.

11.7. Alternatively (**and whenever this is possible**), the police and/or the CPS will ask the Local Authority allocated lawyer (or SPOC if details of allocated lawyer are not known) to request that the Family Court considers the issue of disclosure to the police and/or the CPS at the next hearing. In this way, the Family Court will be in a position to make any orders as appear appropriate without the need for police and/or the CPS to make application to the Family Court. When requesting the Family Court to make an order in accordance with this paragraph, the Local Authority will put the other parties to the proceedings on notice; and will provide the court with details of the officer to whom disclosure is to be made and the purpose for which it is to be made.

11.8. In rare cases, where it considers it appropriate to do so, the Family Court should make orders for disclosure to the police and/or the CPS without application having been made by the police or the CPS.

12. TEXT OR SUMMARY OF JUDGMENT IN FAMILY PROCEEDINGS[19]

12.1. The Local Authority will forward to the CPS copies of relevant Family Court judgments (and summaries thereof) in the possession of the Local Authority. The judgments may be appropriately redacted.

12.2. Where the Local Authority is not in possession of a judgment which appears to be relevant to the concurrent criminal proceedings (e.g. fact-finding judgment), it will notify the CPS in order that the CPS can obtain the judgment directly from the Family Court. In these circumstances it will not be necessary to make formal application for disclosure on Form C2; the CPS will request release of the judgment under Practice Direction 12G above.

12.3. Where it appears to the Local Authority that the judgment will be relevant to the criminal proceedings, the Local Authority will request that the Family Court expedites the preparation of the judgment for release to the CPS (and if possible at public expense). Alternatively, the issue of disclosure of the judgment to the CPS under Practice Direction 12G can be considered at a linked directions hearing.

13. DISCLOSURE BY THE CPS TO THE CRIMINAL DEFENCE

13.1. The Criminal Procedure and Investigations Act 1996[20] requires the prosecution to disclose to the defence any material (including sensitive material) that could reasonably be considered capable of undermining the prosecution case

---

[19] Rule 12.73(1)(c) Family Procedure Rules 2010 and Practice Direction 12G permits the disclosure of the text or summary of the whole or part of a judgement given in family proceedings to a police officer or a member of the CPS for the purpose of a criminal investigation or to enable the CPS to discharge its functions. The Police Officer or CPS lawyer may only communicate the information for the purpose for which he/she received the information.

[20] Section 3 and section 7A.

against the accused or of assisting the case for the accused (the "disclosure test"). Where appropriate, application can be made to the criminal court to withhold sensitive material which satisfies the disclosure test on the grounds of public interest immunity (PII application).

13.2. PII applications to the criminal court for the withholding of sensitive material should be rare. Fairness ordinarily requires that all material which weakens the prosecution case or strengthens that of the defence should be disclosed. There is no basis for making a PII application except where the prosecutor has identified material that fulfils the disclosure test, disclosure of which would create a real risk of serious prejudice to an important public interest[21]

13.3. All material obtained from the Local Authority will be listed by the police on the sensitive disclosure schedule MG6D. The lists of material not disclosed by the Local Authority to the police will also be included on the MG6D (see paragraph 10.3 above: material relating to Family Proceedings; and paragraph 10.7 above: material withheld on the ground of confidentiality).

13.4. Material obtained by the police in accordance with Rule 12.73(1)(a)(viii) Family Procedure Rules 2010 (see paragraphs 10.5 and 10.6 above) must not be disclosed to the CPS. The police will reveal the existence of the material on the MG6D (without describing it). As appropriate, the CPS will seek the permission of the Family Court to access the material.

13.5. Where the material has been obtained following an application by the police to the Family Court, the police must indicate to the CPS whether the Family Court has given permission for the material to be shared with the CPS and with the defence. Further application to the Family Court may be required by the police and/or the CPS as appropriate.

13.6. The CPS will review the material in accordance with its statutory duties[22] and under the Attorney General's Guidelines on Disclosure. Only material which might undermine the prosecution case or might reasonably assist the defence case will fall to be disclosed. There will in no circumstances be "blanket" disclosure to the defence.

13.7. Where in accordance with paragraph 10.7 above a Local Authority document is not made available to the police on the basis of confidentiality (e.g. consent has not been obtained from the person to whom the document relates), the CPS will consider whether it is appropriate to seek access to such material by means of a witness summons in the criminal court[23].

---

[21]   R v H and C [2004] 2 AC 134.
[22]   Under Criminal Procedure and Investigations Act 1996.
[23]   Section 2 Criminal Procedure (Attendance of Witnesses) Act 1965.

13.8. Where in these circumstances application is made by the CPS for a witness summons, the CPS will serve the application on the criminal court and the Local Authority, identifying the Local Authority SPOC as the person who is required to produce the document(s)[24]. In addition, where the Crown Court so directs[25], the CPS will, in accordance with the Criminal Procedure Rules, serve the application on the person to whom the confidential document relates.

13.9. Where any Local Authority material reviewed by the CPS falls within the statutory disclosure test under the CPIA, the CPS will write to the Local Authority SPOC, within 2 working days of review whenever possible, setting out the reasons why the material falls to be disclosed and informing them of that decision. The form at Annex E to this 2013 protocol will be used by the CPS. The CPS will provide to the Local Authority proposals for the editing or summarising of the material for the purposes of disclosure to the defence. Where no material falls for disclosure, the CPS will inform the Local Authority that this is the case.

13.10. Within 5 working days of receipt of that notification, the Local Authority shall be given an opportunity to make any representations in writing to the CPS on the issues of disclosure. This will include objections to disclosure on the basis that the person to whom the material relates has not consented. Note that disclosure of documentation which has been created under the auspices, and for the purposes, of the LSCB, can only be made with the prior consent of the LSCB Chair[26].

13.11. The form at Annex F to this 2013 protocol will be used for this purpose. Where, exceptionally, the Local Authority is unable to meet the 5 working day timescale, the Local Authority will contact the CPS to discuss whether the timescale can be extended in the particular circumstances of the case.

14. PUBLIC INTEREST IMMUNITY (PII) APPLICATION

14.1. If the Local Authority does not agree to disclosure of Local Authority material to the defence, the CPS must negotiate with the Local Authority to explore whether disclosure can be made in edited form or by summarising in another document the issues arising in the material[27]. Whilst recognising that the prosecution must always comply with its statutory duty of disclosure, the sensitivity can often be removed in this way. PII applications in the criminal court will be rare. Local Authority material relating to a child is no longer a "class" of material to which PII applies. Depending on the sensitivity of the material,

---

[24] Rule 28.5(3)(a) Criminal Procedure Rules 2013.
[25] Rule 28.5(3)(b)(i) Criminal Procedure Rules 2013.
[26] For example, reports or documentation related to a Serious Case Review belong to the LSCB, rather than the Local Authority or other member agency of the LSCB.
[27] R v H and C [2004] 2 AC 134.

the Local Authority may itself agree that the public interest in the prosecution of crime overrides the interests of confidentiality[28]. In highly exceptional cases, the CPS may need to make disclosure to the defence of the edited/summarised document without the consent of the Local Authority.

14.2.   If a PII application is appropriate, the CPS will make a PII application to the criminal court as soon as reasonably practicable. The CPS will notify the Local Authority of the date and venue of the PII application and inform the Local Authority of their right to make representations to the criminal court[29].

14.3.   Where PII is sought on the basis of lack of consent from the person to whom the confidential document relates, CPS must in accordance with the Criminal Procedure Rules notify the person to whom the document relates[30] (as above, notification of date and venue of PII application and the interested person's right to make representations to the court).

Part C: Linked Directions Hearings

15. LINKED CRIMINAL AND CARE DIRECTIONS HEARINGS – CRITERIA

15.1.   This 2013 protocol will apply where a person connected with the child who is the subject of the care proceedings or the child himself is to be tried at the Crown Court for any violent or sexual offence or for an offence of child cruelty against the child, or any other child or any person connected with the child; and either:

(i)   The Local Authority, CPS, or any party to the care proceedings (including the child's guardian) considers that the care and criminal proceedings do, or may, impinge on one another; or

(ii)   In any public law proceedings in the High Court or County Court or in any proceedings in the Crown Court, a judge is satisfied that the protocol does, or may, apply.

16. ARRANGEMENTS FOR LINKED DIRECTIONS HEARINGS

16.1.   The allocated case management judge in the Family Court (ACMJ)[31] will consider whether or not there is likely to be a need for a linked directions hearing in respect of the criminal and family cases. If the ACMJ considers that a linked directions hearing is likely to be appropriate he/she shall liaise with the relevant Resident Judge to invite him to nominate a judge to be responsible for the management of the criminal case.

---

[28]   R v Chief Constable of West Midlands ex parte Wiley [1995] 1 AC 274.
[29]   Rule 22.3(b)(ii) Criminal Procedure Rules 2013.
[30]   Rule 22.3(b)(ii) Criminal Procedure Rules 2013.
[31]   In the Family Proceedings Court this will be the legal adviser.

16.2. In the care proceedings it is expected that the ACMJ will issue directions for the linked hearing which will spell out the respective parties' obligations, and which may include, but will not be limited to, recordings and, orders in the form at Annex I to this protocol (use of which by the Family Court is mandatory). At the same time, the ACMJ will consider giving permission to the Local Authority to serve its case summary on the CPS and the Crown Court (in accordance with paragraph 16.6 below).

16.3. Once a judge has been identified to manage the criminal proceedings, the Resident Judge shall direct the listing officers to liaise with family listing to agree the listing of the criminal and care cases for a linked directions hearing before the nominated criminal judge and the ACMJ. In an appropriate case the Resident Judge may agree to the ACMJ undertaking the responsibility for the management of the criminal case if he/she is authorised to try criminal cases, and, where appropriate, serious sexual offence cases.

16.4. If on receipt of criminal proceedings sent from the Magistrates' Courts and consideration of that case by the Resident Judge, or if during a Case Management hearing[32] or other pre-trial hearing listed before the Crown Court, the Resident Judge or judge (as the case may be) is satisfied that this Protocol does or may apply but that no reference has yet been made to the ACMJ for consideration in accordance with paragraph 16.1 above, the judge shall notify the Designated Family Judge accordingly who shall consider with the relevant Resident Judge and the ACMJ, whether a linked directions hearing is required. If there is agreement on the need for a linked directions hearing, the Resident Judge shall nominate a judge to be responsible for the management of the criminal case and arrangements shall then be made for the criminal and care cases to be listed for a linked directions hearing in accordance with paragraph 16.3 above.

16.5. The criminal case shall be listed before the judge at the Crown Court in public with the linked directions appointment in the care proceedings listed for hearing in private immediately thereafter. Subject to any specific objections raised by the parties, the advocates appearing in the criminal case may be invited to remain during the directions appointment in the care proceedings.

16.6. In every case involving a linked directions hearing the Local Authority's legal representative, **by no later than 4.00pm not less than 5 working days prior to the linked directions hearing**, shall with the permission of the family court prepare and serve on the CPS and the Crown Court a case summary setting out the basis of the Local Authority's application, its contentions in respect of findings sought in relation to the "threshold criteria" (Local Authority's "threshold document"), the current position in respect of the child, details of

---

[32] Case management hearings in the Crown Court will include Preliminary Hearings and Plea and Case Management Hearings.

the proposed assessments and/or expert(s) assessments being undertaken and the timescales for the same and the timetable (if any) set for the proceedings within the Family Court.

16.7.   The Local Authority's legal representative and the CPS shall agree a schedule of issues identifying those matters which are likely to be considered at the linked directions hearing. The Local Authority shall circulate the Schedule to the solicitors for the other parties in the criminal and care proceedings **by no later than 4.00pm not less than 2 working days prior to the linked directions hearing**.

16.8.   On the day of the linked directions hearing the advocates in the criminal and care proceedings shall meet **no later than one hour prior to the time fixed for the hearing** to discuss the schedule of issues with a view to identifying what directions may be required with particular reference to the trial timetable, disclosure and expert evidence and such other matters as may be identified by this Protocol.

16.9.   The respective court files in the criminal and care proceedings shall be cross referenced and shall be clearly marked as "linked" cases.

16.10. The directions hearing will be linked but not wholly combined because of the different parties and different procedural rules (such as with regard to privacy and rights of audience) which apply. The judge shall determine whether it is appropriate for some or all of the directions to be issued at a joint hearing or separately and the order of any directions to be issued.

16.11. At the conclusion of the hearing in the criminal case, counsel for the Crown will be invited to draw the minute of order, to be agreed with the defence, which will be submitted to the judge on the day of the hearing, for his/her approval.

16.12. The approved minute of order made in the criminal proceedings will be copied to the parties in the care proceedings by the CPS.

16.13. With the permission of the family court, the order made in the care proceedings will be copied by the Local Authority to the CPS and defence lawyers in the criminal proceedings.

16.14. The timing of the proceedings in a linked care and criminal case should appear in the Timetable for the Child[33].

16.15. **Judicial continuity**: Any adjourned linked directions hearing shall be listed before the same judge (unless the judge otherwise directs) but the judge who is the ACMJ shall not preside over the trial in the criminal proceedings, or pass sentence if there is a guilty plea, nor shall the judge give a "Goodyear

---

[33]   In accordance with the Public Law Outline.

indication". The judge in the criminal trial or who passes sentence if there is a guilty plea shall notify the ACMJ of the outcome.

17. MATTERS TO BE CONSIDERED AT THE LINKED DIRECTIONS HEARING

17.1. The timetabling[34] of both the criminal and care proceedings (with a view to such timetabling being coordinated to ensure the most appropriate order of trial and that each case is heard as expeditiously as possible).

17.2. Disclosure of evidence with particular reference to disclosure of evidence from one set of proceedings into the other with such permission as may be required by the relevant procedural rules.

17.3. Expert evidence with particular reference to the identification of expert witnesses, their willingness to act within the court timetable and the requirements of the Practice Direction concerning the instruction of Experts, their availability and role in the criminal and care hearings.

17.4. Any directions to be given in relation to issues of public interest immunity and for any witness summonses required for third party disclosure (Rule 28 Criminal Procedure Rules 2013).

17.5. Arrangements for the interviewing of children in care for the purpose of the criminal proceedings and any arrangements for the child to give evidence at any criminal or family hearing.

17.6. To ensure where appropriate that a transcript of relevant evidence or judgment in the trial heard first in time is available in the subsequent proceedings.

17.7. Issues relating to any question of assessment or therapeutic input required by any child involved in the proceedings.

17.8. Issues in relation to restrictions on publicity which it is considered may be required.

17.9. Issues in relation to any relevant material which may be pertinent to the issue of bad character (in respect of previous convictions or other alleged "reprehensible behaviour"), whether of defendants or non-defendants.

17.10. Other legal or social work related steps in the Family Court proceedings.

---

[34] Re TB [1995] 2 FLR 801 makes it clear beyond peradventure that the starting point is that the existence of criminal proceedings is not a reason to adjourn the care proceedings. For an exception see:
Re L [2010] 1 FLR 790: in the particular circumstances, the welfare stage of Family Proceedings should have been delayed until after the criminal proceedings.

18. REVIEW

18.1.   The parties to this 2013 protocol and Good Practice Model and the organisations at paragraphs 1.1 and 1.2 above supporting the 2013 protocol will continuously review and monitor the operation of the provisions. The protocol will be subject to a formal review 12 months after the date of implementation.

19. LOCAL PROTOCOLS

19.1.   Local agencies should agree and adopt a local protocol to give effect to this 2013 protocol signed by the Crown Court Resident Judges, Designated Family Judges, Police Forces, CPS and Local Authorities in each CPS Area. A local protocol must not depart from the requirements of the PLO and must require that orders used are in the form of Annex H and Annex I.

19.2.   Each Police Force signatory to the local protocol will provide on the form at Annex A details of a suitable single point of contact (SPOC) for the receipt by secure email of the Annex D disclosure request from the Local Authority.

19.3.   Each Local Authority signatory to the local protocol will provide on the form at Annex B details of a suitable single point of contact (SPOC) for the receipt by secure email of the Annex C disclosure request from the police.

20. SIGNATORIES

20.1.   The following are signatories to the protocol:

Date of agreement: .... **17 October 2013**

Senior Presiding Judge for England and Wales

Lord Justice Gross...

President of the Family Division

The Rt. Hon Sir James Munby...

Director of Public Prosecutions, Crown Prosecution Service

Keir Starmer QC...

The following support the protocol:

Association of Chief Police Officers, Association of Directors of Children Services, Association of Independent Local Safeguarding Children Board Chairs, Department for Education, HM Courts & Tribunals Service, Local Government Association, Welsh Government.

Attorney General's Guidelines for Prosecutors: Section 18 of the Regulation of Investigatory Powers Act 2000 (England and Wales)

SECTION 18 RIPA: PROSECUTORS' GUIDELINES

1. These Guidelines concern the approach to be taken by prosecutors in applying section 18 of the Regulation of Investigatory Powers Act (RIPA) in England and Wales.

Background

2. It has been long-standing Government policy that the fact that interception of communications has taken place in any particular case should remain secret and not be disclosed to the subject. This is because of the need to protect the continuing value of interception as a vital means of gathering intelligence about serious crime and activities which threaten national security. The Government judges that if the use of the technique in particular cases were to be confirmed, the value of the technique would be diminished because targets would either know, or could deduce, when their communications might be intercepted and so could take avoiding action by using other, more secure means of communication.

3. In the context of legal proceedings, the policy that the fact of interception should remain secret is implemented by section 17 of RIPA. Section 17 provides that no evidence shall be adduced, question asked, assertion or disclosure made or other thing done in, for the purposes of, or in connection with, any legal proceedings which discloses the contents of a communication which has been obtained following the issue of an interception warrant or a warrant under the Interception of Communications Act 1985, or any related communications data ("protected information"), or tends to suggest that certain events have occurred.

4.   The effect of section 17 is that the fact of interception of the subject's communications and the product of that interception cannot be relied upon or referred to by either party to the proceedings. This is given further effect by sections 3(7), 7(6), 7A(9) and 9(9) of the Criminal Procedure and Investigations Act 1996 (as amended). This protects the continuing value of interception whilst also creating a "level playing-field", in that neither side can gain any advantage from the interception. In the context of criminal proceedings, this means that the defendant cannot be prejudiced by the existence in the hands of the prosecution of intercept material which is adverse to his interests.

Detailed Analysis

First Stage: action to be taken by the prosecutor

5.   Section 18(7)(a) of RIPA provides,

> "Nothing in section 17(1) shall prohibit any such disclosure of any information that continues to be available for disclosure as is confined to ... a disclosure to a person conducting a criminal prosecution for the purpose only of enabling that person to determine what is required of him by his duty to secure the fairness of the prosecution"

If protected information is disclosed to a prosecutor, as permitted by section 18(7)(a), the first step that should be taken by the prosecutor is to review any information regarding an interception that remains extant at the time that he or she has conduct of the case[1]. In reviewing it, the prosecutor should seek to identify any information whose existence, if no action was taken by the Crown, might result in unfairness. Experience suggests that the most likely example of such potential unfairness is where the evidence in the case is such that the jury may draw an inference which intercept shows to be wrong, and to leave this uncorrected will result in the defence being disadvantaged.

6.   If in the view of the prosecutor to take no action would render the proceedings unfair, the prosecutor should, first consulting with the relevant prosecution agency, take such steps as are available to him or

---

1   Section 15(1) of RIPA provides that it is the duty of the Secretary of State to ensure that arrangements are in place to ensure that (amongst other matters) intercept material is retained by the intercepting agencies only for as long as is necessary for any of the authorised purposes. The authorised purposes include retention which, "is necessary to ensure that a person conducting a criminal prosecution has the information he needs to determine what is required of him by his duty to secure the fairness of the prosecution" (section 15(4)(d)).

her to secure the fairness of the proceedings provided these steps do not contravene section 18(10). In the example given above, such steps could include:

(i)   putting the prosecution case in such a way that the misleading inference is not drawn by the jury;

(ii)   not relying upon the evidence which makes the information relevant;

(iii)   discontinuing that part of the prosecution case in relation to which the protected information is relevant, by amending a charge or count on the indictment or offering no evidence on such a charge or count; or

(iv)   making an admission of fact[2].

There is no requirement for the prosecutor to notify the judge of the action that he or she has taken or proposes to take. Such a course should only be taken by the prosecutor if he considers it essential in the interests of justice to do so (see below).

SECOND STAGE: DISCLOSURE TO THE JUDGE

7.   There may be some cases (although these are likely to be rare) where the prosecutor considers that he cannot secure the fairness of the proceedings without assistance from the relevant judge. In recognition of this, section 18(7)(b) of RIPA provides that in certain limited circumstances, the prosecutor may invite the judge to order a disclosure of the protected information to him.

8.   If the prosecutor considers that he requires the assistance of the trial judge to ensure the fairness of the proceedings, or he is in doubt as to whether the result of taking the steps outlined at para 6 above would ensure fairness, he must apply to see the judge *ex parte*. Under section 18(8), a judge shall not order a disclosure to him except where he is satisfied that the exceptional circumstances of the case make that disclosure essential in the interests of justice. Before the judge is in a position to order such disclosure the prosecutor will need to impart to the judge such information, but only such information, as is necessary to demonstrate

---

2   This is acceptable as long as to do so would not contravene section 17 i.e. reveal the existence of an interception warrant. Prosecutors must bear in mind that such a breach might conceivably occur not only from the factual content of the admission, but also from the circumstances in which it is made.

that exceptional circumstances mean that the prosecutor acting alone cannot secure the fairness of the proceedings. Experience suggests that exceptional circumstances in the course of a trial justifying disclosure to a judge arise only in the following two situations:

(1) **Where the judge's assistance is necessary to ensure the fairness of the trial**

This situation may arise in the example given at paragraph 5 above, where there is a risk that the jury might draw an inference from certain facts, which protected information shows would be the wrong inference, and the prosecutor is unable to ensure that the jury will not draw this inference by his actions alone. The purpose in informing the judge is so that the judge will then be in a position to ensure fairness by:

(i)   summing up in a way which will ensure that the wrong inference is not drawn;

(ii)   giving appropriate directions to the jury; or,

(iii)   requiring the Crown to make an admission of fact which the judge **thinks essential in the interests of justice** if he is of the opinion that **exceptional circumstances** require him to make such a direction (section 18(9)). However, such a direction **must not** authorise or require anything to be done which discloses any of the contents of an intercepted communication or related data or tends to suggest that anything falling within section 17(2) has or may have occurred or be going to occur (section 18(10)). Situations where an admission of fact is required are likely to be rare. The judge must be of the view that proceedings could not be continued unless an admission of fact is made (and the conditions in section 18(9) are satisfied). There may be other ways in which it is possible for a judge to ensure fairness, such as those outlined at (i) and (ii) above.

In practice, no question of taking the action at (i)–(iii) arises if the protected information is already contained in a separate document in another form that has been or can be disclosed without contravening section 17(1), and this disclosure will secure the fairness of the proceedings.

(2) **Where the judge requires knowledge of the protected material for some other purpose**

This situation may arise where, usually in the context of a PII application, the true significance of, or duty of disclosure in relation to, other material being considered for disclosure by a judge, cannot be appraised by the judge without reference to protected information. Disclosure to the judge

353

of the protected information without more may be sufficient to enable him to appraise the material, but once he has seen the protected information the judge may also conclude that the conditions in section 18(9) are satisfied so that an admission of fact by the Crown is required in addition to or instead of disclosure of the non-protected material.

Another example is a case where protected information underlies operational decisions which are likely to be the subject of crossexamination and it is necessary to inform the judge of the existence of the protected information to enable him to deal with the issue when the questions are first posed in a way which ensures section 17(1) is not contravened.

What if the actions of the prosecutor and/or the judge cannot ensure the fairness of the proceedings?

9. There may be very rare cases in which no action taken by the prosecutor and/or judge can prevent the continuation of the proceedings being unfair, e.g. where the requirements of fairness could only be met if the Crown were to make an admission, but it cannot do so without contravening section 18(10). In that situation the prosecutor will have no option but to offer no evidence on the charge in question, or to discontinue the proceedings in their entirety.

Responding to questions about interception

10. Prosecutors are sometimes placed in a situation in which they are asked by the court or by the defence whether interception has taken place or whether protected information exists. Whether or not interception has taken place or protected information exists, an answer in the following terms, or similar should be given:

> "I am not in a position to answer that, but I am aware of sections 17 and 18 of the Regulation of Investigatory Powers Act 2000 and the Attorney General's Guidelines on the Disclosure of Information in Exceptional Circumstances under section 18."

In a case where interception has taken place or protected information exists, an answer in these terms will avoid a breach of the prohibition in section 17 while providing assurance that the prosecutor is aware of his obligations.

11. For the avoidance of doubt, any notification or disclosure of information to the judge in accordance with paragraphs 7–10 must be *ex parte*. It will never be appropriate for prosecutors to volunteer, either *inter partes* or

to the Court *ex parte*, that interception has taken place or that protected information exists, save in accordance with section 18 as elaborated in these Guidelines.

Further Assistance

12. Should a prosecutor be unsure as to the application of these guidelines in any particular case, further guidance should be sought from those instructing him or her. In those cases where a prosecutor has been instructed by the Crown Prosecution Service, the relevant CPS prosecutor must seek appropriate guidance from the relevant casework division in CPS Headquarters.

Reformatted on 29 November 2012

Index

All references are to paragraph number.